Women drinking out in Britain since the early twentieth century

Manchester University Press

STUDIES IN POPULAR CULTURE

General editor: Professor Jeffrey Richards

Also published in this series

Christmas in nineteenth-century England Neil Armstrong

Healthy living in the Alps: the origins of winter tourism in Switzerland, 1860–1914 Susan Barton

Working-class organizations and popular tourism, 1840–1970 Susan Barton

Leisure, citizenship and working-class men in Britain, 1850–1945 Brad Beaven

Leisure and cultural conflict in twentieth-century Britain Brett Brebber (ed.)

The British Consumer Co-operative Movement and film, 1890s–1960s Alan George Burton

British railway enthusiasm Ian Carter

Railways and culture in Britain Ian Carter

Darts in England, 1900–39: a social history Patrick Chaplin

Relocating Britishness Stephen Caunce, Ewa Mazierska, Susan Sydney-Smith and John Walton (eds)

Holiday camps in twentieth-century Britain: packaging pleasure Sandra Trudgen Dawson

History on British television: constructing nation, nationality and collective memory Robert Dillon

The food companions: cinema and consumption in wartime Britain, 1939–45 Richard Farmer

Songs of protest, songs of love: popular ballads in eighteenth-century Britain Robin Ganev

The BBC and national identity in Britain, 1922–53 Thomas Hajkowski

From silent screen to multi-screen: a history of cinema exhibition in Britain since 1896 Stuart Hanson

Smoking in British popular culture, 1800–2000 Matthew Hilton

Juke box Britain: Americanization and youth culture, 1945–60 Adrian Horn

Popular culture in London, c. 1890–1918: the transformation of entertainment Andrew Horrall

Horseracing and the British, 1919–39 Mike Huggins

Popular culture and working-class taste in Britain, 1930–39: a round of cheap diversions? Robert James

Scotland and the music hall, 1850–1914 Paul Maloney

Amateur film: meaning and practice, 1927–77 Heather Norris Nicholson

Films and British national identity: from Dickens to *Dad's Army* Jeffrey Richards

Cinema and radio in Britain and America, 1920–1960 Jeffrey Richards

Looking North: Northern England and the national imagination Dave Russell

The British seaside holiday: holidays and resorts in the twentieth century John K. Walton

Women drinking out in Britain since the early twentieth century

DAVID W. GUTZKE

Manchester University Press

Published by Manchester University Press
Altrincham Street, Manchester M1 7JA, UK
www.manchesteruniversitypress.co.uk

British Library Cataloguing-in-Publication Data is available

Library of Congress Cataloging-in-Publication Data is available

ISBN 978 0 7190 5265 1 *paperback*

First published by Manchester University Press in hardback 2014

This paperback edition first published 2015

Printed by Lightning Source

STUDIES IN POPULAR CULTURE

There has in recent years been an explosion of interest in culture and cultural studies. The impetus has come from two directions and out of two different traditions. On the one hand, cultural history has grown out of social history to become a distinct and identifiable school of historical investigation. On the other hand, cultural studies has grown out of English literature and has concerned itself to a large extent with contemporary issues. Nevertheless, there is a shared project, its aim, to elucidate the meanings and values implicit and explicit in the art, literature, learning, institutions and everyday behaviour within a given society. Both the cultural historian and the cultural studies scholar seek to explore the ways in which a culture is imagined, represented and received; how it interacts with social processes; how it contributes to individual and collective identities and world views, to stability and change, to social, political and economic activities and programmes. This series aims to provide an arena for the cross-fertilization of the discipline, so that the work of the cultural historian can take advantage of the most useful and illuminating of the theoretical developments and the cultural studies scholars can extend the purely historical underpinnings of their investigations. The ultimate objective of the series is to provide a range of books which will explain in a readable and accessible way where we are now socially and culturally and how we got to where we are. This should enable people to be better informed, promote an interdisciplinary approach to cultural issues and encourage deeper thought about the issues, attitudes and institutions of popular culture.

Jeffrey Richards

For Trevor, David,
and my mother and father,
Leone and Edward

Contents

List of plates

List of figures

List of tables

General editor's introduction

The 'local', the beloved neighbourhood public house which is the focal point of the community, has an iconic role in British popular culture. As The Rover's Return, The Queen Vic and The Woolpack, it is at the heart of the most popular and long-running television soap operas, *Coronation Street*, *EastEnders* and *Emmerdale*. But, according to David Gutzke – and it is only one of the many fascinating revelations in this book – the concept of the 'local', even the actual term, came into general use only during the Second World War. It then became a potent symbol of the class and gender egalitarianism that was seen as a characteristic of the democratic struggle against Fascism.

The pub has traditionally been seen as a bastion of masculine leisure activity. But in this ground-breaking book, David Gutzke, who has already published two notable studies on the role of the public house, *Protecting the Pub* (1989) and *Pubs and Progressives* (2006), shifts the focus to women and their relationship to the drink culture.

He traces in detail the evolution of the pub from the old-fashioned, brown-painted, spit and sawdust, men-only establishments of Edwardian England to the brightly coloured, family-friendly, food-serving Wetherspoon pubs of the 1990s. In assessing the appeal of such institutions to women and the extent of their patronage of them, he examines the changing architecture of the buildings, the attitudes and mentality of the brewers, the impact of the two world wars, the nature of advertising and promotion, the role of women in pub management and the nature of the drink being sold.

Significant rivals to the pub began to appear and are analysed perceptively by Gutzke. From the 1960s onwards wine bars develop to meet the rise in wine-drinking and the perceived need to provide somewhere different and distinctive for women drinkers. More recently there has been the emergence of the clubbing culture of which age rather than class or gender has been the determining feature. This and the associated practice of binge-drinking has led since the 1980s to city centres becoming infested with teenage drunks both male and female and turning into no-go areas for respectable citizens at weekends. Gutzke takes the 'moral panic' which this latest development has provoked and sets it firmly in historical context by comparing and contrasting it with similar 'moral panics' about youth and female drinking in Edwardian England and the two world wars, with fascinating results.

Drawing on a wide range of sources, including memoirs, opinion surveys, newspapers, the trade press, novels, films and advertisements and vigorously engaging with previous commentators on the subject, Gutzke charts and analyses in illuminating detail the rich, complex, enduring and evolving role of women drinking in twentieth- and now twenty-first-century British culture.

Jeffrey Richards

Acknowledgements

This book has been decidedly longer in preparation than anyone anticipated, and for their seemingly inexhaustible patience and unshakeable confidence in its ultimate appearance I want to express my profound gratitude to Jeffrey Richards, the Series Editor, and Emma Brennan, MUP's Acquisitions Editor. The book I had planned writing is entirely different in scope, content and argument from what emerged – I know that it has benefited from this longer gestation period. Illness partly interrupted my progress, but so did other books, which I think gave me shrewder insights into drinking habits.

I have incurred other numerous debts in researching and writing the book which I am grateful to knowledge. John Greenaway provided keen insight into Chapter 9; Jane McGregor kindly lent me her dissertation, a perceptive study of Nottingham's pivotal position as the 'binge capital of Britain'; and Victor Bailey suggested sources on the 1950s, while Tim Hall and Jane McGregor generously guided me through the ever-expanding literature on drinking habits in the era of 'binge' Britain.

Two scholars immeasurably improved this book. Trevor Lloyd, my dissertation adviser so long ago at the University of Toronto, mentor and cherished friend, scrutinized every chapter, bringing his deep knowledge of modern Britain to bear on what I wrote. He continues to amaze me with his acuity, breath of knowledge and ability to assimilate new ideas. I regard Trevor as the quintessential scholar, historian and author. Another life-long and precious friend is David Fahey. Far more facile with the computer than me, he gave me new references, answered queries and suggested topics worth exploring. No one could have been more selfless than David in critiquing my prose. Like Trevor, he read ever chapter and all the various revisions that emerged. Looking back over my career, these two scholars, mentors and intimate friends – more than anyone else – have been responsible for my development as a historian.

I want to thank the following for permission to consult private records: Nicholas Redman (Whitbread Archives); Kenneth Thomas (Heineken UK Archives); Diana Lay (National Brewery Centre); Glasgow University Archives Services; and David Wilson (British Pub and Beer Association). For information about *The Tap, Pease Pottage,* I would like to thank Chloe Johnson (Leamington Spa Art Gallery & Museum).

Shannon Conlon and Deborah Williams continually amazed me with their ability to locate key sources and order them through Interlibrary Loan. Patient and creative, they enormously facilitated my research.

I am also pleased to thank former executives of the brewing industry who participated in oral history interviews: Tony Avis and James Lloyd (both Bass Charrington); Stuart Aitken, former Sales Director with Whitbread Beer Company; and Neal Hyde, former chairman of Hydes' Anvil Brewery.

I am grateful to Missouri State University, which awarded me a sabbatical in which to write some of the manuscript and a research grant to travel to Britain.

As I have been writing about alcohol in Britain for some thirty years, I am acutely aware of change. Many brewing archives have closed, with some sources alas lost. Where possible, I have identified the current repository holding the archives; otherwise, I have recorded where I originally consulted them.

David W. Gutzke

Introduction

Regardless of the country or period, anthropological studies have clearly established that most people drink alcohol without causing serious health problems. Abusers constitute a minority, though never to be minimized. As anthropologist Dwight Heath remarked in 1987, 'the importance of drinking as a "normal" (and not necessarily "deviant") behavior has rarely been recognized in other disciplines'.[1] When I began researching this book a few years later, therefore, I focused exclusively on women who drank responsibly, which covered the overwhelming proportion of females. Emergence of a distinct youth subculture of drinking, repudiating traditional drinking norms of restraint, self-control and orderly behaviour that for the first time encompassed both sexes, compelled me to widen my focus. Including youths separately in Chapter 9 afforded an opportunity to juxtapose the promotion of alcoholic products in two quite dissimilar periods: modern drink wholesalers and retailers, on one hand, and Progressive brewers in interwar England, on the other. Assumptions, attitudes and policies of drink sellers could not have been more strikingly different.

This is the first book about women's advance into the man's world of pub, club and beerhouse that examines drinking habits covering a century. Useful preliminary studies – John Burnett's *Liquid Pleasures* and *England Eats Out* – have provided a logical point of departure, but even the wider outlines of the subject have remained obscured, with many topics, such as wine bars and new private social clubs, neglected.[2] More attention has been devoted to the interwar era and the more recent years associated with 'binge drinking' than to the rest of the century. Yet, without exploring Edwardian England, the Second World War and the ensuing four decades of the postwar period, how, when and of course why women's culture of drinking evolved cannot be fully understood.

Several scholars have disputed continuity in women's drinking patterns before the First World War. Mark Girouard argued that some respectable women began drinking in saloon bars from the 1890s, while Stella Moss has gone further in disputing the historical consensus that respectable women shunned public drinking.[3] Chapter 1 examines these interpretations.

Fears of a postwar backlash against women's recent entry into pubs and beerhouses motivated leading brewers to promote the improved public house in 1919, I argued in *Pubs and Progressives* (2006).[4] The gender imbalance owing to male deaths in the war created a context in which many women lacked ties of husbands and dependent children and so avoided the 'settled' mature state of adult women in the 1920s. Men in uniform, in fact, promoted growing anxiety over women's behaviour during the war.[5] To ensure that women's newly won freedom in drinking habits, acquired during the war, would persist and be transformed from a wartime trend into a postwar tradition proved the galvanizing factor for drink sellers. Brewers correctly anticipated powerful ideological pressures would exalt family life as pivotal in the return to peacetime society. 'Implicit in such reconstruction', remarked Judy Gies, 'was the return of women to their prewar domestic roles as wives or mothers or as domestic servants, and the re-establishment of a gendered division of labour both at home and in the workplace'. At the same time, the emergence of the companionate marriage offered wives and courting women the chance to share with the men in their lives wider leisure activities. Hence, brewers' pursuit of improved public houses enabled widening numbers of women to drink out without risking their respectability.[6]

Critical to public house reform was Progressivism. As a transnational movement, social Progressives embraced pragmatism, scientific methodology, the cult of efficiency, experimentation, and cross-class alliances as strategies for addressing the ills of industrialization. As remedies for urban evils, social progressives championed moral uplift, order, discipline and environmentalism. In their attack on society's problems, they sought social justice as a remedy to class conflict. As white-collar, non-partisan middle-class professionals, social Progressives extolled regulation of capitalism and rejected outright radical solutions, such as redistributing wealth or reorganizing economic institutions.[7]

Another group of Progressives later emerged, rooted in the business community and keen to enforce restraints on unregulated capitalism. In response to cut-throat competition, unethical behaviour besmirching the industry's image, relentless pursuit of profits, and excessive numbers of licences as well as their uneven distribution, frustrated brewers also turned to the government to achieve what eluded them, the reordering of their industry. To distinguish them from social Progressives, such individuals could be called economic Progressives. With all traders forced to meet the same guidelines, regardless of size, bigger businesses could use higher standards as a technique for driving smaller, less efficient and less ethical competitors out of business. Without government intervention, Edwardian brewers had faced virtually insoluble problems that would compel Sydney O. Nevile (soon Managing Director of Whitbread & Co.) and W. Waters Butler (Managing Director of Mitchells & Butlers) to advocate the industry's nationalization. Economic Progressives appeared in both the United States and Britain during or soon after the First World War, underlining again the transnational nature of the movement.[8] These economic Progressives held similar attitudes to manufacturers like Sir Robert Peel the elder a century earlier, who supported factory legislation so that their efforts to provide decent working conditions for their employees should not be undercut by less scrupulous competitors who ran their factories for very long working days.[9]

Some enlightened British brewers, espousing new Progressive beliefs, embraced the improved public house as a method of restoring respectability to public drinking, rehabilitating their own reputations and expanding the pubs' clientele. Owners of hundreds, sometimes thousands, of tied houses, they invested huge sums to reinvent the public house. Sydney Nevile, the movement's de facto leader, characterized public house improvement as a 'progressive policy' which he and other prominent brewers, the 'progressive spirits', energetically pursued.[10] His fellow London Progressive, E. W. Giffard, Chairman of Barclay Perkins, explained in 1930 that all improved pubs must include 'suitable seating accommodation, the provision of food of some kind, the supply of beverages other than beer and spirits, and some opportunity for recreation'. In pursuing Progressive traits – order, social control, discipline, moral uplift, environmentalism, pragmatism and experimentation – public house reformers had a philosophy for eradicating the old regime, so closely associated in the public's mind with drunkenness, violence and disreputable behaviour.[11]

In this transformation from boozers to improved pubs, brewer reformers introduced new amenities as a calculated strategy to remake the pub into a truly family venue. Food played a critical role, not just to generate profit and custom, as one recent historian would have it, but to act as an antidote to insobriety.[12] Drawing on their Central Control Board wartime experience, Nevile and Butler knew that ingestion of food facilitated metabolizing alcohol.

Consumption of food as much as chairs and tables served the same ends – retarding the impact of alcohol consumption.[13] Brewers also introduced food, games, children's play areas, non-intoxicating drinks and, reminiscent of the late Victorian era, entertainment featuring famous music hall performers. Of these new features, the garden functioned as a critical agency for promoting family sociability because only here could children under thirteen join parents who consumed alcohol.[14] Where space permitted, pubs held theatrical plays and poetry recitals, which drew impressive audiences, even in working-class areas.[15]

Traditional drinking in pubs and beerhouses in what historians later called the masculine republic involved standing at the bar and ordering drinks, participating in buying rounds, chewing tobacco and spitting it into spittoons amid the most austere surroundings. Bare wooden floors or flagstones, shabby décor, walls lined with sporting themes and, most pre-eminently, disgusting toilets, often lacking soap, toilet paper, hand towel and mirrors, characterized all save the most upmarket establishments. Cleaned infrequently, often grimy and predictably repellant, toilets symbolized all that women loathed about drinking, male companionship and masculine public space.

Progressive brewers appealed directly to middle class and upper-working-class women with the creation of the lounge, a separate room with bourgeois norms of sociability. The ambience of the gentlemen's club prevailed: people at tables, chatting intimately to friends or spouses, placed orders with waiters or waitresses who fetched drinks and food from the counter, no longer propped up by drinkers. Short service bars, and the expectation that people would sit placidly at tables, summoning waiters or waitresses with bar pulls, governed drinking etiquette. Patrons would, in short, imbibe bourgeois social norms. Conspicuously absent too were drunkenness, disorderly behaviour, fraternizing with barmaids, and elbowing at the bar. Another feature closely associated with masculinity, the playing of billiards, was a direct casualty of the need to convert existing space into a lounge. As lounges became a standard feature of improved pubs during the 1920s, billiards playing declined as an activity. 'By 1930', commented two sport historians, 'billiards in pubs was almost dead'. Fears of mixing with social inferiors had prevented the middle and upper classes from frequenting pubs into the 1920s. But when assured of respectable social standards in the lounge, with its bourgeois notions of order, discipline and efficiency, the propertied classes discarded their inhibitions.[16]

Women readily perceived different drinking cues in improved pubs. Sobriety, restraint, good taste and sociability soon became synonymous with the lounge. In an era where clothing denoted class and dictated behaviour, lounge patrons came properly attired. For men, this meant bowlers, trilbies, ties and good suits, never soiled or spotted clothing, scarves, caps or threadbare suit, or work uniforms; for women, respectable dresses were mandatory, with curlers and caps banished. How and what one drank equally signified class (and class pretensions). Men consumed premium bottled beers, served in small 8–ounce glasses, or whisky, while women drank wine, cocktails or stout (drunk also in small 8–ounce glasses). In other rooms at improved pubs, men could down draught beer in pint glasses and chew tobacco, but not spit into sawdust or spittoons. Décor of lounges sent encoded messages as important as those of clothing, beverage and drinking vessels. With the most refined ambience as well as best furnishings, lounges projected respectability, incompatible with drunkenness and disorder. Only here would women find carpeted floors, plants, non-alcoholic advertisements, tasteful prints and new female cloakrooms. New light oak panelling, décorated walls, upholstered furnishings and chintz for chair coverings and curtains – all emblematic of middle-class homes – similarly greeted women.

Again, in other bar rooms males encountered much of the typical masculine culture and exclusiveness of traditional boozers. Nothing in fact was done to challenge directly the masculine republic of drinking in the public or saloon bars. Nevertheless, pronounced differences prevailed. 'Fixed furniture, wall papers, heavy hangings, and such "work of art" as famous racehorses, prizefights, almanac portraits of departed statesman and other mural eyesores', commonplace in Edwardian boozers, were banished from all parts of interwar improved pubs. Thus, reform-minded brewers displayed another key Progressive trait, environmentalism, a commitment to changing the surroundings of drinking as a way of modifying drinking habits.[17]

The government's nationalization of the brewing industry, together with all licensed premises at Carlisle during the First World War had deeply influenced Progressive brewers. Whitbread's Sydney Nevile had become a strong exponent of tables, chairs and bar service as part of the improved pub philosophy. 'People most certainly drink less and they drink more slowly if sitting down than standing up', he told the Royal Commission in 1930. As he disclosed, environmentalism, a key Progressive trait, shaped drinking habits. Generally throughout the country, Nevile observed, 'a far larger number of people sit down than used to be the case'.[18]

Progressive brewers also sought to entice respectable working- and middle-class women to new improved pubs with dance halls, rivalled only by the cinema as the most vital leisure activity for young working women.[19] Despite the fact that the First World War decimated the number of unmarried middle-class men in their late twenties, both marriage rates and the age of marriage in the interwar era altered little. One explanation, J. M. Winter has suggested, is that many middle-class women chose spouses socially beneath them as a way of compensating for demographic changes. In her study of these women, Virginia Nicholson pointed to the crucial role of dance halls in facilitating romance. 'Young women', she remarked, 'certainly saw dance halls as the best place to meet and mate'. Cognizant of the role of pubs as a venue for potential courtship, enterprising brewers turned to dance halls as a logical amenity for combining two key forms of leisure, drinking in pubs and dancing.[20]

Much of the subsequent historical debate on women's drinking habits pivots on what other factors might have actuated public house reform in interwar England. Stella Moss and Alistair Mutch portrayed brewer pub improvers as primarily profit-maximizers who focused on areas in which inhabitants' patronage would defray cost of investment.[21] This new research is appraised in Chapter 1.

Currently, historians view enduring changes in women's drinking habits as a product of the last half of the twentieth century.[22] Claire Langhamer pointed to the Second World War as the cause of an influx of females whose presence tripled in pubs and beerhouses. Women in postwar licensed premises, she argued, persisted as a predominant force in the following decades, providing the basis for the emergence of youth culture. 'By the late 1950s, advertisers actively targeted the young as a lucrative potential market for drink and this included young women', she believed.[23] Terry Gourvish, though discounting the Second World War's impact, also situated changes in women's drinking habits from the 1950s.[24] Stella Moss agreed with Langhamer and Gourvish that new women's drinking habits now became permanent. Once women began patronizing licensed premises in greater numbers, she felt this trend thereafter assumed an upward trajectory.[25]

Our present understanding of women's drinking in the first half of the twentieth century is based on uncertain assumptions and limited statistical evidence. Scholars often have not grasped several vital facets of drinking central to explaining drinking behaviour. Referring generically to all on-licensed premises as pubs confuses two quite different categories of drinking establishments. Beerhouses, created in 1830 and numbering some 47,000 before magistrates assumed control over them in 1869, sold only beer and wine. The second category, licensed victuallers' premises, more commonly called pubs or public houses, retailed the full range of alcoholic beverages and required higher-rated premises to operate as well as two or more rooms. Beerhouses flourished especially in Northern towns, where masculinity and drinking were synonymous. Respectable Northern women would not have considered drinking with husbands in beerhouses; pubs (before the 1890s) provided seating, sometimes food and other attractions, chief among them different drinking rooms. Each category had its own separate licence. Beerhouse licences cost less than licensed victuallers' licences for several reasons. The former were allowed to set up business in cheaper premises, usually no more than one room.[26] To beerhouses, their lower overheads, cramped austere premises and unadorned tables and chairs all reflectors of their neighbourhoods, went those at the base of the social structure. Impoverished women would have frequented beerhouses, situated commonly in slums, more easily than pubs. But geography could override even this distinction in the North when beerhouse keepers upheld the masculine republic with bans on women.[27] These distinctions are critically important because beerhouses remained a key feature of drinking until the 1950s.

Beerhouses assume a central role in historians' attempt to estimate the proportion of women patronizing licensed premises in interwar England. Bolton, York and London have loomed large in interpretations because contemporaries compiled detailed statistics just for these three urban areas. Historians have cited these findings without assessing their compatibility or reliability. Two thirds of on-licences in Bolton but just one-tenth of those in York consisted of beerhouses, vast differences which shaped drinking patterns.

That beerhouses receive short shrift in historical accounts should not surprise in some ways. Their numbers began declining sharply in the late 1950s and 1960s so much that when Robert Roberts came to write his memoir of Salford, *The Classic Slum*, in 1971, he mentioned them just once as a feature of Edwardian England. Yet, in his youth, beerhouses greatly outnumbered public houses in his 'village', as in adjoining Manchester and many other Northern cities.[28] For Roberts, as for later historians, the two terms came to be interchangeable.[29]

Comparing three urban areas irrespective of their geographic locations is also misleading because antipathy to women on licensed premises rose as distance from London increased.[30] Both for drinking in Bolton in the 1930s and more generally for the the Second World War years, historians, notably Drs Moss and Gleiss, have attached weight to the statistics collected by Mass-Observation. Yet, modern polling using sophisticated random sampling techniques to analyse drinking behaviour occurred first in 1949. Tom Harrisson, co-founder of Mass-Observation, had a predilection for impressionistic over statistical evidence that profoundly influenced how it collected and interpreted evidence.[31]

Fixation with numbers has meant that historians have overlooked Ernest Selley's study, *The English Public House as It Is*, published in 1927. Such was his unrivalled knowledge of drinking habits that, when the New Survey of London sought an expert on the topic, it naturally turned to him. Much misunderstanding and inaccuracy would have been subsequently avoided had he been well enough to accept the task of writing about London licensed premises rather than the individual chosen, who knew remarkably less about the topic. In the instance of *The Public House as It Is*, impressionistic evidence, carefully collected, broadly based and skilfully evaluated, was vastly superior to numbers collected rather haphazardly, lacking any comparative basis or awareness of the impact of economic developments.

Historians have also misinterpreted women's interwar drinking habits because they overlooked the lounge, a new room which Progressive brewers introduced following the First World War.[32] This room was not merely new but entirely unprecedented: for the first time a separate, well-furnished room with tables created an atmosphere of gender-neutral space in which women socialized free of leering men, prowling prostitutes and offensive male habits of swearing, disorderly behaviour and drunkenness (at least in public bars). In the lounge middle-class drinking norms – patrons dressed properly and seated at tables covered with tablecloths, beverages served by staff, spittoons banished and bourgeois behaviour exhibited – enabled the sexes to socialize without fear of women being accosted as prostitutes, a powerful factor underestimated by historians in deterring respectable females from frequenting late Victorian and Edwardian pubs. Overlooking the lounge's role in facilitating women's use of pubs explains why Pamela Horn could conclude that 'entry into public houses was discouraged' in the 1920s.[33]

Recent studies have challenged this interpretation, arguing that pub improvement often consisted of mere cosmetic changes, that new or rebuilt pubs were located in middle-class enclaves and that brewers did not install or improve women's toilets because the licensing laws stipulated with what tied-house owners had to comply. But the evidence tells another story altogether, as Chapter 1 demonstrates.

For the years since the mid-twentieth century, public opinion polls and marketing surveys provide key information about beverages, places of consumption, age cohorts, geography and gender. With them, changes over time can be tracked. Although modern public opinion polls and marketing surveys began appearing regularly and over time more frequently from the late 1940s, they have been largely ignored by scholars.

To explore the nature of and changes in the cultures of drinking, other sources were used. Understanding the mentality of drink sellers meant reading not just drink wholesaler and retailer newspapers but the in-house magazines privately circulated inside the companies. Insights also came from oral history interviews with brewing executives and marketers, with Tony Avis (Bass Charrington) and Neal Hyde (Hyde's Anvil Brewery) the most helpful. Surveys of advertisements of alcoholic beverages have also appeared. Of these, Penny Dade's *Drink Talking* is by far the best, its coverage chronologically broad and scope comprehensive.[34]

In seeking to grasp why so many women disliked, even loathed, pubs and beerhouses, I adopted an interdisciplinary approach in which I incorporated material from studies in psychology, sociology and marketing. Novels also provided considerable insights. From *Wonder Woman: Marketing Secrets for the Trillion-Dollar Customer*, I borrowed an analytical framework in which drinkers were divided into birth generations: baby boomers, Generation X and Generation Y. Viewing advertisements within this context reveals much about how some drink sellers wooed women as customers. Emergence of style bars as a part of the widening subculture of drinking in the 1990s proved successful in drawing growing numbers of women. Specialized periodicals – *Flavour: The Magazine of Bar Professions*, *Town and City Magazine*, *Pubchef*, *Morning Advertiser Wine Supplement* and *Glass: The Publican Newspaper Wine Magazine* – offered considerable insight into how these venues targeted Generation X and Y women.

Generation Y women subdivided into two groups, and the drinking habits of the youngest members fortunately have received voluminous study because of scholarly interest in binge drinking, summarized in Chapter 9.

Numerous historians have accepted the importance of moral panics as an analytical concept in explaining historical events, but not examined the characteristics of this phenomenon to establish its validity.[35] Stanley Cohen's book *Folk Devils and Moral Panics: The Creation of the Mods and Rockers* (1972) first popularized the idea, and his thesis has been refined in Eric Goode and Nachman Ben-Yehuda, *Moral Panics: The Social Construction of Deviance* (1994). More recently, David Garland's 'On the Concept of Moral Panic', in 2008 outlined specific stages through which moral panics typically passed.[36]

With this literature, I identified moral panics as a recurring theme of the male response to women's new drinking habits across a century during wars – the Boer War, and the First and Second World Wars. Traits of moral panics are examined in the light of events, clearly establishing for the first time that new women's behaviour aroused recurring anxieties and fears that fostered powerful societal pressures to reassert male control. Though many scholars have interpreted portrayals of binge drinking as a moral panic, no one saw a historical parallel extending back more than a century.[37]

By the end of the period, it was female drinking habits that endured; instead of men converting women to consuming more beer, women induced men to turn increasingly to imbibing wine. As a beverage that could be shared and was less bloating, wine became the drink of choice for both sexes. But it was not so much that women prevailed finally in this one context as that they assumed precedence in other related areas. Women chose where to drink and what meals and wine to order, not just for themselves but for their male partners. In wooing females as customers, shrewd retailers understood that women were far more exacting in evaluating drinking premises than men. Only slowly was this insight recognized in traditional pub culture, and in one important sense mattered much less than in previous decades. The chief competitor to pubs and various types of bars was now ironically the home: almost as much alcohol was being consumed there as in public venues.

Notes

1 Dwight B. Heath, 'A Decade of Development in the Anthropological Study of Alcohol Use: 1970–80', in Mary Douglas (ed.), *Constructive Drinking: Perspectives on Drink from Anthropology* (Cambridge: Cambridge University Press, 1987), pp. 18–19.

2 John Burnett, *Liquid Pleasures: A Social History of Drinks in Modern Britain* (London: Routledge, 1999), and *England Eats Out: A Social History of Eating Out in England from 1830 to the Present* (Longman: Longman/Pearson, 2004).

3 Mark Girouard, *Victorian Pubs* (London: Studio Vista, 1975), pp. 59–69; Stella Maria Moss, 'Cultures of Women's Drinking and the English Public House, 1914–39' (D.Phil., University of Oxford, 2009), p. 72.

4 David W. Gutzke, *Pubs and Progressives: Reinventing the Public House in England, 1896–1960* (DeKalb, Illinois: Northern Illinois University Press, 2006); David W. Gutzke, 'Gender, Class and Public Drinking in Britain during the First World War', *Histoire Sociale/Social History*, 27 (1994), pp. 381–3.

5 See below Chapter 11, pp. 248–55. Carolyn Jackson and Penny Tinkler, '"Ladettes" and "Modern Girls": "Troublesome" Young Femininities', *Sociological Review*, 55 (2007), p. 265.

6 Judy Gies, '"Playing Hard to Get": Working-Class Women, Sexuality and Respectability in Britain, 1918–40', *Women's History Review*, 1 (1992), p. 240; Gutzke, *Pubs and Progressives*, pp. 163–8, 185.

7 For discussion of environmentalism, see Gutzke, *Pubs and Progressives*, pp. 3–4, 16–22; David W. Gutzke, 'Historians and Progressivism', and 'Progressivism in Britain and Abroad', in David W. Gutzke (ed.), *Britain and Transnational Progressivism* (London: Palgrave Macmillan, 2008), pp. 11–64.

8 Gabriel Kolko, *The Triumph of Conservatism: A Reinterpretation of American History, 1900–16* (Chicago: Quadrangle Books, 1963), pp. 2, 14, 284; Robert D. Cuff, *The War Industries Board: Business-Government Relations During the First World War* (Baltimore: Johns Hopkins University Press, 1973), pp. 271–2.

9 I am grateful to Trevor Lloyd for this point.

10 Sydney O. Nevile, *The First Half-Century: A Review of the Developments of the Licensed Trade and the Improvement of the Public House During the Past Fifty Years* (London: n.p. [1949]); *House of Whitbread*, 3 (1926), p. 2. Moss, however, claimed that Progressive brewers never made a 'self-conscious and specific declaration about the pursuit of progressive policies' (Moss, 'Cultures of Women's Drinking', p. 300).

11 *Anchor Magazine*, 10 (June 1930), p. 121; David W. Gutzke, 'Sydney Nevile: Squire in the Slums or Progressive Brewer?', *Business History*, 43 (2011), pp. 6–8.

12 Moss, 'Cultures of Women's Drinking', pp. 295–6; Gutzke, *Pubs and Progressives*, p. 142.

13 Gutzke, *Pubs and Progressives*, p. 64.

14 Licensing law prohibited children under thirteen from being on licensed premises, even with parents, since the 1908 Children's Act. For the origins of this legislation, see David W. Gutzke, '"The Cry of the Children": The Edwardian Medical Campaign Against Maternal Drinking', *British Journal of Addiction*, 79 (1984), pp. 71–84.

15 Gutzke, *Pubs and Progressives*, pp. 111–12, 127, 158–86, 241.

16 Ibid., pp. 159–61; Tony Collins and Wray Vamplew, *Mud, Sweat and Beers: A Cultural History of Sport and Alcohol* (Oxford: Berg, 2002), pp. 25–7. Where the smoke room assumed the trappings and amenities of the lounge, women might venture into it on their own (Pauline Mannion and Bernard Mannion, *Pub Memories of Summer Lane and Newtown between the Wars* (Birmingham: Pauline and Bernard Mannion, [?]), pp. 25, 43).

17 Gutzke, *Pubs and Progressives*, pp. 161–2.

18 Evidence of the Royal Commission on Licensing, 12 Nov. 1930, pp. 2110, 2131. For a discussion of the state management scheme, see Chapter 10, pp. 219–21.

19 Claire Langhamer, *Women's Leisure in England, 1920–60* (Manchester: Manchester University Press, 2000), pp. 58, 63, 70; J. M. Winter, *The Great War and the British People* (London: Macmillan, 1986), pp. 256–60.

20 Virginia Nicholson, *Singled Out: How Two Million Women Survived without Men after the First World War* (rept, 2007: London: Penguin, 2008), p. 69; David W. Gutzke, 'Gender, Class and Public Drinking in Britain during the First World War', in Jack S. Blocker, Jr and Cheryl Krasnick Warsh (eds), *The Changing Face*

of Drink: Substance, Imagery, and Behaviour (Ottawa: University of Ottawa, 1997), pp. 310–11.

21 Moss, 'Cultures of Women's Drinking', p. 297; Alistair Mutch, 'Shaping the Public House, 1850–1950: Business Strategies, State Regulation and Social History', *Cultural and Social History*, 1 (2004), pp. 194, 199.

22 Deirdre Beddoe, *Back to Home and Duty: Women between the Wars, 1918–39* (London: Pandora, 1989), p. 120; Barbara Gleiss, 'Women in Public Houses: A Historic Analysis of the Social and Economic Role of Women Patronising English Public Houses, 1880s-1970' (Ph.D. Dissertation, University of Vienna, 2009), pp. 69, 80, 82.

23 Claire Langhamer, '"A Public House Is for All Classes, Men and Women Alike": Women, Leisure and Drink in Second World War England', *Women's History Review*, 12 (2003), pp. 430, 437; Langhamer, *Women's Leisure in England, 1920–60*, pp. 71–3, 154–5, 189.

24 Terrence R. Gourvish, 'The Business of Alcohol in the US and the UK: UK Regulation and Drinking Habits, 1914–39', *Business and Economic History*, 26 (1997), pp. 613–14; T. R. Gourvish and R. G. Wilson, *The British Brewing Industry, 1830–1980* (Cambridge: Cambridge University Press, 1994), p. 435.

25 Moss, 'Cultures of Women's Drinking', p. 327.

26 David W. Gutzke, *Protecting the Pub: Brewers and Publicans against Temperance* (Woodbridge: Royal Historical Society/Boydell Press, 1989), pp. 46–7.

27 Lyn Murfin, *Popular Leisure in the Lake Counties* (Manchester: Manchester University Press, 1990), pp. 80, 82; Brian Harrison, *Drink and the Victorians: The Temperance Question in England, 1815–72* (1971; rept ed., Keele: Keele University Press, 1994), p. 81; Gourvish, 'The Business of Alcohol in the US and the UK: UK Regulation and Drinking Habits, 1914–39', pp. 609–16; Gourvish and Wilson, *The British Brewing Industry, 1830–1980*, p. 18.

28 Robert Roberts, *The Classic Slum: Salford Life in the First Quarter of the Century* (1971; paperback ed., Harmondsworth: Penguin, 1980), pp. 76, 88, 103, 112, 120–1; *Evidence of the Select Committee of the House of Lords on Intemperance*, 1877, 11 (171), apps b, e, g, I and (271), app. b, c, k, n.

29 Roberts wrote of Salford's 15 beerhouses at the book's beginning, but later called them public houses (Roberts, *Classic Slum*, pp. 16, 120).

30 National Repository, HO 190/843, J. S. Eagles to A. F. Harvey, 19 Dec. 1922, Central Control Board (Liquor Traffic).

31 Gleiss, 'Women in Public Houses', pp. 76–8.

32 Gleiss, 'Women in Public Houses', pp. 69, 80, 82. Moss, however, erroneously asserted that the vault was combined into larger rooms where men and women would occupy the same drinking space. Well into the 1950s, in fact, vaults remained as much a feature of drinking as sex-segregated rooms (Moss, 'Cultures of Women's Drinking', p. 266).

33 Pamela Horn, *Women in the 1920s* (Stroud: Alan Sutton, 1995), p. 176.

34 Penny Dade, *Drink Talking: 100 Years of Alcohol Advertising* (London: Middlesex University Press, 2009).

35 Moss, 'Cultures of Women's Drinking', ch. 1; Lucy Bland, '"Guardians of the Race"

or "Vampires upon the Nation's Health"? Female Sexuality and Its Regulation in Early Twentieth-Century Britain', in Elizabeth Whitelegg, Madeleine Arnot, Else Bartels, Veronica Beechey, Lynda Birke, Susan Himmelweit, Diana Leonard, Sonja Ruehl and Mary Anne Speakman (eds), *The Changing Experience of Women* (1982; rept ed., Oxford: Basil Blackwell, 1985), pp. 381–2; Susan Pedersen, 'Gender, Welfare and Citizenship in Britain During the Great War', *American Historical Review*, 95 (1990), p. 996; Robert Duncan, *Pubs and Patriots: The Drink Crisis in Britain during World War I* (Liverpool: Liverpool University Press, 2013).

36 *Crime, Media, Culture*, 4 (2008), pp. 9–30.

37 C. Critcher, 'Moral Panics and Newspaper Coverage of Binge Drinking', in Bob Franklin (ed.), *Pulling Newspapers Apart* (London: Routledge, 2008), pp. 154–62.

1

From the late Victorian boozer to the interwar improved public house

Late eighteenth-century brewers developed a new relationship with licensed premises, the tied house. Adopting a strategy known today as vertical integration, brewers began acquiring taverns and inns for diverse reasons: specialized retail shops emerged; brewers obtained surplus capital to supply innkeepers and tavern owners with credit; and the licensing bench imposed tougher restraints which, in reducing the number of drink shops, sent their prices soaring. As owners of their own distribution network, brewers wrote provisions into tenancy contracts stipulating that tenants had to sell just their lessee-owners' beers. But the brewer as the lessor assumed responsibility for structural alterations, such as general repairs, reconstruction and rebuilding. Such restrictive covenants led to the licensed premises being called tied houses.[1]

In response to these efforts to corner the beer market, Parliament enacted the Beer Act (1830), opening up sales to a new form of retailer, the beerhouse keeper. Outside the traditional licensing system and aiming at a clientele one step below inns and taverns, beerhouses could with a mere excise licence set up shop in cheaper premises but sell only beer, wine and cider. By 1869, when Parliament finally gave magistrates jurisdiction over newly licensed beerhouses in the Wine and Beerhouse Act, thereby ending the period of free licensing, 47,000 beerhouses had opened their doors, together with 18,000 new licensed victuallers' licences (now informally being called public house licences). Compared with 1829, the aggregate number of licences had more than doubled.[2]

Brewers' monopolistic habits were stifled, but not for long. Diverse motives – from erratic beer demand, falling licensed property values, local rivalries and fears of market exclusion – drove brewers to resume buying licensed property. Speculative gains, too, prompted purchases. Acquisitive-minded brewers equally received impetus from the expansion of the railway network, enabling the distribution of beers, especially of pale ales from Burton, with their higher profit margins.[3] By the 1880s, available non-tied licensed premises now quite diminished, breweries engaged in what one historian has called the 'Brewers' Wars'. Scrambling to control the remaining pubs and beerhouses, brewers intensified competition and drove up prices as sales of licensed property boomed. To fund escalating prices, breweries floated their stock and went public. With this new capital, large breweries aggressively took over smaller concerns and their tied house chains. By 1900, breweries had spent some £200 million on licensed property, all but £30 million within the previous three decades. Precise statistics do not exist, but most specialists would accept the estimate that just a minority of pubs and beerhouses, fewer than 25 per cent, had resisted pressure to sell out.[4]

In so doing, brewers' reputations plummeted. Accused of fostering acute commercial competition, participating in unethical behaviour and fomenting drunkenness, British breweries soon became compared to gigantic US firms such as Carnegie Steel or Rockefeller's Standard Oil. Central to each was vertical integration, the controlling of ancillary businesses as a calculated strategy for manipulating prices, competition and consumer choice. Huge British brewers, critics charged, had become vastly wealthy and exploited their network of pubs and beerhouses across the country to corrupt politics at the local as much as the national level, making meaningful reform impossible. To clinch the analogy, prohibitionists like T. P. Whittaker characterized British brewers as wielding 'a kind of British Tammany [Hall]', the notoriously crooked political machine in New York city synonymous with corruption.[5]

The dominant code of respectability and sexual morality, the embodiment of the morals and attitudes of the foremost social groups, powerfully shaped how women enjoyed leisure in late Victorian and Edwardian Britain.[6] Class thus placed a crucial role in attitudes to public drinking.

Temperance attacks stigmatizing drinking had successfully discredited pubs and beerhouses as popular venues for socializing. From the 1850s, the respectable classes, influenced in part by a cult of domesticity, began withdrawing from licensed premises, turning instead to wine merchants, off-licence shops, private clubs or restaurants for wines and spirits.[7] 'By the 1860's', wrote historian Brian Harrison, 'the respectable classes were drinking at home, or not drinking at all'. Novelist Charles Dickens, in an article about pubs in large towns published in 1864, related that working-class men 'are apt to regard any woman who shows herself in such a place as no better than she should be'. He noted the consequences: 'The public-house system shuts out the great mass of [respectable] women of the middle and lower classes'.[8] Prostitutes prowling or drinking on licensed premises also deterred respectable women from being seen in their company. Brewers themselves were disinclined to view females as potential customers since per capita beer consumption rose steadily in the 1860s and 1870s in England and Wales. This was not so much the result of increased temptation as of rapid urbanization, which created an entirely different environment for labourers.[9]

To promote rapid turnover of customers, publicans stripped tables, chairs and seats from their premises and prohibited games. By forcing patrons to stand, liquor sellers discouraged social intercourse. In London, such revamped establishments earned the name gin palaces; in the provinces, they were called vaults. Conversion into the new layout went speedily forward. By the late 1870s, four-fifths of Manchester's nearly five hundred pubs had acquired vaults. Whether in or outside the capital, licensed premises had been transformed simply into dram shops, with long service bars for quick service. Customers leaned against lengthy bars, drinking a shot or two of spirits. 'The minute you have finished your glass it is whipped away', remarked Dickens. No one doubted the meaning of the gesture. 'You are made to feel that you have no right to remain in the place another moment, unless you renew your consumption', he observed. Dubbed perpendicular drinking, this new approach maximized turnover, and put liquor consumption in the forefront – neither food nor accommodation mattered to dispensers of alcohol. To ensure privacy, pubs came to be designed so that customers, especially lower-class women, could enter one of several entrances which led to partitioned areas surrounding the bar. Such compartments in vaults resembled pawnbrokers' shops. Counter screens, blocking vision between customer, on one hand, and retailer as well as other patrons across the bar, on the other, protected drinkers from public disclosure. 'Few women would frequent a public-house if they had to go into rooms and sit down, open to the observations of all classes', maintained Thomas Higson, Clerk to the Manchester Justices.[10] Even so, only women of the lowest class, usually labourers' wives, used these partitioned spaces. They had no choice: 'A woman would hardly be tolerated in an ordinary inn; she would not be allowed to go and sit among a lot of men and drink', knew Chester's Chief Constable, George Lee Fenwick.[11]

Yet, as Fiona Fisher has recently argued, women could drink in some London pubs provided they avoided traditional male space. From the 1870s and into the 1880s, respectable women were being drawn into the jug and bottle department, a separate compartment where customers purchased liquor for home consumption. Here, ladies[12] of the neighbourhood could gather and socialize freely, drinking alcohol privately without challenging men's presence elsewhere on the licensed premises. Patronage of ladies, better-class districts and a flourishing jug and bottle compartment – these became hallmarks of such establishments. Privacy still remained a concern, so publicans placed counter screens in this bar, its heyday apparently over by the late 1880s.[13]

Nothing changed in the ensuing decades to diminish this masculine republic of drinking's pervasiveness (figure 1). A respectable woman, reflected one knowledgeable source late in the 1890s, 'would not expose herself in the bar of a public-house or spirit vaults'. This even applied to a bar in a first-class hotel. Such attitudes extended downwards into the lower middle and upper working classes.[14] Work as unskilled labour combined with domestic responsibilities occupied such women's time, not choices about how to spend their leisure.[15]

Notwithstanding these pervasive attitudes, Stella Moss recently asserted that many respectable women patronized licensed premises before 1914.[16] Copious evidence indicates, however, that women among the labouring poor aspiring to respectability had no greater freedom in using licensed premises than those socially above them. Too many circumstances, from widespread drunkenness, prowling prostitutes and austere premises to absence of seating, food and even toilets, discouraged females from patronizing drinking premises.

Liverpool authorities' treatment of women as second-class citizens exemplifies how pubs could become virtually unapproachable to most females.

The masculine republic of drinking, James and George Temple, The Tap, Pease Pottage, late victorian watercolour on paper. 1

Prostitutes were ubiquitous in the city's pubs, fostering repeated campaigns to regulate their behaviour. Unescorted women, however irreproachable their conduct, provoked attacks because their presence challenged the pub's well-known masculinity as much as patriarchal control of wives. Harassment of prostitutes culminated in demands in 1911 from the magistrates' clerk, who instructed publicans that female patrons could neither be served alcohol more than once nor treat each other to drinks. Given these rigid guidelines, all women – regardless of their purpose for drinking – found their access to pubs drastically circumscribed, their so-called rights little more than male forbearance towards social inferiors. Demeanour, clothing and drinking habits all served as basis for determining respectability, not prostitution. Thus, a woman with unblemished morality who sought to patronize pubs discovered that authorities regarded her as indistinguishable from prostitutes.[17] Long-standing hostility to women drinking publicly contributed materially to the moral panic over women using pubs throughout the North in the First World War.[18]

Liverpool may well have been an anomaly in its aggressive control of women drinkers, but other circumstances, such as pubs' overwhelming maleness, also powerfully deterred females from venturing into licensed premises. In the Lake District, historian Lyn Murfin discovered, women using pubs before the First World War were regarded as 'low'. A Carlisle woman relished one Edwardian slum pub because 'I could nip in and have a glass and come out again without anybody knowing'. The stigma against drinking went still further in Newcastle-upon-Tyne, where novelist Catherine Cookson recollected that either in retrieving alcohol or consuming it her mother forfeited respectability. Pubs in Craigneuk, near Glasgow, made the prohibition blatant with signs posted outside boozers: 'No Women allowed'. Desperate females violating the ban, seeking money from errant husbands, got beaten then and there for their audacity. At the other end of the country, the few females patronizing London licensed premises 'were written off as déclassées', recalled one brewer.[19] Villagers displayed no greater tolerance for women transgressing the inner sanctum of pubs.[20] Sometimes only the innkeeper's wife broke the gender barrier in rural Lancashire. Women, outfaced by male patrons at the Wagon and Horses in Juniper Hill on the Oxford/Northamptonshire border, discreetly ordered beer in a jug or bottle at the back door.[21] According to London brewer Sydney Nevile in 1939, who had known Edwardian pubs and beerhouses intimately, the improved pub movement instituted since the war's end 'seems to be killing the old prejudice that no respectable women ever went into a public house'.[22]

The working-class trinity – sport, beer and betting – likewise served as powerful deterrents to women venturing into the male republic of the pub, where men defined and projected their sense of masculinity. Brewers understood this relationship, investing in the stock of English football clubs, funding facilities for footballers and offering opportunities for players to supplement incomes. Even before retirement, some football players combined their careers with tenanting or managing public houses, where the ambience and conversation bespoke this sporting ethos. In drinking at the pub, men reinforced work, kinship and neighbourhood ties in public bars or vaults throughout the country, free to talk, joke and confide uninhibitedly without women present. Games played on or around licensed premises, notably billiards, bird shooting, rabbit coursing, dog racing, and knur and spell, as much as those using pubs as headquarters, such as football, all excluded females from this male fraternity. So did friendly societies and trade unions, which typically met on licensed premises because accommodating publicans allowed use of rooms for meetings in exchange for beer sales.[23]

Whether in urban or rural areas, unescorted women frequenting pubs were regarded as trolling for customers. Age became a key component in assessing respectability. Young women visiting pubs would have been denigrated as 'hussies', remembered a licensee's daughter in St Helens. Only on weekends, and then in male company, could respectable middle-aged and elderly women – shielded from charges of prostitution – gain admission to drinking premises without incurring public odium.[24]

Where respectability was most contested – industrial slums – women might experience the least amount of restraint.[25] With men in tow, labourers' wives bolstered the drinking clientele on Saturday and Sunday nights, sitting with husbands for all or part of the evening or separately with other women. In either case, men ordered beverages and paid for them at the bar. Depending on the area, women might drink outside licensed premises on pavements, alleyways, yards, streets or the outdoor (bottle and jug) departments, areas which males avoided. Inside pubs, such women might escape male supervision entirely, but just on Monday mornings when they drank with other females after retrieving goods pawned in the previous week.[26]

Unconcerned about or perhaps contemptuous of claims of respectability, impoverished women in slums certainly visited beerhouses, less often pubs, in greater numbers than other females. Whether they thought themselves respectable was not the issue; visiting pubs and beerhouses carried a social stigma antithetical to their recognition as such individuals outside their own neighbourhoods.[27] George Cruikshank's engraving 'The Boys in the Beer-Shop' (1848) vividly captures the pervasive drunkenness and presence of some slum women in beerhouses. According to a government survey of huge cities in 1908, numerous poverty-stricken mothers patronized some pubs and beerhouses, where they represented one-third or more of all customers on the days surveyed.[28] Women in other localities, social investigators confirmed, comprised significant proportions in some licensed establishments, constituting one-quarter and as many as one-third of the total.[29]

Here and elsewhere, women wage earners had greater freedom in visiting the pub. One contemporary felt that they had fewer inhibitions about drinking publicly because they had often fetched beer for parents' meals. 'The public-house was never a forbidden place to them, and as soon as they became wage-earners, it was their first resort', she remarked. Not surprisingly, when Jack London went down and out to explore London's East End in 1901, he found equal numbers of men and women in licensed premises.[30]

From the 1880s new group of drinkers, respectable members of the lower middle class, began entering pubs, which altered their layouts. To what extent did women modify their own drinking habits?

London, its size and diversity offering most scope for expanding the drinking clientele, displayed this development sooner and to a greater extent than other places, though even here increasing middle-class patrons represented a growing trend rather than a revolutionary transformation. Introduced into pubs was a new room, the saloon bar, the largest room with all the trappings of respectability – upholstered seats, tables and chairs, carpeting, a fireplace, wallpaper and flower vases. Higher alcohol prices supplied some of the financing for what became the apex of the hierarchy of drinking rooms. Multiplying in the 1870s and 1880s, compartments and snugs now began contracting in numbers, replaced with one or more public bars, followed by the most plebean, the private bar, and finally the jug and bottle area, which acted as an off-licence. Saloon bars and billiards rooms arrived together, with the former serving as the entrance to these separate game areas.[31]

In his study of Victorian pubs, Mark Girouard contended that more refined saloon bars in many pubs meant that 'respectable women started coming to pubs for the first time in their history' beginning in the 1890s.[32] This generalization went well beyond his evidence. With the collapse of the brewers' building wars around the turn of the century and the fall in total beer consumption, London brewers faced tight financial circumstances deterring heavy investment in pub alterations, save in upmarket vicinities with customers capable of paying more for alcohol.[33] Further down the social scale pubs and beerhouses remained much as before. Writing in the mid-1920s, one brewer could still admit that 'the average "pub" in working-class residential districts is not an inspiring institution'. Women would not have been drawn into such premises, where, notwithstanding requirements of licensing laws, often no toilets for them existed. Social values likewise inhibited public drinking. Many men and women from the lower middle classes aggressively embraced respectability, and viewed drinking as an unacceptable habit.[34]

Another historian has also advanced the argument for new women's drinking habits in London pubs in the 1890s. Unlike Girouard, Fiona Fisher made a more compelling case for this change, though her thesis focused largely on middle-class women in some of the capital's pubs. Women had displayed new shopping habits from the 1860s to the 1880s in West London, especially around Westbourne Grove, where diverse transformations in retailing, entertainment, catering, publishing and transportation produced what Erica Rappaport called 'a new type of mass public'. Critically from the perspective of women's drinking, 'new ideas of femininity and female public places developed', she maintained.[35] For Fisher, shopping acted as a catalyst a decade later for middle-class women to begin patronizing pubs in this vicinity which facilitated their entry with special 'ladies bars', reserved solely for respectable females. Physically small and partitioned off from the public or private bars, such bars were strategically placed, with a separate entrance to the street.[36] Big pubs along Buckingham Palace Road, Shaftesbury Avenue and Great Portland Street also introduced these special rooms. Lady Henry Somerset told the Royal Commission in 1898 that 'respectable women who would otherwise probably not have gone into public-houses at all' utilized these 'women's only' bars, underlining how public drinking and respectability were regarded as incompatible.[37]

Fisher, however, portrayed these bars as representing a 'turning point of some significance' in women's drinking habits in the 1890s, but this overstated the new trend's impact. There is no evidence of large provincial towns or cities undergoing a parallel development. Ladies' bars facilitated entry into a designated part of the pub, enabling female patrons to drink on the premises without challenging the stigma against the public house. In a revealing story on the ladies' bar at the Royal Oak, located in the centre of Westbourne Grove, the *Licensed Victuallers' Gazette* noted that 'ladies as a rule do not care to be seen entering a public-house'.[38] Proprietor of the Oak was Henry Finch who proposed altering another premises, the Hoop (Notting Hill Gate), with the addition of a 'ladies' bar'. In justifying his application to the magistrates, he stressed how this space allocated for women would not redraw gender boundaries. Women welcomed this bar 'because they know they will not come into contact with men'. Nor would the ladies' bar lead to intermixing on the rest of the premises, he emphasized. 'No women are ever served in any of my gentlemen's bars', he declared.[39] Drinking space, therefore, remained gendered, with women allocated a defined area. Ladies' bars did not overthrow the barriers of sex segregation. That such bars became fashionable primarily in reputable neighbourhoods from the 1890s suggested that gender conventions of public drinking had somewhat relaxed, not been fundamentally redrawn. Nomenclature adopted for these bars – ladies' saloon bars, ladies' only or simply ladies' bars – betrayed how promoters sought ladies, genteel, well-bred, cultured and respectable females, not women.[40]

This clear social distinction between ladies and women limited the scope of new drinking habits. Even in better-off neighbourhoods the influx of women can be easily exaggerated. Apart from West London, refined ladies would not typically drink publicly near their homes because off-licences easily outnumbered pubs or beerhouses. Brian Harrison's article closely correlated London's prosperous neighbourhoods with high levels of grocers' licences and poorer districts with heavy densities of on-licences.[41]

2 Wives' day out, 1928, the one day in which local women freely socialized among themselves.

Edwardian pubs and beerhouses, the preserve chiefly of the working class, thus asserted a pronounced masculinity. The culture of drinking in traditional pubs and beerhouses, their overpowering masculinity, depressing austerity and filthiness, and popular image as dens of alcoholic iniquity repelling social reformers, drinkers' wives and temperance advocates alike, did not long survive the First World War intact (Plate 2).

Government wartime regulations, women's entry into the economy, disappearance of male companionship, loneliness, and grief at lost loved ones – all acted as catalysts for the large influx of respectable women on to licensed premises during the First World War. So did publicans' restrictions of off-consumption sales, which compelled stout-drinking women who formerly drank at home to venture into pubs. 'After a while', Ernest Selley recorded, 'self-consciousness and reticence disappeared. The ice was broken', he learned, 'and what at first was a shamed faced and furtive act became open and unashamed.' These attitudes toward visiting pubs, of course, underscored how anxiety about risking respectability had kept respectable women out of pubs and beerhouses. From the middle class and, to a lesser extent, the upper working class, young women began frequenting licensed premises in unprecedented numbers from mid-1916 onwards, the first major change in women's drinking habits in three-fourths of a century.[42] Thus, this entry of females with a distinct emphasis on youth widened considerably both the gender and age composition of public drinking establishments. Shifting gender boundaries during the war also prompted respectable women's visiting of London night clubs for the first time. Another indication of changing female social behaviour was the increasing acceptance of smoking, formerly confined to bohemians and those scorning the code of respectability.[43]

In building and modernizing tens of thousands of pubs across the country in the interwar era, brewers displayed strong commitment to widening the pub's clientele, with women and men from the respectable working and middle classes being grafted on to a broader working-class male base.[44]

To what extent were they successful? Rising numbers of retailers applying for wine licences afforded one sign of women's growing patronage of improved pubs and beerhouses. In London, 'women customers', remarked one newspaper, 'like to accompany their husbands to an inn in the evening without being required to partake of stronger drink than wine'. Family sociability, more commonly called the 'continental' style of leisure, flourished, with gardens stocked with tables and chairs. In 1932, the Bullfinch in Riverhead, refurbished five years earlier for £1500, demonstrated the link between upgraded premises and wider women's custom. 'In the olden days', reflected the *Beer and Skittles*, 'the wife was content to sit at home while her husband went out. Now', the journal added, 'they went together and the wife preferred to drink a glass of wine instead of a glass of beer'.[45] Given these new habits, domestic drinking of beer 'in working-class homes is negligible', concluded a detailed study of five thousand budgets in seven large urban areas late in the 1930s.[46]

To suburban London saloon bars, now more refined with upholstered chairs and carpeting than public bars, came respectable women for whom brewers specifically catered by feminizing the décor with wooden tables, chairs, even flowers and newspapers. Assaulting masculine drinking culture entailed transforming billiard rooms into lounges with gramophone music played sedately in the background. Lewis Melville's book *The London Scene*, published in 1926, left no doubt about the consequences: 'More and more women "drop in" to the better-conducted [public] houses', owing to the decline of drunkenness. B. D. Nicholson reached similar findings when studying inner and outer London pubs in the following decade for H. Llewellyn Smith's *New Survey of London*. In 'most of the public-houses which have made improvements', he noted, 'women customers are of more than average importance'. Again women turned to less masculine rooms, especially private and saloon bars, regardless of both their class and higher prices for the same beverages.[47]

Recently, Terry Gourvish has challenged the extent to which improved pubs transformed women's leisure. Because reformed pubs were confined primarily to middle-class areas and the affluent South-east, masculine culture in pubs scarcely altered, he argued. To support his contention, he cited Mass-Observation's statistic of women constituting 16 per cent of Bolton's pub and beerhouse patrons late in the 1930s. For Gourvish, therefore, this one economically depressed Northern industrial town stood as representative of the whole country for the entire interwar era.[48]

Progressive brewers fully understood the powerful male citadel in the public bar, and wisely left it unchallenged.[49] Instead, in improved public houses they drew respectable women and men to the lounge, with waiter service, meals, music, flowers, pleasant surroundings and plush seating (Plate 3). Clearly, décorating a new pub in Hull with pale green colour and brown moquette seating had little appeal to heterosexual men. Such colours were, the *Brewers' Journal* commented, 'essentially designed to suit the taste of the ladies'.[50]

In its study *The Pub and the People* in the mid-1930s, Mass-Observation reckoned that just 16 per cent of customers were females in some Bolton pubs and beerhouses, but it would be surprising if this were taken as a representa-

Garden lounge, Rose & Crown, Huyton, Lancashire, 3
rebuilt by Peter Walker & Son, 1936.

tive figure for the whole country.[51] Typically, as one went north from London, masculinity became more pronounced and hostility to women drinking publicly rose commensurately.[52]

Two-thirds of Bolton's on-licenses were beerhouses, their furnishings austere, premises small, drink selection limited and clientele confined to the impoverished. So powerful in fact was masculine opposition to women that beerhouse keepers sometimes excluded them altogether from specific drinking spaces by designating 'men-only' drinking bars, a feature which persisted throughout the region well into the 1940s and beyond. This in turn reflected women's confinement to the home as wives dependent economically on husbands. When newspaper columnist J. B. Priestley spent several days in a similar Northern town, he dismissed the drinking establishments out of hand. 'They were', he wrote, 'gloomy and dingy beerhouses, which offered you a chance to swill and nothing more'.[53]

Predictably, local and regional brewers thought it economically unwise to upgrade interwar premises during the depression. Because the town's leading local brewery, Magee Marshall & Co., a medium-sized company with several hundred tied houses, chose to rebuild just two of its Bolton premises, only one non-local brewery committed minuscule funds of £1010 to reconstructing one establishment. That few women, estimated at 16 per cent, could be found in Bolton pubs should have surprised no one.[54]

However interesting, thought-provoking and wide ranging, Mass-Observation's research was nevertheless highly impressionistic. 'There was a conflict in Mass-Observation from the outset between a populist wish to show "us" to "us" and "us" to "them" and a determination to be scientific', wrote Angus Calder in a perceptive appraisal. 'There was a further dilemma', he added, 'arising from the notion that an unbiased social science must be unselective'. These incongruities became conspicuously transparent when generalizing on a national level. Returning to Bolton in 1960 to reprise what had changed in the intervening years since research was finished on *The Pub and the People*, Mass-Observation concluded that 'there is unarguable evidence in Mass-Observation's comparative observations and in "general experience", that *more women are drinking more alcohol than ever before*'. That same year the British Market Research Bureau's survey, using sophisticated statistical analysis with random sampling techniques, calculated that the percentage of women drinking in licensed premises nationally had contracted to a low of 17 per cent, with just another 16 per cent consuming alcohol elsewhere. Two-thirds of all women now abstained from all alcohol. Nothing better illustrated the limitations of Mass-Observation's statistical methodology as an accurate indicator of national trends than this disparity.[55]

Bolton exemplified one extreme of a continuum which characterized women's interwar drinking, but even in the North it was atypical of towns and cities of some size. Nearby, Manchester brewers invested considerably in improving many pubs and beerhouses with impressive results: 'if the customers could be counted, I should imagine the women would outnumber men', said one councillor.[56] Salford women likewise no longer felt inhibited about frequenting pubs without male escorts. 'To the shocked stares of the respectable', recalled Robert Roberts of the early 1920s, 'housewives with husbands away or on night work could now be seen going off in pairs to the pictures or sitting with a glass of stout in the Best Room at the pub'. Young housewives accompanied husbands, and drank with them, 'bitter for bitter', in the Best Room. Overall, thought Roberts, 'more young people began to frequent public houses'.[57]

Though high unemployment depressed living conditions in the industrial North, some brewers still improved many pubs. Labour as well as building costs, together with interest rates from banks, were all low; profits for these breweries remained solid; and upgrading licensed premises with wider and better amenities, including lounges, served as a marketing tactic for driving smaller competitors out of business and pre-empting rivals entertaining ideas about encroaching on markets. For all these reasons, some Northern brewers committed sizeable sums to upgrading tied house estates, despite Terry Gourvish's view of pub reform as a primarily South-eastern phenomenon.[58]

York, dependent on wool and so less affected by the depression, represented the other end of the continuum. Beerhouses, so plentiful in Bolton, were here virtually absent, accounting for just 10 per cent of the total on-licences. Here women, too, worked outside the home, many of them employed in the town's model factory, New Earswick, run by B. Seebohm Rowntree who ironically studied their drinking habits as well as those of other females for his investigation *Poverty and Progress* (1941). Unlike Bolton, brewers, notably the Tadcaster Tower Brewery, John Smith's and John J. Hunt, spent impressive sums building new and rebuilding old establishments in York. Of the fourteen new or rebuilt pubs, the Hop Inn cost Tadcaster Tower Brewery £7400 to rebuild, nothing even remotely comparable being undertaken in Bolton.[59] Respectable working- and middle-class women flocked to these modern places more than to any of the others. 'There is not the old hesitation in entering public-houses, especially those which have been improved in recent years', Rowntree observed. Young women under twenty-five preferred these up-to-date premises, with fully three-fourths of them counted as frequenters. Rowntree tabulated that in York 'in the most modern house I found almost as many women as men'. Even after marriage, wives displayed independence remarkable for interwar women, much less for those in the North. Employed outside the home, York wives refused to remain there alone while husbands went out drinking, and, asserting their own autonomy, began visiting pubs, occasionally several times a week. All of these factors explain why the proportion of women in York's pubs vastly exceeded those in Bolton.[60]

Were York's hotels, not pubs or beerhouses, principally responsible for drawing exclusively middle-class patrons who were wrongly credited as the cause of rising numbers of women in pubs? Throughout the interwar years, publicans, eager to project their establishments as more refined than mere watering holes, renamed them 'hotels' and listed them as such in county directories. By defining hotels as licensed establishments where proceeds from drink did not trump profits from everything else, Rowntree himself contributed to confusion.[61]

Nothing, however, was said about the lounge, the quintessential feature of interwar 'improved pubs' and the sole gender-neutral space where some upper-working-class and more middle-class couples went without fear of violating powerful masculine drinking norms. The term itself was associ-

4 Dining room, Bridge Hotel, Greenford, Middlesex, built by Young's Brewery in 1935.

ated with upmarket hotels and ladies' clubs for fashionably attired women.[62] Unlike other public or saloon bars, lounges had only either small or service bars, together with waiter service. Food too characterized such establishments (Plate 4). Many genuine pubs and some hotels fell into this category. Courting couples from the upper working class would have frequented them because they offered an ambience with amenities and music unavailable in traditional pubs. In this behaviour of drinking upwards socially, the young resembled their parents. Married working-class men drank in public bars with male friends during the week, but on weekends, when accompanied by wives and dressed in better clothes, chose a plusher room for drinking, the saloon bar, sometimes called the smoke or sitting room depending on geography, or, if available, the lounge.[63]

Rowntree's data, however, must be used cautiously. His 'sample' really consisted of just one licensed house, which he thought representative of dozens of houses in this group. Not more than one of his pubs forming the third category would probably have been an 'improved pub'. Rowntree thus documented rising numbers of young women in drinking establishments in the 1930s, but failed to see improved pubs, class, the lounge and dating behaviour as critical determinants of drinking behaviour.[64]

By no means were changes in the pub's clientele confined to just York or Manchester in the North. In Sheffield, a grammar school headmaster reported having witnessed 'young men and women who would not have gone anywhere near a public house of the old type entering and leaving these ultra-modern public houses'. One Yorkshire publican exemplified these changes. John Sheard, former coal miner for thirty years, retired from his beloved Robin Hood Hotel, Altofts, near Normanton, Yorkshire, for long an oasis from civilization. But now entry of women had changed the pub's clientele: '"I don't like these modern places filled with young women"', and vowed he would look '"for an old inn where women don't go"'.[65] Public house improvement had transformed women's perspective of drinking in public, declared the *Yorkshire Evening News*. Because improved pubs projected a more respectable image, 'women are patronising them in greatly increased numbers', not just in the North but throughout the country.[66]

Another interwar study, *The New Survey of London Life and Labour*, disagreed. No one has previously placed Sir Hubert Llewellyn Smith's discussion of drinking in its proper historical context. In characterizing patrons as idlers consuming both time and alcohol, he came to the topic of the pub with distinct biases. For their part, brewers earned his disapproval for fostering quick turnover of patrons with 'perpendicular drinking', publicizing a few 'model' improved premises, and being generally apathetic towards pub reform. Magistrates, he believed, moreover, obstructed brewers' applications for improvements, and so stultified efforts to upgrade premises.[67]

Llewellyn Smith's assertions sit oddly with the facts. By the time volume nine on life and leisure appeared in 1935, magistrates had approved thousands of projects which involved entirely new or rebuilt premises, including hundreds in London. Still more pubs and beerhouses embraced the improved pub ethos as brewers spent £1000 or more on each project. Far from being indifferent to pub reform as Llewellyn Smith would have it, they had devoted vast sums of money to improvements. They deliberately engaged in social engineering to modify the prevailing drinking culture as a necessary prerequisite for discouraging drunkenness, and promoting conversation as well as family sociability. Central to this reform philosophy was the introduction of tables and chairs and waiter service. Perpendicular drinking, with customers leaning against long service bars, had been a hallmark of the old drinking regime, now under serious attack for causing drunkenness. Llewellyn Smith's depictions of London pubs in 1935 were 15 or 20 years out of date.[68]

Why did the chapter on drink in the *New Survey* not offer him accurate, informed material? Nicholson's lack of expertise and time in which to explore the topic explain his anachronistic views of drinking in the 1930s. This was especially true of his description of London pubs as having three different drinking rooms – public, private and saloon. Well over one thousand 'improved pubs' appeared in London during the interwar years, with many, perhaps most, containing a new room, the lounge, the defining feature of these new architecturally designed premises. Here women foregathered with men in truly gender-neutral space. In pointing to frosted windows, drinkers with cloth caps, proprietary drink advertisements, sawdust, standup (perpendicular) drinking and austere walls, Nicholson betrayed himself rooted in the pub culture of the 1890s and early 1900s, not of the interwar era. Even in public bars, for example, sawdust, still ubiquitous in the Edwardian era, had disappeared from most London pubs, except for the most traditional, by the 1930s. Mindful of these anachronisms, his generalization that 'there are fewer women to be seen in the public-houses than before the War' must be viewed with great scepticism.[69]

Other factors prompt serious questioning of Nicholson's judgements. Of some six hundred pubs surveyed, none selected on a statistically random basis, Nicholson compiled figures from just eight of them over a two-night period in 1933–4, chosen again on an unspecified basis and with locations unidentified.[70] These eight pubs provided data for his table. Given this limited, unrepresentative group, the notion of women constituting one-fourth of the clientele in London pubs becomes virtually meaningless. In reviewing this volume, the *Brewers' Journal* dismissed Nicholson's assertion that women were patronizing licensed premises in decreasing numbers. 'Whilst women of the working classes – particularly during the mid-day session – do not use licensed premises to the extent they did in prewar days, we are sure that licensed houses are patronized to-day much more by women of the middle classes.' In seeking an explanation for this development, the *Journal*, echoing Selley's conclusions several years earlier, pointed to the attractions of improved public houses for respectable women.[71]

Why then had not Selley been appointed to draft the drinking section in the *New Survey*?[72] Well into the project's development, the organizers were still vainly seeking an expert to write on drink. Finally, in the year before the last volume appeared, they selected a relative unknown, B. D. Nicholson, appointed as a distant second best to Ernest Selley, author of the impressive survey of drinking some years earlier, who declined owing to illness.[73] Selley would have brought to the survey's exploration of drinking unrivalled knowledge of the entire country from extensive travels in the mid-1920s.

Table 1 Selley's investigation of drinking habits, 1925–6.

Area	*City/District*
North	Bolton, Carlisle, Chorley, Leeds, Maryport, Middlesbrough, Newcastle, Preston, North Shields, South Shields, Sunderland, and Wallsend
Midlands	Birmingham, Burslem, Coventry, Hanley, Leek, Longton, Stoke, and Tunstall,
South	Cheltenham, Glouceste, Luton, and Southgate
Greater London	Wapping, Whitechapel, Wood Green, and West Ham

No other book exploring the nation's drinking habits in the entire interwar era could claim as much authenticity as Ernest Selley's *The English Public House as It Is*, and none has received as little scholarly attention! Published in 1927, the culmination of two years and more of detailed field research, it offered conclusions painstakingly gathered from some twenty provincial cities dispersed over the country and, most importantly for the *New Survey* writers, greater London (Table 1). Already drinking habits had changed visibly, Selley had discovered. 'Large numbers of women who took their glass of supper beer or stout at home', he commented, 'now take it in public houses'. It was not so much that women who visited pubs went to them more often, as that 'a greater proportion of women visit public houses'. The base of women pub drinkers had already enlarged considerably as a result of Progressive brewers' improved pubs. Aware of subtle class distinctions, Selley observed that 'the increase has occurred chiefly in the better-class public house and among the more respectable types of women'. In his classification, such women stood socially a distinct level above 'the harridan type'. The former were emphatically not, as Gourvish claimed, solely middle-class women, but included respectable upper working-class ones as well.[74]

Pub culture had become more fragmented since Edwardian England. According to Selley, women's presence in such pubs varied enormously, ranging from outright exclusion and consignment to segregated snugs, bottle and jug departments, kitchens and alley ways, on one hand, to fraternization with female friends while husbands joined their mates elsewhere on the premises, on the other. Groups of older or elderly women also came unescorted to pubs and beerhouses. London dockland pubs banned women, unless they worked on the docks and sympathetic licensees served them tea in a separate room. On special occasions, when husband and wife went for a night out together, they did visit dockland pubs, where each had a glass of Guinness and a twopenny sandwich. Nevertheless, leisure still remained segregated in these traditional licensed premises. No wives accompanied husbands on annual pub outings (called Beanos) to the seaside – they were allowed to wave spouses goodbye as they sped off on what became an extended tour of by-pass pubs. North-eastern miners likewise refused to admit women to pubs and beerhouses. Strongest opposition by far came in Scotland, where tradition as much as prevailing sentiment 'effectively prevents a woman going into a public house'. Much depended on whether women, as in Lancashire textile districts, earned money, which conferred some measure of economic independence, including freedom to patronize local pubs.[75] On this disparate culture of female drinking was now imposed another layer in which respectable upper-working-class and middle-class women occupied special space to socialize with male companions.

Had Selley shared his expertise with Llewellyn Smith for the *New Survey*, an entirely different analysis, more accurate, nuanced and broad based, would have appeared pointing to a new drink culture's emergence. In retrospect, Selley's approach would have avoided many of the shortcomings inherent in those who derived their conclusions from quantitative material.

Given the serious limitations of both evidence and types of urban centres that Mass-Observation, Rowntree and Nicholson studied, any attempt to extrapolate from their findings to estimate the influx of women into pubs in Britain generally is meaningless.

There is too another, still more critical, methodological flaw, as unappreciated by contemporaries as by scholars. Whatever proportion women comprised of the total clientele in certain pubs in any locality, no valid inference can be drawn about the total number of women in the area covered who drank in licensed premises. To derive a trustworthy figure of what proportion of women drank, the critical data must be based on the answers given by an actuarial sample drawn randomly from the whole female population who, when asked whether they frequented local pubs, described how and where they drank throughout the year. Put another way, in assessing how many women drank, focus should be, not on what proportion they constituted of those physically in pubs at any given moment, but on what per centage of females in the broader community drank in such establishments over a period of time. Pubs could doubtless be found, for example, in which women comprised one-fourth of the patrons on a given day, but across the country females composed overall a much higher figure of pub goers over the course of a month or year. Perhaps one-third or even two-fifths or more of all women frequented pubs at some time during the year in the interwar era. Undercounting was a vital component of these proportions. Certainly, the proportion of all women who went to pubs was higher than the proportion of people seen in pubs at any time who were women. Sharply contrasting with the present day, men visited pubs more often than women in interwar England. Whatever the precise proportion, respectable upper working- and middle-class women were patronizing pubs in unparalleled numbers in response to tens of thousands of improved public houses, with superior amenities, more capacious premises, food, tea rooms and the lounge, the quintessential sign of genteel drinking (Plate 5).

Because Gourvish equated reformed pubs with 'middle-class enclaves', he equally misinterpreted the nature of pub improvement. In Whitbread's in-house journal, Sydney O. Nevile wrote that 'it is in the working-class residential neighbourhoods where the need for a change is most felt and where the scope is extensive'.[76] Pub improvement, however, did not consist merely of the massive outlay of capital on newly built premises. With 78,000 pubs and beerhouses in the country, such an undertaking was financially impossible. Less expensive but still useful improvements – higher hygienic standards and greater floor space as a prerequisite to installing tables, chairs and catering equipment – could still be pursued with beneficial results in slums.

Ladies' tea room, Reindeer, Peckham, London, 1932. 5

That Progressive brewers sold bigger quantities of beer in working-class districts overall than elsewhere naturally prompted their keen interest in retaining and indeed expanding this clientele base, especially since total beer consumption continued falling from 25 million barrels (1920) to 14 million barrels (1932). To argue otherwise displays a misunderstanding of the economics of brewing. Sydney Nevile, quintessential leader of public house improvement, told the Royal Commission on Licensing in 1930 that 'in every district, in poor districts especially, the general policy ought to be one of general improvement'.[77]

Class proved critical in brewers' thinking about working-class pub improvement. 'If you take the price paid by the industrial consumer', noted Sydney Nevile, 'you could not build improved [public] houses to supply him unless you had better class people with more money in their pockets to spend in the saloon bar to help the [brewer-owner] carry the expenses'.[78] Redistribution of licences became vital to reducing cut-throat competition and offering residents in new outlying districts attractive places in which to drink. 'The removal of redundant houses from poor districts', commented a brewer, 'renders the remaining houses more profitable and thus it becomes economically possible to improve the survivors'.[79] Running a broad gamut from minimal improvements, through reconstruction and finally to rebuilding or even a new building, improved pubs thus were found throughout all types of urban and suburban areas in working- and middle-class districts as well as in slums and propertied neighbourhoods. Repeatedly, Nevile and other Progressive brewers reiterated that investment in pub reform earned at best modest returns, sometimes nothing at all. 'We want to give the working man better surroundings … but it is not easy to keep it on an economic basis', he admitted.[80]

Why then not ignore slum pubs and concentrate on the propertied classes who could afford more expensive drinks? Stella Moss suggested that brewers in fact did so, abandoning their Progressivism for profits. For brewers, she maintained, 'a new layout … was more important as a commercial proposition, than as a spur to social amelioration'.[81]

It is indeed on this issue that Progressive brewers challenged several historians' assertions about the relationship between class and pub reform. For Progressive brewers, as Cecil Chapman explained in a letter to the press, the overriding issue was the desire to be businessmen with a social conscience, not profit maximisers. As a former London JP and Chairman of an organization dedicated to transforming the drinking culture in slums, Chapman could shield these brewers from baseless accusations of self-interested and avaricious motives.[82] Had these been their primary inspirations, pub improvement would have been extremely limited in scope, confined to propertied districts and – overlooked in this debate – markedly less costly owing to limited numbers of licensed premises located in middle-class enclaves.

But many brewers, whose outlook reflected their Progressive beliefs, had entirely different goals. Pre-eminently, they sought much less drunkenness, a clientele as diverse as refreshments and amenities being introduced at improved licensed premises, and regained public esteem. In embracing a policy of 'sobriety plus good service' in 1919, Progressive brewers displayed their mentality, which Sydney Nevile contended, arose solely from 'patriotic and purely domestic motives'. Pride became a key factor propelling these men to advocate public house reform. As Nevile declared before a meeting of brewers in 1919, he and other leading brewers were committed to 'influencing for good the destinies of our own and future generations'.[83]

Progressive brewers spent prodigiously on transforming slum and working-class pubs.[84] Notwithstanding the perception associating improved pubs with

Table 2 Improved pubs in London's interwar slums.

Borough	*Poverty, 1929–30 (%)*	*Number of new or rebuilt premises*
Poplar	24.1%	12
Shoreditch	18%	10
BethnalGreen	17.8%	9
Bermondsey	17.5%	32
Stepney	15.5%	17
Deptford	14.6%	7
Southwark	13.5%	23
Finsbury	13.2%	24
Greenwich	11.8%	14
St.Pancras	11.8%	37
Islington	9.6%	22
Woolwich	8.8%	25
Lambeth	8.5%	41
Camberwell	8.2%	30
Total		303

Sources: Sir Hubert Llewellyn Smith, *The New Survey of London Life and Labour*, vol. 3: *Survey of Social Conditions: The Eastern Area* (London: P.S. King & Son, 1932), pp. 343–412; vol. 6: *Survey of Social Conditions: The Western Area* (London: P.S. King & Son, 1934), pp. 379–462; Gutzke, *Pubs and Progressives*, pp. 243–5.

bourgeois areas, Progressive brewers devoted considerable sums to upgrading licensed premises in slums, where families's income fell below what the *New Survey of London* defined as the 'poverty line', 38s–40s weekly. [85] London boroughs with the highest proportions of poverty, averaging 12.9 per cent, were also those in which Progressive brewers built or rebuilt the most pubs (Table 2).[86] Nearly three-fifths of rebuildings were located in just half of London's districts, the most poverty stricken in the capital. Part of these improvements at Whitbreads, for example, entailed providing new or improving existing water closets: 55 tied houses received them and another 27 acquired improved ladies' toilets just in the 1930s.[87]

Stella Moss recently alleged that Progressive brewers should not be credited with improving women's toilets, a facet of licensed premises dictated by licensing law.[88] What was legally specified and actually existed, however, diverged widely in many instances. 'Some of these [unreformed] places are decrepit, with … no accommodation for women', complained Newcastle's Chief Constable in 1930. Decades later in the mid-1950s the *Brewers' Journal* knew that many licensed premises still had 'no lavatory accommodation for either sex save an outside unroofed urinal'.[89] London certainly did not escape censure. 'The worst of the little places', commented one woman about the capital's smaller licensed premises in 1943, 'is that often there isn't a ladies'. Moss, moreover, overlooked the fact that licensing law did not stipulate the quality of facilities required, especially since women had not historically constituted a significant part of the clientele of licensed premises. In one of the first statements on public house improvement in December 1920, the *House of Whitbread*, the brewery's in-house magazine, laid stress especially on toilets. It was therefore not just a question of whether they existed on licensed premises, but of their location and provisions. Here, the magazine instructed that women's lavatory facilities be placed on the ground floor, and provided with wash basins! Given the primitive conditions often in men's toilets, it is hardly surprising that the brewery had to specify how it proposed to upgrade women's water closets. Hence, improved women's toilets, as I have argued elsewhere, provided another indication of women's vital importance in Progressive brewers' promotion of pub reform.[90]

In transforming pub culture, Progressive brewers not merely changed bricks, mortar and layout but engaged in somewhat more sophisticated social engineering than the London County Council. Moral uplift, the conviction that enriching the environment would elevate the individual, motivated many reforms. Two repertory companies performed 'working-men's cabarets' at some of Barclay Perkins pubs, and, notwithstanding an entrance fee, generated huge audiences, running to five thousand monthly with families in large attendance. Bringing highbrow culture to the masses at improved pubs was the Committee for Verse and Prose Recitation, which used volunteers to recite poetry. Whether performing Shakespeare's *The Two Gentlemen of Verona* or reciting poems by Hilaire Belloc and Rupert Brooke, the 'V & P' ventured into traditional, in some cases rough, working-class pubs where audiences received them enthusiastically. 'We have discovered audiences for good poetry and plays in the most unsuspected places and some of our most cordial receptions have come from those for whom it was a first experience', confirmed John Holgate, the 'V & P's' organizer.[91]

Another indicator of women's use of the lounge or refurbished saloon bars was the disappearance of the ladies' bar. Popular especially in some central London pubs, ladies' bars became relics of the prewar era. No less of an authority than Maurice Gorham, who summarized the state of public houses just before the Second World War, thought that 'no rebuilt pub is likely to have one'. He was somewhat premature in pronouncing the death of these sex-segregated rooms. Of 54 new pubs featured in the *Architects' Journal* in 1938, three still contained women's bars.[92]

As in so much else, the North proved quite conservative, though not entirely immune to changes in national drinking habits.[93] Ladies' or men-only bars still flourished in many Northern watering holes, including six new wartime Carlisle pubs. Even more restrictive was the total prohibition of women from Middlesbrough pubs, begun in 1917 and upheld until 1926.[94] Bona fide working-men's clubs, numbering some 16,000 late in the 1930s with their geographic base in the North, seldom admitted women as members. Three-fourths of them, in fact, specifically banned them.[95]

But many Northern cities still embraced the new subculture of respectable female drinking. Filson Young had reported seeing larger numbers of women in Carlisle's improved pubs on his visit in 1926. This influx in part revealed altered attitudes to women's rooms, where men joining women had desegregated drinking in the 1920s. Residents came to view these sex-segregated rooms as abhorrent and so took the initiative in instituting sexual equality in drinking.[96] Elsewhere, sexual equality also made headway. 'It is very noticeable, especially in the north, how an improved licensed house meets the needs of women customers', remarked Sydney Nevile in an interview in 1939. 'It seems', he added, 'to be killing the old prejudice that no respectable woman ever went into a public house'.[97]

6 Advertisment, *Gloucestershire Echo*, 27 Oct. 1938, Cheltenham (Original) Brewery.

Underlining the heightened importance of females as pub customers, brewers' advertising aimed directly at women as potential pub customers for the first time in the 1930s (Plate 6). Cheltenham Original Brewery, for example, designed an advertisement in which two well-dressed men sat at a table with a correspondingly attired woman. At the bar, one of them ordered a bottle of Cheltenham Ale, which the barmaid prepared to pour into a half-pint glass, both the bottle and glass size crucial indicators of drinking in the lounge. Other breweries, such as Eldridge Pope, prepared publicity literature for openings of new premises showing couples walking from their motor cars to the new premises. Where sales promised sizeable profits, Northern breweries likewise advertised. At the grand opening of the newly built Aintree Hotel, Bent's brewery depicted two middle-class women accompanying a man emerging from the premises in its publicity literature. On these premises, the brewery laid out £16,000, a vast sum especially in the depressed North.[98] Using an innovative approach, Guinness's advertising agency interviewed women who revealed that they drank Guinness over other brands because, as the brewery's advertisement proclaimed, the stout was 'good for them'. Guinness's chief rival, Mackeson's stout, also targeted women in its advertisements.[99]

Similarly, cider manufacturers for the first time began targeting female drinkers with advertisements. Henley's, for instance, linked its Devonshire Cyder with medicinal advantages, including greater energy, youthful skin and twinkling eyes. 'There's no healthier drink than Henley's Cyder', boasted its advertisement, which portrayed a young women seated at a table drinking the product. This was no one-off effort. 'The Modern Girl Votes for Cyder', the advertisements' caption, appeared in the *Daily Mail* for six consecutive years from 1922. Schweppes likewise suggested its cider would give female athletes 'health and slimness'. By the late 1930s, such advertisements had achieved considerable success. Women's consumption of cider, urged one periodical, had propelled the industry's rising sales.[100]

Symptomatic of women's visible and accepted presence on licensed premises was their new role as dart players. Darts playing became a craze in the 1930s, with 'hundreds of applications for alterations to the bars of licensed premises' filed to create room for the sport. At their tied houses, breweries sponsored Darts Leagues, and some adventurous companies even hired a games organizer.[101] Some breweries took the next step in sponsoring leagues and darts championships solely for women. Patrick Chaplin's recent study of the growth of darts in interwar England revealed how the National Darts Association accepted women as participants in the Licensees' Charity Cup, provided they qualified as the licensee or wife of the licence holder. Simultaneously, the Association allowed women to compete in the *News of the World* Individual Darts Championship, with the first female, Mrs Morgan, winning an area title in 1937. As wife of a licensee, Morgan could practise darts freely whenever she wanted in the public bar, the masculine stronghold which monopolized the game. In inaugurating the desegregation of darts as a male activity, Chaplin declared, the Association however tentatively 'began to undermine the status of the public bar as an exclusively male domain'. This in turn enabled the pub's image to be seen as less of an enclave for men only, inspiring new attitudes to women drinking publicly. Geography, however, still proved critical in this progress. Northern men remained less receptive than those in the South to women participating in the sport on an equal basis. Nowhere was the backlash against darts as a gender-neutral activity more intense than in South Shields where men banned women altogether from official league play.[102] But in a larger perspective, women, though not always welcome and sometimes still excluded from male recreational activities in public bars, made definite headway in gaining acceptance in the lounge, where competition between the sexes simply did not exist.

Women frequented reformed pubs for other reasons as well. At Birmingham's new suburban pubs, 'each of the model houses runs its own particular social activities', such as dance classes, glee clubs, musical societies and tea meetings, commented the *Daily Express* reporter. Leeds magistrates encouraged women's use of pubs for afternoon teas and wireless concerts. 'One immediate result of the movement has been to increase enormously the number of women who visit licensed premises', remarked one newspaper. As these functions testified, women visited pubs for numerous events, not all, or even most, of which entailed drinking alcohol.[103]

British mystery writers, often keen observers of social behaviour, promptly recorded changes in women's drinking norms in contemporary novels. Here again was compelling evidence of Progressive brewers' success in challenging traditional gender barriers in public drinking. Of the many novelists whose plots focused on the pub, Joanna Cannan ranked as one of the most astute, partly because of her intimate personal knowledge. In her wartime novel *Death at the Dog*, placed near her home in Reading, Cannan depicts novelist Crescy Hardwick arriving alone to drink in the Dog's lounge, the bar with the 'club-like atmosphere' where other middle-class habituates gather to consume whisky and halves of bitter or mild. Strict class segregation prevails, with labourers drinking in the public bar, their dart board, rudimentary furnishings and cheaper prices all reassuringly working class. Only when enticed with the promise of a darts game did some middle-class lounge patrons venture across the class divide into largely unexplored territory. Unless accompanied by men, women never left the safe class confines of the lounge.[104]

Looking back on these interwar years, a knowledgeable observer reflected that 'a tremendous revolution has taken place in the attitude of the womenfolk of the English middle classes towards the public house'. For him, as for many others, the reason was obvious: newly built or renovated 'improved public houses' had facilitated the entry of huge numbers of women. Such women now frequented pubs with male friends as easily as visiting a cinema or playing tennis in a park.[105] Here there is an interesting parallel with food. As John Walton argued in his well-researched study, fish and chips customers moved upwards socially into middle-class residential neighbourhoods during the interwar years. What was said about this business equally applied to improved pubs. 'Business men, women shoppers, cinema fans, and now motorists, are being catered for', commented one trade journalist.[106]

This thesis of the metamorphosis in drinking habits for such women supports recent historiography that emphasizes how female roles in interwar England became modified as a result of the 'articulation of a self-consciously "modern" femininity that drew upon real changes in the political, social, economic, and sexual position of women'.[107] For women as respectable public drinkers, there was a social revolution that affected much of England and parts of Wales, as regional and national breweries vied for public acclaim and larger market shares by laying out vast sums of money.[108]

In spending about £100 million, brewers built or rebuilt about six thousand pubs and beerhouses and significantly improved tens of thousands more, with well over half of the total on-licences in England and Wales involved in pub improvement on a significant scale. One historian has recently dismissed this huge figure as little more in most cases than window dressing, 'simply the removal of a snug or an internal passageway'.[109] Given that brewers could construct new or rebuild old licensed premises for as little as £3000–3500, the outlay of £1100–1200 on alterations constituted far more than such cosmetic changes. Often, applications sought more space for introducing tables, chairs, catering facilities and converting a billiards room into a lounge. Pub reform was a genuine effort on a massive scale to transform, indeed destroy, the overwhelming masculine culture of drinking. Nothing less than a huge financial commitment implementing the reform philosophy, Progressive brewers realized, would draw the respectable classes, including women, to licensed premises.[110]

As the bulk of beer drinkers consisted of males largely from the working class, with a smaller group from the lower middle class, their drinking premises stood a strong likelihood of undergoing improvement, as gardens, lounges, dining and assembly rooms, entertainment and other amenities transformed the masculine drinking culture. To tens of thousands of improved pubs respectable middle- and upper-working-class women would flock in greater numbers throughout the interwar era. 'The improvement which had taken place in the public house during recent years had made it possible for people to use them who formerly would have felt they would lose caste by doing so', Mrs Edgell, a suburban housewife, remarked on a BBC programme in 1938.[111]

Thus, Progressive brewers did in fact foster a new subculture of female drinking. Historically dominant masculine pubs, threatened with changes in layout, décor and room function, survived, though in diminished numbers. Latent violence characterized the uneasy standoff at Carlisle's Goliath between two factions, coal carters and railway workers. Periodically, strife between them escalated in outright conflict; women had no place in such an environment.[112] Gender equality in drinking therefore prevailed primarily in reformed pubs throughout the country, but certainly had not supplanted the masculine republic in public bars and indeterminate numbers of traditional, unreformed pubs. Rapid changes in drinking habits during the Second World War would enlarge the already considerable numbers of respectable women patronizing licensed premises.

Notes

1 Peter Mathias, *The Brewing Industry in England, 1700–1830* (London: Cambridge University Press, 1959), pp. 117–34, 228–43; Peter Clark, *The English Alehouse: A Social History, 1200–1830* (London: Longman, 1983), pp. 254–60, 263–7, 283–4.

2 The standard accounts of the Beer Act and its impact are Brian Harrison, *Drink and the Victorians: The Temperance Question in England, 1815–72* (1971; 2nd edn, Keele: Keele University Press, 1994), ch. 3; and T. R. Gourvish and R. G. Wilson, *The British Brewing Industry, 1830–1980* (Cambridge: Cambridge University Press, 1994), ch. 1.

3 David W. Gutzke, *Protecting the Pub: Brewers and Publicans against Temperance* (Woodbridge: Boydell & Brewer, 1989), pp. 17–21; *Evidence of the Select Committee on Sales of Liquors on Sunday Bill*, 1868, 14 (402), pp. 47, 50, 54, 56; C. C. Owen, *The Development of Industry in Burton upon Trent* (Chichester: Phillimore, 1978), pp. 79, 229.

4 Gutzke, *Protecting the Pub*, pp. 19–25; Kevin Hawkins and C. L. Pass, *The Brewing Industry: A Study in Industrial Organization and Public Policy* (London: Heinemann Educational Books, 1979), pp. 25–30, 36; Richard G. Wilson, *Greene King: A*

Business and Family History (London: Bodley Head & Jonathan Cape, 1983), pp. 117–18, 141.

5 David W. Gutzke, *Pubs and Progressives: Reinventing the Public House in England, 1896–1960* (DeKalb: Northern Illinois University Press, 2006), pp. 26–7; *Hansard Parliamentary Debates*, 4th series, 89 (19 Feb. 1901), col. 558; David W. Gutzke, 'Rhetoric and Reality: The Political Influence of British Brewers, 1832–1914', *Parliamentary History*, 9 (1990), p. 81; Joseph Rowntree and Arthur Sherwell, *British 'Gothenburg' Experiments and Public-House Trusts* (London: Hodder & Stoughton, 1901), pp. 141–2.

6 Lynda Nead, *Myths of Sexuality: Representations of Women in Victorian Britain* (Oxford: Blackwell, 1988), p. 190; Françoise Barret-Ducrocq, translated by John Howe, *Love in the Time of Victoria: Sexuality and Desire among Working-Class Men and Women in Nineteenth-Century London* (1989, translated and republished, London: Penguin, 1992), pp. 4, 9, 33, 122, 179–81.

7 John Tosh, *A Man's Place: Masculinity and the Middle-Class Home in Victorian England* (London: Yale University Press, 1999), p. 125; Brian Harrison and Barrie Trinder, 'Drink and Sobriety in an Early Victorian Country Town: Banbury, 1830–60', *English Historical Review*, Supplement 4 (1969), pp. 8–9; J. J. Rowley, 'Drink and the Public House in Nottingham, 1830–60', *Transactions of the Thoroton Society of Nottinghamshire*, 79 (1975), p. 81; Harrison, *Drink and the Victorians*, pp. 46, 309; Gutzke, *Protecting the Pub*, p. 32; Robert Thorne, 'Places of Refreshment in the Nineteenth-Century City', in Anthony D. King (ed.), *Buildings and Society: Essays on the Social Development of the Built Environment* (London: Routledge & Kegan Paul, 1980), pp. 231, 233.

8 Charles Dickens, 'You Must Drink', *All the Year Round*, 18 June 1864, p. 439; Brian Harrison, 'Pubs', in H. J. Dyos and Michael Wolff (eds), *The Victorian City: Images and Realities* (London: Routledge & Kegan Paul, 1973), 1:166.

9 Harrison and Trinder, 'Drink and Sobriety', pp. 8–9; Gourvish and Wilson, *British Brewing Industry*, pp. 28–33.

10 *Evidence of the Royal Commission on Liquor Licensing Laws*, 1897, 34, C 8356, pp. 234–5; *Evidence of the Select Committee of the House of Lords on Intemperance*, 1877, 11 (171), pp. 147, 150, 158, 184, 188, 191–2, 304–5; Dickens, 'You Must Drink', p. 438.

11 *Evidence of the Select Committee of the House of Lords on Intemperance*, 1877, 11 (271), p. 43.

12 Until well into the interwar era, some middle-class observers and those socially above drew a clear distinction between ladies – refined females with proper dress, manners and behaviour – and women. In response to publicans posting a sign, 'Ladies are not served in this House', a Seaham Harbour magistrate urged the substitution of 'women' for 'ladies'. 'A respectable woman calling herself a lady would never be seen drinking in a public-house', he argued. Barclay Perkins reiterated this point, designating a room for females in its rebuilt Reindeer pub a 'ladies' tea room' in 1932 (David W. Gutzke, 'Gender, Class and Public Drinking in Britain during the First World War', *Histoire Sociale/Social History*, 27 (1994), p. 388; see below Plate 5).

13 Fiona Elizabeth Fisher, 'In Public, in Private: Design and Modernization in the London Public House, 1872–1902' (Ph.D. dissertation, Kingston University, 2007), pp. 186–200; *Evidence of the Select Committee of the House of Lords on Intemperance*, 1877, 11 (418), p. 141.

14 *Evidence of the Royal Commission on the Liquor Licensing Laws*, 1898, 36, C 8694, p. 526; Mark Girouard, *Victorian Pubs* (London: Studio Vista, 1975), p. 12; Carl Chinn, *They Worked All Their Lives: Women of the Urban Poor in England, 1880–1939* (Manchester: Manchester University Press, 1988), p. 119; Richard Church, *Over the Bridge: An Essay in Autobiography* (London: William Heinemann, 1955), pp. 73, 97; Helen Corke, *In Our Infancy: An Autobiography*, Part 1: *1882–1912* (Cambridge: Cambridge University Press, 1975), pp. 97, 186; George Grossmith and Weedon Grossmith, *The Diary of a Nobody* (1892; rept edn, Aylesbury, Penguin, 1979), pp. 31–2, 34–5.

15 Chris Waters, *British Socialists and the Politics of Popular Culture* (Manchester: Manchester University Press, 1990), p. 166.

16 Stella Maria Moss, 'Cultures of Women's Drinking and the English Public House, 1914–39' (D.Phil., University of Oxford, 2009), p. 72.

17 David Beckingham, 'Gender, Space, and Drunkenness: Liverpool's Licensed Premises, 1860–1914', *Annals of the Association of American Geographers*, 102 (2012), pp. 647–66; Alethea Melling, 'Wicked Women from Wigan and Other Tales: Licentious Leisure and the Social Control of Working-Class Women in Wigan and St Helens, 1914–30', *North West Labour History*, 24 (1999/2000), p. 37

18 For discussion of moral panics, see below Chapter 11, pp. 249, 252–6.

19 Ernest Selley, *The English Public House as It Is* (London: Longmans, Green and Co., 1927), p. 88; Lyn Murfin, *Popular Leisure in the Lake Counties* (Manchester: Manchester University Press, 1990), p. 80; Catherine Cookson, *Our Kate: An Autobiography* (1969; rept edn, London: Corgi, 1974), pp. 29, 43, 47–8, 61; Patrick McGeown, *Heat the Furnace Seven Times More* (London: Hutchinson, 1967), pp. 41–2; Sydney O. Nevile, *Seventy Rolling Years* (London: Faber & Faber, 1958), p. 67; B. Seebohm Rowntree, *Poverty: A Study of Town Life* (London: Macmillan and Co., 1901), pp. 371–82.

20 There were, of course, exceptions. See, for instance, George Bourne [George Sturt], *Change in the Village* (1912; rept edn, Harmondsworth: Penguin, 1984), pp. 47–8.

21 Margaret Penn, *Manchester Fourteen Miles* (Cambridge: Cambridge University Press, 1947), pp. 22, 150; Flora Thompson, *Lark Rise to Candleford: A Trilogy* (1939–41; rept edn, London: Penguin, 1979), pp. 64–5; also see Maud F. Davies, *Life in an English Village: An Economic and Historical Survey of the Parish of Corsley in Wiltshire* (London: T. Unwin,1909), pp. 279–80.

22 F. J. Dawson, 'Mr. Sydney O. Nevile Discusses Improved Licensed Houses', *Hotel Review: Supplement, Inns of Today: A Survey of Public House Improvement*, April 1939.

23 Tony Collins and Wray Vamplew, *Mud, Sweat and Beers: A Cultural History of Sport and Alcohol* (Oxford: Berg, 2002), pp. 12–25; Gutzke, *Protecting the Pub*, pp. 221–2; Andrew Davies, 'Leisure in the "Classic Slum", 1900–39', in Andrew Davies and Steven Fielding (eds), *Workers' Worlds: Cultures and Communities in*

Manchester and Salford, 1880–1939 (Manchester: Manchester University Press, 1992), pp. 107–8; Pamela Dixon and Neal Garnham, 'Drink and the Professional Footballer in 1890s England and Ireland', *Sport in History*, 25 (2005), pp. 375–6.

24 Charles Forman, *Industrial Town: Self Portrait of St. Helens in the 1920s* (London: Cameron & Tayleur, 1978), p. 200.

25 Except in Scotland, where they had to travel some distance to become 'bona fide travellers'.

26 Selley, *English Public House*, pp. 125–6; Eileen Baillie, *The Shabby Paradise: The Autobiography of a Decade* (1958; rept edn, London: Readers Union, 1959), p. 28; George R. Sims, 'The Cry of the Children', *Tribune*, 4, 7, 11, 14, 18, 21 Feb. 1907; Evidence of the Royal Commission on Licensing, 30 Jan. 1930, p. 457; Elizabeth Roberts, *A Woman's Place: An Oral History of Working-Class Women, 1890–1940* (Oxford: Basil Blackwell, 1984), p. 115; *Return of Women and Children in Public-Houses: Information Obtained from Certain Police Forces as to the Frequenting of Public-Houses by Women and Children*, 1908, Cd 3813, pp. 4, 9–10.

27 But Susan Kling argued that working-class women in London patronized pubs which they regarded themselves as entirely respectable behaviour. Unfortunately, most of her evidence came from the mid-Victorian era, when strictures against female presence in licensed premises were less rigid than after the respectable classes withdrew from pubs and beerhouses. Women would have frequented beerhouses, situated commonly in slums, more easily than pubs, though Kling failed to differentiate between these two distinct types of licensed premises (Susan Margaret Kling, 'Time … Pub Culture in Nineteenth Century London: A Social and Cultural History of Working Class Pub Patronage' (Ph.D. dissertation, University of California, Los Angeles, 2001), pp. 199, 204–6.

28 *Return of Women and Children in Public-Houses*, p. 9.

29 James Kneale, 'The Place of Drink: Temperance and the Public, 1856–1914', *Social and Cultural Geography*, 2 (2001), p. 51; Lady Bell, *At the Works: A Study of a Manufacturing Town* (London: Edward Arnold, 1907), p. 132; Rowntree, *Poverty: A Study of Town Life*, pp. 314–26; Arthur Sherwell, *Life in West London: A Study and a Contrast* (London: Methuen & Co., 1897), pp. 130–6.

30 Jack London, *The People of the Abyss* (1903; rept edn, London: Journeymen Press, 1978), pp. 120–1; Mrs Bertrand Russell, 'Four Days in a Factory', *Contemporary Review*, 84 (1903), p. 61. Women's autobiographies later confirmed his observation (A. S. Jasper, *A Hoxton Childhood* (1969; rept edn, Slough: Hollen Street Press, 1971), pp. 7, 9, 29).

31 Girouard, *Victorian Pubs*, pp. 59–69; Arthur Shadwell, 'The English Public House', *National Review*, 25 (1895), p. 378; *Evidence of the Royal Commission on Liquor Licensing Laws*, 1897, 34, C 8355, pp. 330–1, 338–9.

32 Girouard, *Victorian Pubs*, pp. 69–70. But he ignored the early nineteenth century when respectable women had patronized licensed premises.

33 T. R. Gourvish and R. G. Wilson, 'Profitability in the Brewing Industry, 1885–1914', *Business History*, 27 (1985), pp. 146–65.

34 Girouard, *Victorian Pubs*, p. 69; *House of Whitbread*, 2 (January 1926), p. 43; Evidence of the Royal Commission on Licensing, 22 Jan. 1930, pp. 431, 436; Hugh

McLeod, 'White Collar Values and the Role of Religion', in Geoffrey Crossick (ed.), *The Lower Middle Class in Britain, 1870–1914* (London: Croom Helm, 1977), pp. 71, 75.

35 Erica Diane Rappaport, *Shopping for Pleasure: Women in the Making of London's West End* (Princeton: Princeton University Press, 2000), pp. 18, 36.

36 Fisher, 'London Public House', pp. 194–5, 242; *Evidence of the Royal Commission on Liquor Licensing Laws*, 1898, 36, C 8694, p. 171; 'Through Practical Spectacles', Pt 2: 'Things as seen by a Licensed Victualler', *British Review*, 2 (1914), p. 391.

37 Anna Martin, 'Working-Women and Drink', *Nineteenth Century and After*, 78 (1915), pp. 1387–8; *Evidence of the Royal Commission on the Liquor Licensing Laws*, 1898, 36, C 8694, p. 171; Girouard, *Victorian Pubs*, pp. 59, 63, 67, 69; 'Through Practical Spectacles', p. 391; Charles Booth (ed.), *Life and Labour of the People in London*, final volume: *Notes on Social Influences and Conclusion* (London: Macmillan & Co., 1902), p. 61; Noel Buxton and Walter Hoare, 'Temperance Reform', in C. F. G. Masterman (ed.), *The Heart of the Empire: Discussions of Problems of Modern City Life in England* (1902; rept edn, New York: Barnes & Noble, 1973), p. 177; James Kneale, '"A Problem of Supervision": Moral Geographies of the Nineteenth-Century British Public House', *Journal of Historical Geography*, 25 (1999), pp. 343–4.

38 *Licensed Victuallers' Gazette*, 3 Jan. 1902, Fisher, 'London Public Houses', pp. 241–2; Fiona Fisher, 'Privacy and Supervision in the Modernised Public House, 1872–1902', in Penny Sparke, Anne Massey, Trevor Keeble and Brenda Martin (eds), *Designing the Modern Interior from the Victorians to Today* (Oxford: Berg, 2009), p. 44.

39 Fisher, 'London Public Houses', pp. 248–92.

40 Ibid., p. 242.

41 Harrison, 'Pubs', pp. 167–8.

42 Gutzke, 'Gender, Class and Public Drinking', pp. 367–76, 385–8; Selley, *English Public House*, pp. 128–9; Chinn, *They Worked All Their Lives*, pp. 118–19; Roberts, *Woman's Place*, p. 122.

43 Mrs C. S. Peel, *How We Lived Then, 1914–18: A Sketch of Social and Domestic Life in England During the War* (London: John Lane the Bodley Head, 1929), p. 66; Matthew Hilton, *Smoking in British Popular Culture, 1800–2000: Perfect Pleasures* (Manchester: Manchester University Press, 2000), pp. 139–43.

44 Gutzke, *Pubs and Progressives*, pp. 210–11. Progressivism and brewers are discussed above: Introduction, pp. 2–6.

45 *Scotsman*, 13 March 1934; *Beer amd Skittles*, 1 (June 1932), p. 364; *Brewing Trade Review*, March 1938; *Brewer & Wine Merchant*, March 1931; Selley, *English Public House*, p. 127.

46 Sir William Crawford and H. Broadley, *The People's Food* (London: William Heinemann, 1938), p. 284.

47 Lewis Melville [Lewis S. Benjamin and Aubrey Hammond], *The London Scene* (London: Faber and Gwyer, 1926), pp. 35–6; B. D. Nicholson, 'Drink', in Sir Hubert Llewellyn Smith, *The New Survey of London Life and Labour*, vol. 9: *Life and Leisure* (London: P. S. King & Son, 1935), pp. 262–3.

48 Terrence R. Gourvish, 'The Business of Alcohol in the US and the UK: UK Regulation and Drinking Habits, 1914–39', *Business and Economic History*, 26 (1997), pp. 613–14; also see Barbara Gleiss, 'Women in Public Houses: A Historic Analysis of the Social and Economic Role of Women Patronising English Public Houses, 1880s-1970' (Ph.D. Dissertation, University of Vienna, 2009), pp. 69, 80, 82; Moss, 'Cultures of Women's Drinking', p. 297.

49 Greenall, Whitley & Co., Magee, Marshall & Co., Archives, Dated photographs of new premises. Joseph Sharman reconstructed the Bowling Green Hotel in 1934 (Merseyside Record Office, 380 PWK/4/1/102–03, Walker-Cain Collection, Minute Books of Peter Walker & Son). This generalization is also based on the archives of brewers listed in Gutzke, *Pubs and Progressives*, pp. 311–19.

50 Gutzke, *Pubs and Progressives*, pp. 179–86; *Brewers' Journal*, 19 Dec. 1956.

51 The methodology involved in estimating numbers of patrons frequenting licensed premises was discussed by Charles Madge and Tom Harrison (eds), *Five Year's Work, 1937–38 by Mass-Observation* (London: Lindsay Drummond, 1938), pp. 24–8.

52 Mass-Observation, *The Pub and the People: A Worktown Study* (1943; rept edn, London: Cresset Library, 1987), p. 38.

53 *Licensing World*, 25 Feb. 1939; Evidence of the Royal Commission on Licensing, 22 Jan. 1930; Selley, *English Public House*, pp.123–4; Nancy Banks-Smith, 'The Pub that We Called Home', in Angus McGill (ed.), *Pub: A Celebration* (London: Longmans, Green & Co., 1969), pp. 182–3; Gutzke, *Pubs and Progressives*, p. 226; Patrick Chaplin, *Darts in England, 1900–39: A Social History* (Manchester: Manchester University Press, 2009), pp. 178–9; *A Monthly Bulletin*, 27 (Dec. 1956), pp. 167–8; Mass-Observation, *Pub and the People*, pp. 144, 148; University of Sussex, FR 3029, Mass-Observation Archives, A Report on Drinking Habits, Aug. 1948, pp. 49–50; *Brewing Trade Review*, April 1947; Chinn, *They Worked All Their Lives*, p. 121; J. B. Priestley, 'Those Dreadful Towns – Gloom and No Play', *Sunday Chronicle*, 1 Oct. 1933.

54 Mass-Observation, *Pub and the People*, pp. 134–5. See above n. 49.

55 Angus Calder, 'Mass-Observation, 1937–49', in Martin Bulmer (ed.), *Essays on the History of British Sociological Research* (Cambridge: Cambridge University Press, 1985), pp. 128–9; Tom Harrisson, *Britain Revisited* (London: Victor Gollancz, 1961), p. 172; British Market Research Bureau Ltd, *Licensed Premises: Report of an Attitude Survey, August 1960* (1960), p. 66.

56 *Yorkshire Herald*, 23 June 1927.

57 Robert Roberts, *The Classic Slum: Salford Life in the First Quarter of the Century* (1971; paperback ed., Harmondsworth: Penguin, 1980), pp. 204, 222, 235.

58 Gutzke, *Pubs and Progressives*, pp. 202–3, tables 5–6. See above n. 48.

59 B. Seebohm Rowntree, *Poverty and Progress: A Second Survey of York* (London: Longmans, Green & Co., 1941), p. 351; Alan Johnson, *The Inns and Alehouses of York* (Beverley: Hulton Press, 1989); York City Archives Office, Acc. 189/2–3, York Licensing Committee Minute Books; Coors Museum, Tadcaster Tower Brewery, Minute Books of the Board of Directors; Whitbread Archives, Bentley's Yorkshire Breweries, Minute Books of the Board of Directors.

60 Rowntree, *Poverty and Progress*, pp. 351–8.

61 Claire Langhamer, '"A Public House Is for All Classes, Men and Women Alike": Women and Drink in Second World War England', *Women's History Review*, 12 (2003), p. 428; Gutzke, *Pubs and Progressives*, pp. 170–1; Rowntree, *Poverty and Progress*, p. 352.
62 Gutzke, *Pubs and Progressives*, pp. 158, 290 n. 2; Sheila E. Braine, 'London Clubs for Women', in *Edwardian London*, 4 vols (London: Village Press, 1902), 1:114–15.
63 Gutzke, 'Gender, Class and Public Drinking', p. 388; Andrew Davies, *Leisure, Gender and Poverty: Working-Class Culture in Salford and Manchester, 1900–39* (Buckingham: Open University Press, 1992), pp. 66–7.
64 *Brewers' Journal*, 19 Jan. 1944; Rowntree, *Poverty and Progress*, p. 352.
65 *Licensing World*, 25 Feb. 1939.
66 *Christian World*, 22 Nov. 1934; *Yorkshire Evening News*, 13 Oct. 1936; *Brewers' Journal*, 15 June 1938.
67 Llewellyn Smith, N*ew Survey*, vol. 9: *Life and Leisure*, p. 29; McGeown, *Heat the Furnace*, p. 45.
68 Gutzke, *Pubs and Progressives*, pp. 159–62, 178.
69 Gutzke, '"Cry of the Children"', p. 78; Nicholson, 'Drink', in Llewellyn Smith, *Life and Leisure*, 9: 244, 248, 251; Gourvish and Wilson, *British Brewing Industry*, p. 366; T. E. B. Clarke, *What's Yours? The Student's Guide to Publand* (London: Peter Davies, 1939), pp. 13–14.
70 Nicholson, 'Drink', pp. 244, 253–4; London School of Economics and Political Science, Meetings of Consultative Committee, New Survey of London, 1/9/2, 30 Nov. 1928, p. 1. The archives are extremely thin, and the methodology must be inferred from the original directive, in which Llewellyn Smith described how the project used 'about 1 in 20 [licensed premises] selected at random'. This was not, of course, a statistical sample drawn from a table of computer-generated random numbers.
71 Nicholson, 'Drink', in Llewellyn Smith, *Life and Leisure*, 9:253–4, 267–8; Langhamer, 'Women and Drink', p. 427; *Brewers' Journal*, 15 Aug. 1935. There were also shortcomings with the *New Survey*'s investigators. They gathered data from these eight pubs in 1933–4, when beer consumption was abnormally low, fully one-fourth less than in 1939.
72 Nicholson, 'Drink', in Llewellyn Smith, *Life and Leisure*, 9:243–69.
73 Meetings of Consultative Committee, New Survey of London, 1/9/2, 21 Oct. 1932, pp. 2–3.
74 Selley, *English Public House*, pp. 126–7, 129. Female drinking in unreformed premises is explored in Moss, 'Cultures of Women's Drinking', pp. 182–259.
75 Selley, *English Public House*, pp. 123–5; Davies, *Leisure, Gender and Poverty*, pp. 62–8; Chinn, *They Worked All Their Lives*, p. 120; 'Public Houses in Dockland', *Fellowship*, 10 (June 1930), p. 202; Pam Schweitzer and Charles Wegner (eds), *On the River: Memories of a Working River* ([London]: Age Exchange, 1989), pp. 49–51; Evidence of the Royal Commission on Licensing, 31 Jan. 1930, p. 476; National Repository, HO 190/843, J. S. Eagles to A. F. Harvey, 19 Dec. 1922, Central Control Board (Liquor Traffic); Moss, 'Cultures of Women's Drinking', pp. 201, 204, 209. For an excellent analysis of women, gender and the Lancashire textile

industry, see Jutta Schwarzkopf, 'Gender and Technology: Inverting Established Patterns. The Lancashire Cotton Weaving Industry at the Start of the Twentieth Century', in Margaret Walsh (ed.), *Working Out Gender: Perspectives from Labour History* (Aldershot: Ashgate, 1999), pp. 151–66.

76 [Sydney O. Nevile], 'The Ideal House', *House of Whitbread*, 2 (Jan. 1926), p. 43.

77 Gourvish and Wilson, *British Brewing Industry*, table VIII; Evidence of the Royal Commission on Licensing, 12 Nov. 1930, p. 2107.

78 Ibid., pp. 2104, 2126, 2130; *Brewers' Journal*, 15 Feb. 1921.

79 'Removal', *A Monthly Bulletin*, 6 (June 1936), p. 91.

80 F. J. Dawson, 'Mr Sydney O. Nevile Discusses Improved Licensed Houses', *Inns of Today, Hotel Review Supplement*, April 1939.

81 She offered just one newspaper article as evidence. Moss also contended that retailers were more concerned with earning profits than instituting reforms. But this argument indicated a misunderstanding of the tied house system. As tied tenants of a brewer, they had no direct financial responsibility for major structural changes to their premises (Moss, 'Cultures of Women's Drinking', p. 297; Gutzke, *Pubs and Progressives*, p. 218).

82 Moss, 'Cultures of Women's Drinking', p. 297; Chapman to Editor, reproduced in *Brewers' Journal*, 15 July 1929; Sydney O. Nevile, 'My Ideals for an Improved Public House', *A Monthly Bulletin*, 3 (Feb. 1933), p. 26; Evidence of the Royal Commission on Licensing, 11 April and 12 Nov. 1930, pp. 988, 2137; Whitbread Archives, Memorandum on the Conference with the Restaurant Association, Nevile Papers, 3 May 1928, p. 4.

83 Dawson, 'Nevile Discusses Improved Licensed Houses'; Sydney O. Nevile, 'The Function of the Brewing Industry in National Reconstruction', *Journal of the Institute of Brewing*, 25 (1919), p. 131.

84 Eric Hopkins, 'Working Class Life in Birmingham between the Wars, 1918–39', *Midland History*, 15 (1990), pp. 137–9; Michael Wise, 'An Early Experiment in Suburban Development: The Ideal Village, Birmingham', in Eric Grant and Peter Newby (eds), *Landscape and Industry: Essays in Memory of Geoffrey Gullett* ([Barnet: Middlesex Polytechnic, 1982]), p. 153; Gutzke, *Pubs and Progressives*, pp. 86, 132–3, 145, 149, 162, 175. Several recent studies, however, alleged that brewer reformers overlooked slum pubs (Gleiss, 'Women in Public Houses', p. 78; Moss, 'Cultures of Women's Drinking', p. 297).

85 When adjusted for changes in the standard of living, these figures corresponded to Booth's poverty line of 21s per week in his survey, *Life and Labour of the People in London* (Sir Hubert Llewellyn Smith, *The New Survey of London Life and Labour*, vol. 3: *Survey of Social Conditions: The Eastern Area* (London: P. S. King & Son, 1932), pp. 70–3).

86 Altogether, brewers built or rebuilt 514 licensed premises in London in the years 1919–39.

87 Calculated from Whitbread Archive, Whitbread & Co., Rebuilding and Alterations Ledgers.

88 Moss, 'Cultures of Women's Drinking', pp. 292, 300; Gutzke, *Pubs and Progressives*, p. 180.

89 *Brewers' Journal*, 18 Jan. 1956; Evidence of the Royal Commission on Licensing, 22 Jan. 1930, pp. 431, 436.

90 Mass-Observation Archives, FR 1611, Social Change: Women in Public Houses, 23 March 1943, p. 7; 'The Improved Public House', *House of Whitbread*, 1 (Dec. 1920), p. 12; Gutzke, *Pubs and Progressives*, p. 180.

91 Gutzke, *Pubs and Progressives*, pp. 111–12, 146, 148–9; Basil Oliver, *The Renaissance of the English Public House* (London: Faber and Faber, 1947), pp. 149–72; Langhamer, *Women's Leisure in England*, pp. 74–5.

92 *A Monthly Bulletin*, 27 (Dec. 1956), pp. 167–8; Maurice Gorham, *The Local* (London: Cassell & Co., 1939), pp. 40–1; E. B. Musman, 'Public Houses: Design and Construction', *Architects' Journal*, 88 (24 Nov. 1938), pp. 833–90.

93 Gleiss, however, asserted that male pub culture had not changed, with Northern men as antipathetic towards women in pubs as in Edwardian England (Gleiss, 'Women in Public Houses', p. 78).

94 Moss, 'Cultures of Women's Drinking', pp. 220, 273.

95 Young, 'Public-House Reform'.

96 Mass-Observation Archives, Report on Drinking Habits, Aug. 1948, pp. 143, 164; Moss, 'Cultures of Women's Drinking', p. 273; Filson Young, 'Public-House Reform: Experiments of Brewers', *Morning Post*, 25 Jan. 1926.

97 Dawson, 'Sydney O. Nevile'; also see Melling, 'Wicked Women', pp. 37, 40.

98 *Gloucestershire Echo*, 8 June and 27 Oct. 1938; Eldridge Pope & Co. Archives, Advertisement of the Opening of the Saxon King Hotel, Dec. 1939–Jan. 1940; Gutzke, *Pubs and Progressives*, pp. 181–2; National Brewery Centre, Bent's Brewery Co., Advertisement, 1934.

99 Moss, 'Cultures of Women's Drinking', pp. 178–9.

100 Alcohol Research Group Library, Berkeley, California, Marcus Grant, 'Infallible Powers: A Study of Health Claims in Early British Alcohol Beverage Advertising', Unpublished Paper, 1983; *Hotel and Catering Management*, June 1937.

101 *Brewers' Journal*, 15 April 1936; *Ind Coope News*, 32 (April 1960).

102 *Sussex Daily News*, 13 May 1938; Chaplin, *Darts in England*, pp. 121–2, 178–81.

103 'Found – The Ideal Public House!' *Daily Express*, 7 May 1930; *Fellowship*, 6 (Feb. 1926), p. 38; *Anchor Magazine*, 12 (March 1932), pp. 22.

104 Joanna Cannan, *Death at the Dog* (1941; rept edn, Boulder, Colorado: Rue Morgue Press, 1999), pp. 7, 11–13, 18–19.

105 'Adolescents in Public Houses', *A Monthly Bulletin* (Supplement), Aug. 1942, pp. 3, 8.

106 John Walton, *Fish and Chips and the British Working Class, 1870–1940* (Leicester: Leicester University Press, 1992), pp. 141–2.

107 Martin Francis, 'Leisure and Popular Culture', in Ina Zweiniger-Bargielowska (ed.), *Women in Twentieth-Century Britain* (London: Longman, 2001), pp. 235–6; Jane Lewis, *Women in England, 1870–1950: Sexual Divisions and Social Change* (Brighton: Wheatsheaf Books, 1984), pp. 133–6; Susan Pyecroft, 'British Working Women and the First World War', *Historian*, 56 (1994), pp. 699–710; Adrian Bingham, '"An Era of Domesticity"? Histories of Women and Gender in Interwar Britain', *Cultural and Social History*, 1 (2004), pp. 225–33.

108 Pub improvement was largely confined to England. Brewers in depressed Wales spent quite modest amounts on upgrading premises, while those in Scotland had little financial incentive since licensing laws prevented them from owning tied houses. Scottish brewers, however, did spend money on improving pubs south of the border (Gutzke, *Pubs and Progressives*, pp. 205–7).

109 Moss, 'Cultures of Women's Drinking', p. 294. Claire Langhamer likewise minimized the extent of women using pubs. Throughout the 1920–60 years, she argued, 'the public house remained, in essence, a male institution'. She reached this conclusion with no understanding of the lounge as a pivotal factor in attracting respectable women to improved pubs (Langhamer, *Women's Leisure*, pp. 72–3, 154).

110 Gutzke, *Pubs and Progressives*, pp. 209–10.

111 Brewers and Licensed Retailers Association, Précis of Newspapers, 9 Nov. 1938; also see *Licensing World*, 26 Nov. 1938.

112 Murfin, *Popular Leisure in the Lake Counties*, pp. 80–1.

2

Women, war and drinking

Though the two world wars were remarkably similar in drawing larger numbers of women into pubs and beerhouses, their ultimate impact differed greatly. Following the 1918 Armistice, leading brewers, embracing Progressivism and fearful of a backlash against women drinkers, launched the improved public house movement. In the aftermath of the Second World War, in contrast, brewers adopted a resigned attitude, unable to counter powerful societal trends urging women to return home to marriage, family and children. As a result, the trend of bigger numbers of women drinking in wartime pubs and beerhouses proved transitory once the war ended. From the Second World War would come a reinforcement of the connection between pubs and their neighbourhoods, symbolized by a new name, 'the local', conveying a closer, more intimate bond with a key social institution.

This reorientation between pub and patron commenced almost from the war's outset. Amid the battle of Britain in the summer of 1940, Britons forged a more personal relationship with the pub. Both Mass-Observation and the *Brewers' Journal* detected changing attitudes towards the neighbourhood public house, its unreformed appearance appealing strongly to local residents. Older patrons greeted each other as genuine friends, with whom they discussed family matters and sought intimacy and 'homeliness'. Here, too, neighbours relaxed social restraints in quest of what Mass-Observation called 'communal enjoyment and good feeling', an atmosphere that produced some drunkenness but no condemnation. In this convivial, socially tolerant environment, with the pubs' clientele swelled owing to dislocated evacuees, women drank alongside neighbours and strangers, and so became part of the pub community. Here more female drunkenness – 'gay communal intoxication' as Mass-Observation dubbed it – occurred than before the war, but criticism both of women's presence and behaviour had become muted. It came as no surprise therefore that, of those prepared to venture into pubs alone, older women outnumbered younger ones by a ratio of almost two to one. Not all, or even most, older women reacted in the same way. Upper working- and middle-class women felt the most, working-class women the least, hesitant about defying social sanctions. Though this represented a significant change in behaviour, more women overall still depended on escorts. 'Minority feeling still remains fairly strongly against [solitary women visitors to pubs], and is based on unrespectability and immorality associations', remarked Mass-Observation.[1]

Famous detective mystery writer Rupert Croft-Cooke (who used Leo Bruce as his pseudonym) discerned a new attitude towards public houses, while travelling in the South-east where he periodically stopped his caravan and spent evenings in the public bars of Kentish and Sussex inns. From his unusual vantage point in the summer of 1940, Croft-Cooke in a lengthy article in Grimsby's *Evening Telegraph*, observed that the war 'has meant, in almost every inn I know, a drawing closer together, a subtle, not easily perceptible, but quite definite new comradeship among men'. Never before, he thought, had inns acquired such a stature among the English. Through its unique role in solidifying commitment to the war effort, 'the inn is a blockhouse on the home front'.[2]

Changing views of the pub instrumentally shaped wartime film making. Over the course of the next several years, a novel approach to British film making emerged, the 'new school of realism'. Directors and producers rejected Hollywood's slick, expensive and bombastic character, embracing instead genuine, common themes as restrained as budgets and style. Central to these films was imagery consciously mobilizing audiences against potential invaders of the homeland. 'Dancing in aircraft hangars, pub drinking, listening to the radio, fighting together, and other scenes of group activity collectively symbolize community strength and the surmounting of class difference in the face of possible defeat', argued Antonia Lant in her study of wartime cinema.[3] *In Which We Serve*, a wartime drama released in 1942, followed the history of a British destroyer, exploring the theme of loyalty not just to the captain but to country and other members of the crew.

James Nicholls's recent study reached a similar conclusion, but saw the transformative impact of the war as critical in modifying perceptions not so much of the pub as of beer consumption:

> It was this 'Beer Street' version of what beer-drinking meant – a version in which beer-drinking was presented as rational, social and civilised – which was shared by pub-improving brewers, social commentators like George Orwell,

> and, ultimately, the policy-makers of a wartime administration who needed to defend all the unifying national myths they could.

For Nicholls, a new national identify arising from the war was thus imposed from above, partly as a deliberate act of myth making. In exploiting beer drinking as 'the people's drink', policy-makers fostered morale as much as forwarded the government's war aims.[4] But the evolution of national identify can also be viewed as emerging spontaneously at the grass roots level, originating among widening numbers of drinkers who, confronting an unprecedented crisis, found one of England's central social institutions under enormous assault. It would be this renewed appreciation of the pub that strengthened the connection between them and their unique national institution, for which a new word came to express these heartfelt sentiments, 'the local'.[5] In their mental landscape, the local, the hub of their universe, became synonymous with neighbourhood and friends, creating a vivid sense of community and shared sacrifice against adversity. Politician and writer A. P. Herbert observed that:

> the British pub, the people's club, has justified its existence as perhaps it never did before. For it has been the one human corner, a centre not of beer but bonhomie; the one place where after dark the collective heart of the nation could be seen and felt, beating resolute and strong.[6]

Not only causing but reflecting the heightened wartime importance of this reorientation between the English and their pubs was the coalition government's remarkable new stance. Reports from Mass-Observation, in its capacity as a source for home intelligence exploring public reactions to the Blitz and the vitality of nightlife in London, Plymouth, Portsmouth and Southampton in 1940–1, prompted authorities to enrol the brewing industry as an important ally against Hitler.[7] Sydney Nevile, managing director of Whitbread's Brewery and former chairman of the Brewers' Society, recounted that

> We were told it was important from the point of view of the morale of the neighbourhood to keep the 'local' functioning, if possible, so after each raid, we took steps to ascertain the extent of the damage both in London and the country and made every effort to help the tenants to get their houses trading again.[8]

Appointed to examine women's wartime drinking habits in the services, Violet Markham's Committee identified new attitudes to alcoholic beverages. 'Alcohol', her Committee's Report concluded, 'has become a symbol of conviviality for women no less than men'.[9]

Well before the war ended, the word had entered common parlance. Appearing in the *New Statesman and Nation* in August 1943, a woman stated what type of person she sought as a flatmate: '"Advertiser would like girl to share light, sunny Hampstead flat with her. Interested in poetry, politics and the beer at the local"'. Wartime fiction equally underlined the word's ever-widening currency. Appearing in 1945, Maureen Sarsfield's novel *Green December Fills the Graveyard* depicts a housekeeper in a Sussex village seizing the opportunity when her employer is away to go to one of her haunts, 'the nearest local for a *Guinness*'.[10] In *Murder by Matchlight,* written by popular detective fiction writer E. C. R. Lorac and likewise published in 1945, a sergeant locates a landlady at the Duke of Clarence, her Notting Hill Gate 'local'. No one, least of all the landlord, thinks the worse of her for a well-deserved reputation as a heavy drinker: 'drinks like a fish'. In fact, the landlord characterizes her as 'highly respectable' and trustworthy.[11] This tolerance towards women drinkers did not long survive the war's end.

While the war and home front have attracted much attention, historians have only recently explored how they affected drinking habits. According to Claire Langhamer, the Second World War acted as the catalyst of momentous changes in female drinking habits, with nearly three times as many young women, often in the services or war work, frequenting urban pubs as in the 1930s. Based primarily on Mass-Observation's reports, her thesis identified increased pub usage as chiefly confined to urban and industrial areas. Women's presence and war mobilization both reached unprecedented levels in 1943, she claimed. 'Entry into the services', contended Langhamer, 'was instrumental in promoting particular forms of leisure amongst young women', most notably in visiting pubs. Diverse factors facilitated women's entry into pubs: the undertaking of service work; the war's disruptive impact; higher wages; disappearance of social constraints when migrating to a new area; and the pub's roles in both people socializing and courtship rituals. While older women patronized pubs without escorts, younger women typically accompanied friends or a boyfriend.[12]

Her thesis of gender usage of pubs during the war is based on limited, impressionistic evidence. Data must be evaluated carefully to document accurate wartime trends in pub usage. What cast considerable doubt on the validity of Mass-Observation's wartime figures are two postwar surveys reaching strikingly different conclusions. On one hand, Mass-Observation with a survey in 1948 concluded that the proportion of all women who visited on-licensed premises reached almost one-half; on the other hand, Market Information Services the following year, in the first survey drawing on sophisticated statistical analysis, thought that just 35 per cent of women frequented pubs or beerhouses.

A logical inference, therefore, is that Mass-Observation over-counted women in pubs following the war, as it had some years earlier during the war itself. How Mass-Observation collected and interpreted information is hence critical to evaluating both wartime reports and divergent postwar surveys.[13]

Key to Langhamer's interpretation is Mass-Observation's Report on Juvenile Drinking, completed in June 1943, which estimated women's presence in pubs as 'about three times as large as it was in 1938'. This report rested on quite limited data: several central London boroughs (Aldgate, Covent Garden and Victoria), two ports (Liverpool and Portsmouth), one industrial town (Bolton) and two villages. Cathedral cities, market towns, industrial centres (save for Lancashire) and villages (outside the South-west), formed no part of Mass-Observation's survey.[14] Langhamer also quoted conclusions of two other Mass-Observation studies finished in spring 1943 as an explanation of women's motivation for frequenting pubs, their drinking behaviour and their drinking habits. From them, she accepted Mass-Observation's statistic that almost three-fifths of women frequented wartime pubs. Langhamer cited results of surveys of five pubs in Fulham and one in a London South-western borough, studied on five occasions over as many years (1939–43), as the basis for her thesis about women's increased wartime drinking behaviour throughout England.[15] But these reports were hardly representative of all London districts, much less of the entire country.

Mass-Observation's research was flawed conceptually as well methodologically. Whether studying drinking behaviour in the war or in Bolton in the 1930s, Mass-Observation attached too much credibility to determining what proportion of patrons in various drinking establishments consisted of women. Instead of focusing on who drank at pubs and beerhouses, Mass-Observation should have surveyed the broader community, asking residents where, when and how often they consumed alcohol. Without a statistical sample using random numbers, Mass-Observation had no reliable basis for generalizing about drinking habits anywhere, whether in a locality or in the entire country.[16]

Young females began turning to pubs in growing numbers first in early 1941 and with increasing frequency the next year, long before what Langhamer argued. Diverse sources – from local officials and newspapers to periodicals and specially commissioned reports – all recognized greater numbers of women on licensed premises. In March 1941, Newport's Chief Constable became the first officially to maintain that more women had started drinking on licensed premises.[17] One organization with local observers, the Fellowship of Freedom and Reform, collected evidence from professional researchers in nine large cities as well as throughout Lancashire.[18] Its findings, published in August 1942, conclusively established that more women were using licensed premises. The war, they carefully stressed, had not inaugurated new female drinking habits, but accelerated existing prewar trends. 'A change of convention in the habits of women has been visible for a long time', contended the Bulletin's editor.[19]

Precisely when women began patronizing licensed premises in rising numbers is a debate not simply on a specific date but more importantly on motivation. Women's patronage of pubs did expand somewhat during the war, but other factors, quite beyond what Langhamer stressed, provided much of the incentive.

Women in the services were only part of a much wider group patronizing pubs in greater numbers. To the local went women as part not just of courtship rituals, but of a calculated strategy of husband hunting. Christianna Brand, in her novel *Green for Danger*, written in 1943 and later made into a film of that name starring Alastair Sim and Trevor Howard in 1947, imputes this motive to women in the services. When Sister Bates joins the military as a nurse, she reflects: '"Perhaps I shall meet some nice officers!"' Brand herself adds: 'Lest anyone be tempted to despise such single-minded devotion to the opposite sex, it may be pointed out that this innocent aspiration was shared in a greater or less degree, by twenty future members of the Sisters Mess, and at least fifty V.A.D.s'.[20] What better place to meet and socialize with available men than nearby pubs. Loneliness, too, certainly drove many women into pubs. 'Strain and anxiety of married women deprived of the society of their husbands', suggested Romford's superintendent of police, explained why growing numbers of females frequented pubs and beerhouses. Wartime dislocation likewise played a role. 'Snatched by the hand of war from their former homes and circles of acquaintances', wrote the *Brewers' Journal*, evacuees 'have gravitated to what in friendly phrase they term "the local", because it is the place most like to home'.[21] One Essex village woman pointed to the evacuation of London's East End women as responsible for greater female use of pubs. Accustomed to frequenting London pubs, these women unhesitatingly resorted to rural pubs, a development which in turn emboldened young village females to do so as well. To village pubs also went wives and sweethearts with husbands or boyfriends stationed nearby in the RAF.[22] The same process of urban evacuees challenging social taboos against local women using rural pubs appeared in Scotland, the most conservative British region. Northern women who worked just south of the border but lived in Scotland also defied prohibitions against women visiting pubs.[23]

Scottish women too, visited pubs as a result of the war's lowering of social taboos, but ironically only in England, not Scotland. From Glasgow came the testimony early in 1943 of a husband who avoided local pubs, dismissed as 'mere drinking dens'. To his surprise and soon delight, he and his wife obtained good meals at London pubs without his wife incurring condemnation as a 'wicked woman or a red-biddy drinker'.[24] Other transplanted Scots compared Scottish pubs unfavourably with inns in London and its suburbs where 'the whole family at week-ends and holidays' gathered.[25]

'Improved' interwar premises, their huge size, brightness and location on main thoroughfares or High Streets easily identifiable, facilitated the entry to licensed premises of adolescents and less affluent young women from unskilled working-class families. As one delighted women customer enthused about her improved pub, 'that's a lovely place now they've done it all up'. 'It's improved them, women coming into them so much, they're cleaner and brighter.' Young women preferred such larger commercial public houses, with their clean, bright décor, separate conveniences, singing or music and available amusements. 'The pubs are nicer than they used to be', commented one impressed London woman. Young women received powerful encouragement to seek out new premises, such as the newly built Unicorn and Old Cross in Chichester, because here they would find other females under thirty, the age group most receptive to their frequenting pubs by a margin of two to one.[26] In these pubs, too, women drank as often in the gender-neutral lounges or saloon bars as in in public bars. As unskilled working-class women, they typically accompanied men from a similar background with definite views on pub etiquette. Where pub rooms allowed, men modified their social behaviour to suit the occasion. One told a Mass-Observation investigator that when alone he patronized the public bar, whereas when escorting a young woman 'I take her to the saloon bar', with its tables, chairs, flowers and other attractions. He left no doubt about his attitude to women going to a public bar: 'They should keep out of those', he emphasized.[27]

War challenged traditional notions of masculine and feminine roles, turning comfortable assumptions upside down. As Gillian Swanson recently argued, 'the rise in illegitimate births, the incidence of venereal diseases and divorce brought the concept of a maternal femininity that was passive, chaste, unworldly and tied to domestic life under pressure'.[28] Women too assumed men's jobs, breaking down sex segregation in the workplace.[29] 'I suppose it is just as right for women to go into a pub as men, seeing they both tackle the same job', remarked a Mass-Observation interviewee. Across a wide spectrum women's behaviour thus defied established societal norms, providing irresistible inducements and powerful precedents for females to invade working-class men's most sacred public space, the public bars of pubs.[30]

As a result, class and gender barriers collapsed. Reacting to a public outcry at the posting of 'Officers Only' signs in licensed premises near military bases, the War Office intervened with an official statement in which it discountenanced such action. Elsewhere similar issues arose. Following established etiquette, when publicans served officers in a bar, they had denied service to enlisted men. To counter this class segregation, the Minister of War went so far as to draft an order advising publicans that the government saw no problem with soldiers and officers fraternizing together in the same bar. Trains to and from London likewise abolished class distinctions; just the third class remained. All classes now intermixed while waiting on platforms as well as in the carriages themselves. Pubs themselves likewise exhibited class and gender egalitarianism. With limited beer supplies, publicans stocked saloon bars, with higher prices, rather than public bars. A migration between bars naturally occurred, reinforced by fuel shortages which again ensured that saloon bars received priority for fires. Hence, class and gender equality marched hand in hand in eroding prewar social and gender distinctions.[31]

As prewar spatial boundaries disappeared, unescorted women entered pubs more easily, especially as they drank beer in the more refined bars with the rest of the customers. Sometimes they wanted to find a man but not for money, a circumstance which blurred the association between solitary women and prostitution. 'I see no harm in a girl drinking in a pub or in company of either sex', one patron told Mass-Observation. 'Before the war', he admitted, 'I was a bit old-fashioned about such things, but war broadens one's outlook somewhat'. The war thus added another justification for women on their own going to pubs. Surveying Metrop, an unidentified southwest London borough early in 1943, Mass-Observation discovered working-class women were almost three times as likely to visit pubs alone as their middle-class counterparts. Strikingly, nearly two of every three working-class women admitted to entering pubs unescorted. Women resorting to the local, moreover, encountered less male antipathy than in larger main street pubs, with their anonymous clientele.[32]

Recognition of women undertaking entirely unconventional work facilitated this breaching of gender lines in leisure. In repeatedly portraying women's war work as a product of a national emergency, officialdom directly addressed societal fears of females sacrificing their femininity through transgressing strict prewar gender boundaries by entering masculine territory.[33] Commentators and officials alike implicitly sanctioned women's drinking in pubs – another incursion into male territory – as an extension of new gender working roles, while simultaneously conveying to females that the ending of the country's crisis would lead to their loss of traditional male jobs as well as restoration of the prewar drinking regime. Women could continue drinking, but where and with whom they drank would be far more restricted. This subtle, unstated message immeasurably helps explain the sudden collapse of women drinking in pubs immediately following the war.

Did the numbers of women increase three fold compared with the prewar era, as Langhamer and Mass-Observation contended, or did men's withdrawal visually exaggerate the pubs' changing clientele? Many factors exaggerated the numbers of women who began drinking on licensed premises either for the first time or regularly. Heavily bombed cities had hundreds of licensed premises destroyed or seriously damaged, forcing the regular clientele to relocate to another pub, where they contributed to overcrowding. Plymouth, one of the hardest hit, lost one-fourth of its pubs over an eleven-day period during March–April 1941. Less damaged was Portsmouth, where nearly one-seventh of licensed premises – 101 of 761 – were permanently or temporarily put out of business by early 1942. More Portsmouth pubs and beerhouses disappeared during the war than as a result of closure owing to redundancy in the previous 25 years. Hull lost 16 per cent of its licensed premises, twice as many as greater London. Losses in the City itself, however, nearly reached one-third, about the same as in Liverpool. Central Swansea topped them all, with about half its pubs and beerhouses demolished. Sheer numbers of damaged or destroyed premises were clearly important, but the amount of custom lost was also a consideration. Bombing levelled three Sheffield High Street houses with brisk trade. 'Thousands of the former "regulars" of these places now crowd into the other central pubs', explained one commentator.[34] Beer shortages became a common feature of wartime life, forcing customers to seek other nearby pubs still serving alcohol. This caused overcrowding as much as early closures of city centre establishments. Fearful of blackouts and being stranded because of limited night-time transportation, publicans closed early in the evening, compelling patrons to flee to more comfortable suburban pubs. These too soon overflowed with customers. At country pubs outside Cardiff, latecomers discovered that 'every room was so crowded that a chance for a drink was hopeless'. A third reason for packed pubs owed to outsiders – troops, war workers and visitors – whose numbers transformed sedate pubs into booming premises with drinking space at a premium.[35]

So much, too, depended on where pubs were located. In June 1943, a Mass-Observation report put the proportion of women in suburban London pubs at 25–30 per cent.[36] Assertions of the tripling of the number of women patronizing pubs therefore seemed highly suspect, so believed many observers. In August 1943, the *True Temperance Quarterly*, while acknowledging rising numbers of women in pubs, thought claims of their huge increases highly exaggerated.[37] One explanation for this came from the *Brewers' Journal*. 'To-day there may be more women in licensed houses than in 1939, but male patrons in many areas are fewer because they are in the Forces, and this makes the number of women present appear by comparison to be larger than it really is.' Mass-Observation lent substance to this view when it conceded that 'the increased proportion of women to be seen in pubs nowadays is only partly due to increased drinking among that sex [and] … partly due to the decreased pub-going of men'.[38] Women's presence accounted for as much as 40 per cent of the pub's total clientele, but the numbers of younger men had shrunk so perceptibly that older men (over thirty) outnumbered them.[39] To quantify changes in the pub's composition, Mass-Observation suggested that female patrons increased 19 per cent while male customers fell 10 per cent. Added together, the disparity between the sexes had fallen by almost one-third, the same figure Mass-Observation itself would offer several months later as the overall increase of women in pubs.[40]

In the light of this evidence, women's patronage of pubs probably rose by about one-fifth, not one-third as Langhamer has contended, during the war. Assuming that about two-fifths of all women patronized pubs by the late 1930s, then well over half, and perhaps as many as three-fifths, of all females were using pubs during the war.

Although Mass-Observation measured a decline in women frequenting pubs after the war, its figures seem irreconcilable with the subsequent statistical market surveys (see Table 3). How could almost 60 per cent of all women visit pubs during the war, but a handful of years later 65 per cent of them shunned the local? Put in another way, the proportion of women drinking in pubs dropped from three-fifths to one-third, yet the one-fourth of females who temporarily drank during wartime had no recollection of this significant behavioural change later in life. As Langhamer herself commented, 'Almost all of the working-class and lower middle-class interviewees asserted that women, particularly young and unmarried women, rarely viewed the pub as a leisure venue'.[41] There is a plausible explanation. Going to a pub in the postwar years was not regarded as respectable by women, so they denied doing it when

Table 3 Women's weekly use of public houses, 1948–56.

	Date	*Women Patrons as a Proportion of All Women*
Mass-Observation	1948	47%*
Market Information Services	1949	8%
Brewers'Society	1956	18%

* M-O measured women as a proportion of the pub clientele rather than women patrons as a proportion of all women.
Sources: Market Information Services Ltd, *What people think about public houses: The results of a large-scale sample survey carried out among the adult population of England and Wales during November, 1949* (Jan. 1950), table 6; S.H. Benson Ltd, *The Brewers' Society 1957 Advertising Campaign Market Research Charts, July 1956*, chart 7.

surveyed. This could not have accounted for all of the change, but in the 1950s the bias would run in favour of under-reporting.

The wartime dichotomies between older drinkers being drawn to unreformed pubs, while the young went to reformed 'modern' pubs, emerged first in the First World War and continued into the interwar era.[42] In this sense, the Second World War inaugurated no new drinking patterns based on generational differences. Nor did the conclusion of the war end these dissimilar generational attitudes towards different types of pubs. Mass-Observation in its postwar national survey maintained that the older generation's view of beer and beer drinking as part of Britain's tradition created a reverence for 'old-fashioned surroundings' and dislike of modern pubs. Bereft of this generation's long-term memory, the young could appraise the merits of reformed and unreformed pubs, unencumbered by tradition.[43]

Women's drinking habits had not eliminated the long-standing taboos against going into pubs with the same insouciance as men. Despite rising numbers of younger women (under thirty) visiting pubs, they displayed an innate conservatism in invariably entering with another person. Two women together would have reduced the likelihood of being regarded as prostitutes. Even older women, their age as well as their marital status both safeguards against charges of prostitution, though almost twice as likely to go alone into a pub, still recognized the social stigma of going unescorted into licensed premises.[44] London publican George Izzard's remark that in the interwar years 'many people assumed that a girl who came into the bar alone was a tart' thus retained its potency. That just a minority of men – no more than one-third –

approved of young women going into pubs under any circumstances whatsoever explains why females felt impelled to patronize drinking premises with another person rather than alone.[45] Suburban women escaped moral reproach only when a man escorted them. Two women entering together still seemed suspicious.[46]

Most women who ventured into postwar pubs regarded themselves as encroaching on public space, widely regarded in many working-class areas as something akin to a male sanctuary. 'There is still some feeling that it isn't quite ladylike to go to pubs', remarked Mass-Observation.[47] The stigma against women entering pubs unaccompanied persisted for decades. In a public opinion survey in 1970, all but a handful of women stated that they always joined other people when patronizing the pub. Even this small minority qualified their behaviour, admitting they attended alone infrequently.[48]

Though increased female patronage of the pub changed the gender proportions of its clientele, some traits continued to shape social interaction. Pub groups typically contained two or three individuals, and consisted overwhelmingly of the same sex, class and age. Of some 1100 pub groups identified, Mass-Observation counted just three with differing components. Surprisingly, investigators observed pub goers selecting more socially exclusive bars in which to drink, with lower prices sacrificed for more amenities. Yet, class segregation persisted. 'It must not be supposed', the Report asserted, 'that the invasion by the working classes of more expensive and more "respectable" bars has resulted in any particular class intermixing'. In short, wartime experience had not led to any long-term social levelling.[49]

Several traits pre-eminently defined female attitudes to and consumption of alcohol. The war had not altered the large numbers of females who disliked pubs. Women who drank but not in pubs made home drinking 'more proportionately popular among women than pub drinking', Mass-Observation remarked in its 1947–8 report.[50] Two postwar public opinion surveys recorded high levels – well over one-third – of women who avoided pubs altogether, the latter figure being the same as a Gallup Poll taken on the eve of the war.[51]

Non-pub-going in fact became an inveterate trait of numerous women. The cohorts of women of drinking age who had shunned pubs in the Second World War foreshadowed astonishing numbers who remained aloof from them nearly three decades later when pub-going had become far more popular among young females (Table 4). Over twice as many women in the thirty-five to fifty-four age cohort in 1970, which included the youngest group of legal drinkers during the war, abstained from visiting pubs compared with their daughters

Table 4 Women's pub avoidance in 1970.

Mothers		*Daughters*	
Age Cohort: 35–54	*Age Cohort: 55+*	*Age Cohort: 18–24*	*Age Cohort: 25–34*
36%	70%	17%	30%

Source: Interscan, Ltd, *Attitudes on Pub Going Habits and Brewery Control and Ownership of Public Houses* (Aug. 1970), p. 6.

in the comparable age cohort of eighteen to twenty-four in that same year. Almost exactly the same proportion of middle-aged and older females in 1970, the fifty-five and over age cohort who had been in their thirties and forties during the war, eschewed the pub as their daughters in the same age cohort of twenty-five to thirty-four in 1970. Though far from conclusive, the inference from this data supports an intriguing hypothesis of the war's profound impact on women. Instead of predisposing women, especially young ones, towards drinking in pubs, the war had an ironic opposite effect: it ingrained deep hostility in many juvenile and young women to ever frequenting drink premises thereafter.[52] The rising percentages of women avoiding pubs in the 1950s and still more early in the 1960s originated then in their wartime experiences, with drinking either on licensed premises or elsewhere.

Why? Historians have argued that how women responded to the ending of the war depended much on age: younger women more willingly accepted the prospects of marriage, children and domesticity than their older counterparts, determined to remain in the workforce. This latter group did continue working, and accordingly would have disliked most the powerful societal rhetoric extolling home, husband and dependency over work, freedom and greater autonomy.[53] Women's subordinate status had been already underlined at popular London social clubs during the war. Concerned about men returning from the front and encountering women seated at the bar allegedly blocking access, El Vino's proprietors had instituted a new rule: 'Ladies should be confined to chairs well away from the bar, mainly the "smoking room" behind a screen at the back of the premises'. Even before the war ended, therefore, women had been relegated to the periphery of drinking space.[54] Wartime rhetoric of egalitarianism had promised women that drinking in pubs was losing its masculine association. According to one commentator, 'the pub was the gossip-shop for the male; "the local" is the gossip-shop for both sexes, plus darts and other diversions'.[55] Resentment at being evicted from public space claimed as their indisputable right owing to their contribution to winning the war antagonized these women forever. Their wartime contribution had been betrayed, and equality in leisure activities fully revoked. No wonder women of the wartime generation unconsciously denied later having visited the pub, the embodiment of postwar Britain's masculine society, during the war.[56]

It is within this context that the generalization by B. Seebohm Rowntree and G. R. Lavers in 1951 that 'a large proportion, probably a majority, of women of all classes of society, never enter public houses' must be evaluated. Women's presence in public houses never involved an unbroken upward linear path from the First World War. In the interwar era, the numbers of women who frequented licensed premises increased sharply, with probably about two-fifths of all adult females visiting pubs or beerhouses at some point in a year.[57] Then, during the Second World War, growth slowed, adding perhaps another 20 per cent to these figures. Overall, women's use of pubs reached well over half and perhaps as many as three-fifths of all women from 1941 or 1942. But wartime officialdom's promise of a return to the prewar gender status quo, together with the dominant postwar ideology extolling home, family and subordination, affronted women deeply. Two years before Rowntree wrote his observation, Market Information Services completed its survey in which it identified just 35 per cent of women still using public houses monthly. A similar proportion of women defined themselves as abstainers.[58] Hence, Rowntree was witnessing the beginnings of women's withdrawal from pubs. Remaining women pub patrons would be literally driven out of public places owing to the moral panic over prostitution in the 1950s. Less than one decade after his comment, women had virtually disappeared from pubs. Another market survey (1960) recorded just 13 per cent of women frequenting public houses monthly, with the level of abstention from alcohol reaching an unprecedented 71 per cent.[59] Women's plummeting presence on licensed premises paralleled slumping beer consumption on a per capita basis, which had declined following the war and then plateaued until the late 1950s. Given these circumstances, it is difficult to see any validity in the argument that women first began resorting to pubs in increasing numbers in the 1950s.[60]

But not everything was transitory. The 'local', a term first applied to nearby neighbourhood pubs in 1942, became one of the most enduring changes resulting from the war. Given the war's aftermath, women were predictably far less likely to have a link with a neighbourhood pub than men. That two of three women never frequented pubs, and just one of five consumed beer, also helps explain why women had not the same relationship with pubs as men.[61]

Following the war, the term gained widespread currency. In 1947 Whitbread's brewery published a pamphlet celebrating the pub, and felt sufficiently confident of the public's general awareness to entitle it simply *Your Local.* Raylant Pictures produced Spotlight on Your Local, a twenty-minute film which began showing in cinemas in 1949. Appearing that same year was *Back to the Local,* Maurice Gorham's updated version of his prewar book. Publicans, brewers, religious leaders and others all quickly embraced the term in the following decade.[62] By then, the word had become ubiquitous, with more people, regardless of age, using it than the term pub.[63]

Notes

1 University of Sussex, FR 1891, Mass-Observation Archives, Report on Juvenile Drinking in Chichester, Aug. 1943, pp. 5, 7. Hereafter, FR citations refer to the Mass-Observation Archive. *Brewers' Journal,* 19 Nov. 1942; also see *Law Journal,* 24 Oct. 1942.

2 Rupert Croft-Cooke, 'A Blockhouse on the Home Front', *Evening Telegraph* (Grimsby), 15 July 1940.

3 Antonia Lant, *Blackout: Reinventing Women for Wartime British Cinema* (Princeton: Princeton University Press, 1991), pp. 33, 41.

4 James Nicholls, *The Politics of Alcohol: A History of the Drink Question in England* (Manchester: Manchester University Press, 2009), p. 190.

5 Maurice Gorham published a pamphlet, *The Local,* in 1939, but I have been unable to find earlier usages of the term in the brewing industry's newspapers, government reports or more generally in the local or regional press. The *OED* identified usage of the term in the mid-1930s (Maurice Gorham, *The Local* (London: Cassell & Company, 1939); Paul Jennings, *The Local: A History of the English Pub* (Stroud: Tempus, 2007), pp. 203–4). The first wartime references to the pub or pubs as 'the local' or 'locals' came in July 1941 (*Brewer & Wine Merchant,* July 1941).

6 Herbert quoted in Brian Glover, *Brewing for Victory: Brewers, Beer and Pubs in the Second World War* (Cambridge: Lutterworth, 1995), p. 20.

7 Brad Beaven and John Griffiths, 'The Blitz, Civilian Morale and the City: Mass-Observation and Working-Class Culture in Britain, 1940–1', *Urban History,* 26 (1999), pp. 82–3.

8 Sydney O. Nevile, *Seventy Rolling Years* (London: Faber & Faber, 1958), p. 257; also see Brad Beaven, *Leisure, Citizenship and Working-Class Men in Britain, 1850–1945* (Manchester: Manchester University Press, 2005), pp. 229–31.

9 *Brewers' Journal,* 18 Nov. 1942; *Report of the Committee on Amenities and Welfare Conditions in Three Women's Services,* 1942, Cmd 6384.

10 *New Statesman and Nation,* Aug. 1943. Sarsfield's novel has been recently republished as *Murder at Shots Hall* (1945; rept edn, Boulder, Colorado, 2003), p. 157.

11 E. C. R. Lorac, *Murder by Matchlight* (London: Collins, 1945), p. 18. Lorac was a pseudonym of Edith Caroline Rivett, who also wrote mysteries as Carol Carnac.

12 Claire Langhamer, '"A Public House is for all Classes, Men and Women Alike": Women, Leisure and Drink in Second World War England', *Women's History Review*, 12 (2003), pp. 423–43; FR 1891, Report on Juvenile Drinking in Chichester, Aug. 1943, pp. 5, 7; FR 1837, Report on Juvenile Drinking, June 1943, p. 23.

13 FR 3029, A Report on Drinking Habits, Aug. 1948; Market Information Services, *What People Think about Public Houses: The Results of a Large-Scale Sample Survey Carried out among the Adult Population of England and Wales during November, 1949*, January, 1950, Table 5.

14 Langhamer, 'Women, Leisure and Drink', p. 430, and n. 84; FR 1837, Report on Juvenile Drinking, June 1943.

15 Langhamer, 'Women, Leisure and Drink', p. 430; FR 1635, Report on Women in Public Houses, March 1943, pp. 3–4, 7; FR 1837, Report on Juvenile Drinking, June 1943, p. 23; and FR 1611, Social Change: Women in Public Houses, 23 March 1943, p. 1.

16 See Chapter 1, above, pp. 32–3.

17 *Licensed Victuallers' Gazette*, 21 March 1941.

18 Newcastle, Sheffield, Liverpool, Leeds, Birmingham, Nottingham, Bristol, Cardiff and Plymouth comprised the nine cities.

19 'Adolescents in Public Houses', *A Monthly Bulletin* (Supplement), Aug. 1942, pp. 2–3, 8; 'Women in Public Houses', *True Temperance Quarterly*, 43 (Aug. 1943), p. 7.

20 Christianna Brand, *Green for Danger* (1944; rept edn, London: Perennial, 1981), p. 10. Established in 1909, the Voluntary Aid Detachment (VAD) supplied field nursing services, primarily in hospitals.

21 *True Temperance Quarterly*, 50 (May 1945), p. 8; *Brewers' Journal*, 16 June 1943; Anonymous rural Essex woman to editor, *A Monthly Bulletin*, 12 (Oct. 1942), p. 80.

22 Anonymous correspondent to Editor, *A Monthly Bulletin*, quoted in *Brewers' Journal*, 18 Nov. 1942.

23 *Brewers' Journal*, 18 Nov. 1942.

24 Special Correspondent to the *Glasgow Citizen*, quoted in *Brewers' Journal*, 17 Feb. 1943.

25 Letter to Editor, *Falkirk Herald*, quoted in *Brewers' Journal*, 16 Sept. 1942; also see *A Monthly Bulletin*, 22 (April 1952), p. 61.

26 'Adolescents in Public Houses', pp. 3, 8; FR 1611, Social Change: Women in Public Houses, 23 March 1943, p. 7; FR 1891, Report on Juvenile Drinking in Chichester, Aug. 1943, pp. 5, 7; FR 1635, Report on Women in Public Houses, pp. 8–9; FR 1835, Report on Behaviour of Women in Certain London Houses, 11 June 1943, p. 16.

27 FR 1611, Social Change: Women in Public Houses, 23 March 1943, pp. 3, 7; also see *Brewers' Guardian*, 19 Jan. 1944.

28 Gillian Swanson, '"So much Money and so Little to Spend It on": Morale, Consumption and Sexuality', in Christine Gledhill and Gillian Swanson (eds), *Nationalising Femininity: Culture, Sexuality and British Cinema in the Second World War* (Manchester: Manchester University Press, 1996), p. 70.

29 Barbara Gleiss, 'Women in Public Houses: A Historic Analysis of the Social and Economic Role of Women Patronising English Public Houses, 1880s–1970' (Ph.D. dissertation, University of Vienna, 2009), p. 85.
30 FR 1611, Social Change: Women in Public Houses, 23 March 1943, pp. 4, 7.
31 Lant, *Blackout*, p. 42; Angus Calder, *The People's War: Britain, 1939–45* (1969; rept edn, New York: Ace Books, 1972), p. 423; Beaven, *Leisure*, p. 229; Brian Glover, *Brewing for Victory: Brewers, Beer and Pubs in the Second World War* (Cambridge: Lutterworth, 1995), pp. 25–6.
32 FR 1611, Social Change: Women in Public Houses, 23 March 1943, pp. 4, 6; FR 1835, Report on Behaviour of Women in Certain London Public Houses, 11 June 1943, pp. 1–6; Gleiss, 'Women in Public Houses', pp. 86–7; FR 1837, Report on Juvenile Delinquency, June 1943, p. 25; *Evening Standard*, 16 Nov. 1942.
33 Penny Summerfield, '"The Girl that Makes the Thing that Drills the Hole that Holds the Spring …": Discourses of Women and Work in the Second World War', in Christine Gledhill and Gillian Swanson (eds), *Nationalising Femininity: Culture, Sexuality and British Cinema in the Second World War* (Manchester: Manchester University Press, 1996), pp. 41–2.
34 'Adolescents in Public Houses', pp. 19, 21; Philip Eley and R.C. Riley, *The Demise of Demon Drink? Portsmouth Pubs, 1900–50*, Portsmouth Papers No. 58 (Portsmouth: Portsmouth City Council, 1991), pp. 21, 24; Jennings, *The Local*, pp. 209–10.
35 'Adolescents in Public Houses', pp. 6, 9–10, 12, 14, 22.
36 FR 1835, Report on Behaviour of Women in Certain London Public Houses, 11 June 1943, p. 5.
37 'Women in Public Houses'.
38 *Brewers' Journal*, 15 Sept. 1943; FR 1891, Report on Juvenile Drinking in Chichester, Aug. 1943, p. 24.
39 FR 1611, Social Change: Women in Public Houses, March 1943, pp. 2, 7–8.
40 FR 1635, Report on Women in Public Houses, March 1943, p. 7, and FR 1837, Report on Juvenile Drinking, June 1943, p. 88.
41 Langhamer, 'Women, Leisure and Drink', p. 424. See below, p. 86, ns. 6–7.
42 David W. Gutzke, 'Gender, Class, and Public Drinking in Britain during the First World War', in Jack S. Blocker, Jr and Cheryl Krasnick Warsh (eds), *The Changing Face of Drink: Substance, Imagery, and Behaviour* (Ottawa: University of Ottawa, 1997), pp. 311–14; David W. Gutzke, *Pubs and Progressives: Reinventing the Public House in England, 1896–1960* (DeKalb: Northern Illinois University Press, 2006), pp. 183–4.
43 FR 3029, A Report on Drinking Habits, Aug. 1948, p. 74.
44 FR 1611, Social Change: Women in Public Houses, March 1943, p. 4.
45 FR 1635, A Report on Women in Public Houses, p. 8; George Izzard, *One for the Road: The Autobiography of a London Village Publican* (London: Max Parrish, 1959), p. 187.
46 *A Monthly Bulletin*, 13 (June 1943), p. 49.
47 FR 1611, Social Change, p. 4; FR 1635, Women in Public Houses, pp. 9–10; FR 3016, Report on Drinking Habits, Aug. 1948, p. 24.
48 Interscan, Ltd, *Attitudes on Pub Going Habits and Brewery Control and Ownership*

of Public Houses (Aug. 1970), p. 7.

49 FR 3029, A Report on Drinking Habits, Aug. 1948, p. 83.

50 FR 3016, A Report on Drinking Habits, p. 24.

51 George H. Gallup, *The Gallup International Public Opinion Polls: Great Britain, 1937–1975* (New York: Random House, 1976), vol. 1, p. 167; Market Information Services Ltd, *What People Think about Public Houses*, table 5; British Institute of Public Opinion, *Survey of Drinking Habits, 1939.*

52 Interscan, Ltd, *Attitudes on Pub Going Habits and Brewery Control and Ownership of Public Houses* (Aug. 1970), p. 6; British Institute of Public Opinion, *Survey of Drinking Habits, 1939.*

53 Penny Summerfield, 'Approaches to Women and Social Change in the Second World War', in Brian Brivati and Harriet Jones (eds), *What Difference Did the War Make?* (Leicester: Leicester University Press, 1993), pp. 73–4.

54 Adam Edwards, 'Street Life', *Morning Advertiser*, 8 July 2004; 'Jostle, Jostle', *New Statesman*, 3 July 1981, p. 12.

55 'Adolescents in Public Houses', p. 3.

56 Langhamer, 'Women, Leisure and Drink', p. 424.

57 See Chapter 1, above, pp. 32–3.

58 B. Seebohm Rowntree and G. R. Lavers, *English Life and Leisure* (London: Longmans, Green and Co., 1951), p. 175; Claire Langhamer, *Women's Leisure in England, 1920–60* (Manchester: Manchester University Press, 2000), p. 157; Jane Lewis, *Women in England, 1870–1950: Sexual Divisions and Social Change* (Brighton: Harvester Wheatsheaf, 1984), p. xi; Market Information Services, *What People Think about Public Houses: The Results of a Large-Scale Sample Survey Carried Out among the Adult Population of England and Wales during November, 1949,* January, 1950, tables 2 and 5. The MIS survey received support from Ferdynand Zweig who estimated that women comprised between 30 per cent and 40 per cent of patrons in London licensed premises in 1948 (Ferdynand Zweig, *Labour, Life and Poverty* (London: Victor Gollancz, 1948), p. 25).

59 Carol Smart, 'Law and the Control of Women's Sexuality: The Case of the 1950s', in Bridget Hutter and Gillian Williams (eds), *Controlling Women: The Normal and the Deviant* (London: Croom Helm, 1981), pp. 49–53; British Market Research Bureau Ltd, *Licensed Premises: Report of an Attitude Survey, August 1960*, p. 66.

60 Terrence R. Gourvish, 'The Business of Alcohol in the US and the UK: UK Regulation and Drinking Habits, 1914–39', *Business and Economic History*, 26 (1997), pp. 613–14; T. R. Gourvish and R. G. Wilson, *The British Brewing Industry, 1830–1980* (Cambridge: Cambridge University Press, 1994), pp. 618, 630.

61 S. H. Benson, Ltd, *Summary Report of Attitudes Towards Public Houses and Drinking Habits* (1958), pp. 4, 6.

62 Whitbread & Co., *Your Local* (London: Whitbread & Co., 1947); *A Monthly Bulletin*: 19 (March 1949), p. 31; 22 (Feb. 1952), pp. 27–9, 63; 25 (Aug. 1955), p. 129; Maurice Gorham, *Back to the Local* (London: Percival Marshall, 1949).

63 S. H. Benson Ltd, *A Test on the Use of the Words 'Pub' and 'Social' Prepared for the Brewers' Society* (London: Nov. 1959).

3

A tough sell: wooing women in the 1950s–60s

Gender relations modified in the 1950s, though here continuity rather more than change dominated, as David Kynaston's recent study argued. Admittedly, there was a distinct shift towards the companionate marriage in the 1950s, discernible especially in some middle- and to a still lesser extent working-class families. But a powerful societal trend towards domesticity, as marriage and motherhood became ascendant, affected women, whose patronage of the pub as a result plummeted to an all-time low in the late 1950s. It was pre-eminently the one-career family that prevented women from using their economic contributions to negotiate greater equality in their marriages, including shared leisure activities. In this, as in so many other senses, the pub reflected Britain's prevailing social norms. Films now exalted marriage, home and the family, eclipsing the golden interwar and wartime eras in which women on screen were revered. Strong feminine characters such as Bette Davis, Joan Crawford and Katharine Hepburn had starred in movies projecting equality with men, with whom they shared courage and initiative.[1]

Standardization accelerated this transformation first in the late 1950s. To acquire a national market for select beverages, brewers promoted keg beer and lager, two new types of beer in which the distinctive flavour of bitter and cask-conditioned ales was diminished. No longer did it matter where the alcohol was consumed or what clothing a drinker wore. As part of this process, prices became as standardized as the rooms of the pub themselves. Ironically, while the masculine culture of pubs underwent gradual change, women's presence in pubs plummeted. Brewers catered primarily to their main drinkers, men from the lower middle and working classes. Through advertisements championing women as second-class drinkers in a male world, brewers reinforced the widespread cultural norms reminding females of their inferior status.

Admitted as members in just one-fourth of the affiliated branches of the

Working Men's Club and Institute Union, the chief organization of reputable social clubs, women fully grasped their second-class status. 'They come there as a privilege not as a right', related the 1948 Mass-Observation report. Denied membership, women entered as guests, sometimes only on special occasions, and even then endured segregation in private rooms, so as not to disturb male members.[2]

One in every five pints was downed in Britain's clubs in the mid-1960s for diverse reasons. Compared to pubs, clubs had bargain-priced beer, which certainly outranked everything else as a male attraction. Clubs also trumped pubs with more flexible licensing hours, rebates from brewers, free or cheaper amenities, more reliable beer supplies, relaxed attitude to purchasing alcohol, and provision of games as well as musical entertainment. Yet, these considerations, though certainly significant, had proved inadequate to forestall the slide of many clubs towards, and sometimes into, insolvency. Hard-pressed club managers in Leicester, for instance, were unable to book entertainers for concert rooms, defrayed cost of newspapers themselves for club members, and fretted as to how to meet breweries' demands for payments on delivery. Two developments transformed the context. First came the legalization of tombola with cash prizes as a draw for players in 1957; next arrived slot machines – commonly called one-armed bandits – in the following decade. Not only did they revive flagging club sales but they together ensured the revenue necessary for survival of many clubs.[3]

For breweries, club accounts, a massive source of beer sales to an overwhelmingly male clientele, stood as a formidable obstacle to women being regarded as important to expanding beer consumption. Why worry about women, so the argument went, when men constituted the mainstay of the beer market? In drinking primarily gin, port, sherry, or Guinness stout rather than mild ale, the stable of beer consumption, women, after all, unwittingly encouraged this view.[4] From the late Victorian era, brewers had financed clubs, offering low-interest loans, subsidizing costs for rebuilding premises, and pricing beer at unbeatable prices, as publicans knew to their costs! Huge beer sales to clubs, then, literally constituted a mental roadblock to enlarging the beer market. Beer, pubs, clubs and men were synonymous in the minds of beer wholesalers; these associations created a mentality antipathetic to marketing beer with gender as a new component. Expenditure on alcohol in pubs and beerhouses accounted for well over three-fourths of the total.[5]

Slumping beer consumption immediately after the war, however, compelled brewers at least half-heartedly to entertain new ideas about marketing their products. In 1949, the Brewers' Society commissioned market research with Market Information Services, the first statistical survey undertaken on the Society's behalf.[6] Some 2400 detailed interviews later produced daunting results: two-thirds of all women avoided the pub altogether, half of them drinking no alcohol whatsoever. About half of the remainder, 20 per cent of all women, frequented pubs occasionally. Two-thirds of all men, in contrast, patronized pubs. Thus, the pub-going clientele constituted no more than half of the adult population. By the time these results emerged the following year, beer consumption had plummeted 20 per cent since 1945. Here indeed was a crisis for one of Britain's central institutions, and those who owned them, the brewers.[7]

The unavoidable, embarrassing problem was that some women heartily disliked both beer and stout, regardless of social class or geography. Nearly half and sometimes as many as two-thirds of all women drank neither beer nor stout.[8]

Even before these findings appeared, brewers reacted to falling beer consumption with a national advertising campaign, aimed at wooing women. Launched in 1948, these newspaper advertisements, drawn by professional artists, discarded the image of an isolated woman shown in a non-pub context, and instead portrayed females of all ages mingling with men in lounges and saloon bars, two areas with tables and more refined décor. Nevertheless, in two important senses the advertisements remained consistent with social norms: women were escorted by men – none drank just with other women – and came from the propertied classes.[9]

Whitbread's advertising of Mackeson's Stout several years later, with the slogan 'the stout that's not bitter', targeted women who shunned the sour flavour of beer, and conspicuously challenged conventional wisdom about marketing beer. Demonstrating an imaginative flair, the brewery photographed local working-class women (not professional models), sometimes unescorted but always conversing with another woman, in the lounge. Not only identified were the customers' real names but the drinking establishments. Still more creatively, the photographs were all published in Northern newspapers, the country's most conservative drinking region where Guinness reigned supreme as the top-selling stout. In offering personal testimonials from female drinkers, the advertisements acquired authenticity as much as credibility. In a lengthy story in the *Yorkshire Evening News*, two women, photographed sitting at a table in Leeds Central Station Hotel, glowingly endorsed Mackeson's Stout: 'I like its smooth flavour', commented Mrs Ethel Price, while her friend, Mrs Greta

Harrison, exclaimed 'Give me *Mackeson*'s every time'. Whitbread shrewdly ensured its material was not easily overlooked. Half-page advertisements with detailed commentary from Leeds, Macclesfied and Preston drinkers appeared in spring 1952. As in the Brewers' Society's campaign, women were photographed drinking in lounges.[10] Other huge breweries, such as Watney and Guinness, also placed women in advertisements for stout subsequently, but the context lacked both Whitbread's ingenuity and setting in a public house.[11]

Faced with a flat beer market which underlined the failure of the advertising campaign, brewers again turned to market researchers for answers. Taking no chances this time on statistical errors arising from a small sample, the Brewers' Society commissioned a still more detailed survey with almost thirty thousand interviews across the country in 1956–7. From the brewers' perspective, the findings could scarcely have been more daunting, given the recent expenditure on advertising to expand beer consumption: the proportion of women visiting pubs had actually fallen slightly from 35 per cent to 33 per cent, and the proportion of those drinking beer had slumped even more, from 40 per cent to 33 per cent.[12]

Brewers had every right to be disturbed about these findings, and, perhaps sensing worse to come, continued closely to track drinking habits. Three years later, in yet another survey, brewers discovered women's patronage of pubs had plunged from 33 per cent to 13 per cent, a decline unprecedented since statistical polling began in 1939.[13] No one previously has observed this remarkable collapse of drinking in pubs by women in the late 1950s, a change which the postwar ideology lauding a woman's true place as in the home both partly caused and powerfully reinforced.[14] Indeed, what appeared irrefutable was that cultural rhetoric more effectively shaped women's behaviour than advertisements aimed specially at females, at least in this decade.

What and where women consumed alcohol cast further gloom among brewers. Only one-fifth of all women drank beer, most of them in the working or impoverished classes. Half of the beer they consumed, moreover, was stout, now a niche sector comprising just 10 per cent of total beer sales. Two brands commanded the market: Guinness, with about half of all sales based primarily among older Scottish and Northern drinkers; and Whitbread's Mackeson's, which accounted for another quarter of sales chiefly to middle-aged women living in the Midlands and the South.[15] Bereft of the middle and upper classes as frequent drinkers, the pub was overwhelmingly working-class (Table 5)[16]

It is not hard to imagine why pubs repelled women so much in the 1950s. In an interview with Egon Ronay, columnist for the *Daily Telegraph*, Charles

Table 5 Class composition of public house patrons, 1960.

Class	*% in Public Houses*	*% of Population*
Middle/Upper (AB)	10%	12%
Lower Middle (C)	24%	17%
Working & Poor (DE)	66%	71%

Source: British Market Research Bureau Ltd., *Licensed Premises, 1960*, p. 103

Clore (Chairman of Sears) offered a damning indictment in 1959: 'Most of our pubs today don't appeal to women'. Reasons abounded for this: 'They are uncomfortable, antiquated and don't attract the younger generation'. The *Daily Express* wholeheartedly agreed: 'Comfort is the very last consideration of the [pub] owners'.[17]

Though breweries were reputedly spending £25 million annually on all kinds of pub improvement early in the 1960s, this hardly addressed the lengthy building moratorium when virtually nothing was undertaken. Too many pubs, thought the *Daily Express*, were in appalling condition: 'the bar furniture worn and shoddy. The walls smoke-stained brown.... The floor coverings threadbare and tattered'.[18] Another innovative feature, designed to save money without sacrificing historic authenticity, at least to the untrained eye, was fake pub refurbishment. Overhead beams and wrought-ironwork on close inspection proved to be made of plastic.[19]

Women regarded nothing as more important than cleanliness and good hygiene at pubs. Whatever advice appeared to the contrary in the trade press, most brewing company executives and landlords remained unconvinced of the direct relationship between toilets of high standards and solid profits.[20] Writing in 1959, pub architect R. P. Shannon acknowledged that 'not long ago it was quite common for licensed houses to be devoid of all sanitary facilities for women'. In that same year, the *Daily Express* supplied a harsher view: present-day toilets, it stated, were 'an insult to a modern hygienic society'.[21] Shannon pointed with pride to the vastly improved toilet facilities in new pubs, where customers could expect to find, perhaps for the first time in such circumstances, 'toilet holders, coat hooks, wash basins with hot and cold water, soap dispensers, towels and mirrors'.[22] A decade later, however, women's toilets in prewar unimproved premises still remained in a class of their own. 'I am amazed at the drab, dirty and generally dilapidated condition of toilets at some establishments', one secretary confessed. After visiting one of them, she exclaimed that 'this is enough to put you off [drinking in pubs] for a lifetime'.

One leading designer of pub package kits, Leslie Kostick, endorsed this assessment, lamenting that brewers generally lacked interest in toilets which he felt redolent of a 'scene of Dickensian harshness'.[23] In her own contribution to an ironically entitled collection of essays, *Pub: A Celebration*, published late in the 1960s, reporter Marjorie Proops described her unforgettable reactions:

> Squalid little rooms with grimy towels (or none at all): dirty washbasins; slimy bits of soap; penny-in-the-slot doors; spotty-looking glasses and nowhere to park your handbag or make-up – that's the picture far too many pub ladies' rooms present.

In fact, it was said that women limited their drinking sessions to no more than two drinks; otherwise, they contemplated the horrors of navigating inaccessible, dark staircases with 'the unspeakable "Ladies"' at the journey's end as their reward.[24] Not surprisingly, such 'nasty little hell-holes' revolted women, regardless of how much brewers spent refurbishing premises with laminated tables and garishly coloured interiors, their walls covered in inexpensive veneers.[25]

That a public house could win a coveted newspaper award as 'pub of the year' in 1970 with deplorable hygiene for women underlined 'the attitude of so many owners to this very vital part of their premises', remarked John Locke, Managing Director of Twyfords. Locke, himself, saw the level of hygiene as a key factor determining the type and number of customers which a pub could draw.[26] Yet, in a survey of attitudes to the pub commissioned by the Brewers' Society that same year, toilet conditions did not warrant a separate category when surveyors questioned customers about what they disliked most in drinking at pubs.[27] Women's views can be inferred, however, from a survey a decade earlier in which they identified new modern pubs, with the most up-to-date toilets boasted about by Shannon, as the most attractive.[28]

Women objected to the public house so much because they saw drinking as boring, unappealing, wasteful of family income and the sole rationale cited by male companions for going on the outing. Given these sentiments, they interpreted their presence as inhibiting menfolk from fully enjoying the experience. 'There is a cultural basis to the resistance to the idea of women drinking, and also to the acceptance of women staying at home, whilst men go out alone – and that this traditional way of thinking is most firmly established by the working classes', contended one national market survey in 1960. Men sensed women's disapproval of visiting their local, despite its proximity to home. This conflict typically ended with working-class men – whether married or courting – being dissuaded from taking females to any pubs: four of five working men patronized a pub without females. Different gender attitudes towards leisure also explain why men typically drank without women in pubs. 'The notion that men earned leisure while women facilitated it framed gendered experiences of leisure within a marriage', concluded Claire Langhamer.[29]

That women lacked the same compelling incentives as men for visiting pubs likewise illuminates why the former drank beer most often at home or a friend's house, where the bottled beer they consumed had not in their eyes the defects perceived by men. There were class differences: middle- and upper-class women preferred bottled beer, whereas working-class or impoverished women opted for bottled stout.[30]

Notwithstanding these deficiencies, a minority of women, though very few in the North, did use the pub in the 1950s.[31] The stage in the family life cycle, class and age, even more than their occupational status, as Langhamer has recently argued, critically shaped whether they accompanied husbands or boyfriends. Such women were more likely to drink in pubs while courting and in the early years of marriage before children arrived. Disavowing the pronounced ideological emphasis on domesticity prevailing in postwar Britain, some middle-class men, together with smaller numbers of young working-class males, did embrace social intimacy with women. These more liberated husbands 'are not only willing to have their wives with them in the pub, but also actually tend to enjoy themselves more if their wife is accompanying them', commented market researchers.[32]

This new leisure habit, confined to less than one-third of women, foreshadowed how pub culture would evolve in the swinging sixties. Brewers interested in maximizing profit thus had compelling reasons to ponder the survey's further observation that 'it is possible for women to enhance their husband's pleasure in the pub, as well as making it possible for him to protract his visit and increase his spending'.[33] Regardless of gender, the pub remained primarily working-class (see Table 5). 'It is (as with men) amongst the middle class women that there is the biggest reserve of potential pub goers; i.e. women who have a drink at least once a month (mainly at home) but do not go to the pub', observed a 1960 market survey.[34] From the late 1950s changes in the British palate would have profound consequences for both women and more widely drinking habits in general.

Historically, consumer taste had registered more frequent, long-standing changes in the twentieth than in the nineteenth century. Porter, which had appeared in the eighteenth century and quickly came to dominate, was supplanted by pale ale in the 1840s–50s, transforming Burton upon Trent into the country's major brewing centre and members of the Allsopp and Bass families into millionaires, with newly acquired peerages in the House of Lords. Towards the end of the century, lighter hopped, less alcoholic, sparkling bottled ales gained popularity, especially among the middle classes.[35] It was not so much the type of beer as its standard gravity, more commonly known as alcoholic strength, that altered during the First World War, as wartime shortages in hops and grain caused rationing and weaker beers, caustically dubbed 'Lloyd George's Ale'.[36] By the war's end, drinkers' palates had fundamentally recalibrated, finding lower-gravity beers now the accepted drinking norm.

Once again drinking taste modified in the 1950s, preparing drinkers for keg beers which had muted bitterness and lager beers with their more mellow flavour. Diverse factors facilitated this change. Immediately following the Second World War, the public, previously deprived of sugar, had devoured eagerly sweeter consumables, but sweetened products – confectionery, biscuits and stouts – soon lost popularity. Introduction of pasteurized bottled or keg beers diminished the importance of naturally conditioned draught bitter beer, distinctive in many instances for its bitterness. Keg beers, pressurized with carbon dioxide and less heavily hopped, together with bottled beers, offered drinkers a blander taste. The shift towards what H. Alan Walker, Chairman of Bass Charrington, called 'a more middle of the road palate', was part of the larger trend of standardization in clothing, food and designs. 'People', he noted, 'want to share the same tastes – to follow fashion'. Cheese, meat and other products, now refrigerated and packaged, had far milder flavours than before the war. 'With this smoothing out of flavours in other goods', recalled Scottish & Newcastle's head brewer in the mid-1960s, 'had gone step in step the flavours of beer – bitter beers were nowhere as bitter today as in 1947–8'. Bouillon, commonly employed to provide a distinct bitterness before 1939 and used by brewers as a substitute for imported American hops, lost popularity, as the British palate shifted decisively towards a mellower, rounded flavour.[37]

In this reorientation of drinking habits, pub habituates ironically received considerable impetus from their landlord, whose indifferent skills literally drove them to despair and ultimately other alternatives. 'I think there were a lot … of sloppy, lazy publicans … [from] the time when I first came into the trade [in 1948]', disclosed Northern brewer Neal Hyde.[38] Cask-conditioned beers required careful handling, expertise in management and, especially, immaculate cellars. Derek Brock recalled his father-in-law's cellar expertise at a Penmark pub in rural Glamorganshire in the 1950s and early 1960s: 'There was no fancy air-conditioning for the ancient Six Bells cellar; he controlled the temperature fluctuations with wet sacks and hosepipes in the summer, and a variety of all available electric fires in the winter, but the beer rarely moved from its perfection of 54°F.' The Six Bells was, as Neal Hyde and other brewers knew so well, an anomaly in the retail trade. By the late 1950s, recalled the *Publican*, 'nothing had been spent on pub cellars for something like 30 years because of war time restrictions'.[39]

As an intermediate step to overcoming deficient cellar conditions and to reassure drinkers that they were buying consistent taste, brewers turned aggressively to marketing bottled beer, and found unexpectedly a group already sold on the idea. To the young, steeped in knowledge about technological changes, increasing numbers of products sold in glass containers in the 1950s evoked strong cultural associations with higher hygienic standards. Products retailed as 'untouched by hand' had made these youthful consumers 'container-conscious'. Whether beer, milk or jams, consumables marketed to adolescents and young adults thus elicited 'an impression of unadulterated cleanliness and virtue', asserted one brewing newspaper. Bottled beer, so brewers gladly learned, had an audience predisposed to their product. Owing to their layout and physical size, numerous working-men's clubs 'can only stock and serve conveniently this class of beer', related the *Brewing Trade Review*. In clubs, as in pubs, sales quickly soared, with Southern brewers selling fully half of their production in bottles.[40]

Overall, drinkers consumed nearly one-third of their beer from bottles by the mid-1960s. Many Cockneys mixed light bottled beer with draught bitter because they had no other choice, given the sad truism: 'bitter was often undrinkable by itself'. As one went further North, bottled beer lost much of its allure, but even here habitual draught beer drinkers began displaying disgust. 'I quite firmly believed that the basic reason that this was happening was a reaction from people coming back after the war to the quality of draught beer during the war', thought Neal Hyde, whose family brewery sold about 20 per cent of output in bottles.[41]

Declining cellar quality and vile-tasting, even unquaffable, beers gave brewers powerful incentives to find a more bacteria- and landlord-resistant beverage. Keg beer – pressurized, pasteurized and utterly predictable – proved to be the solution. A filtered, carbonated, sparkling beverage, with a longer shelf life than its cask-conditioned predecessor, keg beer required of the retailer far fewer skills to serve and maintain. To recapture the market for draught beers, brewers became committed to promoting keg beers aggressively. As a brand of keg beer all tasted the same from the same brewery, landlords' cellar-keeping skills became radically devalued.

Mass-produced, standardized beers were antithetical to the old masculine drinking culture, based on individual taste and beers revered for their distinctive aroma, quality, and deeply rooted sense of local identity. Not only would small numbers of national keg beers replace thousands of brands brewed for local or regional markets but they would eliminate one important rationale for separate bars, the different beverages popular with varying social classes. Mild ale, drunk overwhelmingly in public bars, would thus be one of the chief casualties of standardizing taste. From the brewers' perspective, mild beer offered little prospect of widening the consumer base. In this emergent trend towards homogenized products, the brewing industry was following exactly the pattern as in the rest of the economy.[42]

Several factors heightened the marketing significance of keg beer's wider dissemination into the beer market late in the 1950s.[43] The two sexes had decidedly different ways in which they consumed beer: men drank draught beer in pubs and clubs much more enthusiastically than women, who consumed far less beer but in cans or bottles at home or friends' homes.[44] Men revered draught beer because manliness involved acquiring the knowledge, taste and eyesight to evaluate the changing condition of unpasteurized beer.[45] Thus, men chose a pub and publican partly on the basis of his beer-keeping skills. Women shared none of these traits. Canned and bottled beers lacked this mystique as they were pasteurized, with more predictable flavours and longer shelf lives. Women, moreover, used an entirely different rationale for selecting pubs. According to one informed commentator, women 'prefer the comfort and amenities of a modern, tastefully appointed bar rather than surroundings that are dreary and outmoded'.[46] Keg beer hence affected drinking habits more of men than of women. Deprived of the traditional motive for frequenting pubs where a favourite beer, kept in superb condition, was on draught, men could more readily accept wives' suggestions that they drink where entertainment and respectability were offered. But wives also responded to subtle marketing psychology by other shrewd women. Women behind the bar as the licensee's wife had considerable insight into what women as wives on the other side of the counter wanted. To her barmaids, Alice Kaye, wife of the landlord at the Horse & Groom (Lincoln), gave the following studied advice: 'Always pay more attention to the wives than to the husbands, especially when they come in together for a drink'. Her logic showed perceptive insight into marriages. 'Once the wife is confident about the atmosphere her husband is in', Kaye confided to a reporter, 'her mind is set at ease'. In respecting their wives' opinion about an appropriate drinking venue, husbands gave further impetus to the emergence of the companionate marriage in postwar Britain.[47]

Given keg beer's indirect assault on masculine drinking culture, it was indeed ironic that Ind Coope relaunched a keg version of its Double Diamond featured in a 1962 national advertising campaign as 'the beer the men drink'. Notwithstanding the attractions of a national market for advertising beer, Ind Coope found it inconceivable to sell one beer to both sexes. Its advertising agents, Hobson Bates, articulated the goal of the new advertising campaign, the instalment of 'Double Diamond as the natural and appropriate drink for "Men Only" occasions'.[48] For Ind Coope, as for other leading breweries, selling beer to men remained paramount. One year before introducing Skol, for example, *Ind Coope News* boasted that the brewery's new pubs possessed 'a dominant air of virility in their conception'.[49] In their own defence, brewers might have pointed to their need to hold on to their main customers.

One brewery also unwittingly assaulted male drinking culture with a new alcoholic beverage. Lager was certainly not the first postwar alcoholic beverage aimed specifically at women.[50] This distinction belonged to Showerings, an established brewery and cider business, which introduced Baby Champion (later shortened to Babycham) in 1950, aimed at those aged eighteen to twenty-four, a cohort of nubile women. Cheaper than a glass of spirits, this sparkling perry-based drink evoked a refined image by being retailed in a small bottle filling a champagne glass to the brim, a point emphasized in its advertisements. Showerings hired young women as the models and used 'I'd love a Babycham' as the slogan. The company's clever marketing strategy paid handsome dividends, with sales of Babycham becoming an overnight sensation in the 1950s; the brewery at one point was unable to fill more than 5 per cent of the massive numbers of orders. An advertisement in 1959, displaying a bride drinking Babycham on her wedding day, testified to Showerings' success in creating an upmarket image, the beverage for those special occasions in a woman's life. By the late 1970s, the company was spending £750,000 annually on television advertisements. Demonstrating the product's staying power, Showerings relaunched Babycham in 1983 with a £3.25 million promotional effort.[51]

As standbys until the early 1950s, women drank a stable of other beverages – wine, port, sherry, Pimm's (a premixed drink) and mixtures of beverages – shandy (beer and lemonade), port-and-lemon and gin-and-tonic.[52] According to a Gallup survey in 1948, women preferred both wine and spirits over beer by a margin of more than two to one.[53] For the cocktail market one of the most popular brands was Campari, an aperitif with continental associations, which

Barclay's Lager Advertisement, 1948. 7

projected an image of sophisticated leisure. Overpriced at 2s 6d a glass, served at room temperature, and the repellant Red Biddy as the sole alternative, pub wines had little appeal to women. When pub manager Sean Treacy introduced clarets and burgundies at Finch's King's Arms (Fulham Road, Chelsea), it was thought worthy enough to merit a story in the *Daily Express*.[54]

From the very beginning of postwar advertising, lager had acquired an image as a woman's beverage. Barclays helped establish this view when it employed women to advertise its own lager from 1946 onwards (Plate 7). Typical of the market the brewery sought was an early advertisement in which a man accompanied an affluent woman, well dressed with a stole, who sat in a lounge drinking lager from a specially designed tall beer glass.[55] Within several years, McEwan's followed suit with an advertisement for its own export lager featuring a man and woman seated at a bar consuming the drink.[56]

Skol, a lager publicly unveiled by Ind Coope in May 1959, became one of the first beers targeted at young women. Part of the marketing strategy focused on serving the beer in a unique glass. 'Special stemmed "Skol" goblets of Waterford glass are being introduced because we feel that many women refuse to drink beer on account of it being served ... unattractively in formidable [traditional pint] glasses', commented the brewery's Marketing Director. Privately, the brewery suspected women had previously resisted lager in the customary beer glasses owing to a desire to avoid seeming 'unfeminine' when in male company in a public house.[57] In the summer of 1960, the brewing industry orchestrated a huge multi-media advertising campaign with newspapers, magazines, television and billboards all mobilized. Advertisements featuring a man and woman drinking Skol appeared in the popular press, *Daily Mirror* and the *Express*. Other advertisements more directly cultivated the female market, with half-page advertisments purchased in such leading magazines as *Woman*, *Woman's Own*, *Woman's Day* and *Woman's Realm*. Reflecting Ind Coope's ambivalent attitude to encouraging women to encroach on male drinking space, some advertisements pictured a solitary female with a Skol set in an unspecific background.[58]

Two factors facilitated lager's introduction into the British market: warmer homes and refrigeration.[59] 'In the summer', reminisced brewer Neal Hyde of the immediate postwar era, 'the beer tasted like warm bath water'. Winter drinking in pubs lacking central heating had its own set of horrors for inveterate drinkers. 'You were', Hyde continued, 'cold from the outside, you were cold in the room you went into, and you got a belly full of cold beer out of the pump'. Change did not come overnight, but gradually living rooms in British homes became 5° (F) warmer in 1970 than in 1950. As central heating spread, drinkers could consume lager in other rooms of the house, too. This was equally true of pubs themselves. One large brewery went so far as to cite better central heating in its pubs as a key factor in patrons' greater willingness to consume lager. For the British market, lager was ideally served between 45° and 48° (F), several degrees cooler than other bottled beers and almost ten degrees colder than how retailers ideally dispensed draught beers. Few pubs, even those owned by Barclays, which had brewed a lager since the 1930s, offered it on draught. Not until the 1950s were pubs, restaurants and domestic homes acquiring the refrigerators necessary for storing bottled beer at optimum temperature. Nevertheless, progress came slowly: Britain's record-breaking hot summer in 1959 caught most pubs without refrigeration. The next step came in the early 1960s with cold shelves, each one capable of storing three to four dozen beer bottles. Still, lager consumption grew incrementally, a fact which owed much to middle-class views of heated rooms as unsuitable and extravagant. Lager's market share increased from 2 per cent in 1960 to just 4 per cent a decade later.[60]

Despite this modest increase, two of five drinkers had tried lager. Scotland led the way, with one in five drinkers committed lager drinkers.[61] South of the border, lager appealed to young and middle-aged women and men aged twenty to forty. One factor remained to retard lager's growth, the absence of a dispensing system using refrigeration for draught lager. When this was overcome in the early 1970s, consumption of draught lager soared, accounting for four-fifths of all lager sales.[62]

As Britons shifted from warm to chilled beer, they participated in what John Burnett has termed a 'cold drinks revolution'. From the late 1950s, warmer restaurants, offices, shops, public transport and motor cars, perhaps aided by global warming, transformed life dramatically. 'Bodies that in the past needed heavy clothes and hot beverages now wear lighter dress and take their milk and soft drinks, lager, cider and white wine from the domestic refrigerator', argued Burnett. Transatlantic exchanges with America may also have fostered this fundamental change in lifestyles. So too did the growing popularity of continental eating habits – salads, lighter meals, more fish and less red meat, consumed ideally, not with hot tea or warm beer, but with cold beverages.[63]

Brewers responded to declining numbers of women pub drinkers with not only the introduction of lager but extensive national advertising. In this new national advertising campaign, brewers again predictably photographed propertied women in pubs. Mindful of the recent warning in a public opinion poll that radically altering the overwhelmingly masculine nature of pubs could alienate men, the backbone of the drinking clientele, brewers went to great lengths to reassure them that women would not violate masculine drinking norms.[64] Hence, advertisers depicted middle-class females as drinking and playing games in male company, consuming halves of beer and relying on men to purchase it at the bar and provide expert advice.[65] The message was unmistakable: women would enter saloon bars or lounges only when properly

8 Brewers' Society Advertisement, 13 May 1961.

escorted and behave as the submissive spouses that husbands expected. Such cautious advertising characterized the approach of nearly all breweries.[66] Guinness, for example, produced its own advertisements targeting women in its 'The Younger Generation' campaign launched late in the 1950s. Holding a glass of Guinness seated at a table in a pub, a well-dressed woman remarked to her male escort: 'Thank you, Mike, for teaching me how good Guinness tastes!' Commercials reiterated the same message when couples drank at home. Clearly, men preferred women to be obedient, deferential and respectful of the masculine culture of drinking. Women were thus being admitted to drinking premises, formally exclusively male, as privileged guests who relied on men to instruct them about male drinking rituals.[67]

In its third advertising campaign, 'Beer is Best', formally inaugurated in 1962, the Brewers' Society targeted young housewives – their wedding rings conspicuously evident – or unmarried women in their mid- to late twenties, demographic groups which had avoided pubs. Drinkers portrayed in the background of the advertisements were of similar age or older. Famous women admitted accompanying husbands to the local for drinks and sometimes a meal. An actress featured in one advertisement with the caption 'Dora Bryan says I Love Pubs', while another showcased a novelist with the caption 'Monica Dickens Looks in at the Local'. These advertisements uniformly were set in saloon bars or lounges.[68] To the public bars, brewers also beckoned women with advertisements in which they appeared as darts players or onlookers. One showed a woman, dart in hand, squinting, with the caption: 'Who said girls can't play darts?' 'Today', the advertisement continued, 'is the first time I've ever played darts. It's easy' (Plate 8). Watneys, together with Guinness and the *People* newspaper, had energetically promoted darts with its Red Barrel League, while Taylor Walker boasted sponsorship of a long-established league with five thousand players and two hundred teams. But the game became the casualty of carpeted lounges as much as the television. In an effort to encourage a National Darts League, Watneys contributed £1200 in 1967.[69]

Whether in eating and drinking or in clothing, standardization characterized the 1950s and 1960s. Keg beer, its flavour uniform, predictable and less bitter than its predecessors, embodied the new consumer taste. This was equally true of lager, its introduction reflecting broader social changes in heating and refrigeration more than continental travel.

Standardization redefined how the British themselves drank. With standardized beverages, now keg beer and soon lager, consumers of all classes would be drinking the same beverages in the same pub, paying the same price, enjoying the same amenities and wearing clothes identifying them broadly as bourgeois. Yet, brewers would discover that they not solved fundamentally the problem of how to sell beer to women while remaining themselves as captive as their overwhelming male patrons to sexist attitudes.

Notes

1 David Kynaston, *Family Britain, 1951–57: Tales of a New Jerusalem* (London: Bloomsbury, 2009); Judith Harwin and Shirley Otto, 'Women, Alcohol and the Screen', in Jim Cook and Mike Lewington (eds), *Images of Alcoholism* (London: British Film Institute, 1979), pp. 46–7.

2 University of Sussex, FR 3029, Mass-Observation Archives, *A Report on Drinking Habits*, Aug. 1948, p. 164; David Nash and David Reeder, with Peter Jones and Richard Rodger, *Leicester in the Twentieth Century* (Stroud: Alan Sutton in Association with Leicester City Council, 1993), p. 177. Hereafter FR citations refer to the Mass-Observation Archives.

3 FR 3029, A Report on Drinking Habits, Aug. 1948, p. 164; Nash and Reeder, *Leicester*, p. 178; Ferdynand Zweig, *The British Worker* (Harmondsworth: Penguin Books, 1952), p. 138.

4 FR 3029, A Report on Drinking Habits, Aug. 1948, pp. 49–50.

5 Northamptonshire Record Office: NBP 103, Northamptonshire Brewers' Association, Minute Book, 10 March 1953, and Northampton Brewing Co., Loans to Clubs; Staffordshire Record Office, D 3163/3, Shropshire Wholesale Brewers' Association, Minute Book, 28 Nov. 1950, p. 25b; David Gutzke, *Protecting the Pub: Brewers and Publicans against Temperance* (Woodbridge: Royal Historical Society/Boydell Press), 1989, pp. 192, 196–8; Modern Records Centre, University of Warwick, MSS 420, Box 320, Memorandum on the Distribution of Beer in 1938, p. 5.

6 T. R. Gourvish, and R. G. Wilson, *The British Brewing Industry, 1830–1980* (Cambridge: Cambridge University Press, 1994), pp. 366–7. The survey utilized what has become standard among statistical studies, a random national sample drawn from electoral registers to guarantee a representative cross-section of the population with a margin of error of just 1.2 per cent (Market Information Services Ltd, *What People Think about Public Houses: The Results of a Large-Scale Sample Survey Carried out among the Adult Population of England and Wales during November, 1949* (Jan. 1950), General Introduction).

7 Market Information Services Ltd, *What People Think*, Table 5; Gourvish and Wilson, *British Brewing Industry*, pp. 366–7; Geoffrey Gorer, *Exploring English Character* (New York: Criterion Books, 1955), p. 69.

8 *Daily Herald Readers and the Market for Beer and Stout, Aug. 1960* (1960), Table 4, p. 12.

9 *Brewing Trade Review*, April and June 1948; Modern Records Centre, University of Warwick, Brewers' Society, MSS 420/BS/4/60/1, Advertisements, 1949–50; *Brewing Trade Review*, May, June and July 1955.

10 *Yorkshire Evening News*, 19 May 1952; *Macclesfield Times & Courier*, [unidentified but April or May] 1952; unidentified Preston newspaper, 7 April 1952, Whitbread Archives.
11 *Caterer and Hotel-Keeper*, 8 Jan. and 19 March 1955; *Guinness Time*, 13:1 (1960), p. 19.
12 S. H. Benson, Ltd, *The Brewers' Society 1957 Advertising Campaign Market Research Charts* (July 1956), p. 3.
13 Odhams Press Survey, 1960, *Financial Times*, quoted in the *Licensing World*, Aug. 1960; British Market Research Bureau Ltd, *Licensed Premises: Report of an Attitude Survey, August 1960* (1960), p. 66. Hereafter BMRI.
14 See above Ch. 2, p. 64.
15 S. H. Benson, *Summary Report on Attitudes Towards Public Houses and Drinking Habits* (Brewers' Society, 1958), pp. 1–4, 6–7; Odhams Press Survey, Aug. 1960.
16 Two-thirds of pub customers came from the working class (BMRI, *Licensed Premises* (1960), p. 103).
17 *Daily Telegraph*, 18 June 1959; *Daily Express*, 27 May 1959.
18 *Daily Telegraph*, 18 June 1959; *Daily Express*, 27 May 1959; Sir Bryan Bonsor and Reginald R. E. Heslewood, 'The Public House in a Modern Society', *Journal of the Royal Society of Arts* (July 1970), p. 454.
19 Michael Roulstone, 'The British Public House and the 1960s', in Alan Roulstone (ed.), *One for the Road: A Complete Collection of Drawings from 15 Guidelines Published Between 1963 and 1967 under the Series Title One for the Road* (Llangynog: Michael Roulstone Publications, 2004), CD-Rom, Appendix 2, pp. 573–4.
20 John M. R. Smart, 'Design – Past and Present', *Brewers' Guardian*, Nov. 1968. The Brewers' Society claimed it understood the relationship between women's attitudes to pubs and the conditions of loos (Lynne Edmunds, 'Décor, that's the Thing which Makes a Woman Pop into the Pub', *Daily Telegraph*, 12 Dec. 1974).
21 Author's italics. R. P. Shannon, 'Public House Trends', *Brewers' Journal*, 16 Sept. 1959; *Daily Express*, 27 May 1959.
22 Shannon, 'Public House Trends'.
23 *Brewers' Guardian*, March 1968; also see Suzy Menkes, 'Merry-Go-Round', *The Times*, 29 Jan. 1968.
24 Marjorie Proops, 'What will You Have, Mrs. Pankhurst?' in Angus McGill (ed.), *Pub: A Celebration* (London: Longmans, Green & Co., 1969), p. 124.
25 Ibid.
26 *Brewers' Guardian*, Dec. 1970.
27 Interscan, Ltd, *Attitudes on Pub Going Habits and Brewery Control and Ownership of Public Houses* (Aug. 1970), p. 11.
28 BMRI, *Licensed Premises, 1960*, Summary.
29 Ibid., pp. 67–71, 75, 77–8, 80; Claire Langhamer, *Women's Leisure in England, 1920–60* (Manchester: Manchester University Press, 2000), pp. 138, 152.
30 *Daily Herald Readers and the Market for Beer and Stout, Aug. 1960* (1960), Tables 16 and 23, pp. 26, 33; Odhams Press Survey, 1960, *Financial Times*, quoted in *Licensing World*, Aug. 1960.
31 Courting couples turned to cinemas rather than pubs in the 1950s (Elizabeth

Roberts, *Women and Families: An Oral History, 1940–70* (Oxford: Blackwell, 1995), pp. 62–3).

32 Langhamer, *Women's Leisure*, pp. 88, 156–7, 159, 180; BMRI, *Licensed Premises, 1960*, pp. 75–7.

33 BMRI, *Licensed Premises, 1960*, p. 77.

34 *The Brewers' Society 1957 Advertising Campaign Market Research Charts* (July 1956), pp. 3–6; BMRI, *Licensed Premises, 1960*, pp. 22, 28, 53, 57, 66–7.

35 Gutzke, *Protecting the Pub*, pp. 12, 203; E. M. Sigsworth, 'Science and the Brewing Industry, 1850–1900', *Economic History Review*, 17 (1965), pp. 540, 543–6; Jonathan Brown, *Steeped in Tradition: The Malting Industry in England Since the Railway Age* (Reading: University of Reading and Institute of Agriculture, 1983), pp. 21–2; Julian L. Baker, *The Brewing Industry* (London: Methuen, 1905), pp. 9, 12.

36 David W. Gutzke, *Pubs and Progressives: Reinventing the Public House in England, 1896–1960* (DeKalb, Illinois: Northern Illinois University Press, 2006), p. 52.

37 H. Alan Walker, 'Good Brews Woo the Wives as Well', *The Times*, 22 April 1968; *Brewers' Guardian*, Jan. 1964; Odhams Press Survey, Aug. 1960. Bouillon or stock cube is dehydrated broth shaped into a cube, and used commonly in cooking.

38 Author's interview with Neal Hyde, 15 Aug. 1998; also see London Metropolitan Archives, LMA/4453/A/09/071; Whitbread Archives, Sydney O. Nevile's Undated Memorandum on Poor Cellar Conditions [1961]. Managers had a reputation for watering and adulterating beer as strategies for making profits, otherwise impossible if they followed the dictates of their brewery owners (Tom Berkley, *We Keep a Pub* (1955; rept edn, London: Arrow Books, 1959), pp. 103, 239).

39 *Publican*, 14 June 1984; Derek Brock, *Cuckoo Marans in the Taproom: An Innkeeper in the Vale of Glamorgan* (London: John Murray, 1985), p. 15.

40 Interview with Richard Courage (Director of Courage Brewery), *Brewers' Journal*, 19 Oct. 1960; *Brewing Trade Review*, June 1954 and March 1957.

41 *Publican*, 14 June 1984; *Brewing Trade Review*, June 1954 and March 1957; *A Report of the Proceedings of the Monopolies and Mergers Commission on the Proposed Merger between Scottish & Newcastle Breweries PLC and Matthew Brown PLC, 1985*, Cmnd 9645, table 2.1; Author's interview with Neal Hyde, 15 Aug. 1998. Combining mild ale with bottled brown ale became temporarily popular in the mid-1950s (*Brewers' Guardian*, Feb. 1959).

42 H. M. Robinson, 'What's Yours?', *Red Hand*, 1 (Jan. 1958), p. 15; David W. Gutzke, 'Runcorn Brewery: The Unofficial History of a Corporate Disaster', *Histoire Sociale/Social History*, 41 (2008), pp. 217–19; L. R. Gofton, 'Social Change, Market Change: Drinking Men in North East England', *Food and Foodways*, 1 (1986), pp. 253–77.

43 Watneys pioneered keg beer in the 1930s, but it was not until the 1950s, with J. W. Green/Flowers Breweries leading the way with Flowers Keg in 1954, that breweries began promoting it seriously (Gourvish and Wilson, *British Brewing Industry*, pp. 457–8).

44 *Daily Herald Readers*, pp. 12, 25–6; *A Monthly Bulletin*, 22 (April 1952), p. 61; Odhams Press Survey, 1960, Aug. 1960.

45 See Chapter 9, below, p. 206.

46 Walker, 'Good Brews'; Shannon, 'Public House Trends', pp. 356–7; J. A. P. Charrington, 'Trends in Taste Reflect Ways of Life', *The Times (Beer in Britain Supplement)*, 22 April 1968; Beverley (Blackpool) to Editor, *A Monthly Bulletin*, 36 (Feb. 1965), p. 16.

47 Penny Summerfield, 'Women in Britain Since 1945: Companionate Marriage and the Double Burden', in James Obelkevich and Peter Catterall (eds), *Understanding Post-War British Society* (London: Routledge, 1994), pp. 58–9; "'It's Sound Psychology to Look After Wives in a Family Trade … '", *Licensed Victuallers' Gazette*, March 1964.

48 *Ind Coope News*, 61 (Sept. 1961); Raymond G. Anderson, 'Allied Breweries', in Jack S. Blocker, Jr, David M. Fahey and Ian R. Tyrrell (eds), *Alcohol and Temperance in Modern History: An International Encyclopedia*, 2 vols (Santa Barbara, California: ABC Clio, 2003), 36.

49 *Ind Coope News*, 1 (June 1957).

50 Women's consumption of stout during the war prompted McEwan's in the 1950s to advertise its Sweet Stout in newspapers displaying contented housewives drinking the beverage.

51 *Licensing World*, Sept. and Dec. 1960, and May and Oct. 1962; Anderson, 'Allied Breweries', 2, 36; *Publican*, 23 June 1983; Christian Davis, 'Showerings of Promotional Material', *Publican*, 16 Nov. 1978 and 28 Nov. 1985; Tom Harrisson, *Britain Revisited* (London: Victor Gollancz, 1961), pp. 178–9; Penny Dade, *Drink Talking: 100 Years of Alcohol Advertising* (London: Middlesex University Press, 2009), p. 68; Asa Briggs, *Wine for Sale: Victoria Wine and the Liquor Trade, 1860–1984* (London: B. T. Batsford, 1985), p. 131.

52 J. W. Fellows, 'Women Drinkers', *Red Hand*, 7 (Jan.–Feb. 1953), pp. 23–5; *Licensing World*, Jan. 1961; FR 3016, A Report on Drinking Habits, August 1948, p. 30.

53 George H. Gallup, *The Gallup International Public Opinion Polls: Great Britain, 1937–1975*, 2 vols (New York, 1976), 167.

54 Katharine Whitehorn, 'Mixing Their Drinkers', *Observer*, 1963; Sean Treacy, *A Smell of Broken Glass* (London: Tom Stacey, 1973), pp. 66–7; Dade, *Drink Talking*, p. 69.

55 Back cover, *Anchor Magazine*, 20 (July 1946).

56 *Brewer & Wine Merchant*, May 1940; Scottish Brewing Archives: SNM 11/2/3, McEwan & Co., Advertisements, May 1955–Aug. 1956, pp. 181a, 190a; SNM 11/2/3, McEwan & Co., Advertisements, pp. 213a–14, 1958.

57 *Brewers' Guardian*, June 1959, April 1962; *Mine Host*, Summer 1960; *Ind Coope News*, 29 (Jan. 1960). Other breweries, such as Tuborg, followed suit with 6–ounce bottles of lager poured into glasses resembling oversized wine goblets (*Licensing World*, Oct. 1960).

58 *Daily Mirror*, 13 July 1961; *Express*, 10 Sept. 1961; *Mine Host*, Summer 1960; *Ind Coope News*, 33 (May 1960).

59 Some contemporaries believed that continental travel, which enabled Britons to drink lager more easily, promoted its consumption in Britain, but the number of foreign holidays, as John Burnett noted, remained small until the late 1960s (T. B. Bunting, 'The Trend Towards Lager Beers', *Financial Times*, 12 Oct. 1959, p. ix;

John Burnett, *England Eats Out: A Social History of Eating Out in England from 1830 to the Present* (London: Pearson, 2004), pp. 269–70).

60 Author's interview with Neal Hyde, 15 Aug. 1998; Bunting, 'Lager Beers', p. ix; Obelkevich, 'Consumption', pp. 146–7; 'Marketing Approach to Keg Puts Cart before Horse', *The Times*, 26 April 1971; *Mine Host*, Spring 1962; George E. Gracie, 'Launching a Lager on the British Market', *Brewers' Guardian*, April 1962; Interview with Martin Chambers (Joint Managing Director of Gaskell & Chambers), *Brewers' Journal*, 15 March 1961. Before refrigeration, publicans had placed lagers and mild ales in ice pails during hot summer months (Gorham, *Back to the Local*, pp. 109–11).

61 Michael Bradley and David Fenwick, *Public Attitudes to Liquor Licensing Laws in Great Britain: An Enquiry Carried Out in October-November, 1970 by OPCS Social Survey Division on Behalf of the Home Office and the Scottish Home and Health Department* (London: Her Majesty's Stationery Office, 1974), pp. 8, 12.

62 Ind Coope Marketing Survey, quoted in *Argosy*, July 1970, p. 7; *Brewers' Guardian*, March 1975.

63 John Burnett, *Liquid Pleasures: A Social History of Drinks in Modern Britain* (London: Routledge, 1999), pp. 2, 187.

64 British Market Research Bureau Ltd, *Licensed Premises, 1960*, p. 77.

65 Modern Records Centre, University of Warwick, Brewers' Society, MS 420/BS/4/60/1, Advertisements. These advertisements were reproduced in the industry's newspapers. See, for example, *Brewers' Journal*, 20 April 1960; *Brewing Trade Review*, June 1960 and July–Nov. 1961; *Licensing World*, June and Aug. 1960; *Licensed Victuallers' Gazette*, March–May, and July 1960.

66 J. Joule & Co., Advertisements: *Evening Standard*, 9 Oct. and 3 Nov. 1969; *Staffordshire Advertiser & Chronicle*, 1969–70; and *Stone Advertiser*, 1969–70; London Metropolitan Archives, LMA/4453/G/01/005, Whitbread Archives, 1957, pp. 90–5.

67 Jim Davies, *The Book of Guinness Advertising* ([London]: Guinness Publishing, 1998), pp. 116, 145.

68 For these advertisements, which appeared in English newspapers, 1962–64, see Modern Records Centre, University of Warwick, MS 420/BS/4/60/1.

69 Michael O'Connor, 'Darts, Dominoes and Daddlums', *The Times* (*Beer in Britain Supplement*), 22 April 1968; *Ind Coope News*, 32 (April 1960). The advertisment appeared in national daily newspapers (*Daily Express*, 2 Nov. 1962; *Daily Telegraph*, 2 Nov. 1962; *Evening News*, 2 Nov. 1962) and on weekends (*Daily Herald*, 16 Nov. 1962, and the *Daily Mail*, 16 Nov. 1962; *Evening Standard*, 18 April 1967).

4

Bikinis, boots and booze

Pronounced manliness, patriarchal attitudes and sexism, all characteristic of drink wholesalers and retailers for centuries, endured, indeed flourished into the 1960s and beyond. Gender largely shaped how consumers responded to alcohol advertising. Drinks manufacturers, especially brewing executives, intuitively saw sex as the pathway to enticing males. They failed to grasp that the product's innate qualities mattered most to women in their evaluation.[1] But even more crucially, seeing the sexes as monolithic groups ignored the formative experiences in their backgrounds that would profoundly influence their attitudes to products, including alcohol.

In a *New Society* survey in 1970 based on detailed interviews, almost six hundred pub landlords throughout the country repeatedly professed their unwavering support for serving unaccompanied female drinkers.[2] Support for this attitude came from Marjorie Proops, columnist for the *Daily Mirror*, who believed that pub culture at least in and around London had changed significantly. 'Women alone in pubs are no longer any more remarkable than men alone in pubs', she wrote in a collection of essays, aptly named *Pub: A Celebration*. Southern suburban pubs became especially popular with middle-class housewives out on shopping journeys, with a Bloody Mary ordered as a reviver. Sherry and gossip at a pub, so her friends said, became a welcome substitute for coffee and biscuits at a café. The old regime persisted strongest the further London receded from view. Special ladies' lounges – restricted to women only – still flourished in the North, where she detected 'a certain smug satisfaction that … women know their place and men know how to keep them there'. Even when Northern couples frequented pubs together, they drank in segregated groups, with women some distance from the bar which men propped up.[3]

Against this image in the *New Society* survey of the all-welcoming, jovial landlord stood large numbers of women who seldom ventured into pubs alone.

London, typically where social changes originated first, hardly upheld this optimistic view. City centre pubs posted notices refusing to serve unescorted women after 9.30 p.m. When women drank in lounges, Ann Garvey noted, 'regular denizens either leer knowingly or look mildly affronted'.[4] Nor was Proops correct in seeing just the North as an anomaly in its persisting masculinity. With copious evidence, Comus Elliot provided his own eye-witness testimony of women's absence from pubs published ironically in the same year as the *New Society* survey. Dedicated to his self-appointed task of drinking daily in a different pub, first begun in August 1954, he frequented some 4200 premises over the course of the next seventeen years, and reached one irrefutable conclusion: strikingly few women drank in pubs.[5]

Indeed, only in bingo clubs from the 1960s could unaccompanied women engage in leisure. That many bingo clubs were located in former cinemas, where women previously had gone unescorted for leisure, facilitated this transformation in leisure habits.[6]

Drinking etiquette powerfully sustained masculine culture and dominance, discouraging most unescorted women from encroaching on men's leisure space well into the 1980s.[7] Should women steel themselves to cross a pub's threshold, they encountered different issues. Having to confront a crowded bar as an uninvited outsider with taller, more aggressive men forming an in-group who displayed male solidarity with the landlord behind the counter, proved a formidable undertaking. Emphasizing this masculine bond and women's subordinate status was the publicans' time-honoured practice of serving men first. When finally served herself, the unescorted woman next had the pressing problem of finding a seat, certainly not at the bar but at a table or booth separate from other male patrons. In crowded pubs, should she ask to share a table, men inferred from this necessity something altogether unwarranted. 'Why do men, in a pub atmosphere, feel that a lone female is fair game to be chatted up?' inquired Ann Steele in an article in the *Publican*. At a detached table, men's privacy would be respected, whereas women were subjected to officious male attention, inquiring whether they needed help with crossword puzzles or about titles of the books they were reading. Elsewhere on buses or the Tube, Steele stressed, women received less attention but not in pubs. 'Why do we women', she asked rhetorically, 'get the definite message that a pub is a predominantly male domain?' She provided her own answer: 'Because, up to now, it always has been'.[8]

Admittedly, this was true, but the vicious circle started with the fact that single women often in the past had been looking for customers, with the publican's connivance or disapproval. A crossword puzzle presumably made it harder for the publican to express disapproval. Would the police worry about a pub that seemed unusually welcoming to single women?

Drinking in licensed premises with male escorts fortified the image of the pub as a masculine republic. On entering their local, male regulars would find the landlord unasked providing them with their standard beverage. Women accompanying men into a pub never paid for themselves, for their male companion or for a round. Whatever the drink, men expected women to consume smaller quantities of alcohol than they did. If they ordered identical amounts, the landlord automatically served women in smaller glasses. The very act of seeking to emulate men in the pub, argued Anne Garvey, affords 'a reckless, if conscious challenge to the man's right'.[9] All of these social cues subtly underlined women's status as outsiders, who as men's guests occupied an inferior position in male drinking space.

National market research likewise contradicted the view of a sea-change in gender drinking habits. 'Even in this day and age', conceded a 1970 Brewers' Society survey, 'the social stigma attached to women going into pubs on their own is still prevalent'. Nine of ten women admitted their unwillingness to enter a pub alone. Regardless of age or marital status, no fewer than 95 per cent of all women confirmed that they visited pubs always with other people. But their opposition to pub culture went far deeper than this. Nearly half of all women, if given a choice, would never frequent pubs at all. More remarkably, about three-fourths of them visited infrequently. Of those who did, sherry ranked as their preferred pub beverage.[10] Brewers themselves adopted a surprisingly resigned attitude to attracting women as customers. One survey in 1972 revealed that drink manufacturers ranked tenth in advertising in women's magazines, with food (first), toiletries and cosmetics (second), clothes (third) and household equipment (fourth) far ahead.[11]

Why was there such an incongruity between the purveyors of beer, on one hand, and women, on the other, towards females' status in pubs? In deliberately exploiting feminine sexual appeal as a marketing tactic for generating male custom, the brewing industry reinforced long-standing sexist attitudes in pub culture that made women feel so unwelcome. Nothing else explains why Brewers' Society beer advertisements appeared in some male pornographic magazines such as *Men Only*.[12]

Among the first objectifying women to sell beer was Hammond's United Brewery. From 1958 onwards, a young woman dressed in a skimpy uniform appeared on a poster exhibited in thousands of barrooms with the caption:

'Something rather special here! A more than ordinary beer. Full of body, pretty strong. Ask for Guards [Ale]'. Hammond's distributed some ten thousand cutout showcards with the same model but a shorter caption: 'Attention Men! Order Guards Ale'. To publicize the beer's twenty-first anniversary, Hammonds arranged for a photograph of three female 'guards' with the beer.[13]

By no means was the brewery alone in exploiting women's sexual attraction to promote beer sales. On some of its advertisements for Magnet Pale Ale, for instance, John Smith's Brewery placed a nubile blonde woman, a low-cut dress and raised skirt revealing nylons and garters, holding a glass of beer. Whitbreads adventurously exploited sexual appeal with an advertisement in 1962. Taking a traditional subject, barmaids, the brewery placed beer glasses filled with Tankard in front of them, with the caption: 'The only way to surprise an experienced barmaid'. The subtle sexual content came when the advertisment gave the ages of three of the women, but the Lara Croft measurements of the fourth, 'Lulu (39–18–38)'.[14]

Hidebound breweries bolstered their tenants' opposition to offering anything but traditional beverages, such as soft drinks, sherry and cider. Rejecting women as pioneers of new gender roles, brewing executives chose instead to cast them in a traditional guise more gratifying to husbands than to career-orientated, overworked, self-sacrificing wives and mothers (Plate 9). In a reactionary, insensitive advertisement in 1969, revealing far more about the male mentality of many beer sellers than the beer's expected consumers, Whitbreads portrayed wives as homemakers and impulsive purchasers, wholly financially dependent on husbands' pay cheques. While showering, a young woman pours a bottle of the brewery's pale ale over her hair as shampoo, thoughtlessly unaware of the beer's capacity for soothing her husband's anxieties that could otherwise lead to a divorce. Wittily, the advertisement admonishes her: 'So for the sake of your marriage, remember. Our flavour is meant to go to his palate. Not to your head'. Here the image of women as independent in outlook, feminist in belief, and potentially (and unwisely) subversive in behaviour is altogether ignored, with the traditional gender roles reasserted as the path to connubial bliss. Have your husband drink Whitbread's Pale Ale, the brewery advised, and all will be right with the world, including your marital relationship.[15] Nothing could have been more condescending, patronizing or offensive, as it trivialized women's efforts not just to define new gender roles but to claim recognition of their contribution to the economy.[16]

There was another dimension to sexist beer advertising. In a hidebound industry, brewers displayed striking apathy towards market research to ascertain

Pat, who appeared on Tennent's lager cans as one of the brewery's 'Lager Lovelies' late in the 1960s. 9

customers' drinking habits. Arthur Seldon observed that '£3,000 or £4,000 spent on consumer research … would make more fruitful the scores of thousands spent telling them [i.e. customers] to buy it'.[17] Ironically, he exaggerated brewers' advertising budgets because nationally brewers spent modest amounts. While brewers' allocation remained fixed at £110,000 annually, other advertisers significantly increased their expenditure, which rose over two-and-a-half times from £22 million (1948) to £59.5 million (1953). Over one-third of what brewers spent went to local newspaper or trade and miscellaneous publications.[18] The brewing industry, furthermore, possessed antiquated views about the market. Compared with significant amounts of money committed to market research in the food industry from the mid-1950s, the brewing industry stayed uninterested in this area until the late 1960s.[19]

The 1970s heralded a sexual revolution with young women alluringly attired in hot pants, miniskirts and high heels or boots. Brazen sexual appeal now replaced sexual innuendo in alcohol advertisements. Breweries quickly capitalized on these trends, hiring young models as the most provocative way of garnering publicity. On the opening of its new pubs, Ushers Brewery, for example, dispatched four 'Ushers Party girls', dressed in miniskirts, silk stockings and high-heeled black boots. Trumans wittily called theirs 'Trumaids'.[20] Reigning beauty queens, sometimes chosen in brewery-sponsored competitions, also appeared. With tabloid page three girls as inspiration, Drybrough's Brewery hired Angie Layne to appear, black corseted and nylon clad, at the first anniversary of the opening of Edinburgh's leading go-go pub, Paddy's of Rose Street.[21] Hot pants competitions became popular, with the winner chosen as the brewery's representative. Even more blatantly, Courage mixed sex and alcohol in publicizing its introduction of an American imported beer, Colt 45, at another iconic symbol of the United States, the Playboy Club. It was a short step to hiring women, outfitted like Playboy Bunnies, to attend publicity functions.[22]

Inside pubs and clubs other sexist images firmly established this era as 'the chauvinistic seventies'. Early in the decade, snack manufacturer Big D put scantily clad, buxom model Beverley Pinkerton on its display cards, and as more and more customers purchased nutty snack packages, more of her was progressively revealed. Pinkerton's 'reign' as pub-men's most desired candidate lasted until political correctness consigned her to memory early in the 1980s. Some years later, 'the Big D peanut board had become less interesting than paint stripper'.[23] But tantalizing women displayed on Tennent's beer cans continued, marketed chiefly in Scotland, as 'lager lovelies'.[24]

According to Mark Luce (Courage Director of Brands Marketing), advertising mesmerized brewing executives: 'Brands', he reflected, 'were sold on an image presented almost entirely by television advertising'. This then became the irresistible forum for enticing men, the prime audience targeted by brewers.[25]

Throughout the 1970s, men's virility became the staple of beer advertisements. This overt masculinity emerged especially in Yorkshire, where 'grimy but bronzed workmen stride assertively across television-set bar rooms'.

Truman's concentrated on London's ITV area with one hundred thirty-second commercials in 1972 alone, seen by all but 5 per cent of men of drinking age. An alluring blonde, provocatively dressed in a plunging neckline, leaned over a man drinking a pint. The caption read: 'What makes a Truman Being?'[26] Worthington's commercials were even more affronting to women, particularly with growing numbers of two-career families. One of them portrayed disingenuous husbands fabricating excuses to wives as a tactic for going out alone specifically to visit their local. Worthington exemplified the recurring theme of beer television commercials: drinking stayed, as in the very distant past, a solitary male activity undertaken to escape intrusive female scrutiny. Even allowing women to appear in a more favourable light won few of them as customers. In selling Tavern, Worthington scripted a young woman, who, though disliking beer, confessed: 'I like the men who drink it'.[27] Whatever the content, breweries placed the emphasis of commercials on men – their attitudes, sexual appeal and, implicitly, role as chief breadwinner.

As a foreign brewery, Heineken embraced a more subtle strategy in the 1970s. Its advertisements relied upon a new slogan, 'Heineken. Refreshes the Parts Other Beers cannot Reach', with understated sexual innuendo. Although women in fact never served as dominant characters, Heineken nonetheless upheld the masculine drinking culture in advertisements, encapsulated in well-understood commandments. Each commercial pivoted around three men situated in a pub, overseen by a male landlord. Commandment six advised that 'women shall, from time to time, be permitted to take part as long as they pose no threat to the camaraderie' of the men. Women were thus cast as subordinates among the actors as well as the pub's clientele. Unthreatening to male drinking culture, women appeared as barmaids, ensconced behind the bar. They seemed invisible in the cast of characters, except in the last frames, where the camera caught 'both a handsome bosom and a pint [of beer]'.[28]

Some breweries attempted to break rank with their competitors. Guinness shed its image as producers of just men's beers in the mid-1960s, with women shown drinking the beer outside pubs in its 'Guinness is Good for You' advertisements. In 1974, the Irish brewery ran advertisements in *Over 21*, a magazine with a readership of young, fashion-conscious women.[29] Yet, the brewery's mentality still remained anchored partly in the past. Guinness's new advertising agency, J. Walter Thompson, employer of a female Art Director, could not resist blatant sexist appeals in some advertisments. Above the rim of a glass of Guinness were the sensual red lips of a 'ladylike' woman. The red lips, far from being innocuous, were '"a metaphor for the sexual act"', argued Dr Janice

Winship, Professor at the University of Birmingham's Center for Contemporary Cultural Studies. Guinness's official historian of advertising conceded only that the lips were 'mildly suggestive', but weakened his case considerably in emphatically denying that the brewery ever stooped to exploiting sexual images to sell beer. In marketing its Dublin-brewed Harp lager in England, Guinness hired attractive women as 'Miss Harp' representatives who toured pubs, and appeared in parades as well as sporting events throughout the 1960s and 1970s. 'Miss Harp' beauty contests were held around the country, sometimes judged by such actresses as June Thorburn. Involved also with the beer's production and marketing, Courage likewise deployed women as 'Miss Harp', but, concerned about its public image, 'dropped the blonde from our advertising' in the mid-1960s. 'Miss Harp', however, had an afterlife: subsequent promotional events still saw her as active and as scantily clad as ever.[30] The overwhelming masculine culture at Guinness, as at other breweries, persisted. Not a single female, for instance, drew a salary from the Marketing Department of the Park Royal Brewery, controlled by Guinness. Ind Coope appointed Britain's first female sale representative in the brewing industry, but not until 1964 and even then she dealt with a small region, the East Midlands.[31]

As the big six breweries emerged through consolidation to dominate the brewing industry from the 1960s, the alluring prospect of national markets promoting limited brands emerged.[32] Breweries seemingly understood the changing nature of retailing, and began extolling the importance of their ideal customer, the 'young brisk, possibly androgenic drinker'. Yet, there was an amazing disconnect between rhetoric and reality – the past proved inescapable as the template for selling beer. 'All the ghosts which the brewers would like to lay to rest in the interests of a wider more heterogeneous market rear up in commercial after commercial', noted David White in 1970. Failed advertising campaigns, however, never shook confidence in this strategy. Some years earlier Bass Charrington, then the country's largest brewery, ran an advertising campaign, which White derided for extolling 'beefy manliness'. Nothing, critics agreed, did more to associate Bass's draught beer with the prowess of working-class male drinkers in the public's mind than these advertisements.[33]

Beer commercials represented a microcosm of the wider sexism that still permeated the cultures of drinking and indeed of society. Treatment of pub tenants revealed much about gender relations in the 1970s and beyond. Though women had since the medieval era been unofficial, unpaid and unrecognized co-partners in running the inn and later pub as a family enterprise, magistrates seldom licensed them, save only in extraordinary circumstances such as the husband's death, an all-too frequent occurrence among beer retailers.[34] Having obtained licences, widows incurred enmity of male publicans who vigorously opposed their admission into local licensed victuallers' associations, the fraternal bodies which fostered solidarity and provided legal advice to members.[35] Even then, allowing wives to succeed deceased husbands proved so unusual and so transitory as to warrant a special name, 'the widow's year'. Once the designated year lapsed, brewers 'shoved the widow out', observed Ben Davis, an estate design consultant with Allied Breweries.[36]

Well into the 1980s, Whitbread's long-standing patriarchal prototype for tenants, typical of the national breweries as a whole, involved a young husband and wife without small children. According to one informed source, 'some brewers will not even grant an interview to anyone unable to produce a marriage certificate'. Consider the case of Gill Storey in 1984. She approached several London breweries for a tenancy, but none granted her one. Raising the capital herself, she bought an East End pub, and christened it appropriately the Alternative, billed as a place where 'women could go and relax with no problem'. Men were banned on weekends, but not on weekdays, though most shunned the compromise. Women still comprised the bulk of the patrons. Nothing had then changed since the *Licensed Victuallers' Gazette*, in a 1961 editorial, wrote that while 'women have become prominent in most trades and professions previously barred to them, there has not been any outstanding increase in the number of women who hold licences'.[37]

Discrimination against women, however, took other guises. Anita Adams's career typified the obstacles women faced in entering the trade. Despite dipping into her own pocket to put up the thousands of pounds to assume the tenancy of a York pub in 1980, it was her husband, not Anita, whose name appeared on the licence and symbolically over the pub's entrance as the official licensee. Given the ubiquitous masculine culture in virtually every facet of the drinks industry, women remained subordinate, invisible and powerless.[38]

But gender relations as enacted daily in drinking rituals at tens of thousands of pubs were hardly an anomaly in British society. When Britain's victorious soccer team in the 1966 World Cup attended a banquet in their honour in Kensington, women – whether players' wives or girlfriends – sat in a segregated dining room.[39] Only in this decade did gentlemen's social clubs allow women to attend private parties – in the evenings. When Brooks's, for example, subsequently modified this restriction and permitted women into the club after 6 p.m., they still could not frequent the bar or the Members Room. On Fleet Street, women were underrepresented and inconspicuous, with most of them relegated to the journalist ghetto otherwise known as the Women's Department well into the 1970s.[40] So the brewing industry conformed to type. Doris Penery had become a brewster owing to the wartime emergency early in the 1940s leading to her post with Tamar brewery (Devonport), a temporary arrangement lasting over two decades. Doing its best to ignore this sole exception, the Incorporated Brewers' Guild continued priding itself on its exclusively male composition.[41]

Even CAMRA (Campaign for Real Ale), founded early in the 1970s to preserve traditional beer and drinking premises, tacitly endorsed the industry's philosophy of perpetuating pubs as a masculine republic. Thus, CAMRA objected not to overt sexism in pubs but to changes in how breweries produced beer.[42]

Sexism permeating the culture of brewing still thrived into the 1990s.[43] There was one notable change. Some at least began questioning the shrewdness of this marketing strategy. Reviewing the use of women in progressive stages of undress in advertisments since the late 1940s, Courage Brewery conceded – albeit privately and in an extremely qualified way – that now such an approach 'would be viewed as being rather dubious and somewhat "sexist"'.[44] Whitbreads put the matter more succinctly. 'There is no point in alienating half the population' with sexual advertisements, commented its Business Development Director.[45]

Bass responded differently to growing numbers of women drinkers. In what it called 'another progressive step away from the past' aimed at wooing women as beer drinkers, the brewery decided to photograph one male model, together with the traditional three female models, on its calendar of 'Tennent Girls' for 1991. This compromise lasted just a year before Bass, belatedly bowing to cultural changes, finally discontinued 'Tennent Girls' on its beer cans.[46] But the concept of semi-nude young women as a basis for advertising was refashioned several years later in the guise of 'Miss Kimberly'. Dubbed 'the Super Ice Maiden', this clearly feminine figure was in fact an androgyny aimed at attracting both men and women. Worthington adopted this same approach in advertisements for its draught bitter, with blonde bewigged Dr Veronica as the androgynous symbol, described as 'a cross between Desmond Morris and sex therapist Dr Ruth'. Another advertisement featured heavy masculine overtones. For those men who shunned the beer, the advertisement warned they chanced the likelihood of becoming women. Traditional sexual images, however, persisted as the staple of advertisments for Bass's biggest seller, Carling Black Label, and sometimes too for Worthington Draught Bitter.[47]

In one revealing strategy, Bass had landlords dispense with every purchase of Carling a special game card containing a photograph of a nubile model, whose clothes could be scratched off, ultimately revealing what prize the drinker had won.[48]

Nothing more offended baby boomer females, born between 1946 and 1965 and representing one-third of all women, than men's condescending attitudes, some perceptive marketers outside the industry knew.[49] Sharply contrasting with crudely sexist beer advertisements were those of spirits manufacturers.[50] Cutty Sark appealed to women while reassuring men in a 1965 advertisement in *Vogue* magazine. A young, well-dressed women sits in a cockpit, with a subtle caption suggesting that whisky, though traditionally a male beverage, now 'is the man's Scotch that women prefer'. In a still more direct appeal to emancipated women, Ballantine drew an analogy between the gender upheaval of the new woman, on one hand, and political and social changes instituted in France over a century earlier, on the other. Three uninhibited women boldly drank whiskey at a bar, with one wittingly invoking and updating the French Revolution as an expression of their common philosophy: 'liberty, equality and Ballantine'. Another women's magazine, *McCall's*, carried Smirnoff's Vodka advertisement in 1965 reflecting the female's new occupational roles. Here the advertisement portrayed a female astronaut. Pimm's mixed drink less directly addressed gender roles in an advertisement juxtaposing female and male glasses. These clever approaches to women help explain why their consumption of spirits was more than twice as great as of beer well into the 1970s. Not to be outdone, Showerings ran an advertisement touting Babycham as vital for any Christmas party. The three women in the picture outnumbered the two men.[51] Mindful of some women's more cosmopolitan self-image in the 1990s, Bacardi cleverly inverted stereotypes with an advertisement in *CQ* in which a young woman drank a glass of rum in one hand, while holding a cigar in the other. The caption went further in challenging strict gender relationships: 'Politically Correct by Day; Bacardi by Night'.[52]

Though spirits manufacturers displayed greater subtlety as well as ingenuity in attracting women through advertising, they also used sex to entice men. Women in bikinis or in nothing save a towel, for example, graced some Hennessy and Dewar advertisements for cognac and whiskey respectively, but the blatant, crude sexual images dominating brewers' advertisments really had no counterparts. For the launch of a new promotional campaign in October 1979, Vladivar Vodka hired a young, scantily clad blonde to pose with boxes of the company's vodka.[53] Manufacturers of vodka, which grew considerably in popularity in the 1960s–70s, more than doubling in volume, ironically believed such themes appealed to the young, especially to women. According to one trade commentator, young females 'can continue to drink their favourite soft drink but a nip of vodka makes them appear, and feel grown up'.[54] Smirnoff's Vodka campaign, 'The effect is shattering', went still further, with erotic scenes matched by a suggestive caption: 'I thought the Karma Sutra was an Indian restaurant until I discovered Smirnoff".[55]

Brewers' attitudes to women drinking in pubs, however, continued to combine conservatism with sexism and, at times, hypocrisy. Pubs ought to remain masculine strongholds, so the industry assumed, despite wider changes in British society towards greater sexual equality. In 1978, for instance, the Brewers' Society challenged the advertising of a new alcoholic beverage, the Stud (a mixture of Cinzano and Vladivar), with a poster showing a provocatively dressed Joan Collins posed on a couch. The drink's name was a tie-in to a recently released movie with the same title and actor. Kenneth Dunjohn, spokesperson for the Brewers' Society, sought the moral high ground, claiming this advertisement clashed with the industry's oft-stated policy of refusing to 'link sex with drink'. 'It is essential to our reputation', he emphasized, 'to register concern'.[56] Such self-righteous assertions sat rather oddly with the fact that brewers for decades had unabashedly exploited women's sexual appeal to sell their products as readily as some other drink manufacturing groups. The Brewers' Society had never protested at its own members' blatantly erotic advertisments. That Dunjohn's views were both paternalistic and patronizing towards women – representative indeed of the industry as a whole – emerged in a *Guardian* interview several years later. If numerous women entered pubs, he contended, these neophyte customers would 'spoil' the atmosphere, redolent in many instances of gentlemen's clubs. Casting aside all prudence, he candidly confided that the industry would not dare entice women into pubs owing to their greater susceptibility than men to alcohol problems.[57]

Sexism in the industry continued as virulent as ever, while consumption trends ironically soared. New drinkers, especially women and those from the middle classes, drove beer consumption's expansion from 25 million (1959) to 42 million barrels (1979), maintained Terry Gourvish.[58] By the 1970s, about one-fourth of the middle and upper classes were drinking in pubs at least three times weekly, with the proportion rising to one-third in the classes below. Age too had fundamentally altered. Whatever the accuracy of Sir Edgar Sandar's observation of middle-aged and elderly men as the dominant pub patrons in the 1930s, the age structure now had moved sharply downwards. Those under forty-four comprised the bulk of regular pub goers, with the proportion of drinkers falling as age rose.[59]

The catalysts for these changes were complex. According to historian Alun Howkins, new middle-class notions of family sociability, together with the quest for higher returns – profit margins on food easily surpassed those on alcohol – led to rising numbers of bourgeois drinkers. Middle-class holiday makers who visited Europe came to see the French café, with its food and accommodation of children, as superior to the English pub. Pressure from these patrons, he reasoned, provided impetus for replacement of traditional inns with 'scampi in the basket' pubs, especially in rural areas. Basic public bars, once good for agricultural labourers and tenant farmers, were eliminated in favour of a new version of 'historic' rustic England. One large bar now became standard, with 'dark red carpet, stained "oak" furniture, horsebrasses and blazing log fire'. Open windows allowing potential customers to peer into premises that projected well-lit, spacious environments were borrowed from wine bars, which had helped guarantee popularity among women.[60] From the early 1970s, 'there was a rapid escalation in opening up existing pubs', commented scholars of a recently published book. 'The tendency has been to design them as a single space', they noted, 'in contrast to the hierarchical stratification that was de rigueur a century before'.[61] Howkins pointed to soaring numbers of licences for restaurants and hotels, nearly eight times greater than for pubs, in the years 1976–86 as evidence of this transformation. Another indicator of the advent of one sprawling bar was the nearly doubling of the average pub carpet order, which expanded from 75 yards (1974) to 130 yards (1979). Merging space from former public bars with the lounge accounted for 'one of the most striking changes in pub interiors over the last few years', observed a *Publican* reporter.[62]

So impressed was *Guardian* reporter H.F. Ellis that he claimed, with much hyperbole, that improved pub food 'has been the greatest advance in civilization in Britain in my lifetime'. Regardless of whether food standards rose quite as dramatically as he portrayed, pub food prices were certainly much cheaper than those at many restaurants. With dinners at upmarket establishments priced at £35 for two, a threesome could eat pleasantly for less than £7 at South-western inns in 1984. Good food, he asserted, had emboldened women to enter previously masculine territory.[63] 'Pubs', felt the *Economist* in 1985, 'have been offering more food, more room to sit down – women are less keen than men on propping up bars – and more things to do'. Of marginal importance in 1950, food sales in pubs had more than doubled in thirty years, accounting now for 13 per cent of total turnover.[64]

Had radically different pub layouts fostered new male attitudes to women drinkers in the 1970s and 1980s? Valerie Hey vigorously denied this contention in her staunch feminist onslaught on pubs as male drinking dens in *Patriarchy and Pub Culture*, which appeared in 1986. In explaining her 'humiliation' and 'harassment', typical of women in general when drinking alone in pubs, she declared that 'it is still practically impossible for single women to consume pints of beer in a pub without their activity being read as a sexually deviant or defiant action'.[65] There was some validity in what she argued, but so many variables – class, gender ratios, region and, critically, landlords – shaped women's perceptions of and treatment in pubs that Hey's generalization merits further examination.

Class differences fundamentally moulded drinking habits, and often determined which pubs an individual selected as the local. Where men vastly outnumbered women in lower-class pubs, the clientele consisted chiefly of men. Both sexes saw the pub as the sole venue for socializing while drinking. Because working-class people drew on family and local neighbourhoods as the social basis for socializing in pubs, reciprocity – round buying – was unnecessary in their local. Working-class husbands and wives never aspired to move beyond the 'local', the key agency for socializing. Among the first serious social investigators to establish class differences in postwar leisure habits was Ferdynand Zweig, Professor of Political Economy, on whose visits to some four hundred London pubs he based his conclusions in *Labour, Life and Poverty*. Since a working man had no money or physical space for parties, regarded his own home as uninviting to guests and had strong beliefs about how to spend leisure time, 'he prefers to meet everybody he likes in the pub rather than at home', Zweig related. These class differences, first identified by Zweig in 1948 and confirmed in Young and Wilmott in their classic study *Family and Kinship in East London* (1962), persisted at least into the 1980s.[66]

In the early 1980s sociologist Michael A. Smith researched some of the most illuminating studies of public house drinking cultures. Influenced by Mass-Observation's *Pub and the People* with its participant-observer approach, he developed a typology of three distinct pub types: the 'rough' underclass pub; its respectable working-class counterpart: and finally, at the end of the continuum, the 'posh' middle-class establishment.[67]

Rough working-class pubs and cider houses were overwhelmingly masculine, their men all heavy drinkers (ten to fifteen pints at a time), often divided into two distinct drinking sessions, who exhibited toughness born of hard physical lives vividly encapsulated in the phrase 'balls over brains'. Some critics perceived them as 'mad buggers and head bangers', though Smith thought this overstated. Nevertheless, the subculture was decidedly rough, with prostitutes ever-present, fights predictable, abusive drinking expected and literally hundreds of patrons barred for a time each month. Of Tyneside pubs, Tony Avis recalled them vividly if not fondly as 'disgusting places'.[68]

Noise, clannishness and raw violence characterized this subculture. Catering often to young unmarried men who relished loud music as ardently as vast quantities of beer or cider, these drinking premises projected a fierce territoriality which resented and expelled outsiders. Young men, together with unattached mature males, coalesced in repelling unwanted intruders. 'Fights break out most between the regulars and those from other areas whose very presence is understood to be provocative', wrote one researcher. Football supporters, their local as base for communication with CB walkie talkies, incited battles on Saturday nights with rival club supporters in the town centre and travel stations.[69]

Attack on this masculine subculture escalated into rare violent confrontation between its defenders, the young regulars, and the new landlord at Casey's, a tough dockland pub in a languishing area in Crossley, Merseyside, early in the 1970s. Arriving as an avowed, unrepentant reformer, the new publican, regarded widely but unlovingly as socially arrogant, instituted changes bitterly resented by regulars. He raised beer prices, habitually short-changed customers, banned skinheads and their friends, and finally proscribed the long-standing habit of young children purchasing soft drinks and sweets. Resistance – broken windows, graffiti on walls, and vandalized toilets as well as jukebox – intensified, culminating in a paint drum being set afire and rolled into the bar. Within months, the landlord left, and, curiously enough in defiance of existing employment customs in the trade, a mature woman, who had lived nearby, was installed. Rescinding the unpopular restrictions, she quickly established rapport with regulars, including the skinheads. Casey's was certainly an extreme example of this subculture's vigorous defence of prevailing norms, but regulars at other rough pubs with their 'balls over brains' clientele clearly had the capacity, when aroused, of thwarting any unwanted reforms.[70]

Nearly all the customers were regulars who frequented this type of pub as 'a place for making and reaffirming their social links', where they met mates with whom they drank in a separate, confined world.[71] Drinking became for them a 'private situation of public interaction', with outsiders unwanted, unwelcomed and unnoticed. Women entered this subculture on restricted terms. On Friday and Saturday nights, wives accompanied husbands and even then sat by themselves at tables with other wives, while husbands interacted with their mates elsewhere in the pub. A second group, nubile women, arrived and stayed in groups. Finally, there were prostitutes, who entered alone but seldom stayed long. In such a pub lone women were regarded as vulnerable. Pornography, openly displayed and freely circulated, indicated male attitudes. Indistinguishable from customers, the landlord drank with them on the other side of the bar, and joined in playing pool and cards. He materially contributed to the misogynistic ambience, with sexist comments, profanity and discussions of work the core of verbal exchanges with male customers. He was in every sense one of them. As a topic, women, absent (save for prostitutes) during the week, were not so much verbally demeaned as simply ignored in this masculine subculture. Weekends temporarily modified the environment, but women never were allowed to disrupt the male bonding ever-present between regulars.

Rough pubs consisted of either communal or non-communal premises. Each drew its custom chiefly from manual and semi-skilled workers who drank heavily with other men, but the communal establishments were physically smaller, quieter, located in back-street residential districts or villages, and depended heavily on local trade. Drinkers too displayed greater interaction with other regulars, playing games, conversing at the bar or with friends, and buying rounds. Fund raising and pub sports also distinguished communal pubs. Key was the landlord's role: in communal pubs he actively intervened to encourage such socializing; in non-communal pubs he stood aloof, offering no direction to his patrons who expected to meet and converse privately with friends, wives or female companions, or relatives, uninterested in other patrons, regardless of whether they were regulars.[72]

A less homogenous clientele signified a respectable working-class pub, with regulars dominant. Men came according to a well-understood routine to socialize with their mates and other regulars, using alcohol as a 'social lubricant'. Three groups were discernible: the bar area of manual labourers who arrived without women; young working-class couples who displayed traditional class norms – they sat side by side at tables and the man retrieved and paid for drinks; and middle-class patrons who showed what Smith called 'strong middle-class norms of private interaction'. Whether couples or not, middle-class customers sat, never at the bar, but facing each other at tables in closed social space, not interacting with anyone else. They totally disregarded activities all popular with working-class patrons – pool, the jukebox or game machines – almost as if such diversions did not register in their mental landscape. Class barriers thus remained as tangible as when the traditional bars physically divided them. Around noon women, married or co-habiting and from nearly factories or other workplaces, ate in the pub and conversed among themselves.

The landlord liked women in his pub as important for sales, and displayed towards them an avuncular but insincere demeanour. He still engaged in private, sexual innuendo with male regulars, and sat with them at the bar. Together with regulars, he viewed women alone as legitimate targets of unsolicited male interest. There were differences, however, from the rough pub. The respectable establishment lacked prostitutes, pornography, violence, pervasive heavy drinking and patrons predisposed to fighting.

Similarities too existed with the 'posh' middle-class pub. Wherever they drank, bourgeois patrons viewed the pub, Smith remarked, 'almost as a service station compared to the working class who saw it as another home'. Never the purpose of an outing, drinking was moderate, usually one to three pints, and stays typically short – thirty minutes to two hours. Not going either to meet mates or to drink as an end in itself, middle-class users had no reason for seeing the pub as a separate, self-contained world. For them, the pub became a place for bringing friends and partners. It was, in fact, 'a public situation of private interaction', and as such the groups stayed intact during the evening, members never seeking to incorporate others into discussions. These conventions also prevailed at restaurants; only at rather specialized restaurants would one speak to strangers or join another table. Regulars, constituting 70 per cent of the patrons, perceived the pub 'as an extension of their existing social relations and time frameworks'. Not for them was there a fixed routine, where men met mates at predetermined times for extended stays to pursue their chief interests, sharing considerable drink, enjoying comradery and denigrating women.

'Paternalistic egalitarianism' defined gender relations in the 'posh' pub. Representing nearly one-half of its regulars, women earned the respect of the landlord, who treated them with 'a strict sense of professional equality'. Conversation between him and other regulars or among male regulars was sexually irreproachable. He set the tone for this atmosphere, establishing himself as the landlord, not one of the mates.

Some publicans recognized their ability to attract female custom, unlike those whom Smith observed. At pubs such as the Bakers Arms (Lychett Minster, Dorset), landlord Tom Porter deemed women 'easily my most important customers' in the mid-1980s. From first-hand experience, he knew, 'it is the women who specify which pub is allowable'. To his pub, women came alone or with other females, confident that, with Porter acting as a protective guardian, 'they won't be chatted up or otherwise annoyed by groups of loud mouthed yobboes who think they are God's gift to the opposite sex'.[73]

Women, in Smith's research, frequented bourgeois pubs with other males, with whom they stayed throughout the visit. At no point, therefore, were women left unattended at the tables or booths where they sat across from male escorts. Men brought their reason for socializing with them, so they had no reason to interact with other patrons. Bar space too was distinctively dissimilar to the other two types of pubs, where an all-male group held sway with the landlord literally one of them. Here, small groups from both sexes congregated around the bar, ensuring much open space for socializing. In sharp contrast to working-class patrons at the other two pub types, middle-class users at the posh pub stayed for short periods before continuing a planned evening elsewhere. Socializing was thus informal and individualized, not regimented or formalized.

Subsequent sociological studies confirmed Smith's interpretation. Middle-class drinkers drank at entirely different pubs dominated by people of their own socio-economic class, and, since they did not see relatives often, went to visit their local, which often involved travelling some distance. Almost equally divided between the sexes, the group meeting at the local possessed two shared traits: members had comparable disposable incomes and a bourgeois lifestyle. In practice, this meant that they had the space to entertain a large gathering at home, the money to dine out with other members at restaurants and pubs, and the desire to drink regularly at the local pub as part of a distinct social grouping. For them, reciprocity within the group took the form of either round buying at the pub or entertainment at alternating houses. They regarded the pub as a forum for establishing initial contact which then shifted to homes of the couples for social interactions. For middle-class married women, the pub became part of a wider constellation of settings for developing friendships.[74] A 1980 Mintel survey corroborated earlier market research of an inverse relationship between class and pubbing: half of the poorest group frequented pubs, whereas just a quarter of the upper and middle classes (AB groups) used them. Well into the decade, middle-class families entertained friends at home on a weekly basis far more commonly than those socially below them.[75] From the 1960s, a trend had emerged in which middle-class couples drank aperitifs or liqueurs as pre- or post-prandial beverages at home, notably among women. Campari, for instance, targeted advertisements at these consumers, carefully avoiding sexist themes.[76]

One key inference is that the low per centage of middle-class women in pubs owed less to their opposition to public drinking than to differing patterns of socializing. These women drank alcohol in a broader range of settings than their working-class counterparts. Class and age both shaped drinking habits. Entertaining guests at home was most prevalent among the middle classes and young childless couples, a Brewers' Society 1984 survey revealed.[77] The phenomenal growth of wine consumption, doubling between 1975 and 1985, reflected changing socializing patterns: fully three-fourths of wine drinkers never visited wine bars.[78] Women, too, had less incentive for frequenting the pub since their first choice of beverage was the ubiquitous soft drink. Of those drinking beer in pubs in the early 1980s, men overwhelmingly dominated women by almost three to one. In fact, more women drank bottled wine, readily available in supermarkets and off-licences, than draught bitter or cider. Why not then drink and socialize in the comfort of their home?[79]

Breweries ventured into new territory in the swinging sixties and seventies with overtly sexist advertisements showing more skin and more titillation. Sexism within the brewing industry mirrored wider societal chauvinist attitudes. Against this background, the cultures of drinking remained virtually unchanged, though more women began patronizing pubs in groups or with male escorts. The physical layout of drinking premises also changed, with the disappearance of separate rooms and the upgrading of amenities with carpeting. Pubs, however, were far from homogenous. Class, gender proportions, geographic regions and even the landlords themselves created distinct subcultures of drinking, determining what reception women received on entry to drinking premises. More dramatic changes in drinking began from the mid-1980s when market segmentation fostered different types of drink venues which undermined the formerly overpowering masculine republic in pubs.

Notes

1 J. L. Le Bel, 'Sensory, Snob, and Sex Appeals in Wine Advertising', *International Journal of Wine Marketing*, 17 (2005), pp. 67–78; also see L. Rappaport, G. R. Peters, T. McCann and L. Huff-Corzine, 'Gender and Age Differences in Food Cognition', *Appetite*, 20 (1993), pp. 33–52.

2 David White, 'The Pull of the Pub', *New Society*, 16 (1970), p. 318.

3 Marjorie Proops, 'What Will You Have, Mrs. Pankhurst?', in Angus McGill (ed.), *Pub: A Celebration* (London: Longmans, Green & Co., 1969), pp. 117–18, 122; Graham Turner, *The North Country* (London: Eyre & Spottiswoode, 1967), p. 361.

4 Anne Garvey, 'Out of the Way: Women in Pubs', *New Society*, 27 (21 Feb. 1974), pp. 459–60.

5 Comus Elliot, 'The Pub's a Pub for All That', *A Monthly Bulletin*, 42 (May 1971), pp. 88–9.

6 Rachael Dixey, '"Eyes Down": A Study of Bingo', in Erica Wimbush and Margaret Talbot (eds), *Relative Freedoms: Women and Leisure* (Milton Keynes: Open University Press, 1988), p. 94.
7 See Chapter 5, pp. 114–15.
8 Ann Steele, 'Is Family Atmosphere Enough?', *Publican*, 24 Nov. 1983; Adrian Franklin, *Pub Drinking and the Licensed Trade: A Study of Drinking Cultures and Local Community in Two Areas of South West England* (Bristol: University of Bristol, 1985), p. 8.
9 Garvey, 'Women in Pubs', p. 460.
10 *Brewing Review*, Aug. 1976; Interscan, Ltd, *Attitude Survey on Pub Going Habits and Brewery Control and Ownership of Public Houses* (Aug. 1970), p. 7; Michael Bradley and David Fenwick, *Public Attitudes to Liquor Licensing Laws in Great Britain: An Enquiry Carried Out in October-November, 1970 by OPCS Social Survey Division on Behalf of the Home Office and the Scottish Home and Health Department* (London: Her Majesty's Stationery Office, 1974), pp. 3, 55.
11 Rosemary Scott, *The Female Consumer* (London: Associated Business Programmes, 1976), p. 217.
12 University of Warwick, Modern Records Centre, MS 420, BS/4/60/1, Press Advertisements, 1949–50.
13 The National Brewery Centre, Hammond's United Brewery, Advertisements, pp. 1, 35 and 49.
14 Postcard, Museum of Advertising & Packaging, Gloucester, John Smith's Brewery, Robert Opie Collection; *House of Whitbread*, 22 (Oct. 1962).
15 Penny Dade, *Drink Talking: 100 Years of Alcohol Advertising* (London: Middlesex University Press, 2009), pp. 92–3; Jeremy Pursehouse, 'Box Clever … ', *Publican*, 9 July 1981.
16 See Chapter 6, p. 131.
17 Arthur Seldon, 'Time, Gentlemen …', *Scope* (Feb. 1951), p. 60. Guinness was an anomaly in pioneering market research in the brewing industry in the 1950s. It also advertised more in proportion to sales. But of course other brewers reckoned their beer 'sold itself' through the tied house system (Modern Records Centre, Brewers' Society, C. E. Guinness' comments, 23 Nov. 1990).
18 Modern Records Centre, MS 420, BS/4/60/1, Memorandum on Brewers' Society Advertising, 1955.
19 John McKenzie, 'Market Research and the Brewing Industry', *Brewers' Guardian*, July 1971.
20 *Things that Affect Us*, 77 (Winter 1970), pp. 30–1; *Argosy*, Feb. 1973, p. 4; *Golden Cockerel*, April 1971, p. 7; *Truman Times*, May/June 1972; *Truman Topics*, May 1973.
21 *Maltster*, Spring, 1984; also see *Tartan Star*, Oct. and Nov. 1986; *Argosy*, July 1970, pp. 9, 12 Oct. 1970, p. 8, and Dec. 1972; *Golden Cockerel*, Oct. 1969, p. 1, and July 1971, p. 9; *Huntsman*, Feb. 1974.
22 *Golden Cockerel*, Winter 1963, p. 27, Oct. 1971, p. 5; June 1972, p. 5, and Sept. 1974, p. 1; *Argosy*, Oct. 1971, p. 7.
23 Adam Edwards, 'Big D Goes for Double G to Drive Men Nuts', *Morning Advertiser*, 4 May 2006.

24 See David W. Gutzke, 'Tennent's Lager, National Identity and Football in Scotland, 1960s–90s', *Sport in History*, 32 (2012), pp. 555–8; Charles Schofield and Anthony Kamm, *Lager Lovelies* (Glasgow: Richard Drew, 1984).

25 John Burbedge, 'Getting on the Brand-Wagon', *Courage News*, 41 (Feb. 1990).

26 Garvey, 'Women in Pubs', p. 460; *Truman Times*, March/April 1972.

27 White, 'Pull of the Pub', p. 318.

28 Peter Mayle, *Thirsty Work: Ten Years of Heineken Advertising* (London: Macmillan, 1983), 'Three Men in a Pub, and Other Golden Rules'.

29 *Guinness Time*, 27 (Winter 1974), p. 14; White, 'Pull of the Pub', pp. 317–18; Dade, *Drink Talking*, p. 90.

30 *Guinness Time*, 15 (1962), pp. 23; 18 (Summer 1965), pp. 17; 22 (Spring 1969), p. 41; 25 (Summer 1972), p. 19; 26 (Autumn 1973), p. 26; 27 (Autumn 1974), p. 26; London Metropolitan Archives, Acc. 2305/26/159, Courage, Barclay & Simonds, Harp Lager Ltd, Sales Information Precis for Representatives, 10 June 1965. During the 1970s, companies in other sectors of the economy used sex to sell products. For example, 'Cadbury Flake girls suggestively ate sticks of the chocolates on TV' (Edwards, 'Big D').

31 Jim Davies, *The Book of Guinness Advertising* ([London]: Guinness Publishing, 1998), p. 116; *Guinness Time*, 22 (Spring 1969), pp. 50–1; *Ind Coope News*, Aug. 1964.

32 David W. Gutzke, 'Runcorn Brewery: The Unofficial History of a Corporate Disaster', *Historie Sociale/Social History*, 41 (2008), pp. 218, 226.

33 *Courage News*, 45 (Aug. 1990); White, 'Pull of the Pub', p. 318. Bass had a long tradition of emphasizing its beers' male proletarian roots. Well into the 1950s and 1960s, the brewery promoted the image of its beers as just for men. This explains why Bass built men-only bars on housing estates, such as those in Hull, moving 'forward like a dinosaur'. Bass was alone, not in having a men-only bar, but in including it in new pubs. 'No other brewer actively pursued it as a policy', remarked Tony Avis (Author's interview with Tony Avis, 26 July 1997).

34 Of the 159 publicans in York in 1929, for example, just 27 were women (Mike Race, *Public Houses, Private Lives: An Oral History of Life in York Pubs in the Mid-twentieth Century* (York: Voyager Publications, 1999), p. 64).

35 Michele Cheaney, 'Jobs for the Girls', *Publican Newspaper*, 28 April 1997; Robert Metcalfe, 'Wanted: Women Who Can Run Pubs', *Publican*, 11 Nov. 1989; Stanley Wright, *Running Your Own Pub* (London: Hutchinson, 1984), p. 8; Lorna Harrison, 'Those Were the Days', *Publican Newspaper*, 25 Sept. 2000; Adam Tinworth, 'Be Irresistible to Women', *Publican*, 3 July 1995.

36 Ben Davis, 'A Woman's Place: Behind the Bar', *Publican*, 25 Aug. 1983; P. Hyde, 'The Occupational Role of Publican' (M.Phil., Univ. of Kent, 1974), p. 124.

37 *Publican*, 22 March 1984; *Licensed Victuallers' Gazette*, Sept. 1961; W. C. Stevenson, *Making and Managing a Pub* (Newton Abbot: David and Charles, 1981), p. 123; Barbara Rogers, *Men Only: An Investigation into Men's Organisations* (London: Pandora, 1988), p. 18.

38 *Publican Newspaper*, 26 March 1996.

39 Richard Weight, *Patriots: National Identity in Britain, 1940–2000* (London: Macmillan, 2002), p. 463.

40 Christopher Wood, 'Brooks's Since the War', in Philip Ziegler and Desmond Seward (eds), *Brooks's: A Social History* (London: Constable, 1991), p. 105; Roger Smith, 'Sex and Occupational Role on Fleet Street', in Diana Leonard Barker and Sheila Allen (eds), *Dependence and Exploitation in Work and Marriage* (London: Longman, 1976), pp. 72–3.
41 *Staff News*, 8 (Summer 1964), p. 9.
42 Rogers, *Men Only*, pp. 21–2.
43 Ibid., pp. 19–20.
44 Burbedge, 'Getting on the Brand-Wagon'.
45 Tinworth, 'Irresistible to Women'.
46 *Bass Brewers News*, Dec. 1991, p. 13, and Feb. 1993, p. 10.
47 Ibid., Dec. 1995, May and Sept. 1996, May 1997 and March 1998. Guinness remained in this sense, as in many others, an anomaly. Though an attractive blonde had helped sell Harp lager from the beverage's inception, Barclays had wanted to 'improve our public image' and so had discontinued this type of advertising.
48 Ibid., Feb. 1997.
49 Iain Ellwood with Sheila Shekar, *Wonder Woman: Marketing Secrets for the Trillion-Dollar Customer* (Houndmills: Palgrave Macmillan, 2008), p. 131.
50 Guinness proved exceptional in depicting women in its advertisements as saucy, emancipated and fashionably attractive, though not sexually arousing, from the 1970s (Davies, *Guinness Advertising*, pp. 118–19).
51 Dade, *Drink Talking*, pp. 94, 100–1, 112, 114.
52 Ibid., pp. 151–2. Guinness television commercials also reversed gender roles in the 1990s (Davies, *Guinness Advertising*, p. 233).
53 Dade, *Drink Talking*, pp. 112–13, 146; *Publican*, 11 Oct. 1979.
54 Christian Davis, *Publican*, 13 Sept. 1984: 'Zany Humour that Sent Vodka Zooming', and 'Sales Fall as Fewer Visit Pubs'; Dade, *Drink Talking*, p. 110;
55 Davies, *Guinness Advertising*, p. 116.
56 Modern Records Centre, MS 420/BS/4/60/4, 'The Stud' Poster, Dunjohn Memorandum, 18 July 1978.
57 Chris Middleton, 'Why Women Can Go for a Drink without Feeling the Pinch', *Guardian*, 27 July 1982.
58 T. R. Gourvish and R. G. Wilson, *The British Brewing Industry, 1830–1980* (Cambridge: Cambridge University Press, 1994), pp. 454–5, 557.
59 MORI, *Attitudes to the British Brewing Industry, 1975* (1975), p. 25; University of Sussex, FR 1837, Mass-Observation Archives, Report on Juvenile Drinking, June 1943, p. 38.
60 Peter Martin, 'How "Revolutionary" Does Pub Design Need to Be?' *Publican*, 8 Nov. 1984; Michael Roulstone, 'The British Public House and the 1960s', in Michael Roulstone (ed.), *One for the Road: Alan Roulstone's 1960s* (Llangynog: Michael Roulstone Publications, 2004), p. 571; Alun Howkins, 'The Ploughman's Rest: Whose Round Is It Anyway? Brewers, Real Ale Campaigners, Lager Louts or the City?', *New Statesman*, 14 April 1989, p. 11.
61 Geoff Brandwood, Andrew Davison and Michael Slaughter, *Licensed to Sell: The History and Heritage of the Public House* (London: English Heritage, 2004), pp. 90–1.
62 Alun Howkins, 'The Ploughman's Rest', p. 11; John Lloyd, 'Colourful Carpets

Keep You One Step Ahead', *Publican*, 22 March 1979. Based on the drawings of Alan Roulstone, an inveterate pub habituate from the 1950s, carpeting had become more common beginning in the 1960s (Roulstone, 'British Public House and the 1960s', p. 570).

63 H. F. Ellis, 'Time, Ladies Please', *Guardian*, 31 Dec. 1984.

64 *Publican*, 12 July 1984; 'Carry on Boozing', *Economist*, 9 Nov. 1985.

65 Bradley and Fenwick, *Public Attitudes*, p. 56; Valerie Hey, *Patriarchy and Pub Culture* (London: Tavistock Publications, 1986), pp. 5, 30; Elliot, 'The Pub's a Pub for All That', pp. 88–9.

66 Ferdynand Zweig, *Labour, Life and Poverty* (London: Victor Gollancz, 1948), p. 30; Michael Young and Peter Willmott, *Family and Kinship in East London* (1957; rept edn, Harmondsworth: Penguin, 1964), pp. 23, 153.

67 Unless otherwise indicated, the next eleven paragraphs are based on the following by Michael A. Smith: *Sex, Gender and Power: The Enigma of the Public House* (Hebden Bridge: Privately Published, 2003); and 'An Empirical Study of a Rough Working Class Pub', in Eric Single and Thomas Storm (eds), *Public Drinking and Public Policy: Proceedings of a Symposium on Observation Studies Held at Banff, Alberta, Canada, April 26–8, 1984* (Toronto: Addiction Research Foundation, 1984), pp. 139–52.

68 Author's interview with Tony Avis, 26 July 1997; Brian Bennison, *Heady Days: A History of Newcastle's Public Houses: The Central Area* (Newcastle: Newcastle Libraries & Information Services, 1996), 1:30; Franklin, *Pub Drinking and the Licensed Trade*, pp. 23, 56.

69 Franklin, *Pub Drinking and the Licensed Trade*, pp. 24, 40.

70 Owen Gill, *Luke Street: Housing Policy, Conflict and the Creation of the Delinquent Area* (London: Macmillan, 1977), pp. 160–5.

71 Also see Paul Thompson, 'Imagination and Passivity in Leisure: Coventry Car Workers and Their Families from the 1920s to the 1970s', in David Thoms, Len Holden and Tim Claydon (eds), *The Motor Car and Popular Culture in the Twentieth Century* (Aldershot: Ashgate, 1998), p. 261.

72 Franklin, *Pub Drinking and the Licensed Trade*, pp. 25, 33–4, 39, 51.

73 Tom Porter to Editor, *Publican*, 10 Oct. 1985; Tom Porter, 'Working the Female Factor', *Publican*, 17 Jan. 1985.

74 G. P. Hunt and S. Satterlee, 'The Pub, the Village and the People', *Human Organization*, 45 (1986), pp. 62–74; Geoffrey Hunt and Saundra Satterlee, 'Cohesion and Division: Drinking in an English Village', *Man*, 21 (1986), pp. 521–37; Geoffrey P. Hunt, 'The Middle Class Revisited: Eating and Drinking in an English Village', *Western Folklore*, 50 (1991), pp. 401–20.

75 Mintel Beer Survey, 1980 quoted in *Publican*, 24 April 1980; MORI, *Public Attitudes to Pubs and Leisure* (June 1984), pp. 54–5; British Market Research Bureau Ltd, *Licensed Premises: Report of an Attitude Survey, August 1960* (1960), p. 66.

76 Dade, *Drink Talking*, p. 95.

77 MORI, *Public Attitudes to Pubs and Leisure* (June 1984), pp. 54–5.

78 *Publican*, 23 Jan. 1986.

79 Adam Tinworth, 'Be Irresistible to Women', *Publican*, 3 July 1995; MORI, *Public Attitudes to Pubs and Leisure* (June 1984), p. 50.

5

The more things change, the more (some) things remain the same

By the mid-1980s Smith's typology of pubs was already being modified, with those upholding the traditional culture of drinking steadily contracting as manufacturing jobs disappeared, service industries replaced them and more women joined the labour market, often in part-time, low-paid jobs. Violence still marked the subculture of rough working-class pubs, but bouncers now acted as a deterrent, forcing aggression out of doors into the streets. Youths with pride, as in Newcastle, perpetuated the 'balls over brains' behaviour of their elders, though they sought self-protection in gangs and moved beyond the local as an informal headquarters and refuge.[1]

Now one could identify six distinct drink venues, dependent more on function than class: youth bars, fun pubs, lounge bars, family pubs, repositioned traditional ale bars and private gentlemen's (sex) clubs.[2] High-tech leisure machines, gambling and video machines, pub sports and perhaps a children's room targeted the young. On weekends, fun pubs became part of the circuit, a series of pubs all within walking distance in which the young would quaff a drink and then move on to the next venue. Loud music and bouncers, off the town centre, distinguished youth pubs. For the more sedate middle classes, three options prevailed. At lounge bars, patrons sat and drank, listening to jukebox music. Unlike traditional pubs, there was little standing room at the bar itself, which as a result shrank considerably in size. Family pubs offered outdoor play facilities, gardens and menus tailored to parents with children. At traditional premises breweries began emphasizing food, real ale and wines.[3]

Some facets of the male subculture of drinking began slowly changing. A Gallup Poll commissioned in 1985 found increasing numbers of women were not only patronizing pubs and clubs but doing so without male escorts.[4] 'One distinct advantage of smartening up a pub and providing music, whether it be a disco or a cocktail-bar image, is that ladies will feel it acceptable to frequent such a place without being accompanied by a male', Wendy Bristow wrote about the most fashionable London pubs in 1980. Even in the conservative North, as one professional librarian at Lancaster University reflected, 'it is now quite acceptable for women to drink on their own, lean on the bar and sup their drinks silently'. Younger Northern women, however, still felt inhibited about entering pubs alone.[5]

Other indicators of greater gender equality also emerged, with women drinking pints (at least in the South) and ordering drinks themselves at bar counters as participants in the buying of a round. Since the 1960s women had drunk pints in the South without inciting much comment, but not in the North, where, as one transplanted soul remarked, it was still 'Andy Capp country'.[6]

But vestiges of sexual inequality remained. On visiting a pub, women, though joining now with their menfolk in sharing costs, still found themselves as often paying nothing as being called upon to participate in buying rounds. More striking was the persistence of traditional gender attitudes in group drinking. When women accompanied men into pubs and joined a large group, men only bought rounds. Women who challenged this convention were told politely 'Ladies don't do that'.[7]

Working-men's clubs also defied changing gender relations in British society. Four million men affiliated in some four thousand clubs, together with two to three million women denied full membership, represented huge numbers of drinkers. Dominated by men from their mid-Victorian beginnings, such clubs had successfully resisted reform, notwithstanding women's long-standing complaints of sexist treatment. Powerful backers in the Labour Party had guaranteed clubs' exemption from legal oversight. Under the Friendly Societies Act of 1974, clubs with 'model rules' could legally discriminate against women. This status was enshrined the following year in the Sex Discrimination Act, which thoughtfully excluded clubs from its provisions. Denied membership and admitted as social appendages of husbands, women had been summarily excluded when they became widows.[8] To underline graphically women's subordinate status, some clubs drew white lines on floors and forbade females to cross them; others threw open games facilities for use by children, never by women. Some one hundred women angrily picketed at the Club & Institute Union's National Convention in 1980. In response, Frank Morris (CIU's General Secretary) declared: 'It is an inherent trait in British men to enjoy the company of their fellow men'. Reiterating the Institute's stance, he stressed men welcomed women's company 'in the right place'. With the battle lines drawn, escalating aggression came one year later at the National Convention, where officials locked the door to women's toilets. Verbal taunts greeted women who picketed the meeting: '"There are only two places for women: one's in bed and the other's in the kitchen."'[9]

The 'men only' rule became even more objectionable when women took up snooker as a serious sport. No other organization sponsored more sporting events than the Club & Institute Union, and use of recreational facilities of affiliated clubs was critical for women darts and snooker players with competitive instincts. For her much-publicized campaign to persuade her local club, the Elmere Social Club, to grant women free access to snooker tables, Sheila Capstick was expelled, one of the conflict's first martyrs. Defenders of the status quo received national support in December: the national organization, to which the Elmere Club was affiliated, organized a ballot of club committees which promptly voted down almost to a man a resolution permitting membership for women. '"The enemy"', as the CIU President dubbed supporters of equal rights, had been vanquished.[10]

Outraged women eventually fought back, with Capstick, one of the country's leading snooker players, in the vanguard. In 1983 she spearheaded formation of the Equal Rights in Clubs Campaign for Action (ERICCA). Her notoriety rallied feminists who accused club members throughout the country of striving to exclude women because men were in some cases losing matches, together evidently with their masculinity, to female opponents. Organizer of the largest groups of sporting leagues in the country, the Club & Institute Union could no longer escape public scrutiny. Snooker, like darts, had gained status as a professional sport, with participants drawn by bigger prizes and possible wider exposure on television. Lucrative national careers beckoned, but only for men, who could exploit their clubs and their facilities as springboards into competitive sports.[11]

Despite passage of the Race Relations Act, racial discrimination persisted. According to Barbara Rogers, who investigated three working-men's clubs in 1983, clubs routinely excluded minorities. As the legislation safeguarded 'members of the public', clubs could exploit this loophole to argue that as membership was private, not public, they were exempted from its provisions.[12]

But the Club & Institute Union faced still more formidable financial problems undermining its discriminatory policies. Cheap beer and popular entertainment were no longer enticements – beer prices lost their margin against pubs, while costs of live shows soared – forcing many clubs to shut their doors. By 1989, there were over four hundred fewer clubs than fifteen years earlier. Changing sociability patterns prompted men to turn to drinking at home with their wives, ironically drawn to televised national darts and snooker matches. Pubs alone now had an advantage in offering customers real ale: it required greater expertise to serve than available at clubs. To bolster flagging profits and membership, some clubs introduced strip shows on Sunday mornings, following the weekly club meeting. But this did not address generational changes in which youth sought disco lights and jukebox music, two demands which ageing club members regarded as anathema.[13]

Well into the 1990s, the annual conference of the Club & Institute Union routinely considered, and just as summarily dismissed, motions granting women full membership rights. Representing hidebound club conservatism, Les Barke, President of the Langham Club, asserted that 'women get very "mannish" if you allow them on committees'. Women eventually won these contested membership rights, but by then it was too late. Many clubs had been forced to close, the Institute's total affiliates for the first time falling well below three thousand, as members increasingly represented elderly men with their white-only drinking regime. Demographic changes in which younger men preferred style bars with expensive premium brands to utilitarian clubs with cheap beers, smoking bans and racist as well as sexist policies all meant that working-men's clubs became 'ageing bastions for a by-gone era'. Coventry, in the club heartland, capitulated, shutting its doors; and in another stronghold one club secretary soon forecast the dismal future in 2008: 'Most clubs in South Shields will be finished in a decade'. It was, as the *Morning Advertiser* reporter aptly observed, 'the end of an era – and the death of a wonderful, but redundant institution'.[14]

This was a conspicuous, though not the only, gender contrast in drinking. Men and women continued appraising pubs for a night out differently. Women attached greater weight than men to socializing in comfort, pride of place going to clean toilets, tasty food and quiet music.[15] Of these characteristics, none loomed larger for women than clean toilets. Little changed over the course of the 1980s, save that surveys sponsored by the Brewers' Society began recording remarkably high numbers – one in three – of female drinkers regularly using pubs who criticized toilets as dirty or deficient.[16] Dorset publican Tom Porter went so far as to declare that 'a lady's first consideration about a pub is what are the toilets like. If they are clean, smell nice and are well décorated', he added, 'she'll consider coming back again'. He followed his own advice, with the ladies' lavatory 'nearly over the top in its smartness'.[17] His shrewd insights anticipated the philosophy of the pioneering female-friendly chains (Wetherspoon and Pitcher & Piano) as well as the findings of voluminous market research.[18]

Championing public demands for better facilities, the *Publican* urged that '"ladies" powder rooms have to be quite beautiful – three star standards'.[19] Most pubs fell somewhat short of this expectation. One of the most damning surveys came from Pinnacle, a hygiene company, in which it found that four-fifths of the nine hundred pubs surveyed had unhygienic toilets. Urban pubs ranked still worse, with almost nine of every ten deemed inadequate. Even railway stations and restaurants, though hardly stellar overall in cleanliness, scored higher.[20] Many women were strongly prejudiced when venturing into pubs. Hardly unusual was Sharyl Garratt, editor of *The Face*, who confessed to shunning pubs partly because 'the toilets are horrible'.[21]

Toilet cleanliness came to rank as a priority for both sexes from the early 1990s. Customers of Mansfield Brewery pubs, for example, considered high toilet hygiene standards as only less important than glass hygiene and beer quality.[22] In a national survey, two out of every five customers cited poor hygiene as the reason for not returning to a pub.[23] Customers were scarcely alone in evaluating not just the beer, proximity or landlord's friendliness but the environmental totality of a pub in their decisions about future drink venues. One Managing Director of a company owning a chain of pubs, Michael Izza, candidly and bluntly condemned the quality of pub toilets as 'appalling'. 'Unkempt toilets' likewise earned the wrath of Stewart Gilliland, Managing Director of Interbrew UK, in 2001, as one of the three most offensive shortcomings in pubs. For every pub giving consumers what they deserved, he contended, two or three failed.[24] Even CAMRA members, generally unconcerned with anything save beer quality and selection, had eventually come to see clean bar areas and toilets as one of their top priorities, a membership survey in 2003 disclosed. CAMRA's Marketing Manager, Louise Ashworth, gave the issue further urgency. Women, she maintained, saw cleanliness, especially in toilets, as one decisive factor in selecting a pub in which to drink.[25] Still more startling, a survey in 2007 discovered that no other factor deterred more women from frequenting a pub than its toilet conditions. 'It's common knowledge among women that the toilets are often the social hub of a night out', remarked Gerard McElvenny, whose company specialized in designing imaginative interiors for the leisure industry. Yet, landlords, though eager to draw more female customers, regarded toilets as largely unimportant compared to so many other matters. For licensees, this was a failure of marketing; others felt that first-rate toilets, not beer selection or quality, prices, or cable television, could woo women. 'It's a typical rule that if a place has nice toilets', argued McElvenny, 'it will bring in the women to use them, and … then the men are not far behind'.[26]

European visitors likewise regarded the hygiene of British pubs, wine bars and fast-food bars as nothing less than deplorable. Dirty premises outranked both price and quality as factors determining whether to return to a pub. British cases of food poisoning reaching some seventy thousand in 2002, for example, gave Europeans reasonable grounds for objecting forcibly to unclean pubs and restaurants.[27]

Whether for European tourists or more generally native British women, changing the culture of brewing and pub drinking proved extraordinarily difficult. Breweries perpetuated the old brewing culture in which beer and masculinity reigned supreme. Male brewery executives shared the same outlook as their chief customers, men. Two market research surveys completed in the 1980s underlined strikingly divergent gender views of pubs. Most men – but significantly not most women – thought pubs catered to the needs of women. Scottish males, in contrast, had no reservations: two-thirds of them saw Scottish pubs as masculine haunts. Men, moreover, regarded issues related specifically to drinking – beer quality, beverage choices, service and hours – as paramount, whereas women saw clean toilets as the overriding issue. Geography likewise shaped men's attitudes. English men thus had no understanding of what women sought in pubs, and could not act as a catalyst for altering the environment.[28]

That no revolution in lavatory hygiene transformed pubs in the ensuing years explains why leading women from the drinks industry could meet in 2008 under the *Morning Advertiser*'s auspices to discuss what changes would ensure females revisited licensed premises. Of the major five factors identified, 'cleanliness throughout, especially in the toilets', ranked first. So important was this issue to Sharon Dickinson, *Morning Advertiser* Group Sales Manager, that when she went in a new pub 'I'm out the door' if she encountered 'anything doggy about it'. Expanding on this criticism, Lisa Harlow (Waverly TBS, a drinks wholesaler firm) noted that 'the doors and all around them are filthy and the handle is dirty'. To her, these shortcomings reflected standards of male cleaners. Feature editor for the paper, Jessica Harvey, specifically complained about broken cubicle locks, and absence of vital amenities – hand lotion, full-length mirrors, cotton buds for straightening mascara and hooks for purses or bags.[29]

Pubs with comfortable seating, pleasant staff offering first-rate service and wide choice of beverages, notably wine, all earned these women's accolades.

Powerful associations between pubs and masculinity still created anxiety for single women. Even in 2008, Lucy Britner, *Morning Advertiser* reporter, could relate feeling apprehensive. 'People', she knew, 'wonder why a woman is in a pub on her own'. She adopted different strategies while awaiting the arrival of her friend to deflect male interest – texting virtually everyone in her telephone book or going for extended periods to the toilets. For this reason, she and other women wanted pubs to furnish complimentary newspapers and magazines so that they could occupy themselves until friends appeared.[30] Carole Seddon, a retired civil servant, expresses this conviction in Simon Brett's novel *The Poisoning in the Pub*, published one year after Britner's comments. 'While she drank her Maipo Valley Chardonnay, Carole was kicking herself for not bringing *The Times* with her. She felt exposed sitting alone drinking in the Hare and Hounds.' As Brett's character was drinking not just wine but fashionable New World wine from Chile, this passage gains additional credibility.[31]

Psychological cues still proclaimed women's second-class status. Writer for the *Morning Advertiser* and former editor of CAMRA's *Good Beer Guide* Roger Protz described two telling experiences when visiting pubs with female friends in 2008. He ordered two pints of bitter at one of them, but while Protz received a pint the landlord served his female friend a half pint in 'a lady's glass'. Worse came in Middlesbrough, where he and another female friend entered a pub and all conversation stopped until they left.[32]

Breweries and the industry more broadly remained fixated on the past, continuing to see working-class men as the mainstay of customers. That one Bass executive, Bob Cartwright, could even comment in 1998 upon the 'long-term decline of the pub traditionalist – the largely male, blue-collar workers who stopped off to rehydrate on the way home from the mine or the foundry', as if evoking the recent rather than quite distant past, exemplified this antiquated mentality.[33] Lest they affront men, breweries marketed low-alcoholic beers, such as Coors Lite to men. After renaming the beer Miller Pilsner, the brewery displayed no greater enthusiasm for females as customers. 'Beer', exclaimed a brewery representative, 'is predominantly drunk by men so we would not position Miller Pilsner as a woman's beer'.[34] Advertisements for John Smith's, Tetley's and London Pride, three leading bitters, ignored females entirely. The overwhelming male culture of beer wholesaling, retailing and consumption in part explained this bias. But it also owed to the failures of Allied and Lacons in the 1980s. Allied had introduced a lager aimed avowedly at women, Bleu de Brasserie, which proved as unpopular as Lacon's own version of a female beverage, a prepackaged lager and lime.[35] Nothing then had really changed since 1993, when a market research survey had found that 'few pubs were willing to admit they were aiming at women for fear of scaring off the men!'[36]

Some drinks manufacturers, in contrast, displayed greater insight into selling women alcohol. DiSaronno, for instance, marketed a liqueur, heavily laced with sugar, targeted at women, the drink's chief consumers. Given that females drank more soft drinks (14 per cent) than any other beverage on licensed premises, this strategy made considerable sense. More women, in fact, drank draught lager (9 per cent) and wine (5 per cent) than draught bitter (2 per cent).[37]

Preoccupation with selling alcohol to men literally still permeated the brewers' mentality from the top downwards in the new century. Greene King epitomized this philosophy with its advertisements showing a naked woman in bed covered with a sheet, above the caption 'Lie back and think of longer queues at the bar'. Placed on the front page of *What's Brewing* and on billboards, the advertisement, as the *Morning Advertiser* admitted, involved bondage.[38] J. W. Lees, reviving the discontinued concept of the Tennent calendars, celebrated its 175th anniversary with a calendar featuring twelve of the brewery's barmaids. A busty, provocatively posed and skimpily dressed woman, for example, appeared as Miss October. Whitbreads, in contrast, claimed the moral high ground, and insisted that it 'would never consider using sexist advertising to promote a brand – there is no point in alienating half the population'. Nevertheless, Whitbreads marketed Murphy's beer, aimed at drinkers in their twenties with an Irish lass, clad in black leather whose plunging cleavage revealed substantial bosom. Mansfield's rebranding of its leading beer aimed at the same target group and approach. From its slogan, 'Man's World, Man's Pint, Mansfield', to its advertisement, in which a naked woman's hands covered her breasts, this Midland brewery overtly sought only male customers. Whether for brewing executives or marketers, beer and men went together. 'According to the vast majority of those who earn their living by promoting the sales of beer', remarked a Midland reporter, 'anything sold in a pint glass is about as macho as you can get, barring a rugby scrum or stag night'.[39]

That rugby had lost much of its aggressive masculinity, if not misogyny, over the preceding several decades only underscored how the brewing industry's machismo had become increasingly anachronistic. Rugby football clubs had traditionally celebrated their masculinity with mock striptease, drunkenness and 'objectification and defilement of women and homosexuals' through obscene songs. Yet, from the late 1960s as a result of economic pressures leading to the introduction of social dances at rugby clubs, the waning of sexism, and greater stress on companionate sexual relationships, the traditional masculine culture gradually diminished.[40]

Beer wholesalers scarcely represented an anomaly in the industry. Virtually all drink manufacturers targeted primarily men utilizing sexist advertisements. At the BBC's Good Food shows in the mid-1990s, for instance, seductive blonde models paraded at all but one of the stalls. Such was the allure of selling to males aged eighteen to twenty-four that Bacardi rum, which had marketed itself primarily as a female beverage, began extolling the virtues of male bonding enacted through boxing with advertisements from the late 1990s.[41]

Sex not only persisted as the promotional tool for selling alcoholic beverages and pub foods but became even more flagrantly raunchy, partly reflecting a general shift in what society would accept. Bass, for example, aired a Carling advertisement in which scantily attired women dribbled beer around a flat which a male eagerly licked up. Watchdog ITC promptly banned the advertisement for 'mimicking oral sex'. Nothing much was left to the imagination in a Smirnoff commercial portraying a woman having an unmistakable orgasm in a theatre box.[42] Men doubtless thought this a seductive advertisement, but from a marketing perspective it was misdirected since remarkably few of them drank the beverage. Over 90 per cent of Smirnoff Ice drinkers, one of the beverages commonly called RTDs (Ready to Drink) in the trade, were young women.[43]

Both pubs and clubs began more aggressively pushing sexist bar snacks. Beginning in 2002, Big D, producers of bagged peanuts, revived the advertising gimmick of a quite buxom, bikini-clad, blonde lass featured on a large display card, covered with peanut packages and hung on a wall easily visible to pub customers. As packages were purchased, progressively more of the titillating Ruth Higham, *Daily Star* pin-up 'Big D' girl, emerged. Sex certainly sold peanuts in pubs; sales skyrocketed by 35 per cent. 'She was a Big D star who helped rebuild the brand', boasted a snack company spokeswoman. Concerned about the concept going stale, along with sales, Big D found a still more endowed female, Danish model Malene Espensen, four years later. A *Morning Advertiser* story caught the company's advertising flair and prevailing views of the cultures of drinking: 'Big D Goes for Double G to Drive Men Nuts'. Scottish publicans later got into the act when Big D held the 'Pull in the Punters' competition. Each customer's purchase of a Big D pub card enabled the landlord's name to be entered in a drawing competition in which the winner received Malene's help serving drinks in the bar for an evening.[44]

CAMRA, the consumer lobby group promoting cask-conditioned beers, proved to be a quite reliable guide to the pervasive sexist attitudes in beer retailing, on both sides of the bar counter. When CAMRA sought more women as members, the predominantly male leadership predictably devised advertisements of questionable appeal to women. In 2002, for example, CAMRA hit upon a new symbol, Ninkasi, Goddess of Beer. She appeared in all her glory as 'a luscious, pouting, busty babe who is apparently intended to appeal to women rather than titillate men'. Two male marketers candidly confessed: '"We like her a lot"'. Females, in contrast, resented what they saw as 'a Lara Croft lookalike'. The *Morning Advertiser*, read by mostly male landlords, defended Ninkasi, and pointed to the advertisement's appearance in newspapers generally as justification. Her replacement advertisement scarcely disarmed female critics. It featured an attractive unclothed blonde model with hops and hop leaves placed strategically on her breasts and lower waist. In response to CAMRA featuring a woman holding a pint of beer on the cover of its *2003 Beer Guide*, one woman wrote to the *Morning Advertiser*'s editor, dismissing this appeal to females as affronting. 'This merely reinforces the stereotype of CAMRA members as being ageing, balding, overweight males who, after a couple of pints of strong ale, fantasise about picking up such nice bits of totty'.[45]

Not until 2004 did CAMRA's newly hired marketing manager, Louise Ashworth, implicitly challenge what she called 'the macho image' of real ale. 'A woman is not going to be turned on to real ale if she sees some semi-naked blonde draped over a beer barrel', she argued in an article published, significantly, not in CAMRA's *What's Brewing* but in the retailers' *Morning Advertiser*. Nor were women much impressed when CAMRA turned to a female as Chair who championed the idea of brewers introducing beers specifically targeting women as customers. This misguided advice ignored previous failed efforts of brewers to market such a gender-specific beverage.[46]

With this advertising culture, beer marketers thus continued to insinuate into the female mind an unmistakably negative view of beer drinking. Fully two-thirds of female drinkers surveyed in 2003 said that they regarded real ale unenthusiastically because of its links with unfeminine behaviour.[47] In response to the North West Pub & Beer Association's invitation to a beer and food tasting luncheon at Heathcotes, Manchester's upmarket restaurant, eighteen female MPs unanimously declined. In conceding that women's replies 'may say something about their general perception of beer', the Association's Secretary betrayed how little male beer retailers really understood the obstacles to overcoming entrenched drinking stereotypes for which they themselves were largely responsible.[48]

New demographic and drinking trends had heightened women's importance as consumers of beer from the 1990s. Four times as many women in South America and two to two-and-a-half-times as many in the US drank beer as in the UK. Yet, market surveys projected that women would comprise at least 40 per cent and perhaps as much as 50 per cent of the pubs' total clientele by 2000. Alarmingly, the proportion of the young (eighteen- to twenty-four-year-olds), previously the backbone of pub drinkers, would plummet to just 20 per cent of pub goers. Here indeed was a marketing crisis in the making, requiring radical reappraisal of current strategy as well as a new customer mix.[49]

Women's wine consumption grew steadily, and reached 55 per cent of the total wine market in 2005, more than twice what they consumed of aggregate beer sales. Such gloomy sales prompted some breweries to embrace a new marketing solution. Mark Hunter, Coors UK Chief Executive, returned from Canada with new ideas and much enthusiasm for transforming beer sales. Ironically, it was Hunter, as a senior executive at then Tennent Caledonian Breweries early in the 1990s, who ended the reign of Tennent girls on the company's beer cans. In an unprecedented move, he appointed five women across the company's departments to a special task force, Project Eve, dedicated to answering the perennial question: Why don't British women drink beer? Avoiding the impolitic issue of why men primarily staffed the Marketing Department at Coors Brewers, the women instead confined themselves to conducting research. Their findings pointed to women's widespread prejudice – against the taste of beer, its fattening properties and its presentation.[50]

Women's aversion to beer proved more complicated than these conclusions suggested. Had the Project Eve team surveyed Europeans, another strikingly different perspective would have been obtained. German women customarily drank beer from the same type of glasses as men. When in her homeland, solicitor and beer lover Jeanette Fahlbusch bought beer and drank it publicly. But she shunned her favourite beverage in English pubs, lest she get beer '"slopped up in a boring old glass, lukewarm, with no head on it and full of chemicals"'. For her, presentation – an attractive glass, a new napkin and beer mat, and the beer's ideal temperature and head – determined where she consumed beer.[51]

Germans and other Europeans did drink beer differently, as Jeanette Fahlbusch rightly noted. From 2004 Punch Taverns began introducing continental beers – Duckstein, Leffe Blonde, Fruli, Paulaner and Franziskaner – into its pubs. 'The way they are retailed, the branded glassware, the theatre of serve, the point-of-sale – it all has a massive impact', contended Geoff Brown, Punch Marketing Manager. But not one apparently made on British licensees, who, though given special training, tenaciously adhered to a 'slurping culture'. In the United Kingdom, wrote broadcaster Janet Street-Porter of the *Independent on Sunday*, 'beer is part of the slurping culture where you down a massive amount of liquid in one go'. Interbrew UK was making similar arguments to landlords in its own attempts to promote Hoegaarden and Leffe.[52] This was not, however, simply a clash between two dissimilar cultures of drinking. Indeed, it had much wider significance. That young British women echoed and endorsed Fahlbusch's sentiments about drinking in pubs indicated that drinking habits were being globalized.[53]

Wholly oblivious of these emergent new attitudes, British wholesalers proposed their own radical and revolutionary marketing remedy, the creation of a special woman's drinking glass![54] In 2005 the British Beer & Pub Association proposed to sell beer in a wine-sized glass as a method of combating the pint's masculine image. Instead of the standard male pint, women could drink from small, one-third pint glasses. This seemingly ingenious solution to appealing to women was ill-suited to a market in which drinking premium beers in either bottles or branded glasses had become popular among both sexes as a bold statement image.[55] Wholesalers, after all, had to look no further for enlightenment than the widely popular Belgian wheat beer, Hoegaarden, served in a distinctive, rectangular container, the same size as men used. 'It is consumed', thought *Flavour*'s reporter, 'almost equally by men and women here and in Belgium, its home market'. Soon Leffe, another Belgian beer, and Stella Artois joined Hoegaarden in being served in branded glasses. 'People are extremely image conscious and have been prepared to pay more to drink bottled beers but now they can do the same with beer from the tap', remarked the sales manager for Charles Glassware, sellers of these bespoke glasses. Treating women differently in pubs with special, smaller glasses smacked of sexism, precisely the behaviour which drinks retailers sought to repudiate.[56]

For their part, Project Eve women inspired Coors UK to strike out on an entirely different path, the introduction of new beverages. Surely women, so the thinking went, would respond to Blue Moon (a Belgian-style wheat ale spiced with coriander), a rose-favoured beer (along the lines of its champagne and beer mixture, Kasteel Cru), or a beer-based cocktail. One Project Eve woman expressed considerable doubt whether these drinks would woo women from wine or spirits.[57] Sharing her scepticism was Debbie Hearne, Project Manager at Box Marketing, a company specializing in drinks marketing. 'A cocktail ingredient would flatten a beer', she observed. But she articulated another powerful explanation for women's views. 'Sexist beer ads over the years have also contributed to putting women off beer.' Nothing changed in the ensuing years, with nearly four out of five weekly female pub goers still not beer drinkers. When Coors sought another approach in 2011 and marketed a new lager beer, Animée, with three different flavours (filtered, rose and lemon) as a female drink, women responded unenthusiastically. Melissa Cole succinctly put their viewpoint: 'If brewers want to entice women to drink more beer, they should stop their sexist adverts aimed solely at men'. This was the same verdict of Iain Ellwood, head consultant at Interbrand, who stridently criticized such beer marketing as 'incredibly sexist'.[58] Brewers fully reaped what decades of sexist advertisements had thus sown: women consumed little beer, a meagre one-fourth of the total sales, but loomed large in the wine market, accounting for just over half of the aggregate consumption.[59]

A masculine mentality still permeated the drinks industry: uppermost in the minds of executives was the male drinker, to whom they repeatedly appealed with sexist commercials and advertisements which became still raunchier and more offensive to women over decades. What this in fact reflected was ingrained traditional assumptions about gender roles in which men earned the family income, while women remained at home as housewives and mothers. Unable to recognize – indeed accept – changes in employment, greater sexual equality and market changes, especially the rise of wine consumption, drink manufacturers resorted to time-honoured methods for attracting women. These failed miserably, ensuring women drank wine at home rather than the pub, and, if middle class, preferred socializing at home to the local.

Notes

1 Blake Morrison, 'Brave New World on the Tyne', *Independent*, 4 Dec. 1994.

2 A seventh type, style bars, began appearing in the early 1990s. See Chapter 8, pp. 172–3, 178–81.

3 Adrian Franklin, *Pub Drinking and the Licensed Trade: A Study of Drinking Cultures and Local Community in Two Areas of South West England* (Bristol: University of Bristol, 1985), pp. 58–9.

4 Gallup Poll, 1985, quoted in *Pub Leader*, Nov. 1985.

5 Jenny Greenhalgh, 'The Licensee and His Pub', in Marcus Binney and Emma Milne (eds), *Time Gentlemen Please!* (London: SAVE Britain's Heritage in association with CAMRA, 1983), p. 39; Leslie R. Gofton, 'Folk Devils and the Demon Drink: Drinking Rituals and Social Integration in North East England', *Drogalkohol*, 12 (1988), p. 190; Wendy Bristow, 'Dazzling Décor', *Publican*, 22 May 1980. A 1988 Brewers' Society survey suggested that attitudes to women's presence in pubs may have differed according to gender: women felt more comfortable going to pubs alone, while men retained reservations about this development (Market and

Opinion Research International, *Public Attitudes to Pubs and Leisure*, April 1988 (1988), p. 66). Hereafter, MORI.

6 *Pub Leader*, Nov. 1985; Graham Turner, *The North Country* (London: Eyre & Spottiswoode, 1967), p. 361; also see Adam Tinworth, 'Be Irresistible to Women', *Publican*, 3 July 1995.

7 G. P. Hunt and S. Satterlee, 'The Pub, the Village and the People', *Human Organization*, 45 (1986), p. 72; MORI, *Attitudes to the British Brewing Industry* (Spring 1981), p. ii.

8 Affiliated clubs could admit women as members, but not issue an Affiliation and Pass Card, entitling them to visit other such establishments, a privilege reserved solely for men. Unlike Labour social clubs, Conservative ones not only discriminated against women but denied them admission on to club premises altogether (Barbara Rogers, *Men Only: An Investigation into Men's Organizations* (London: Pandora, 1988), pp. 54, 68–70).

9 Barbara Rogers, 'Men Only, Please', *New Statesman*, 107 (3 Feb. 1984), p. 9; Rogers, *Men Only*, pp. 63–4; Sandra Salmans, 'Women vs. British "Men-Only Pubs"', *New York Times*, 25 June 1980.

10 Rogers, *Men Only*, pp. 55–6, and 'Men Only', pp. 9–10; Salmans, 'Women vs. British "Men-Only Pubs"'. Not all working-men's clubs excluded women. The Greasbrough Social Club, near Rotherham, one of the country's largest and most prosperous, specialized in first-rate entertainment, and women came with husbands, 'very conscious of being on parade'. Clubs on Tyneside and Teeside had been flourishing since the 1960s, with the total number reaching some 1500, each worth on average £50,000 to £100,000. To these clubs, representing a merging of clubs, music halls and pubs, went wives of members (Turner, *North Country*, pp. 245–52; Ronald Faux, 'Much Bending of Elbows in North-East', *The Times*, 26 April 1971).

11 Rogers, 'Men Only, Please', p. 10.

12 Ibid., p. 9.

13 Rogers, *Men Only*, pp. 64–6; 'Girls in the Club', *Economist*, 1 April 1989.

14 Dominic Roskrow, 'Whatever Happened to the Working Men's Clubs?' *Morning Advertiser*, 30 Oct. 2008; 'Girls in the Club'.

15 MORI, *Public Attitudes to Pubs and Leisure, April 1988* (1988), p. 57; also see MORI's 1981 survey quoted in Rogers, *Men Only*, p. 18.

16 MORI, *Public Attitudes to Pubs and Leisure (June 1984)*, p. 7. Throughout the 1970s and 1980s, pollsters repeatedly identified cleanliness as one of the three most salient factors ranked by customers (MORI, *Attitudes to the British Brewing Industry* (Spring 1981), p. iii). Even men had begun to object to vile toilets and unemptied ashtrays, their complaints establishing a new record in the annals of *The Good Pub Guide* in 1988 ('Time Again, Gentlemen', *Economist*, 16 April 1988).

17 Tom Porter to Editor, *Publican*, 10 Oct. 1985; Tom Porter, 'Working the Female Factor', *Publican*, 17 Jan. 1985.

18 See for example, Paul Allonby, 'Half a Million Spent to Make Women Happy!' *Licensee and Morning Advertiser*, 12 April 1999; Catherine Quinn, 'Where Small Is Beautiful', *Morning Advertiser*, 14 Feb. 2008.

19 *Publican*, Dec. 1985.
20 Robert Metcalfe, 'Survey Finds Most Pub Loos Unhygienic', *Publican*, 14 Oct. 1989.
21 Garratt quoted in Alex Spillius, 'The Bitter End?', *Observer*, 7 Nov. 1993; Ann Steele, 'Is Family Atmosphere Enough?' *Publican*, 24 Nov. 1983.
22 *Publican*, 22 Nov. 1993.
23 Publican/Carling Pub Goers Report, quoted in 'What your Customers Want', *Publican Newspaper*, 4 March 1996.
24 Tinworth, 'Irresistible to Women'; Mike Bennett, 'Interbrew UK Head Slams Sloppy Pubs', *Morning Advertiser*, 24 May 2001.
25 Claire Hu, 'Cleanliness Is Next to Godliness Say Punters', *Morning Advertiser*, 26 Feb. 2004; Louise Ashworth, 'What Women Want', *Morning Advertiser*, 4 Nov. 2004; Lorna Harrison, 'Pub-Goers Survey', *Publican Newspaper*, 12 Nov. 2002; Sally Bairstow, 'Increase Your Pulling Power', *Morning Advertiser*, 19 June 2003.
26 Quinn, 'Where Small Is Beautiful'.
27 MORI survey, quoted in the *Morning Advertiser*, 1 April 2004.
28 *Mintel Report on Alcoholic Drinks, 1983*, quoted in the *Publican*, 26 May 1983; MORI, *Public Attitudes to Pubs and Leisure (June 1984)*, p. vii.
29 Jessica Harvey, 'What Women Want', *Morning Advertiser*, 28 Aug. 2008.
30 Ibid.
31 Simon Brett, *The Poisoning in the Pub* (2009; paperback ed., London: Pan, 2010), p. 315.
32 Roger Protz, 'Ladies Who Brew', *Morning Advertiser*, 28 Aug. 2008.
33 The economic collapse of manufacturing, shipbuilding, steel and mining had been a product of the tumultuous Thatcherite 1980s. By the early 1990s, just 1 per cent of Newcastle workers, for example, were employed in heavy manufacturing, compared with 30 per cent in 1980 (Morrison, 'Brave New World').
34 John Willman, 'Make Mine a Family Pub with a Twist of Real Ale', *Financial Times*, 31 March 1998; David Flockhart, 'Beer', *Flavour*, 12 (June 2001), p. 36.
35 Ben McFarland, 'One for the Ladies', *Publican Newspaper*, 16 April 2001.
36 Franklin, *Pub Drinking and the Licensed Trade*, p. 54; Caroline Nodder, 'Female Market Up Over "Friendly" Bars', *Publican Newspaper*, 10 Aug. 1998.
37 Tinworth, 'Irresistible to Women'.
38 *Morning Advertiser*, 12 Sept. and 17 Oct. 2002.
39 Catherine Turner, 'It's Your Round, Girls!', *Coventry Evening Telegraph*, 28 Sept. 2000; *Publican Newspaper*, 15 April 2002; John Porter, 'Keeping Abreast of the Beer Market', *Town & City Magazine*, Nov. 1998; also see Wolverhampton and Dudley's advertisements (*Publican Newspaper*, 8 May 2000); Scottish Courage's Kronenbourg 1664 advertisement (*Morning Advertiser*, 27 June 2002); *Publican Newspaper*, 19 Jan. 2004; *Publican*, 26 April 2004.
40 K. G. Sheard and E. G. Dunning, 'The Rugby Football Club as a Type of "Male Preserve": Some Sociological Notes', in John W. Loy, Jr, Gerald S. Kenyon and Barry D. McPherson (eds), *Sport, Culture and Society: A Reader on the Sociology of Sport*, 2nd rev. ed. (Philadelphia: Lea & Febiger, 1981), pp. 158, 160–5.
41 Tinworth, 'Irresistible to Women'; Andrew Burnyeat, 'Pubs Transformed by the Gentle Touch', *Publican Newspaper*, 8 May 2000.

42 *Morning Advertiser*, 19 Sept. 2002; Ashworth, 'What Women Want'.
43 Adam Withrington, 'RTDs – What Would Licensees Like to See?' *Publican*, 19 Sept. 2005.
44 Adam Edwards, 'Big D Goes for Double G to Drive Men Nuts', *Morning Advertiser*, 4 May 2006.
45 *Morning Advertiser*, 12 Sept. 2002; Rhoda Waygood to Editor, *Morning Advertiser*, 12 Sept. 2002; Simon McQuiggan and Pete Brown, 'What Women Don't Want', *Morning Advertiser*, 28 Aug. 2003.
46 Ashworth, 'What Women Want'.
47 Hall & Woodhouse survey, quoted in *Beer* (*Supplement to Morning Advertiser*), Oct. 2003.
48 *Morning Advertiser*, 26 Feb. 2004.
49 Gemma Charles, 'Coors Seeks Feminine Touch', *Marketing*, 27 March 2008, p. 16; BLRA Survey (1994) and Whitbread Inn's *The Changing Face of the British Pub* (1994) quoted in Kate Oppenheim, 'Success in Quality and Equality', *Publican*, 8 Jan. 1996; *Publican Newspaper*, 4 March 1996.
50 John D. Pratten and Jean-Baptiste Carlier, 'Wine Sales in British Public Houses', *International Journal of Wine Business Research*, 22 (2010), pp. 63–4; Charles, 'Feminine Touch', p. 16.
51 Flockhart, 'Beer', pp. 35–6; also see Bennett, 'Interbrew UK'.
52 *Publican*, 31 Jan. 2005; *Publican*, 31 Aug. 2009; 'Panel: Why the Majority of Women in the UK do Not Drink Beer?' *Publican*, 23 March 2009; *Morning Advertiser*, 24 Jan. 2008.
53 See below, pp. 177, 182, 205, 207.
54 Some years earlier Fuller's had sought wider feminine appeal for its Organic Honey Dew beer with pils-style glasses. In marketing its popular London Pride, in contrast, Fuller's directed its appeal solely at men, the main consumers of the beverage. McFarland, 'One for the Ladies'.
55 Author's interview with Stuart Aitken, former Sales Director of the Whitbread Beer Co., 4 Aug. 2000; Ben McFarland, 'A Glass of Their Own', *Publican Newspaper*, 23 Sept. 2002.
56 Sarah Swainson (Marketing Managing of Bavaria UK) to Editor, *Publican*, 21 March 2005; Roger Protz, 'Women's Glasses Idea Is a Non Starter', *Morning Advertiser*, 17 March 2005; Flockhart, 'Beer', p. 36; McFarland, 'Glass of Their Own'.
57 Charles, 'Feminine Touch', p. 16; Zoe Wood, 'Sinking Brewers Aim to Give Women a Taste of Beer', *Observer*, 20 July 2008.
58 Charles, 'Feminine Touch'; Wood, 'Sinking Brewers'; www.guardian.co.uk/lifeandstyle/wordofmouth/2011/jul/19/lager-for-ladies-again.
59 John Harrington, 'Report Links Women to Surge in Pub Wine Sales', *Morning Advertiser*, 7 Oct. 2004.

6

Drinking habits of their own

Per capita consumption of wine doubled within a decade, rising from 5 (1975) to 10 litres (1985), contributing to what some observers called 'a wine revolution'. 'Wine', remarked John Burnett, 'has passed from a drink of privilege to one of mass consumption, and Britain has been at least partially converted to an Europeanization of taste'. Symptomatic of wine's growing popularity were weekly columns in national newspaper detailing recent market developments.[1]

Soaring wine consumption, however, had not led to new wine bars. Per capita consumption of wine increased two-and-a-half times between 1960 and 1975, yet interested patrons outside London would have looked vainly for a wine bar, even in large cities or cathedral towns. *Kelley's Directories*, for instance, recorded no wine bars in Oxford, Chichester, Edinburgh or Glasgow in the 1970s, and none in Cambridge until 1973.[2]

Wine consumption's phenomenal growth thus underlined changing socializing patterns: in 1986 fully three-fourths of wine drinkers admitted never having visited wine bars.[3] Women, too, had less incentive for frequenting pubs since their first choice of beverage was the ubiquitous soft drink, more acceptable than cheap, unpalatable wine. More women bought wine by the bottle, readily available in supermarkets and off-licences, than draught bitter or cider. Why not then drink and entertain comfortably in their home?[4] The fashion for cooking pointed towards inviting friends in for a simple little four-course dinner, and wine seemed a natural accompaniment.

Absence of choice, quality and competitively priced wines certainly handicapped efforts to expand women's patronage in pubs. There was also the vicious circle that pubs sold relatively little wine, so an opened bottle would not be drunk fast enough to remain in good condition: either the publican had to charge for getting only three or four drinks from a bottle that should provide six, or he had to pour a couple of glasses that left people saying 'Never again'. Eventually the circle was broken when wine sold quickly so as not to spoil. Other factors equally deterred women from patronizing pubs.

Middle- and upper-class women prized a sedate atmosphere in which to eat tasty meals complemented with good-quality wine. No wonder, then that, when such women did drink outside the home, three-and-a-half times as many frequented large hotels, where amenities such as toilets reached the highest standards, as frequented ordinary pubs. Beneath them socially, women resorted to traditional pubs, followed closely by working-men's social clubs, far more often than to big hotels.[5]

Longer life expectancy and fewer children per family acted as key demographic catalysts to wine bars' rapid expansion from the late 1970s. Having reached twenty, women could now anticipate living into their mid-seventies. Two-child families became the norm, half the number born per family at the turn of the century. Both factors facilitated women's entry into the job market. So did the fact that a much larger proportion of the new jobs were regarded as open to women. Unlike their predecessors, mothers resumed work when their children began school. The proportion of women in the workforce for the twenty-five to thirty-four cohort, when they typically had pre-schoolers, rose sharply from 30 per cent early in the 1960s to almost 50 per cent within two decades. Husbands, on one hand, decided in the 1970s that the choice to work belonged to wives. Women's career prospects, on the other, improved significantly owing to their qualification for university degrees, enabling them to enter professional and scientific fields in expanding numbers. These two critical demographic changes created growing numbers of paid women workers who for the first time had both the disposable income and the freedom to establish new drinking habits.[6]

Legislation accelerated these social trends. Passed in 1970 in response to Britain's entry into the European Common Market, the Equal Pay Act made women's work better paid.[7] Several years later the Sex Discrimination Act outlawed discrimination in vital areas of education, public facilities and advertising. Finally, the Employment Protection Act, enacted also in 1975, gave motherhood legal protection in the job market: no longer could an employer either sack women for taking maternity leave or refuse them their former jobs if they returned within four months.

Globalization also engendered new drinking habits. Foreign travel introduced Britons to an entirely different drinking context, and this, together with rising incomes, encouraged eating out. Precisely how many did so is undocumented, but by 1999 over two-thirds of all British adults ate out regularly.

Demographic, legal and global developments had created a growing potential market for new drinking venues aimed specifically at women. Wine bars themselves, however, had to feature amenities appealing to this clientele.

This new subculture of drinking began with shrewd advertisement. Proprietors choose names distinguishing their wine bars from both pubs and their overwhelming male clientele. Some London wine bars adopted conventional names – Old Bottlescrew, Vats, In Vino Veritas, and Cork & Bottle – while others had proved more imaginative and gave nothing away – Catch Twenty Two, Downstairs, Frogs Legs and Loose Box. Still better as an infallible indicator of the nature of the business was to use 'wine bar' in the name. Not quite half of those in London did so in 1984, suggesting many proprietors hedged about the public's awareness of both their existence and differences with pubs.[8]

Unlike pubs, women came to wine bars, as one patron observed, to engage in 'a lot more talking than drinking'.[9] Devoid of such traditional trappings of pubs as public bars, drunkenness and stereotypic trawling prostitutes in a man's world, wine bars exorcized women's fear of insecurity, embarrassment, humiliation, and absence of what I would call 'inviolable public space'. Here, they were not 'fair game' for male attention, salacious comments and mockery. Into wine bars went no leering beer-swilling men who, as 'regulars' imposing and asserting their unwelcome masculinity, would freely hassle women. Draught beer, in fact, was rarely available in wine bars, itself a strong deterrent to men seeing these venues as logical alternatives to pubs. What women wanted most was a place where 'they don't feel they're going to have to take pot luck with the kind of people who are there'. In redefining gender boundaries, the wine bar gave them sanctuary of an unprecedented kind. They had no compunction – either alone or with company – about patronizing wine bars where owners were mindful of their customers' desires, notably privacy and anonymity in a feminine environment.[10]

The 'feminine' atmosphere as much as the beverages drew custom. Wine bars consciously targeted a professional, upwardly mobile, female clientele; many of their entrepreneurs adamantly refused to employ anyone with prior pub experience. This was the case with John Davy's Boot and Flogger, opened in Southwark in 1962, and his understanding of the emergent new female subculture of drinking explains why he owned 19 of the 250 wine bars in London alone within two decades. Julia Carpenter became the first woman to open a wine bar, Wolsey's (Fulham Road, London), in 1972. In its proprietor, purpose, attitudes, staff, and outright repudiation of the brewing industry's masculine ethos, Wolsey's typified wine bars. The unmistakable feminine culture of wine bars thus reflected large numbers of women who served either as proprietors or as members of the staff.[11]

Class status likewise fostered rapid expansion. At Motcomb's (Motcomb Street), opened in 1974 across from Sotheby's auctioneering house in Belgravia, Susie Gwyn offered her exclusive customers a sumptuous décor (including stained glass, gothic arches, historic pews and William Morris carpeting), together with cheeses flown from Paris. Winner of the wine bar of the year award in 1985, Le Metro in Knightsbridge had an authentic French atmosphere, including a wine list of some seventy French wines, all priced between £5 and £8 a bottle, and fillets of smoked goose. Even in the provinces wines bars made a mark. The Vintner in Bristol provided live piano or guitar music, and boasted a wine list of twenty, all priced under £6 a bottle. Sixteen other wines were sold by the glass. Middle- and upper-class professional women visited pubs infrequently, if at all, and even then with great reluctance; wine bars fundamentally changed their attitudes to public drinking. Unlike boozers with their traditional pronounced masculinity, wine bars provided tables and waitress service, eliminating the need for women to elbow their way through densely crowded men to place orders at bars. Wine bars, free from powerful connotations with men-only drinking, offered women a gender-neutral space in which their presence signified nothing sexually. Sharply contrasting with most pubs, wine bars ensured that 'a woman is not made to feel so "available"'. Women began patronizing wine bars with an enthusiasm that pubs had never generated, save perhaps in wartime. In retrospect, one journalist noted, wine bars 'created a whole new retail sector', and with this phenomenon 'publicans and brewers have still to come to terms'. By the mid-1980s, about one in four Britons, many of them women, were frequenting wine bars.[12]

There were other reasons why wine bars surpassed pubs as better venues for many professional women and men. High hygiene standards especially attracted women patrons. At the most exalted level, the distinguished wine merchants Corney & Barrow ran an upmarket wine bar chain in the City of London competing for well-heeled city executives. Mindful of women constituting as much as 30 per cent of the customers, the chain went so far as to install alarms in toilets, summoning staff at forty-minute intervals for an inspection, as a fail-safe method of guaranteeing hygienic standards rivalling a McDonald's outlet. To prevent busy staff from disregarding the reminder, only in the toilet areas could alarms be reset.[13] Kathryn McWhirter's *Good Wine Bar Guide* (1986) cited both wine bars' lower prices than restaurants and food, generally reliable and sometimes even superb, as compelling factors. Provincial wine bars commonly opened late, around 7.30 p.m., when patrons arrived to dine while drinking. Eating out at wine bars, however, developed slowly as a habit. In 1984 they ranked eleventh as most popular dining places, capturing just 4 per cent of the market and ranking well behind the leading venues – Chinese or Indian restaurants (29 per cent), steak restaurants (26 per cent) and pubs (25 per cent). Even hamburger restaurants and fish and chip shops enjoyed slightly bigger custom. Pubs, in contrast, still saw themselves as purveyors of alcohol, and with good reason – it still accounted for well over four-fifths of all their takings into the mid-1980s.[14]

By the late 1970s, growing numbers of wine bars appeared: one informed source estimated between five and six hundred had been opened in the country. In the next decade their numbers exploded as they captured 20 per cent of the on-licensed drinks market. Author of a guide for aspiring bar owners published

Figure 1 Growth of London wine bars, 1974–2000

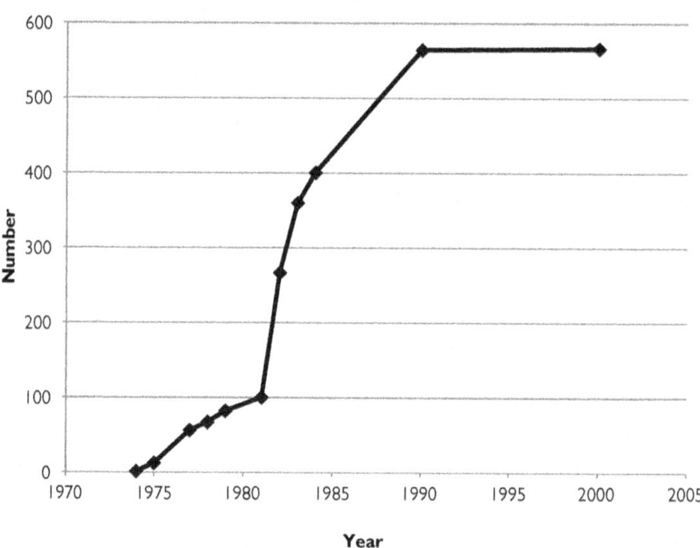

Sources: Compiled from *Post Office Directories of London*, 1974-84, and *London's Yellow Pages*, 1984-2000.

in 1984, wine proprietor Judy Ridgeway thought wine bars had more than tripled numerically in just six years. London offered impressive corroborative evidence on an even larger scale (see Figure 1).[15]

In every sense an anomaly, London attracted disproportionate numbers of wine bars, but these were far from randomly distributed. From the outset, central London held pride of place as the unofficial wine bar headquarters. 'It is the single women who have led the march to wine bars as central London pubs have found', remarked the *Economist*.[16] Accounting for between 25 per cent and 30 per cent of the capital's wine bars in the 1980s, this predominance grew to over 40 per cent a decade later. By 2000, central London dwarfed all other districts combined. In all London's other six districts, wine bars were to be found in roughly equal proportions, with the lowest numbers in the capital's south-east.[17]

Wine bar chains, primarily in London and South-east England, represented just a fraction of all wine bars. Elsewhere, two chains, physically resembling pubs, easily dwarfed them: Heneky Bars (48) and Yates Wine Lodges (35). Of the 566 wine bars in London in 2000, chains accounted for less than a quarter, with All Bar One (35) in first place, followed distantly by Pitcher & Piano (10).[18]

Pubs and wine bars were roughly distributed in the same proportions around the country. Informed estimates placed pubs as most numerous in the South (50–60 per cent), with the Midlands and Wales a distant second (20–30 per cent), and the North and Scotland last (15–25 per cent). Compared to this distribution, slightly higher numbers of wine bars were concentrated in the South (65–70 per cent), similar numbers in the North and Scotland (20–25 per cent), while fewer were found in the Midlands and Wales (10–15 per cent).[19]

Rapid growth had not changed the nature of the ownership. 'Roughly 65 per cent of the wine bars operating in Britain are single operations which are owned and run by private individuals', concluded one market research report. None of them, of course, had prior experience, at least initially, in running such establishments, and some paid dearly for this lack of expertise.[20] Of the twelve wine bars listed in the *Post Office Directory of London* in 1975, for instance, half did not survive a decade. Steady attrition continued. By 2000, just two – the City Boot (7 Moorfields High Walk, EC2) and Vats (51 Lamb's Conduit Street, WC1) – could celebrate their first quarter-century of business.[21] Whatever the uncertainties of the market, wine bar proprietors often matched the enthusiasm and educational attainment of their customers. 'A London wine bar may well be run by a university man who wants to discuss his wines as much as he wants to sell them', wrote a *New York Times* reporter.[22]

High turnover of proprietors also reflected the desire to make a killing in the marketplace. Kathryn McWhirter's *The Good Wine Bar Guide, 1986*, an authoritative compilation published by the Consumers' Association, criticized two-thirds of all wine bars for stocking 'the cheapest wines they can dredge up from the local-cash-and-carry or the latest passing rep[resentative]'. This is the fate of Horace Rumpole, who has to content himself with Chateau Fleet Street at Pommeroy's Wine Bar, near the Old Bailey, in John Mortimer's chronicles of the famous barrister. McWhirter also contended that wine bar owners and bar managers displayed woeful ignorance about wine and insouciance towards becoming better informed. This damning indictment applied to about 250 of the nearly 500 wine bars highlighted in her guide, a list of the trade's elite establishments. Two-thirds of all wine bars evaluated – some 900 – fell well below what she deemed 'good', the minimum threshold for inclusion.[23] Another national guide, prepared by the Automobile Association the previous year, stressed divergent standards of meals. 'Mass-produced quiches, so-called pâtes, and ready-prepared salads of the cole-slew variety, accompanied by a glass of anonymous and nondescript "house wine", are too often encountered'.[24]

Publicans' one standard response to these competitors – objecting to grants of new wine licences – demonstrated their unimaginative attitude to new drinking habits. Desperate publicans even tried enlisting customers on behalf of this misguided campaign, including Derek Cooper. Approached at his local to write to magistrates opposing a licence application of a new wine bar nearby, Cooper symbolized precisely why pubs had failed so miserably in selling wine. As a wine expert, he was an unlikely opponent of wine bars. Moreover, he thought so little of the wine served in his local that there he instead drank bitter![25]

'Publicans and brewers alike', complained one trade newspaper in January 1979, 'seem still to be baffled as to how to serve wine in pubs'. Instead of being chilled, white wine arrived at room temperature, and, adding insult to injury, unreasonably priced. Publicans so disliked opening a large wine bottle to obtain just a glassful that they often refused to stock it. Reliable estimates suggested that many publicans took a pragmatic approach: two of five pubs had no wine for sale.[26]

Retailers' failure to serve wine in palatable condition was striking given the *cruover*, a new French invention introduced in 1979. Now, opened wine bottles, preserved with nitrogen gas and stored in a refrigerated cabinet, enabled customers to be served wine with vastly improved flavour.[27] That this had not occurred generally was obvious to pub customers interested in ordering wine. Amid the swinging seventies, the proportion of women who visited pubs in the decade rose to 30 per cent, just a 10 per cent increase.[28]

Host of Radio Four's 'Food Programme' and author of a respected wine book, Derek Cooper wrote a devastating critique of wine in pubs published in the *Publican* in 1986. Mediocre quality, outrageous prices for cheap vintages, and inexpert staff handling – these too often described wine sales, even in his beloved local. He speculated that one reason why the brewer-tied house owner stocked such dismal wine was because 'he didn't want any competition from anything as tedious as wine'.[29] Yet, Egon Ronay's annual survey, the *Coca Cola Pub Guide*, repeatedly established that wine did not so much compete as complement beer, when served in pubs doing a brisk food trade. That just 217 pubs met Ronay's standard for inclusion in his 1990 guide underlined just how few brewers and publicans recognized this argument's validity.[30] One exception had been Whitbreads. Its wines and spirits division, Stowells of Chelsea, for instance, had provided compelling evidence a decade earlier that, with proper attention to quality and display, pub wine sales could easily increase by 200 per cent. Nothing could have been more damning to retailers than what Stowells of Chelsea's Managing Director asserted: 'There is no such thing as a pub which cannot sell wine'.[31]

Corroborative statistical evidence from across the country came in 1987. In an embarrassing *Which?* survey, 60 per cent of adults – all periodically wine drinkers – visited pubs but eschewed wine. Of the total wine market of £20 billion, customers drank £1 billion – just 5 per cent – in pubs, the same percentage as in 1980. Tied tenants were often restricted to purchasing just their lessor's wine, and so breweries could not escape responsibility for wines either of very poor quality or with unrealistic wholesale prices. Publicans, who controlled retail prices, proceeded to charge exorbitant amounts for the 'featured' white or red plonk. Inexpensive, acceptable wines could be had, said the survey, but not, significantly, in most pubs. Yuppies, the term coined that same year for young urban professionals, showed their awareness of this fact by popularizing wine bars.[32]

Admittedly, owing to EEC directives at the end of the 1980s, brewers had to release tenants, though not managers, from the tie, which should have widened wine selections. But landlords proved no more adventurous than brewers.[33] 'Nothing but the cheapest will do' characterized publicans' marketing strategy, remarked Nick Hyde, Marketing Director of W. & A. Gilbey, the wine shipping firm, in 1988. He knew this all too well from recent experience. To promote wine sales in pubs, Gilbeys had organized seminars devoted to informing landlords of what quality wines they could sell. Their response was predictable: 'We got zero interest'. This caused no surprise from Andrew Jones, wine correspondent for an independent radio station. 'Licensees', he observed, 'are not interested in wine'.[34] Indeed, the very fact that the following year

Eldridge Pope merited a story in the *Publican* substantiated this conclusion. In pioneering wine education classes for its tenants, Eldridge Pope won coveted mention for six of the brewery's pubs in *Egon Ronay Good Pub Guide*, which used sale of good wine as one of its criteria.[35]

The long-standing and previously unbeatable combination of beer and men, the mainstay of global breweries' profits from the US and UK, continued plummeting. Sales from beer accounted for 66 per cent of the overall drinks market in 1970, whereas nearly forty years later the figure had slumped to about 40 per cent. Declining beer consumption became reminiscent of levels during the Great Depression when men had earlier turned from their favourite tipple. Wine now claimed one-third of the entire alcohol beverage market.[36] So uninterested in this subject was the Brewers' Society, the industry's chief lobbying agency, that wine got no mention whatsoever in the statistics collected regularly on retail sales in pubs well into the 1990s.[37] One deterrent to enlarging the proportion of women in pubs was the pessimistic conclusion of public opinion surveys that the women's market for alcoholic beverages had crested, with growth unlikely save in wine sales. This perspective partly explains why twenty times as much wine was being consumed at home than in pubs in the 1980s. Just one-tenth of all pubs accounted for four-fifths of wine sales.[38]

Consider another example of the industry's reactionary response to consumers wanting drinkable wine in pubs. 'Many wine drinkers', maintained the *Publican Newspaper* in May 1997, 'would rather order something else in a pub, than risk being faced with a glass of cheap oxidised wine'. This was indeed incongruous, given that wine sales were booming in the off-trade, especially in supermarkets, as wine selections widened, and women had become more frequent pub patrons. Eight of ten Britons quaffed wine, but just one of ten did so in a pub. Publicans had only themselves to blame. 'They don't take wine seriously enough', complained one wholesale representative for South African wineries. The story was the same among Californian wine producers: 'There is a lot to be done before pubs become the natural home for Californian wines'. Such was the dismal image of wine offered in pubs that one big wine producer, E. & J. Gallo, fearful of besmirching its reputation, shunned this retail market altogether in the 1990s. No wonder then that wine sold in pubs remained 'very poor to the consumer', as the *Publican Newspaper* admitted.[39]

Nothing really changed in the ensuing years. Wine consumption rose sharply from 14 to 17 litres per capita between 1998 and 2003 largely owing to women, the beverage's largest consumers who drank 27 per cent more wine. Little of this higher consumption, however, occurred at pubs, where men felt inhibited about ordering wine and women were infrequent patrons. At the end of a five-year spurt in rising wine consumption, wine thus still accounted for only 11 per cent of sales in pubs.[40] Soaring wine consumption was revolutionizing drinking habits of Britons solely in the off-trade. Supermarkets and off-licences sold seven of every ten wine bottles, so customers drove this remarkable change in drinking habits.[41]

By then, too, drinkers were consuming more alcohol at home than at pubs, clubs or bars. Television, videos and compact discs were critical in encouraging drinkers to shift to home consumption, and also causing a substitution of beverages: beer became abandoned for wine, cider or spirits.[42] Wives too saw distinct advantages in staying home and drinking. Previously, when drinking out at a pub together, he selected her as a designated driver lest he lose his licence. For some wives, this meant an abstemious evening. Drinking at home allowed wives the same freedom as their husbands: they could drink without fear of violating drunken driving laws.[43]

This striking paradox of soaring wine consumption, on one hand, and stagnant wine sales in pubs, on the other, derived primarily from new women's drinking habits. Not only were women drinking more wine and doing so at home, often with husbands or male friends, but increasingly they were turning to New World wines as their first choice, with far-reaching consequences.[44]

Old World wines from France, Germany and Italy had virtually monopolized what Britons had formerly purchased, accounting for over four-fifths of the wine sold. In the mid-1990s consumers began abandoning them in ever-growing numbers for New World wines produced in Australia, and, to a lesser extent, the US, South Africa and Chile. Within less than a decade, total sales from wineries in the New World became a dominant force (41 per cent) in the UK wine market. A benchmark of a kind was reached in 2002, when for the first time Australian outsold French wines in the UK. Yet, in that same year, just half of the country's pubs stocked Australian wine.[45]

Women's enthusiasm for New World wines certainly constituted an important new consumption trend, but of greater value, at least within the drink industry, was what it represented in alcohol retailing. Market researchers attached great weight to women as consumers for two compelling reasons: their predisposition to experiment and their role as 'early adopters' of new beverages. As Bacardi Martini's Category Development Manager remarked, 'women have a wider repertoire of drinks and are more likely to try new drinks where males are more likely to default to their usual'.[46]

Wine marketed for the off-trade outsold that for the on-trade by a factor of almost four to one. Why were landlords still so unsuccessful at drawing women, the wine market's trend setters, into pubs? Historically conservative, landlords had stocked European wines from time immemorial, knew surprisingly little about New World wines and so saw every reason for discounting what may have appeared as a flash in the pan craze for exotic products. Publicans thus had no insight into how brands had come to dominate the market, making country of origin irrelevant. Unable to appreciate how wine retailing had evolved from a marketing system in which multiple Old World small players negotiated with wholesale distributors to literally a New World where a handful of companies bankrolled global brands – E. & J. Gallo, Stowells of Chelsea and Jacob's Creek – to establish market leadership, they lacked the expertise to pick wines that consumers most wanted. Consider one large Californian producer, Ernest & Julio Gallo. Its sales for off-consumption in the UK grew an astonishing 40 per cent annually in the early 2000s, catapulting it into seventh place among the country's biggest drinks brands. 'Until recently you couldn't find it in many pubs', complained *Glass*, the *Publican*'s annual wine magazine in 2002.[47]

Not surprisingly, landlords miserably showcased wine. Four of every five pubs had no displays for wine, with nearly two of the four going so far as to conceal it from customers! Compared with abundant varieties of wines stocked (and sold in steadily multiplying amounts) at supermarkets, the typical pub could seldom offer patrons more than five choices, often as few as three. Too many publicans – one of three – betrayed their real attitude in disdainfully putting two choices before customers, a red and a white wine.[48]

To lack of displays and choice, critics added a third conspicuous fault with pub wines. Remarkably few customers surveyed – just 20 per cent – were satisfied with the present range and quality of wine in pubs. A Whitbread survey (1997) discovered that 30 per cent of people spurned pub wine owing to its inferior quality, and, even more staggeringly, fully half of non-wine drinkers indicated a willingness to drink wine if landlords improved their offerings and cooled wine vintages correctly.[49]

Other marketing problems hampered sales. When stocking wines, publicans focused on percentage margins, not the more important cash margins. As a result, Kym Milne (director of the Waverley Group's wine marketing) observed in 2002 , 'you see the unfortunately still prevalent dodgy bottle of cheap French plonk with a huge mark-up sitting on the shelf gathering dust'.[50] One decade after Whitbread's survey the complaints had not changed much.

Adam Withrington, reporter for the *Publican*, quipped that wine 'sells well in pubs but it's not well sold'. Pubs, he thought, greatly benefited from the fact that wine had become a popular beverage and been successfully marketed by supermarkets. It was ironically a brewer (and wine lover), Simon Loftus, Chairman of Adnams brewery, who summarized widespread discontent with wine served in pubs. 'Two or three wines will be on offer, chosen on price not quality – and the measures will be mean, the glasses cheap, the mark-up exorbitant', he wrote in the retailers' *Morning Advertiser*.[51]

Repeatedly market research established that consumers would willingly order well-known wines in pubs at twice the prices asked at off-licences. As consumer taste became more informed, customers sought good-quality, well-known wines. Two surveys in 2001–2 established that wine drinkers knew what they wanted to consume in pubs: the exact same wines – Stowells of Chelsea and Lindemans, for example – that they quaffed at home, even if this meant landlords charged more than supermarkets, the most competitively priced wine retailers.[52] Landlords ironically dreaded the consequences of carrying well-known wines. 'Pubs', grumbled Graham Donald (Matthew Clark Wholesale), 'avoided listing any wines that could easily be found in supermarkets or off-licences because of the fear that consumers would compare prices and complain at the large on-trade mark up'. Notwithstanding this expanding lucrative sector of the drinks market, two-thirds and more of the wine sold still came from supermarkets.[53]

Landlords as much as brewing executives proved unable to adapt to a new, evolving marketing environment. Wine sales fared badly in pubs simply because many publicans, in part in response to breweries that insisted their tied houses give primacy to beer, retained strong antipathy towards other alcoholic beverages than beer. Drawn overwhelmingly from the lower middle and middle class, landlords had deep-seated prejudices themselves against wine as a toff's drink, served to the propertied classes in restaurants, private social clubs and wine bars, more suited for women and pansies than real men. Here they shared the prejudices of some male customers, who, commented a Mintel Senior Market Analyst in 2005, 'feel there is still a stigma attached to drinking wine down the pub or in a [working-men's social] club'.[54]

In their defence, landlords confronted powerful social norms which deterred many men from switching from beer to wine when drinking with wives or female companions in pubs. Drinking at home, in contrast, left men free to consume wine with women. There were the long-standing related problems too of range and quality. Home consumption, said John Band, author of

Datamonitor's 2003 report, 'allows people a much wider choice of wine, which is important, given the limited and often unpalatable wine selection available in many pubs'.[55] Red wine, chiefly drunk by men in pubs, was more often served in an inferior state than white, typically consumed by women. Hence, men expected the worst wine in pubs, and so ordered lager. By 2008, escalating wine consumption in Britain was predicted to place it second only to France as a global consumer of the fermented grape.[56]

Brewers as much as retailers failed repeatedly to incorporate wine and women into the male subcultures of drinking in public houses, leaving condescending stereotypes of females intact with disastrous results for retailing alcohol. Even before the Thatcher government's intervention against the tied house system late in the 1980s, the opening of wine bars had challenged the old brewing order sustaining a masculine culture in pubs and working-class clubs. The end result was not just the founding of wine bars but their steady expansion, helped by the brewing industry's feeble responses to yet another competitor more adept at selling women an alcoholic product than public houses.

Notes

1 Richard Weight, *Patriots: National Identity in Britain, 1940–2000* (London: Macmillan, 2002), pp. 652–3; John Burnett, *Liquid Pleasures: A Social History in Modern Britain* (London: Routledge, 1999), p. 156; *Publican Newspaper*, 19 May 1997.

2 Burnett, *Liquid Pleasures*, p. 154; compiled from *Kelley's Directories: Cambridge*, 1960–75; *Oxford*, 1972–6; *Chichester, Edinburgh and Glasgow*, 1974–78. MORI, *Public Attitudes to Pubs and Leisure* (June 1984), p. 20; Acumen Marketing Group Ltd, *A Report on the British Market for Food in Pubs and Wine Bars* (London: Acumen Marketing Group, March 1978), p. 4.

3 Mintel Market Research Survey, quoted in *Publican*, 23 Jan. 1986.

4 Adam Tinworth, 'Be Irresistible to Women', *Publican*, 3 July 1995; MORI, *Public Attitudes to Pubs* (June 1984), p. 50.

5 MORI, *Public Attitudes to Pubs* (June 1984), p. vii; Interscan, Ltd, *Attitude Survey on Pub Going Habits and Brewery Control and Ownership of Public Houses* (Aug. 1970), p. 13. This was a rare survey that analysed class, age, gender and types of drinking establishments.

6 Deidre McCloskey, 'Paid Work', in Ina Zweiniger-Bargielowska (ed.), *Women in Twentieth-Century Britain* (Harlow: Pearson Education Limited, 2001), pp. 168–70.

7 Heather E. Joshi, Richard Layard and Susan J. Owen, 'Why Are More Women Working in Britain?', *Journal of Labor Economics*, 3 (1985), pp. S147–76.

8 *Post Office Directory of London*, 1980 and 1984.

9 Barbara Rogers, *Men Only: An Investigation into Men's Organizations* (London: Pandora, 1988), pp. 10–11.

10 Ibid., p. 18; John Arlott, 'Clearly Women's Bibulous Rights Are Respected – Except, Perhaps in Pubs', *Guardian*, 29 Jan. 1982.

11 Chris Middleton, 'Why Women Can Go for a Drink without Feeling the Pinch', *Guardian*, 27 July 1982; Beryl Hartland, 'At Last, Places for the Women Who Hate Pubs', *Daily Telegraph*, 19 June 1974.

12 Middleton, 'Drink without Feeling the Pinch'; Christian Davis, 'Sales Fall as Fewer Visit Pub', *Publican*, 13 Sept. 1984; Hartland, 'Women Who Hate Pubs'; Mintel Market Research Survey, quoted in the *Publican*, 23 Jan. 1986; Ben Davis, *The Traditional English Pub: A Way of Drinking* (London: Architectural Press, 1981), p. 83; Rogers, *Men Only*, p. 15; *Bistros, Inns and Wine Bars in Britain* (Basingstoke: Automobile Association, 1985), pp. 8–9.

13 *Publican*, 4 July 1994.

14 Judy Ridgeway, *Running Your Own Wine Bar* (London: Kogan Page, 1984), p. 8; Kathryn McWhirter, *The Good Wine Bar Guide, 1986* (London: Consumers' Association, 1985), p. 8; Lorna Harrison, 'Those Were the Days', *Publican*, 25 Sept. 2000; MORI, *Public Attitudes to Pubs* (June 1984), p. 68.

15 Acumen Marketing Group Ltd, *Food in Pubs and Wine Bars*, p. 4; Ridgeway, *Running Your Own Wine Bar*, p. 74. Wide discrepancies exist between Post Office directories and yellow pages in London. Some wine bars chose not to advertise in the latter in the 1970s, but early in the 1980s wine bar proprietors made this publication their listing of choice, though some remained loyal to Post Office directories. In 1984 the *Post Office Directory of London* listed 185 wine bars, compared with the 400 in *London's Yellow Pages* (calculated from *Post Office Directories of London*, 1975–84, and *London's Yellow Pages*, 1975–84).

16 'Time Again, Gentlemen', *Economist*, 16 April 1988.

17 Calculated from *Post Office Directories of London*, 1974–84, and from *London Yellow Pages*, 1984–2000; Acumen Marketing Group Ltd, *Food in Pubs and Wine Bars*, p. 20.

18 Calculated from the *London Yellow Page Directory*, 2000–2.

19 Acumen Marketing Group Ltd, *Food in Pubs and Wine Bars*, p. 21.

20 Ibid., pp. 15, 20–1.

21 *Post Office Directory of London*, 1975 and 1984; *Directory of London Yellow Pages, 2000*.

22 Frank J. Prial, 'A London Awash in Wine Bars', *New York Times*, 2 Dec. 1987.

23 McWhirter, *Good Wine Bar Guide, 1986*, pp. 7–8; John Mortimer, *Rumpole of the Bailey* (1978; rept edn, Harmondsworth: Penguin Books, 1980), pp. 103, 106.

24 *Bistros, Inns and Wine Bars*, p. 7.

25 Derek Cooper, 'I Like Pubs, but ...', *Publican* (*Pub Wine Supplement*), 13 Nov. 1986.

26 Davis, 'Sales Fall'; Katharine Whitehorn, 'Mixing Their Drinkers', *Observer*, 1963. In that same year, Showerings sought to exploit increasing women's demands for good but inexpensive wine by introducing four small wine bottles, each capable of filling the standard wine glass (*Publican*, 25 Jan. 1979).

27 Roger Protz, 'Suffolk Surprise', *Publican* (*Pub Wine Supplement*), 13 Nov. 1986. Cabinets were, however, relatively expensive, costing £4280 for a single compartment and £4590 for a double compartment. Each compartment held ten wine bottles.

28 MORI survey, published in the *Brewing Review*, Jan. 1986.
29 Cooper, 'I Like Pubs, but …'.
30 *Publican*, 23 Sept. 1989. To earn inclusion, pubs had to serve four acceptable good-quality wines of varying styles.
31 *Publican*, 11 Sept. 1980.
32 Ibid.; 'Wine in Pubs', *Which?*, June 1987, pp. 266–8; Christian Davis, 'Price and Quality Turns Wine Drinkers Off Pubs', *Publican*, 11 June 1987; Christopher Pope, 'Everywhere but the Pub', *Publican*, Autumn 1988; Jetske van Westering, 'Developments in UK Pub Wine Sales: Responses to Growing Public Consumption of Wine', *International Journal of Wine Marketing*, 5 (1993), pp. 35–41; Harrison, 'Those Were the Days'.
33 Lewis Ragbourn, 'Poor Wine not the Brewers' Fault', *Publican*, 22 July 1989.
34 *Publican*, 14 April 1988.
35 Pope, 'Everywhere but the Pub'. Young's Brewery aggressively promoted licensee training programmes a decade later with astonishingly successful results (F. Sims, 'Clare to Be Different', *Morning Advertiser*, 5 Aug. 2004).
36 Zoe Wood, 'Sinking Brewers Aim to Give Women a Taste of Beer', *Observer*, 20 July 2008.
37 Westering, 'UK Pub Wine Sales', pp. 35–41.
38 *Publican*, 11 Sept. 1980; R. Mansukhani, *The Pub Report: British Pubs in the 1980s* (London: Euromonitor, 1985); *UK Market for Beers, Wine and Spirits to 1990*, quoted in Rogers, *Men Only*, pp. 13–14.
39 *Publican Newspaper*, 19 May 1997; *Publican*, 15 Nov. 1999; also see Peter Martin, 'The Best of Britain's Pub Wines', *Publican*, 28 March 1994.
40 Mintel Survey, quoted in Adam Withrington, 'Men: Drink More Wine', *Publican*, 14 Feb. 2005; John Harrington, 'Report Links Women to Surge in Pub Wine Sales', *Morning Advertiser*, 7 Oct. 2004.
41 'Pub Wine Matures', *Glass: The Publican Newspaper Wine Magazine for 2002*, p. 11.
42 Mintel surveys, quoted in the *Publican*, 28 Jan. and 4 Feb. 2002. In 2003, home drinking accounted for 43 per cent of the total drinks market.
43 Arlott, 'Women's Bibulous Rights'.
44 Harrington, 'Surge in Pub Wine Sales'.
45 'Pub Wine Matures', p. 11; 'Grape Expectations', *Glass: The Publican Newspaper Wine Magazine for 2003*, p. 9.
46 Sally Bairstow, *Morning Advertiser*: 'The Female Drinker', 19 June 2003, and 'Increase Your Pulling Power', 19 June 2003.
47 'Pub Wine Matures', *Glass, 2002*, pp. 7–11.
48 John Harrington, 'Report Links Women to Surge in Pub Wine Sales', *Morning Advertiser*, 7 Oct. 2004; 'Grape Expectations', pp. 8–11; John D. Pratten and Jean-Baptiste Carlier, 'Wine Sales in British Public Houses', *International Journal of Wine Business Research*, 22 (2010), p. 65.
49 Whitbread Inns' Wine Drinking Survey Conducted by Audience Selection, quoted in *Publican*, 19 May 1997.
50 Claudia Dowell, 'Grape Expectations', *Publican Newspaper*, 19 May 1997; Kym Milne, 'Grape Expectations', *Glass: The Publican Newspaper Wine Magazine for*

2002, p. 5.

51 Adam Withrington, 'With a Bit of Effort…', *Publican*, 1 Oct. 2007; Simon Loftus, 'Why It Pays to Be Generous', *Morning Advertiser*, 23 May 2002.

52 Dowell, 'Grape Expectations'; 'Pub Wine Matures', *Glass, 2002*, p. 11; *Morning Advertiser Wine Supplement*, 4 April 2002.

53 *Glass: The Publican Newspaper Wine Magazine for 2003*, pp. 7, 9; Leonardo Casini, Alessio Cavicchi and Armando Maria Corsi, 'Trends in the British Wine Market and Consumer Confusion', *British Food Journal*, 110 (2008), p. 548.

54 MORI, *Public Attitudes to Pubs and Leisure* (June 1984), pp. 48–9; 'Grape Expectations', *Glass: The Publican Newspaper Wine Magazine for 2003*, p. 7; Mintel Survey, quoted in Withrington, 'Men: Drink More Wine'.

55 Harrington, 'Surge in Pub Wine Sales'.

56 Withrington, 'Men: Drink More Wine'.

7

Men are from Mars, women from Venus: understanding the psychology of selling alcohol in the 1980s–90s

Ben Davis, licensed estate design consultant with Allied Breweries for some thirty years from 1949, epitomized the reactionary attitudes of many in the brewing industry to wine bars' explosive growth. According to his convoluted diagnosis, modernized pubs had lost business owing to their becoming more like wine bars, which had in turn gained custom by mimicking traditional pubs. To these trends he pointed as evidence of why 'a good proportion of the wine trade bar trade consists of people who would marginally prefer to drink beer or spirits, but cannot find in a convenient pub the sort of atmosphere they prefer'. However much the physical layout of pubs changed in the 1970s, their interiors endured largely unchallenged, much to Davis's satisfaction.[1]

As design consultant for a national brewery for thirty years, Davis played an influential but unacknowledged role in perpetuating the industry's masculine drinking culture in pubs, which alienated numerous potential female patrons. 'Feminine décorations', he sneered, 'can only succeed in a pub when the commercial attention … is to cater deliberately for an available trade of homosexual males'. He relished his status as an unregenerate curmudgeon, and remorselessly reiterated his unshakeable belief in brown as the colour for public and saloon bars. Nothing else for him would do. Any attempt at feminizing the environment with curtains, cushions or flowers he regarded with anathema. 'What brings women customers into a pub', he intoned, 'is either the men themselves or the masculine atmosphere'. Even after he retired, Davis remained steadfastly opposed to altering the masculine atmospheres of pubs, which he still regarded as a powerful factor attracting female customers. Nearly three years later he could still be found stridently denouncing introduction of drapes, carpets, cushions and overall 'lush furnishings' as responsible for transforming pubs into 'poofs' parlours', a development which had driven beer drinkers into wine bars.[2]

His influence at Ind Coope and later Allied Breweries cannot easily be exaggerated. Personally, he designed numerous pubs not just in England but in the Netherlands and Belgium. As an architect, he was responsible for the Hotel Leofric (Coventry), the first principal hotel erected after the Second World War. As a teacher, he conceived a series of courses on pub interiors, taken by those within the Allied Breweries Group. In his dust jacket notes, he argued that through his teaching 'the influence of work carried out on the same principles [as his own]' had a discernible impact on British pub interiors. But his philosophy extended into the broader reaches of the industry. In 1981, the prestigious Architectural Press published his lengthy book, *The Traditional English Pub: A Way of Drinking*, which summarized his ideas. Another indicator of respect, though not agreement, was the willingness of the *Publican*, the leading retail newspaper, to print several of his articles and letters. Finally, other major trade periodicals, notably the *A Monthly Bulletin* and *Interior Design*, lent credibility by publishing many of his articles. Because Davis was a major figure in formulating the culture of drinking in postwar Britain, conservative breweries had no incentive for reappraising their approach to selling alcohol.[3]

Critics assailed such views as curmudgeonly, 'trying to drag us down into a tyrannic fantasy of dark brown snubs'. To them, Davis and his supporters pursued an appalling goal: 'They want to sink down into a dark brown hell'. Davis had invited this criticism, confessing that he would be 'very happy in a totally brown pub'. Even a reporter for the retailers' newspaper, the *Publican*, implicitly rebuked Davis. Brightly coloured, well-ventilated bars, together with transparent entrance windows – all borrowed from the experiences of wine bars – offered the way to generating wider female custom, contended Peter Martin. Neither Davis nor the brewing industry had apparently learned anything from wine bars' remarkable appeal. 'Wine bar owners have come from nowhere into the licensed trade and created a whole new retail sector', wrote one reporter in 1984. 'The market', he added, 'is there and publicans and brewers have still to come to terms with it'.[4]

Whether in consumer products or interior décorations, subsequent consumer research discovered, women clearly saw light, bold (primary) colours with elaborate exterior designs and curved lines as powerful attractions, whereas men 'preferred straight, rectilinear shapes, darker colours and plain surfaces'. Marketers and advertisers had to be heedful of these differences if seeking to woo the female customer. 'The more they consider the gender of the audience and creator as part of their communications process, the more likely they are to be effective', commented Iain Ellwood, widely known as an authority on branding who headed Consulting at Interbrand.[5] Some entrepreneurs outside the brewing industry understood this observation. Jonathan Downey, a young (thirty-four) corporate lawyer, determined to establish adult entertainment featuring cocktails, superb wines and food, and club nights, established a pubco, Matchbar. MatchEC1, the first of the chain, opened in London in 1997. When he hired Dick Bradsell as consultant, the latter's first remark showed enormous insight into the psychology of retailing: 'You've got no red in here, women won't come'. Accepting this as a truism, Downey made red a standard colour of at least one wall in all his bars. He was not disappointed with the result. Within four years, the chain's three bars were generating £4 million annually, and, to the envy of adherents of the old brewing culture, had a gender split of 65–70 per cent women, 30–35 per cent men.[6]

In the 1960s–70s, the emergent field of environmental psychology established that individuals did react to the nature of the built environment, and that this awareness in turn would affect their behaviour in that setting.[7] But the next step in research, demonstrating environmental influences on consumption habits, came a decade or two later. These studies, though extremely suggestive, generated little interest in the field of marketing until the late 1980s. What had considerably wider implications, as one leading scholar realised, was research showing that 'recurring social behavior patterns are associated with particular physical settings and that when people encounter typical settings, their social behaviors can be predicted'. Even minimal alterations in the built environment had discernible impact on behaviour.[8]

While not specifically directed at marketing alcohol, these findings did much to explain many women's antipathy to visiting traditional pubs, and offered a strong rejoinder to Ben Davis's homophobic, sexist and antiquated views of public drinking. For women, the physical layout, colours, décor and furnishings characterizing conventional pubs evoked deep-seated, powerful emotions against invading male space. No seats, Spartan furnishings, smoky atmospheres, thick crowds, dreary or dull colors, noisy music, standup drinking and much physical movement – all these smacked unmistakably of men-only places, with 'high-load environments'. Embedded in the built environment of traditional pubs were also cues enabling women to predict whether they would be emotionally and physically comfortable using the drinking premises. Women, studies of drinking learned, heartily disliked shabby, dark surroundings, redolent of heavy drinking monopolized by males. In fact, research on environmental psychology discovered that strong feelings about the built environment could also be transmitted to products consumed there. Hence, women's dislike of the traditional pub environment could also create prejudice against beer consumption.[9]

In determining where to drink, women viewed the environment as outranking virtually everything, from the type of beverages served to whether they accompanied male companions. Women pre-eminently wanted a venue wholly different from what men prized. 'Low-load environments' – soft colours, muted lights, simplicity, little noise, dispersed customers in stable surroundings – all suggested female-friendly venues. Outside, they valued pubs which looked more like cafés and restaurants: readily accessible parking areas, gardens and vast windows allowing unobstructed views within and without. Inside, they sought pubs where they could socialize and eat while seated comfortably in neat, radiantly light rooms. Not surprisingly, they preferred pubs with female-friendly environments – flowers and plants, attractive décor and smaller drinking areas – everything Davis passionately loathed. In attracting women as customers, 'cleanliness is paramount', observed Allied Domecq's Marketing Manager, late in the 1990s, years after Davis had retired.[10]

Women drinkers dreaded three features of traditional pubs. Vast undifferentiated open spaces inside the front door made it 'very difficult to walk in on your own', and created a sense of vulnerability, with males propping up the bar and gazing at newcomers who instinctively felt like intruders. Once seated, women confronted another unnerving aspect of pubs, the male phalanx serving as sentinels around the bar, who symbolically blocked access to unwanted (female) drinkers. Taller and more aggressive men also put women at a disadvantage. So did well-understood pub etiquette which ordained that bar staff grant male regulars priority in getting served. Bar staff and proprietors, frequently men, unwittingly excluded women by displaying camaraderie with male regulars, sometimes making females the butt of male humour. Unable to hear soft-spoken women in a noisy bar, staff would chide them: 'Speak up love or you'll die of thirst in here'. Nearby men would jeer at such witticism, mortifying the women. Finally, women disliked sitting alone at tables, fearful of being mistaken as either prostitutes or on the prowl for men. 'Aspects of the physical environment', wrote two scholars specializing in marketing research, 'serve as signals denoting the predominance of either the traditional male or the more socially-oriented female view of pubs'. More succinctly, drink wholesalers and retailers could target female customers with a radically different physical environment in public house premises. Reconstructed, rebuilt or new pubs could substitute circular or U-shaped bars for those with long, straight counters, reducing the impact of men's overpowering presence. Pubs also needed to embrace many of the trappings of restaurants along continental lines, where huge transparent windows at entrances and gardens in the back, together with plants, flowers, tables, chairs and gardens inside, all projected an image that women could easily decode as female-friendly. Etched glass, obscuring vision of the pub interior and emblematic of the enduring Victorian masculine republic, disappeared.[11]

But the environment encompassed more than physical surroundings. Bar staff assumed a key role in allaying women's anxieties about public drinking with a new bar etiquette in which customers were treated with the same familiarity as regulars, and received equal respect as well as treatment regardless of gender. Where bar layout could not easily be altered, women could avoid male attention and physical obstruction at the bar, on one hand, and enjoy 'a positive bar experience', on the other, by ordering through a waitress.[12]

Anticipating this research and its important findings, several outsiders rejected the sterile attitudes of conventional drinking and instead grasp the possibilities of a changing market, vividly demonstrated by the wine bar revolution. Nobody did more to redefine the culture of public drinking in the late twentieth century than Tim Martin and Crispin Tweddle, two entrepreneurs who not only shared ambition and business acumen but recognized the commercial potential of another group of outsiders, women. Martin and Tweddle, far from responding to new drinking habits in pubs, created an entirely new subculture of drinking through innovative integration of space, materials, colour, services, staff and amenities. They pioneered the emergence of pubcos, chains of pubs owned by a company that had no brewing interests and, as a result, no reason to concentrate on beer in selling services. This novel approach to liquor retailing, recalled the *Publican*, brought 'new ideas and concepts specifically attractive to women and families'.[13] These men's careers, ideas and assumptions must be viewed in the light of subsequent market research, which drew on the new field of environmental psychology, exploring women's attitudes towards drinking. What Martin and Tweddle intuitively sensed about women would be validated later by numerous academic studies in the 1990s.

With funds from the sale of several flats and his father's inheritance, Tim Martin, a twenty-four-year old solicitor wholly inexperienced in retailing alcohol, bought a small pub in Muswell Hill, North London, one of the most unpropitious areas for experimenting with retailing alcohol, in 1979. This pub inaugurated J. D. Wetherspoon, a pubco that would top seven hundred pubs thirty years later. Unafraid of being unconventional, he purchased another pub, Tanners Hall, Stoke Newington, near the site of a recent race riot, in 1983. With the pub transformed by Martin's philosophy, beer sales tripled in less than a decade, rising from 450 to 1500 barrels annually. Soon, he would add another component to the mix: a range of discounted real ales, a boon to CAMRA members. This commitment, as one reporter recollected, 'became a key driver of business in the 1980s'.[14]

Fifteen of his pubs would be named or renamed The Moon under Water, Martin's personal tribute to George Orwell's mythical but ideal pub recorded in a 1946 essay which inspired much of the Wetherspoon philosophy. From Orwell, Martin would come to see the critical importance of making the pub's environment the paramount consideration, even over the beer. Customers, reflected John Hutson, Wetherspoon Managing Director, 'wouldn't choose a Wetherspoon if it had dirty toilets, rude staff and dirty tables. It's our core values that lead to success'.[15] No music, no television, no pub games, no smoking at the bar, inexpensive but good wines, hot food throughout the day and a good selection of discounted but superbly served cask-conditioned beers – these would come to characterize his approach to retailing, making Martin a maverick in the industry, and soon a multimillionaire in society. Like Orwell, Martin prized conversation, and so banned music; like Orwell, Martin regarded good food as an essential ingredient to a sociable pub; and finally like Orwell, Martin saw the pub as a family venue with fathers, mothers and children transforming the atmosphere. Licensing laws had rendered this difficult but not impossible to achieve. Hence, Orwell attached great weight to a garden. 'It allows whole families to go there instead of Mum having to stay at home and mind the baby while Dad goes out alone', he shrewdly observed.[16]

For Martin, as for his iconoclastic interwar predecessors, the interwar brewer pub improvers, gardens loomed large as key factors in environmentalism, an attitude in which changes in the environment could promote sobriety, respectable behaviour and safe places to consume alcohol. Almost as if borrowing the text of a speech from interwar pub improvers, Martin argued that 'customers' behaviour seems to be better in an environment where food is being served, even if they do not consume food themselves'. Just over a decade after he started his chain, Martin, ever the iconoclast, introduced food throughout the day, save for the last hour, the first pubco to adopt this approach. Food, of course, had been widely understood since the First World War to delay the metabolism of alcohol, reducing the likelihood of drunkenness, but the drive to promote catering had faltered sharply from the 1950s. Ultimately, Martin would come to articulate another controversial stance, the entire banning of smoking in all pubs. Inside the industry, this heretical idea provoked fierce opposition, as wholesalers and retailers foretold plummeting sales. Food and smoking atmospheres, he contended, were interrelated. Smoke-free environments 'made pubs more attractive to diners and this has played a part of the big increase in our food sales', Martin maintained. Approaching the goal of sobriety from another direction altogether, he became a strong advocate of security cameras in pubs as a restraint on drunkenness, and voluntarily installed CCTVs in the entire chain at considerable cost. This same logic prompted his banning of alcopops, happy hours and incentive drinking, such as specials advertising two beverages for the price of one, all of them associated in his mind with fostering irresponsible drinking, potential violent behaviour and unseemly conduct. Like the interwar brewer pub improvers, Martin assiduously sought respectable, moderate drinking. Martin, though he never spoke of it himself, would doubtless have subscribed to their movement's slogan: 'We do not want people to drink more beer – we want more people to drink beer'. That distinction still powerfully underlined differences between him and so many contemporaries in the trade.[17]

Repudiating the prevailing strategy of market segmentation, in which brewers designed pubs specifically targeting one group, whether the young, middle-aged, families or students, Martin thought of the pub as part of a broader community encompassing everyone regardless of age, gender, occupation, class or ethnicity. Market research had informed this attitude, confirming that pubs catering primarily to young drinkers had far more behavioural problems. Music, integral to youth drinking culture, was likewise banned as a strategy for deterring the young from dominating a pub's clientele.[18]

Though averse to focusing on one specific drinking group, Martin deliberately sought far more women as a proportion of his overall clientele than at traditional pubs. Like interwar pub improving brewers, he had become convinced that 'the presence of both sexes can have a beneficial effect on behaviour'. Critical to attracting women was the introduction of a pseudo-Victorian entrance, with large transparent windows. 'Women in particular, we've found, like to be able to check out a pub's clientele before deciding to enter', noted the chain's chief designer, Shuna Le Moine. Once inside, women could find booths, providing additional privacy. Because Wetherspoon's pubs prohibited barstools (and later smoking) at the bars, men did not congregate there, allowing women to order themselves without feeling intimidated. This strategy became the prototype of other non-traditional bar chains. Wetherspoons, however, carried the female-friendly philosophy one step further. In its pubs, females would have been just as likely to order from women as from men, again reducing the gender barrier at the sales nexus. To create a sales rapport between customer and staff, Martin had cash registers set into the bar, facing forward and so facilitating eye contact when ordering. In pouring beverages from a bottle, staff were instructed to display plainly the label.[19]

Wetherspoon also borrowed ideas from McDonald's as well as Marks and Spencer: public premises ought to have clean and hygienic lavoratories of the highest standards. Mindful of market research, Martin had come to see impeccable toilets as a key attractor of women. As one Wetherspoon manager remarked shrewdly, 'a lot of women will judge a pub on how clean the toilets are'. Men, too, came to dislike disgraceful toilet conditions: poor hygiene repelled two of five potential pub goers, according to a 1996 industry survey. For this reason, high hygienic standards in toilets – ensured with hourly inspections, an idea inspired by TGI (Thank God It's) Friday – became a trademark. Still more compelling evidence of the vital importance of toilet hygiene emerged. Women, Wetherspoon research revealed, had come to see the quality of the loos as the *chief determinant* in selecting a pub. No other consideration proved more critical in dooming a pub as a possible venue for a night out than dismal toilets. Peter Martin, in the *Observer*, deemed the JDW loos worthy of 'royal-visit standard'. Repeatedly, one of his pubs won 'loo of the year' for the entire country, an achievement in which Martin took as much pride as offering a diverse range of discounted beers. As the company evolved, Wetherspoon loos became still more impressive, costly and sumptuous. Martin could allocate as much as £20,000–£30,000 to producing first-rate toilet facilities, including sofas and lounging areas. One of the leading experts in the area, Gerard McElvenny, specialized in designing interiors for the leisure industry. 'It's a typical rule that if a place has nice toilets', he explained, 'it will bring in the women to use them, and … then the men are not far behind'.[20]

McDonald's, together with Marks and Spencer, equally inspired Martin because of their dominant presence among London's High Street retailers, one key area of intense competition where he himself wanted to become a powerful player. By converting shops, banks, cinemas, theatres and even an opera house into pubs, he would obtain vital High Street sites facilitating his applications for new licences. Through this strategy, he was conscious of 'invading a monopoly' of liquor retailing, with all the characteristic hallmarks – high prices, poor service and little investment in retail premises.[21] Martin, like interwar brewers, though on a vastly larger scale, purchased sites before obtaining licences. As Wetherspoon expanded, the pipeline of sites awaiting licensing stretched to some three hundred, with just a handful annually being developed after receiving licenses. This upstart in the industry provoked intense opposition, as breweries and soon pubcos mobilized forces to thwart him. Yet, in offering local inhabitants greater choice, better service, lower prices and décor superior to surrounding pubs, Martin sought licences from a powerful position. And, as a trained solicitor, he invariably won: of the first twenty licensing applications, for example, Martin, who had intensely researched each location, succeeded in all but one. But, as he himself acknowledged, there were enormous costs to expansion: instead of each application costing £20,000, opponents raised the outlay appreciably from £50,000 to £100,000.[22]

Capitalizing on outlets situated on the High Street, Martin transformed them into a hybrid pub, restaurant and coffee house. Aware of the lure of coffee houses to women, he consciously catered to their tastes with cappuccino, espresso and lattes, often including chocolate muffins and other delectable sweets, at rock-bottom prices. Banished were emblematic signs of the traditional boozers – dartboards, televisions, music and scruffy carpets. Instead of traditional pub furniture, he introduced comfortable sofas, fresh flowers and lustrous wood panelling.[23] By 2004, in its list of the industry's key personalities, the *Morning Advertiser* ranked Martin first for the third consecutive year because he 'has shaped the high street in his own image. JD Wetherspoon's super-sized pubs came to dominate every town and city in the UK during the 1990s'.[24]

Whether in promoting 'state-of-the-art air filtration' systems to remove smoke, proposing a total ban on smoking which outraged the industry, championing first-rate hygienic toilets or introducing all-day food (and later inexpensive breakfasts from 9 a.m. at £1.99), Wetherspoon justly earned the reputation as a pace setter, the pubco spearheading the industry's most innovative changes Within less than thirty years, Martin fulfilling his ambition had matched his competitors on the High Street. Of all the eating outlets, Wetherspoon ranked second only to McDonald's in popularity. Just Starbucks and the four dominant fast-food chains had better visibility than JDW. No other pub or restaurant group had higher brand recognition than Wetherspoon. Central to this success were his focus on meals and women as customers. 'Wetherspoon's', wrote the Peach Factory 2008 Survey, 'is now the second most popular eating-out destination in the country, on a par with KFC and ahead of Subway, Pizza Hut, Burger King and Starbucks'. Reminiscing about the *Publican*'s first twenty-five years of publication in 2005, its editor paid Martin the ultimate accolade, characterizing him as 'the founding father of the modern pub' and the inventor of the multiple chains. Another reporter recognized him as 'the first independent to have made it big-time in pubs'. But none of these tributes really matched in importance a poll of senior industry executives and licensees in 2005 in which Martin was placed first 'as the individual from the pub trade who has made the biggest impact on the industry in the past 30 years'.[25]

Breaking with regular practice in the trade in another area, Martin hired two managers, each working alternating shifts as a tactic for ensuring cleanliness and first-rate service. Finally, after finding that cigarette smoke killed plants and flowers in the pubs, Martin eventually perfected air ducts for removing smoke, and feminized the environment by reintroducing flowers.[26]

Another unheralded visionary, Crispin Tweddell, equally sensed how he might position his pubs between wine bars, with their calculated appeal to women, and pseudo-traditional pubs, the industry's attempt to rediscover the past to bolster flagging profits. When he established Pitcher & Piano, one of the first pubcos specifically aimed at introducing what would soon be called 'female-friendly' venues, he drew heavily from ideas outside the industry. Trained in business at Manchester University, he became associated with several companies specializing in design consultancy, and gained investment capital from a health food chain and shoe shop, before founding Pitcher & Piano in 1986. Brewers, he saw, had nothing to offer young, middle-class professionals, especially women, in their twenties and late thirties who, as Tweddell's Managing Director observed, 'go to bars to meet people and have a good time with friends'. Women disliked pubs for numerous reasons: queuing for drinks with men at the bar while awaiting service from an irascible barman; the overpowering masculinity of dark furnishings, with high tabletops and uncomfortable chairs; and repulsive toilets, dirty, dingy and devoid of mirrors.[27] There was another powerful deterrent for females. 'We realized that a woman on her own waiting to meet a friend would rarely go into a pub', recollected Duncan Watts, co-founder of Pitcher & Piano. Recent market research had identified collusion between male customers and male landlords as vitally important too. 'Women customers', stated the *Mintel Report on Alcoholic Drinks* in 1982, 'were frequently subjected to unwanted male advances without any kind of intervention or protection from the landlord'.[28]

Turning the received wisdom about pub design on its head, Tweddell and Watts offered the pub 'as a house open to the public rather than as a place to show off, in the gin palace sense which has made all the running recently', asserted reporter Deyan Sudjic in *The Times*. Pitcher & Piano's philosophy pivoted on transforming the bar area into a female-friendly environment, without alienating men with feminized décor. Tweddell broke with tradition in employing a female design consultant, Sarah Ward, to create 'a home from home' atmosphere in the outlets, with one design called 'home by the fire' employing the traditional table and chair. Instead of seeking to attract customers with superior décoration, as commonly embraced in the brewing industry in the 1950s–70s, Ward opted for furnishings typical in middle-class homes. But she unhesitatingly rejected British furniture companies which refused to modify chair design and so went abroad to the US for supplies. All furniture and fittings were simple but appealing, with sofas handmade and solid light oak used for tables and chairs. Interiors thus bespoke quality, without tacky artificial, inexpensive veneers or plywood.[29]

Tweddle knew his market well. 'Toilets', a *Publican* reporter confirmed, 'are excellent; well spaced and appointed, large mirrors and spotlessly maintained'. He also introduced table service owing to women's prior experience with eating out at restaurants and sandwich bars. With this amenity, virtually unknown at pubs, he also appealed to women in two other ways: women needed no longer fear being hassled by male customers or rude barmen; and he projected an image as an entirely different type of venue, one which violated trade norms in openly seeking female patrons, unlike national breweries.[30] Fresh cut flowers, together with newspapers and magazines read by professionals, likewise characterized outlets. Staff, dressed to company standard, greeted customers. Tweddle anticipated later consumer research that pointed to the role of the staff as critical in creating a safe female-friendly environment, free of bouncers.[31]

Andrew Bonnell, Tweddell's Managing Director, had served an apprenticeship with John Lewis, Allied Domecq and Nigel Ward, owner of a pubco. He made shrewd staff recruitment integral to the concept, another point of departure from the industry. Bonnell chose people with the same socio-economic background as the customers they served: young (twenties and thirties), intelligent, primarily women, middle-class, well paid and incentive-driven. These traits came to typify other female-friendly venues, embodying the assumption, as one manager later said, that 'women will feel more at home with like-minded staff'. About staff requirements Bonnell certainly had no doubts. 'We want qualities not normally found in the catering trade', he asserted. Rejecting the idea of retraining experienced bar staff, he opted for untrained workers who could imbibe the new philosophy required. In this regard Pitcher & Piano was not just far ahead of practices in the industry but embracing a philosophy followed by Britain's most progressive businesses. 'As the best employers know', commented Iain Ellwood, recognized specialist in branding goods, 'hiring for attitude and training for skills is a more effective route to powerful customer connections [than recruiting only experienced staff] and this is especially true for women customers'. It was not a career ladder that Bonnell offered so much as an apprenticeship for women eager to establish their own companies: he expected managers, though paid £20,000 annually and offered as much as £9000 in bonus, to burn out in three years.[32]

Pitcher & Piano lavished huge sums on creating the ideal setting and reaped commensurate rewards. Trafalgar Square, its interior alone costing £400,000, became the company's flagship outlet, covering 5000 square feet and accommodating over five hundred customers. Sprawling licensed premises harkened back to the interwar improved public houses. To address critics of the interwar pubs who damned them for their open, undifferentiated spaces, Ward designed square booths. By 1995, the company's five London venues had generated £1 million profits on a turnover of £5 million, an impressive return of 20 per cent on investment. So too concluded Marston's Brewery which paid £20 million for the chain the following year, a testament to the perceived appeal of female-friendly pubs.[33]

Tweddell had the foresight to pioneer a new retailing concept as Britain had become a service-oriented economy. The young market, the eighteen- to twenty-four-year-olds who hitherto had formed the backbone of the pub's clientele, contracted by almost 20 per cent, while the middle-aged and middle-class group expanded by 10 per cent.[34]

Pitcher & Piano would later earn accolades as the prototype for female-friendly venues, the first of what came to be called chain bars, positioning themselves between traditional pubs, on one hand, and wine bars, on the other. The chain itself entered the mainstream of big alcohol producers when Marston's Brewery purchased it, and expanded the outlets to 38 within a decade.[35] Bass embraced the same approach with its All Bar One chain, created in 1994; another 52 outlets opened in the following decade. On Friday nights, its customers consisted of almost equal numbers of women as men. Females staffed most of the managerial positions. Bar 38 (Scottish & Newcastle), Carpe Diem Quo Vadis (Allied Domecq) and Peppers (Whitbread) followed the same formula. Pubco Grosvenor Inns also established its own female-friendly chain, Slug and Lettuce.[36]

Regardless of the chain or its creator, the formula became standardized: newspapers, choice of food, table service, wines (together with soft drinks and coffee), music (save at Wetherspoon pubs), clean and pleasant toilets, and good ventilation. Large clear windows dominated entrances, and comfortable furniture as well as attractive décor distinguished interiors. Small tables and soft chairs prevailed, except at All Bar One, where vast open floor spaces and trestle tables created, thought the *Publican Newspaper*, 'a warehouse-feel inside'.[37] All chain bars rejected a conscious effort to feminize interiors, 'with Laura Ashley curtains and pictures of kittens on the walls'. Had pubcos embraced this transparently patronising approach, two *Morning Advertiser* reporters later observed, 'women wouldn't have gone near' the chain outlets.[38]

For the female-friendly pub, designers consciously chose light colours to reflect and refract light, making interiors seem more inviting and fostering women's 'accessibility'. From the *Morning Advertiser* came advice that the bar be 'light, bright, open and airy'. Equally anathema to Davis would have been its recommendation that such pubs stock a broad range of wines, cocktails and speciality beers. The perceptive, subtle way in which pubcos sought female custom stood in sharp contrast to how breweries themselves saw class as the ultimate marketing tool for women.[39]

Nothing short of a revolution in design transformed drink venues in the 1980s and 1990s. Historic pubs – their dark brown colours, crowded counters with male drinkers, cramped drinking space, entrance windows largely obscured by etchings and overwhelming male presence – had alienated women. The new generation of designers, grasping the shortcomings of these features, created interiors antithetical to what Davis had advocated. Davis's book, *The Traditional English Pub*, his homage to masculine drinking in a masculine environment, appeared in 1981. Strikingly, throughout his book, he always referred to drinkers and retailers in the masculine, reflecting his conservative views of women's subordinate status in the pub, as in the rest of society.

Cumulatively, the impact of these pubcos was enormous. Female-friendly chains, recalled Caroline Nodder, editor of the *Publican*, 'led to a revolution in standards and consumer demand for food, wine and range of drinks brands [that] transformed the market almost beyond recognition'.[40]

Attracting more female customers became part of a wider strategy in which breweries and many pubcos – J. D. Wetherspoons being a prominent exception – developed segmented markets with pubs branded according to occupations. Bass's All Bar One targeted women, especially office workers, while its O'Neill's pubs wooed students. Huge profits drove this transformation. Branded pubs represented about a quarter of Bass's managed estate premises, for example, but accounted for nearly half of its profits. Since companies structured retailing around branded divisions, not geographic areas, outlets abandoned the historic identification with specific breweries and beers, and instead enticed customers with branded images projecting lifestyle experiences. From a retailing perspective, it gave the company broad flexibility to create multi-identities each appealing to different consumer types, while avoiding competition between venues in the same area. Each venue, moreover, adopted a 'chameleon' policy in which the environment was altered during the day to draw different types of clientele.[41] No longer would drink venues position themselves in the marketplace at a specific demographic group. 'These outlets', remarked the *Publican* in 2000, 'can do a quiet morning coffee but also dim the lights and crank up the music for a Friday night on the town'.[42] Such bars became concentrated in decaying city centres of Northern industrial towns.

Throughout the 1990s, female-friendly concept chains 'made a killing' in the marketplace. In characterizing the All Bar One outlets as 'our jewel in the crown', one Bass official acknowledged these outlets' enormous commercial success. Market research agreed, attributing rising female drinking to the chain's feminine appeal. Public recognition of its leading role as a 'female-friendly' chain came early in 2000 when Datamonitor, public opinion surveyors, credited All Bar One with expanding drinking among women in the 1990s.[43]

Ironically, therefore, its calculated appeal to women 'was played down slightly so as not to deter men' when the chain first appeared. To accommodate growing numbers of female consumers, drink sellers began marketing PPS (premium packaged spirits), which easily outdistanced rivals, including lager. Three times as many women drank PPS beverages as beer, the least popular beverage. Class played a vital role in determining drinking habits. 'Older men', observed one reporter in May 2000, 'are close to unwelcome in the female-friendly bars of today, unless they are wearing a suit'.[44]

The concept, however, did not long remain static. Fullers unveiled its own new interpretation, the Fine Line, an upmarket chain brand, in the summer of 1998, with seven more outlets opened in the following three years. Here, more than in other chains, the Fine Line was the product of cross-fertilization: from Pitcher & Piano came its head of Bars Division, Harri Owen, while from All Bar One came Rupert Clark as Operations Manager. Fullers even poached staff from Slug and Lettuce and Henry's Café Bars.[45]

Fine Line marked a significant departure in this market. From a well-known London brewer of outstanding cask conditioned beers came premises wholly devoid of them. Upmarket wines and spirits instead dominated. Colours were carefully chosen to 'refract and reflect the light to make the whole bar feel open', observed Rupert Clark. For women in shirt sleeves and skirts, Fullers thoughtfully provided furniture with soft fabric and tables of suitable heights. Likewise, Fullers demonstrated cognizance of women's eating habits, introducing light snacks, nutritious selections and seasonal foods. Men came appropriately attired in suits. Staff became well versed in giving advice on suitable wines for both the meal and the palate. The *Publican* praised the first outlet at Battersea as a 'stylish bar-restaurant in West London that has been visited by an unusually high number of senior management from Britain's regional brewers'. They were rightly intrigued: *Time Out*, adjudicator of fashionable London, characterized the chain as 'smart, sleek and modern', and bestowed an award.[46]

Regardless of their differences, these female-friendly chains, concentrated overwhelmingly in London with some outlets in the South-east, selected locations in towns and city centres, easily visible to pedestrians. In sharp contrast with traditional pubs, the staff at female-friendly pubs – young, intelligent, educated, personable and energetic – 'are mirror images of the customers'. These innovative approaches experienced considerable success in retailing alcohol to women. Women constituted half of the clientele in pubs with hybrid pub, restaurant or wine bar formats, compared with a gender split of 80 men to 20 women in traditional pubs.[47]

Undoubtedly the Beer Orders in 1988 shaped the brewing industry, but in ways wholly different from what critics have depicted.[48] Sexist, homophobic, conservative, even reactionary, the brewing industry steadfastly resisted change, a remarkable posture given changes in demography, employment, education and attitudes more generally towards women since the 1960s. The Beer Orders thus did not so much inaugurate as accelerate transformation in the cultures of drinking. New chains were at hand to buy up the tied houses when the brewers began unloading them, and, moreover, had a new concept of what to do with them. Had brewers been forced to sell in 1960 (or had chosen to sell to liquidate the capital locked up in pubs), they might have found that their successors had just the same values and ran pubs as individuals in just the same way as brewers had done. Once outsiders came with money and ideas as novel as Progressive brewers had championed in the 1920s and 1930s, the old regime began declining. So long ignored, patronized and marginalized as drinkers by brewers and retailers alike, women ironically acquired the power and influence formerly denied them. Losers in the long run would be promoters of the old drinking culture, brewers and retailers, who so deservedly reaped what they had sown through decades of perpetuating the male status quo.

Notes

1 Ben Davis, 'Pubs Losing Out on Atmosphere', *Publican*, 22 May 1986; Geoff Brandwood, Andrew Davison and Michael Slaughter, *Licensed to Sell: The History and Heritage of the Public House* (London: English Heritage, 2004), p. 90.

2 Iain Ellwood with Sheila Shekar, *Wonder Woman: Marketing Secrets for the Trillion-Dollar Customer* (Houndmills: Palgrave Macmillan, 2008), pp. 148–50, 158; Jane McCallion, 'Does New Design Improve a Pub?' *Publican*, 11 Aug. 1988; Peter Martin, 'How "Revolutionary" Does Pub Design Need to Be?', *Publican*, 8 Nov. 1984; Ben Davis, *Publican*: 'A Woman's Place: Behind the Bar', 25 Aug. 1983, and 'Pubs Losing Out on Atmosphere'.

3 Ben Davis, *The Traditional English Pub: A Way of Drinking* (London: Architectural Press, 1981), dust jacket.

4 McCallion, 'New Design'; Martin, 'Pub Design'; Davis, *Traditional Pub*, p. 74.

5 Ellwood with Shekar, *Wonder Woman*, pp. 148–50, 158.

6 Kate Oppenheim, 'Match Maker', *ICE*, Oct. 2000.

7 Bernard H. Booms and Mary J. Bitner, 'Marketing Services by Managing the Environment', *Cornell Hotel and Restaurant Administration Quarterly*, 23 (May 1982), pp. 35, 38–9; Mary Jo Bitner, 'Servicescapes: The Impact of Physical Surroundings on Customers and Employees', *Journal of Marketing*, 56 (April 1992), p. 57. For an earlier example of how interwar brewers used one form of the built environment to attract custom, see David W. Gutzke, *Pubs and Progressives: Reinventing the Public House in England, 1896–1960* (De Kalb: Northern Illinois University Press, 2006), ch. 9.

8 Mary Jo Bitner, 'Servicescapes', pp. 57–61, 63, 67; James Ward, Mary Jo Bitner and Dan Gossett, 'Seem: A Measure of Service Environment Meaning', in Mary Jo Bitner and Lawrence A. Crosby (eds), *Designing: A Winning Service Strategy* (Chicago: American Marketing Association, 1989), p. 34.

9 Ruth A. Schmidt and Roger Sapsford, 'Issues of Gender and Servicescape: Marketing UK Public Houses to Women', *International Journal of Retail and Distribution Management*, 23 (1995), pp. 35–9; Bitner, 'Servicescapes', pp. 63, 66; Booms and Bitner, 'Marketing Services by Managing the Environment', p. 39.

10 Schmidt and Sapsford, 'Marketing UK Public Houses to Women', pp. 35–7; *Adventure*, 12 (Oct.–Dec. 1998), pp. 18–19; Booms and Bitner, 'Marketing Services', p. 39.

11 Schmidt and Sapsford, 'Marketing UK Public Houses to Women', pp. 37–8; Geoff Brandwood, 'The Vanishing Faces of the Traditional Pub', *Journal of the Brewery History Society*, 123 (Summer 2006), p. 122; also see Paul Allonby, 'Half a Million Spent to Make Women Happy!', *Licensee and Morning Advertiser*, 12 April 1999.

12 Schmidt and Sapsford, 'Marketing UK Public Houses to Women', pp. 37–9.

13 *Publican*, 26 Sept. 2005.

14 *Publican*, 13 May 1991; Michelle Stanistreet, 'Pulling Pints with Passion', *Sunday Express*, 20 Feb. 2000; Paul Charity, 'Profile: Wetherspoon's Chairman Tim Martin', *Morning Advertiser*, 2 May 2002.

15 George Orwell, 'The Moon under Water', *Evening Standard*, 9 Feb. 1946; Lorna Harrison, 'Dear John', *Publican*, 3 Jan. 2004; Nils Pratley, 'An Orwellian Vision Pays Off for the Pub Iconoclast', *Daily Telegraph*, 20 Sept. 1997.

16 Orwell, 'Moon Under Water'.

17 Tim Martin, 'Responsibility Rules at JDW', *Morning Advertiser*, 10 Nov. 2005; Tim Martin, 'Memo to All JDW Staff: "We Are Responsible Retailers"', *Morning Advertiser*, 30 Sept. 2004; Gutzke, *Pubs and Progressives*, pp. 18, 55–6, 59–60, 91–2, 96, 98, 109–11, 117–18, 132–4, 159–62, 170, 175–6, 187, 197, 229, 232, 235–6, 241, 257, n. 8; Robert Thorne, 'Good Service and Sobriety: The Improved Public House', *Architectural Review*, 159 (Feb. 1976), pp. 107–11; *One Hundred and Fifty Years of Brewing, 1788–1938: Souvenir Book of the Bristol Brewery Georges & Company* (Bristol: Bristol Brewery, Georges & Company, 1938), handwritten comments by its chairman, N. Hadley, inside back cover.

18 Martin, '"We Are All Responsible Retailers"'.

19 Adam Tinworth, 'Be Irresistible to Women', *Publican*, 3 July 1995; Catherine Turner, 'It's Your Round, Girls!' *Coventry Evening Telegraph*, 28 Sept. 2000; Stanistreet, 'Pulling Pints'; Martin, '"We are Responsible Retailers"'.

20 Martin, 'We Are All Responsible Retailers'; *Publican*, 13 April 1992; Peter Martin, 'Eat, Drink and Be Merry: But You Can't Play Darts', *Observer*, 25 May 1997; Catherine Quinn, 'Where Small is Beautiful', *Morning Advertiser*, 14 Feb. 2008.

21 *Publican*, 13 April 1992.

22 Gutzke, *Pubs and Progressives*, p. 201; Mark Stretton, 'Wetherspoon Woes', *Publican*, 8 July 2002; Caroline Nodder, 'We're 30!' *Publican*, 26 Sept. 2005; Peter Martin, 'Eat, Drink and Be Merry'.

23 David Flockhart, 'Beer', *Flavour* 12 (June 2001), pp. 35–6; Martin, 'Eat, Drink and Be Merry'.

24 *Morning Advertiser*, 3 June 2004.

25 Ibid.; *Morning Advertiser*, 5 April 2007; Daniel Pearce, 'Tim's the Man', *Publican*, 26 Sept. 2005; Peter Martin, 'Out of the Wet and into the Dry', *Morning Advertiser*, 17 April 2008.

26 Tim Martin, 'We Are All Responsible Retailers'; Martin, 'Eat, Drink and Be Merry'; Publican/Carling Pub-Goers Report, 1996, quoted in *Publican Newspaper*, 4 March 1996.

27 Andrew Palmer, 'Cashing in on Women', *Publican*, 4 April 1994; *Publican*, 28 Feb. 1994.

28 Roger Tredre, 'Pubs See Light in Battle for Women', *Observer*, 6 Aug. 1995; *Mintel Report on Alcoholic Drinks, 1982*, quoted in Chris Middleton, 'Calling Women to the Bar', *Guardian*, 13 Aug. 1983.

29 Deyan Sudjic, 'Call that a Pub?', *The Times*, 5 Nov. 1988; *Publican*, 28 Feb. 1994.

30 See Chapter 4, above, p. 102.

31 Palmer, 'Cashing in on Women'; Grosvenor Inn's internal report, quoted in Tredre, 'Battle for Woman'. See also the extensive survey commissioned by Archers

(*Morning Advertiser*, 20 June 2002).

32 *Publican*, 28 Feb. 1994; Sally Bairstow, 'Increase Your Pulling Power', *Morning Advertiser*, 19 June 2003; Ellwood with Shekar, *Wonder Woman*, p. 184; Karan Bilimoria, *Bottled for Business: The Less Gassy Guide to Entrepreneurship* (Chichester: Capstone Publishing, 2007), p. 60.

33 *Publican*, 28 Feb. 1994; Palmer, 'Cashing in on Women'; Rupert Richard Halstead, 'Drunk on Success', *Independent*, 30 June 1996.

34 Henley Centre Social Survey, quoted in *Courage News*, 60 (Dec. 1991).

35 Paul Charity, 'New Tune for Pitcher and Piano', *Morning Advertiser*, 17 July 2003.

36 Tinworth, 'Irresistible to Women'; Tredre, 'Battle for Women'.

37 Caroline Nodder, 'Female Market Up Over "Friendly" Bars', *Publican Newspaper*, 10 Aug. 1998; Bairstow, 'Pulling Power', *Morning Advertiser*. All Bar One had no bar stools, making it easier for women to place orders.

38 Simon McQuiggan and Pete Brown, 'What Women Don't Want', *Morning Advertiser*, 28 Aug. 2003.

39 Bairstow, 'Pulling Power'.

40 Nodder, 'We're 30!'

41 'Are Publicans Serving at Last Change Saloon?', *Express*, 13 Dec. 1998; Robert Hollands, Paul Chatterton, Bernie C. Byrnes and Cait Read, *The London of the North? Youth Cultures, Urban Change and Nightlife in Leeds* (Newcastle-upon-Tyne, Centre for Urban and Regional Development Studies, Department of Sociology and Social Policy, University of Newcastle-upon-Tyne, 2001), pp. 15–16.

42 *Publican Newspaper*, 25 Sept. 2000.

43 Andrew Burnyeat, 'Bass to Cut Size of Its Flagship Chain', and 'Pubs Transformed by the Gentle Touch', *Publican Newspaper*, 1 and 8 May 2000.

44 Burnyeat, 'Pubs Transformed by the Gentle Touch'; Ben McFarland, 'One for the Ladies', *Publican Newspaper*, 16 April 2001.

45 *Publican Newspaper*, 9 July 2001.

46 Bairstow, 'Pulling Power'.

47 Turner, 'It's Your Round, Girls!'; India Knight, 'Say No to the Nice Pub', *Sunday Times*, 27 Feb. 2000; 'What's Your Pleasure?', *Economist*, 21 Dec. 1996, p. 83; 'Last Change Saloon?'; *Sunday Express*, 13 Dec. 1999; Craig Thatcher, 'All Bar None', *Leisure & Management*, 16 (Dec. 1996), pp. 40–1; John Willman, 'Make Mine a Family Pub with a Twist of Real Ale', *Financial Times*, 31 March 1998.

48 For the Beer Orders, see Chapter 8, below, pp. 164–5.

8

New money, new ideas, new women

Within the brewing industry, Margaret Thatcher's Beer Orders, issued in 1989, acquired infamy for causing incalculable harm, fatally undermining the historic if controversial tied house system. When Lord Young, her Secretary of State for Trade and Industry, laid down that no brewery could own over two thousand tied houses, some national breweries reacted not by selling off the requisite number of pubs to comply with the fiat but by disposing of their entire tied estates (Courage) or all their breweries (Watneys).[1] *Morning Advertiser* reporter Derek Pain expressed the industry's consensus in damning the misguided reforms for destroying the old order to benefit just newly formed pub companies, soon called pubcos, financed by foreign investors to create pub chains as extensive and antithetical to competition as the old tied house system. From the customers' perspective, he contended, 'the Beer Orders have been a waste of time – and money'.[2] The most recent, detailed assessment, *Intervention in the Modern UK Brewing Industry*, written by several authors closely associated with breweries, saw no reason to disagree: the Thatcher government's 'intervention has brought virtually no benefit to the millions of people who enjoy drinking beer in the comfortable ambience of a British pub'.[3] Curiously, this monograph, written by four men and over three hundred pages in length, contains no listing of 'women' in its index.[4]

Outside the hallowed precincts of the brewers' Boards of Directors, a dissenting view of the Beer Orders certainly existed. For these critics, the traditional order was monopolistic, sexist, homophobic, often racist, exceedingly conservative and hidebound, unresponsive to consumer pressure and exclusively male from the Boards of Directors downwards. Females, seldom seen and never heard, hovered inconspicuously on the periphery as secretaries. Espousing the interests of their own sex, brewing company executives blocked entry of women into pub tenancies, hired managers whose wives received no remuneration and employed estate managers who presided over many licensed premises as notable for their overwhelming masculinity as for their vile hygiene. Wherever one looked – from the appallingly filthy, germ-ridden toilets often devoid of soap, hand towels, mirrors and recent paint to the plain, unimaginative food and overpriced, poorly served, insipid Chateau plonk – traditional pubs had remarkably little to offer women.

Accordingly, the industry's own pessimistic analysis of the Beer Orders attaches far too much weight to governmental policy, minimizing new trends in the industry preceding the Beer Orders, which in fact accelerated rather than inaugurated changes. Pubcos had already demonstrated how the cultures of drinking would change. Because they saw drinkers as more sophisticated in their habits, pubcos responded quickly to customer needs, fundamentally transforming the brewing industry's culture. Their executives, as one study conceded, 'were prepared to challenge the norms and expectations of a fairly conservative industry'.[5]

Even breweries, notoriously unimaginative, reflected the impact of the emergent new culture. The quintessential example involved the reverse takeover of Devenish Weymouth, a long-established Dorset brewery with 330 tied houses, by Inn Leisure, a pubco owing forty pubs and wine bars, in 1986. Analysing this merger, three years before the Beer Orders' proclamation, the *Publican* observed that 'currently many of the best and most successful ideas in the pub trade are coming from the free trade and in particular the growing number of fast expanding groups like Inn Leisure'. The merger's role reversal was certainly not lost on the reporter: Devenish sought out an independent pubco as a means of acquiring 'the business expertise it needs to revive its flagging pub sales'.[6]

Symptomatic of new career paths opening for women was the career of Claire Varlett, who began as a part-time secretary for Regent Inns in 1986. As this pubco acquired 45 pubs and floated its stock over the course of the next decade, she rose to become Personal Assistant to David Franks, Managing and Financial Director. On being recognized as Business Woman of the Year in 1995, Varlett was paid the ultimate accolade when Franks acknowledged her as the company's 'real' Managing Director.[7] Nothing then paralleled her upward career mobility in the traditional brewing industry.

Long before the Beer Orders cast gloom on the brewing industry, the catalysts transforming the brewing industry had either already appeared or soon would emerge, having nothing to do with restrictions on tied house ownership. Over-capacity and excessive numbers of licences in fact would have fostered changes, regardless of whether the Beer Orders had been implemented.[8] Slumping beer consumption since 1979 created surplus capacity of some 14 million barrels annually, roughly 25 per cent of the total. Less beer being drunk in turn meant pubs with marginal turnover, primarily in villages, in rural areas and on housing estates with high unemployment, would ultimately accept market realities and close. Experts estimated the imperiled pubs numbered about ten thousand, about 15 per cent of the total. Demographic trends carried the most far-reaching consequences. The eighteen- to twenty-five-year-old cohort – representing one-seventh of the population but responsible for over one-third of total beer consumption – had sustained brewery profits, but would not for much longer. By the mid-1990s, this group was expected to contract by 25 per cent, leading to the closure of thousands of pubs. Although the thirty-five to fifty-five age cohort would expand by 15 per cent, this group was expected to consume less alcohol and drink it at home. Single households were likewise projected to rise appreciably, together with home ownership, making domestic drinking more attractive than the local. Already a pronounced shift from public to private drinking was threatening pubs, as domestic consumption had more than doubled in a decade, with one-fourth of beer consumption now in homes.[9]

Structural changes in the economy also shaped consumption habits. Since the 1960s and 1970s, unskilled and semi-skilled manufacturing and coal mine workers had steadily contracted in numbers. Thatcher's subsequent policy of deindustrialization had accelerated this development, depriving many pubs of their traditional masculine subcultures of drinking. Some had closed, but many more sought survival through a vital metamorphosis. 'Boozers are being transformed into pubs with restaurants, pubs with family rooms, and ancillary leisure facilities such as ten-pin bowling alleys', wrote John Shepherd in the *Independent* in 1993.[10]

Survival of drink outlets often depended not on the Beer Orders restrictions but on obtaining more physical space, making village inns far likelier to endure than their urban counterparts, unable to expand outward owing to cramped quarters. Over two-thirds of town and suburban pubs drew their profits primarily from selling alcohol well into the 1990s, with food accounting for just one-seventh of the takings. These too were the establishments with the highest annual turnovers, averaging some £230,000, £45,000–£50,000 more than rural or village counterparts. The latter sold less alcohol but twice as much food as town and suburban pubs, and spearheaded the drive for attracting families, introducing a family room and banning smoking. Motivation for these changes came from non-tied independent licensees. Brewer-owned urban premises, their 'wet' profits the highest among the categories, had little incentive to anticipate future market changes.[11]

The Beer Orders undoubtedly had an impact, though much exaggerated by the industry itself. With literally thousands of pubs changing hands, the Orders afforded 'new opportunities for a mini-generation of pushy young entrepreneurs', concluded Linda Bain, spokeswoman of Scottish and Newcastle.[12] In fostering a booming market in licensed property, the Orders recast alcohol retailing and employment. Nowhere was the industry's new culture of mobility more apparent than in gender relations. Again much impetus for change originated outside the brewing industry. 'The pub business is attracting a lot of single women now because of the opportunities the pub companies are offering them', knew Barbara Johnson, Human Resource Manager at Allied Domecq Retail.[13]

Women's influx into executive managerial positions fundamentally transformed attitudes, assumptions and aspirations in the retailing of alcohol within the traditional brewing fraternity as well. In hiring Liz Morgan as its Marketing Director, Carlsberg-Tetley grasped the previous shortcomings of its retail policies. 'Men', declared Morgan, 'don't appreciate the slight insecurity women feel' in entering pubs. Mindful of widening the base of females in pubs, Ind Coope began hiring women as Marketing Managers in the 1990s. Kathryn McNamara had filled this role at Boddingtons, promoting innovative advertisments. Not surprisingly, women in such managerial roles concentrated, not on the type of beer served, but on improving the ambience and expanding the range of both wines and non-alcoholic beverages. Retail Business and Operations Manager at All Bar One, Mary Jane Brook, stated emphatically and proudly that its pubs 'smell clean – not of stale beer'.[14]

Women behind bar counter received different treatment, too. Bass became the first national brewery to change the age-old tenancy system in which the husband received the licence with his wife as the unpaid, full-time largely silent partner. Under a new scheme, christened the 'New Deal', both the manager and his or her partner received a part- or full-time salaried position, with wages now guaranteed in individual contracts. To help the licensee, Bass hired another individual altogether as an assistant manager. Should the partner want and be qualified for a managerial position, Bass would hire each to run separate pubs. Skill in managing an outlet, not gender, age or prior experience, now became paramount.[15]

Women's entry into retailing alcohol as managers rather than as appendages of husbands paralleled another change in the industry, the employment of women as tenants. Previously, 'only in exceptional circumstances will single men or women be considered for tenancies or management positions', maintained Stanley Wright in his book, *Running Your Own Pub* (1984).[16] The following year Wright's confident assertion about the masculine monopoly in retailing alcohol became challenged in the heartland of male drinking, Newcastle's Quayside. Tetley's placed one of its first single female licensees – at twenty one of the youngest such women in the UK – to run Christies, a trendy wine bar/pub. Her rigorous apprenticeship included a stint as substitute manager at a traditional male boozer. That Tetley's turned to her as a licensee of a pub imitating a wine bar in an area undergoing gentrification both underlined and foreshadowed how wine bars and pubcos subverted the historic gender boundaries perpetuated by masculine drinking culture.[17]

Inside the brewing industry, increasing numbers of brewers endorsed Tetley's policy of discarding gender stereotypes in employment. Mark Woodhouse, Vice Chairman of Hall & Woodhouse, drew a shrewd analogy between women as customers and employees. 'It is ludicrous that at a time when brewers are trying to encourage more women to drink beer that women do not have a more significant representation within the industry', he observed. Acting on these beliefs, his family brewery inaugurated employment of single women or women in same-sex relationships to run pubs in the 1990s, partly as a response to growing numbers of outlets advertising themselves as family-friendly.[18]

'The days have gone when running a pub was seen as a male preserve', pronounced Grey Philips, Secretary of the Swansea Licensed Victuallers' Association, which had equal numbers of women and men as members.[19] By 1999, one national survey suggested that single women comprised one-seventh of all pub managers. Overall, one in every ten licensees was a female.[20] Women comprised one-fourth of the unmarried licensees at Allied, though this still represented a quite small proportion of the overall licensees. Similarly, women constituted one-fifth of the licensees at Whitbread Pub Partnerships. Promoting change at Friary Meux was Julian Cartwright, named Managing Director in 1980. On his arrival, he recalled, 'we hardly gave any thought to single women running pubs alone'. In the ensuing years, gender attitudes had modified. Cartwright expressed the new assumption in 1989: 'It is only commonsense that women are more than capable of running businesses every bit as well as their counterparts'. Women's success as landladies had prompted hiring more of them than single men, and in the process challenged sexism. But progress across the industry, even among pubcos, was slow and uneven. Of Vanguard's 1600 pubs, just eighty were run by non-married women by the late 1990s.[21] Sexism, too, had far from vanished. Male licensees turned up in force to object to some single women applying for licences. Early in 2004, the *Publican* could still characterize the liquor business as 'traditionally a male-dominated industry'.[22]

Bigger profits as much as expertise motivated breweries to move towards gender-neutral hiring policies. At Nicholson's, another Allied subsidiary, female licensees increased profits by 21 per cent, vastly more than what men had achieved. Women also earned distinction and awards for skills in the cellar, traditionally a male preserve. It was London's Dog & Duck – tenanted by Gean Bell – that won the Soho Society's Pub of the Year award in 1994. Nicholson's Director, David Kelham, had no doubts of either women's abilities or their impact. 'People these days', he reflected, 'still assume that the pub trade is dominated by men but this is no longer the case'.[23]

Other factors equally made women's employment in pubs as managers or licensees attractive to liquor wholesalers. Many in the industry had come to see women's presence in licensed premises as playing a civilizing role in the masculine culture of drinking. 'When it is not an all-male atmosphere you get less posturing and extreme positions taken by the men', urged Michael Izza, Managing Director of John Labatt Retail. Customers, he added, frequently displayed greater respect towards female rather than male licensees. Women, too, more often had greater emotional skills than men in dealing with customers' divergent personalities. Tim Williams, recruiter for Whitbread Pub Partnerships' pub lessees, saw women as 'less confrontational so there is less hostility and this calming influence creates a more welcoming place for women to drink in'. Women behind the bar as the 'landlady' thus fostered an environment conducive to female customers feeling safe and unthreatened.[24]

Rising numbers of pub meals similarly affected the culture of drinking for women in diverse, unexpected ways. Seen as a traditional feminine skill, catering broadened the scope for women's employment in the drinks industry, providing one important catalyst for women's entry into managerial or tenancy positions. Reinforcing new hiring and promotional policies was the widening proportion of females in the workforce, cresting at almost one in two, a development which in turn encouraged women's resort to public drinking. Between 1994 and 2000, the number of women visiting bars regularly more than doubled, with over half of females now engaged in this leisure habit. Not only did one-third of all women patronize a pub regularly but significantly four-fifths of them indicated a willingness to venture into it alone.[25]

By the 1990s, well over eight of every ten pubs served food, and virtually all of these offered lunches. Demonstrating this trade's potential profitability, food sales accounted for one-third of turnover at Greene King's six hundred managed houses.[26] Pubs assumed the trappings of restaurants, a change which reinforced consumption of beverages more associated with food, dining and sociability. Unlike conventional wine bars, these hybrid restaurant bar-pubs had a much broader selection of wines, and also sold coffee, soft drinks and premium packaged beers. 'Gastro-pubs', offering cuisine more sophisticated than typical pub grub, first appeared in London in the 1990s, with the Eagle and the Landsdowne pioneering the trend. A decade later London still retained undisputed lead, and alone accounted for 67 of the well over a thousand entries appearing in *Which? Pub Guide*. Though gastro-pubs remained a phenomenon primarily of London, pubs across the country likewise elevated standards.[27]

Distinctly reversing the accepted wisdom of running pubs, food, not drink, generated profits for other purchases. Food and a range of coffees proved irresistible as incentives for women to use pubs. By the early 1990s, well over half of women ate lunches at pubs, and food takings had doubled in value in a decade to claim almost a quarter of all sales.[28]

But marketers carefully differentiated between different age cohorts of women. A 1991 Key Note market survey forecast two vital demographic changes in the following decade: drinkers in the sixteen to twenty-four age group – hitherto the mainstay of pub goers – would shrink in numbers by 15 per cent, while there would be a matching increase in the number of married women aged thirty-five to forty-four. This was far from an even tradeoff, however. Such older women not only drank less alcohol than the sixteen to twenty-four age cohort, but displayed no preference whatsoever between drinking in pubs or at home, much to the displeasure of publicans.[29] To compound the difficulties of publicans, women generally avoided beer altogether and instead drank wine and spirit-based beverages. One of the most popular, Bacardi Breezer, a pre-mixed rum-based beverage served in a bottle with 12.5 per cent alcohol, outstripped sales of many bottled beers, with women accounting for 60 per cent of its drinkers.[30]

With more people taking alcohol with meals in restaurants and gastro-pubs, male diners felt fewer inhibitions in opting for wine over beer. Diverse surveys confirmed the continuing failure of pubs to sell men wine, though ironically wine consumption in pubs overall was rising.[31] Eating out became a critical factor in wine consumption's expansion. 'It is the increasing importance of food in pubs that is driving wine growth there', remarked Hew Dalrymple, Marketing Director of Waverley Wines & Spirits, in 2003. In response to widening numbers of consumers eating prepared food and venturing into wine bars as well as female-friendly pubs, the culture of selling alcohol to women became quite elaborate, with market segmentation the pivotal feature. Targeting those under thirty-five (especially women) with high disposal incomes and from the higher socio-demographic groups, wine bars sought patrons desiring 'somewhere aspirational serving high quality food in social surroundings'.[32]

By the 1990s seven different drinking venues existed. At the most exclusive came private gentlemen's clubs, often of great antiquity with members drawn from Britain's traditional landed governing classes. Sexual equality remained a quite novel, even alien, concept at London gentlemen's clubs. Brooks's epitomized the discriminatory attitudes of many male members. Women of all social ranks had been effectively excluded until the Second World War. Even Queen Mary entered the sacred sanctum of Brooks's Library, escorted by a member, as an exceptional guest in 1938. The Duke of Devonshire, recumbent on the sofa, greeted this intrusion with the ungallant utterance, 'My God, a woman!' Overcoming his shock, jumping to his feet and finally regaining his dignity, he expressed the expected social greeting: 'Ma'am'. Well into the 1980s at Brooks', men upheld their male monopoly on club premises, save for special occasions such as private parties, when after 6 p.m. they retreated to the bar and members' room, the sole remaining male sanctuaries.[33] Exclusively male in composition and specifically excluded as private clubs from the Sex Discrimination Act (1975), these institutions, save in one instance, still proclaimed their masculinity with minimal rights granted women. Even Prime Minister Margaret Thatcher was allowed into the Carlton Club's hallowed halls only as a special concession, signified in her status as an associate member. Just one, the Reform Club, granted women membership on the same basis as men.[34]

These conservative private clubs sharply contrasted with another type of private social club which began emerging in the mid-1980s without acquiring a distinguishing name. Both types required members to nominate individuals for membership, ensuring the club's selectivity. The Groucho Club (1985), Soho House (1994), Townhouse (1998) and Black's (1992) also saw themselves as catering to a social elite, but of another type altogether, drawn from the media, the film industry and publishing and advertising. Membership too was quite dissimilar: women had full rights and, allegedly at least, joined in almost as many numbers as men; members' ages averaged in the thirties, some twenty years lower than in traditional social clubs; the menus revealed more health-conscious, trendy executives; and alcohol and cinemas displaced chess and backgammon. Nevertheless, a strict dress code prevailed and was sometimes brutally enforced: members turning up with pony tails could have them summarily cut off; and mobile telephones, baseball caps and gum chewing were all proscribed. Soho House, in contrast, banned ties. Open to qualified minorities in theory, these new social clubs, whether deliberately by design or unintentionally by reputation, counted few members of minority ethnic groups as members in reality. Other private clubs, requiring membership fees but no sponsors, and less exclusive hotel bars, where service ranked as a priority and bouncers excluded plebeians, constituted two other categories.[35]

Below such exalted drinking venues, style bars specialized in exotic, expensive cocktails, imported vodkas, premium gins, rums and speciality beers, either imported (primarily from Europe, especially Germany, Belgium and Italy) or brewed by indigenous micro-breweries. Shots and shooters too were another mainstay of such bars. Older 'female-friendly' bars, All Bar One and Pitcher & Piano in London and Fat Cat Café Bars in the provinces, now comprised a less exclusive rank as chain bars. Finally, at the base and steadily contracting in numbers as much as in profits, though still the largest overall group, stood traditional pubs.[36]

Following a US consumer fashion for 'small is good', style bars began appearing in Britain early in the 1990s.[37] Changing public taste had induced women increasingly to abandon themed bars and turn to style bars (also called concepts bars or pre-club venues) – individual outlets run by autonomous entrepreneurs who created unique atmospheres in the establishment.[38] 'The introduction of style bars', observed a Stoke-on-Trent nightclub owner, 'has created a whole new niche market of more affluent customers and the pubs and bars have tried to keep up branding and re-branding'. Style bars rose in numbers paralleling sale of a widening diversity of imported beer brands. Previously, 'most pub-goers were in for a treat if they had a choice of anything more than a bottle of Beck's or Holsten Pils'.[39]

Such was the persisting masculine culture in the brewing industry that national breweries, keen to open trendy style bars, hired experienced personnel outside their own companies.[40] There was, however, one significant problem: recruitment of as many men as women as cocktail managers, more commonly called mixologists. As one ascended the hierarchy of drink outlets, from traditional pubs, chain bars, style bars and finally members' bars, the number of women in managerial positions declined. An area manager of Casa, one leading style bar, expressed his conundrum: 'We try and get a 50:50 split [between the genders], because that's a reflection of the clientele that we're trying to attract'. Despite this goal, women accounted for just 20 per cent of managers, the same proportion of females who submitted applications. Numerous factors perpetuated the masculine culture in style and members' bars. Bartenders had been exclusively males when the profession emerged in the interwar era. As in other professions in which women sought job mobility, female bar managers confronted animosity from bar staff. Lengthy work shifts and unsociable hours likewise deterred females. But women also faced special gender difficulties. Some style bar owners doubted whether women could handle drunks and feared marriage and pregnancy would make females unreliable as employees. According to Claire West, Operations Director of the Breakfast Group, there was a far deeper problem. 'Women', she knew, 'tend to be pigeon-holed as waitresses rather than mixologists'.[41] Ironically, then, in a new sector of the retail market in which women might have been expected to encounter fewer obstacles to social mobility, style bars replicated many of the problems for women employed in pubs.

Staff recruitment was not the only problem in attracting female customers to diverse types of drinking bars. Several factors – generation, image and outlook – proved instrumental in marketing products to different groups of women. There was ample evidence that selling alcohol to women was incompatible with employing overtly sexist advertisements, that women need not be targeted as a special marketing group and that advertisements could be gender-neutral without alienating male drinkers. One of the shrewdest analyses of women as consumers, *Wonder Woman: Marketing Secrets for the Trillion-Dollar Customer* (2008), written by Iain Ellwood and Sheila Shekar, adopted a generational approach to gaining insights into retailing alcohol.

Generation X women, born between 1966 and 1977 and representing one-fifth of the total female population, were less optimistic than their parents or children and more conservative than their own children. But simultaneously they were guilt-ridden owing to abandoning their parents' priority given to work. They were caught between two generations, the baby boomers (1945–65), on one hand, and Generation Y, on the other (1977 to present). Though they espoused the traditional values of their parents, insecurity and uncertainty – fostered by AIDS, pessimistic long-term career prospects and financial responsibility for parents – prevented them from embracing the more carefree, liberated lives of their children. Such woman displayed striking self-reliance: almost 40 per cent of all women between sixteen and sixty-four were non-married, and this group would eventually comprise half of all women by 2010. Keenness to blur gender lines (as a reflection of their self-reliance), quest for independence, scepticism about exaggerated advertisers' claims, and a overriding interest in asserting control over their relationships, all made Generation X women distinctive, requiring considerable perception from marketers. The four Manhattan women in *Sex and the City* who embodied these traits explain why Guinness sponsored it. Guinness market research in 2000 led to the dubbing of such women as SASSY – single, affluent, successful, sensual and young – and to the reorientation of Bailey's as a feminine drink. Women accounted for three-fifths of sales of PPS (premium packaged spirits) beverages, the leading female drink category that easily outsold cider, lager and ale. 'Factual endorsements help to persuade Generation X women that performance claims are both true and significant', observed Iain Ellwood and Sheila Shekar. Indeed, they thought few other approaches rival personal testimonies as an advertising strategy.[42]

No one demonstrated the truth of this statement better than Timothy Taylor's brewery. Witness the astounding consumer reaction late in the 1990s to Madonna's offhand (and quite unsolicited) praise for the Yorkshire brewery's award-winning beer, Landlord. Though not having a high alcohol content, Landlord had as much flavour and distinctiveness as stronger beers. So great was the impact that the brewery had difficulty keeping up with soaring demand in what became one of the most successful, if unplanned, advertisements in modern history. The advertisement on the brewery's company vans had read 'For Men of the North', but, in response to female staff, the new strapline was 'Brewed for Men of the North and Now Liked by Madonna'.[43] Thus, as Madonna graphically demonstrated, women and men could respond to the same stimuli and product in identical ways. Madonna appealed to Generation X women for numerous reasons: her endorsement embodied the anti-marketing approach so appealing to this generation – she was widely known but an unpaid sponsor of the beer; as a beer drinker, she provided an honest, straightforward, factual and (unprompted) account that resonated with these women; and, in extolling this particular beer, she asserted women's right to assume roles formerly associated exclusively with men. In drinking Taylor's Landlord, Generation X women proved their self-reliance, displaying the initiative to redraw gender boundaries between men and women.

Some marketers understood and cleverly exploited Generation X women's ironic attitude towards advertising. Such women 'appreciate the self-conscious attitude that says overtly, "We know we are trying to sell to you but we think you'll like this product"'.[44] No advertisement illustrated this insight better than Boddington's 'Cream of Manchester' campaign late in the 1990s, which took self-mockery of advertising aimed at males to an entirely new level by inverting gender stereotypes. Imaginative, unconventional and wholly uncharacteristic of the industry, Boddington's featured actress Melanie Sykes, 'totally in charge and totally female, slurping her way through pints of creamy Boddies'. Soaring sales to both sexes clearly demonstrated the unrealized potential of unisex advertising, when targeted at one generation of women.[45] According to Natalie Glover, manger of the Flying Standard (Coventry), 'the Melanie Sykes adverts made it more acceptable for women to drink bitter'. Another example of skilfully wooing Generation X women came when the drinks manufacturer DiSaronno set up a stall at the BBC Good Food Show in 1995. Other drinks competitors had predictably hired seductive blondes, but not DiSaronno. It too cleverly inverted gender stereotypes by hiring male hunks attired in dinner jackets to parade in front of the booth. 'It created quite a stir', remarked the company's brand manager, Angela Curry, with a classic understatement.[46]

Generation Y women, however, were less homogeneous than Ellwood and Shekar depict, and must be divided into two groups, reflecting their birth cohort. The youngest drinkers, born between 1985 and 1991, drank for different reasons than their older siblings. Determination to get drunk ranked fourth as a motive for drinking for over half of these young women.[47]

Older women in this generation, born between 1978 and 1984, rejected drunkenness as an avowed object, and consumed alcohol primarily for sociability and taste.[48] These women fundamentally shaped the emergent new drinking culture in which style bars played such a pivotal role. To these women, where they worked, what they bought and where they socialized all defined their identity. Because brands embodied their values, these women choose those which, after thorough research, demonstrated corporate social responsibility, called CSR in the trade.[49] 'Choice of drink remains highly gendered ... illustrating how drinking alcohol is linked with self-image, identity and consumer marketing for young people', commented one leading survey of drinking habits.[50]

Tim Martin's J. D. Wetherspoon Company exhibited CSR, too. He spearheaded the transformation of big buildings – initially carpet warehouses, car showrooms, Woolworth's stores, and later banks, post offices, even theatres and cinemas – into big pubs, across the company. Because he built drinking premises, dubbed superpubs, within the existing structure and restored the original premises to former glory, Martin could rightly depict himself as preserving Britain's historic heritage. So too, for example, concluded the Tunbridge Wells Civic Society, which bestowed an award for his restoring a former opera house. In this instance, Martin reclaimed the glories of the past from the dinginess of the present: the opera house had descended down the social scale, becoming an unheralded bingo hall.[51] He aimed to make money and did; but his vision, dovetailing with Generation Y women's interest in projecting corporate social responsibility, went well beyond drinking in a salubrious watering hole. In yet another sense, he qualified as an innovator in promoting healthy surroundings for all customers. Well before virtually anyone else in the industry, Martin created non-smoking areas in each pub spanning one-fourth of the floor space throughout his chain of JDW pubs. As drinkers steadily turned to drinking at home in the ensuing years, market research confirmed that smoky atmospheres ranked alongside price as two of the chief deterrents to frequenting pubs. 'There are', noted the *Publican* reporter, 'thousands of discontented ex-pub-goers out there, unwilling to spend their leisure time in smoky pubs'.[52] Grateful letters primarily from women vindicated Martin's strategy. Environments permeated with smoke undoubtedly affected such women's quest for sociability and relaxation, two of the three key factors motivating them to consume alcohol. By far the most important factor, the sheer enjoyment of tasting alcohol, could also be thwarted in a repulsive smoky atmosphere.[53]

Wetherspoon earned Generation Y women's respect also as a model employer. No other pubco matched its success as one of Britain's foremost employers. Across a wide spectrum – salaries, benefits, diversity, training, career opportunities, environmental sustainability and CSR – Wetherspoon clearly impressed judges. Exemplifying his sensitivity to women as his employees, Martin learned that his barmaids felt uneasy when male customers used their names listed on name tags, so he dropped the practice altogether. His impact easily transcended JDW. 'Other operators watch what he's doing like hawks', confessed one such competitor. On publication of *Britain's Top Employers, 2008*, a story and picture appeared in the company's magazine. Posed in front of a Wetherspoon pub were ten employees, all of them women, including the firm's legal director.[54]

His origins as a progressive employer had deep roots. Martin learned much from the founder of Wal-Mart, Sam Walton, whose autobiography, *Made in America*, he had read with abiding interest.[55] Walton had introduced a profit sharing scheme with employees, and Martin in 1998 emulated him with a bonus scheme in which bar staff received a monthly bonus of 6 per cent, the only pubco to adopt such a policy. Martin literally paid for his commitment twice over: the City punished his generosity with a slump in share price, but his decision remained unchanged. He equally borrowed from Walton the importance of incorporating staff ideas, a principle which provided the genesis of his unexpected strong public support in 2004 for a total smoking ban in all pubs in the industry from January 2006. As a former smoker and current drinker, Martin had suspected strongly that if he took the initiative and banned smoking in his Wetherspoon chain, widespread customer dissatisfaction would ensue, driving many disgruntled customers out of his pubs. But, as Walton himself had found earlier on other issues, an informal poll of staff at headquarters disclosed another story: numerous employees who drank had boycotted his competitors' pubs and restaurants during rush hours owing to pungent smoking odours. Though the industry in general excoriated him, Martin pointed to the successful implementation of a smoking ban in Scotland, where higher food sales had largely offset declines in alcohol sales, as offering a powerful example to the industry.[56] Martin's advocacy of a national ban and his adoption of one in JDW pubs proved instrumental in convincing the government to embrace a blanket smoking prohibition throughout the industry from 1 July 2007.

His commitment to eliminating smoking throughout the country's pubs derived from several factors. First, Martin believed in listening to staff concerns, a conviction that provided the impetus for his business philosophy of institutionizing change. 'A culture of continuous improvement and trying new ideas was emerging in the 1980s, which underpinned continued success in the 1990s', recalled Paul Charity in a profile published in 2002. Second, California had proscribed smoking several years earlier without confronting economic disaster. There, after a two-year period of adjustment, bars and restaurants regained ground lost owing to the ban. It was no accident, therefore, that Martin saw what had happened in California, for here he had formed an overseas partnership years earlier with Fetzer Vineyards in what would become a classic example of Anglo-American exchange and globalism.[57]

In associating his own company with a cutting-edge environmentally conscious winery, Martin dramatically expanded the concept of CSR. Founded in California in 1968, Fetzer Vineyards acquired a well-earned reputation as an outstanding 'green' company. 'It is our responsibility to work in a way which treads lightly on the land, so it is important that our wine-making practices be as environmentally friendly as possible', asserted Dennis Martin, the vineyards' winemaker. Among producers of organic grapes, Fetzer ranked not only first in California but as one of the world's leaders. From its installation of an immense solar panel decreasing the company's electrical needs by 75 per cent and so reducing the company's greenhouse gases, to recycling virtually everything – glass, cardboard as well as grape skins, stems and seeds – the winery aggressively sought sustainable practices. With its waste sent to landfill cut by 95 per cent, Fetzer became one of the state's major recycling companies.[58] Martin, too, perhaps influenced by Fetzer, embraced environmentalism: 'I am sure we're recycling more than anyone else and I am sure we can do better'. By 2007, Martin had opened his first 'green pub' in Melton Mowbray, and instructed other pubs in his company to turn off curtain heaters, common in restaurants and pubs for heating and cooling, to save electricity.[59]

Fetzer became Wetherspoon's house wine in 1998, giving his pub chain a new world wine from a region enormously popular in Britain.[60] That it was organic and from a company with strong CSR credentials meant that Generation Y women, who were far likelier to drink wine than men, had strong reasons for consuming it. Within a decade the two companies collaborated in inaugurating a draught wine system. 'The wine is stored chilled in a sealed container and, when a glass is requested, the required amount is "pulled through" a cooling system, delivering the precise temperature required', commented Wetherspoon's magazine.[61]

Supermarkets and off-licence retailers also grasp the psychology of selling women beer far better than most breweries. Tesco became the first supermarket chain to establish a panel of women who recommended beers for female drinkers.[62] This interest reflected significant changes in consumer habits. In less than a decade beer sales in shops and especially supermarkets soared, growing from 30 per cent (1998) to 41 per cent (2005) of the market.[63] Hiring Liz Moran as Marketing Director seemingly helped give Carlsberg-Tetley a different marketing approach to females. 'Women are also more discriminating', she emphasized. 'They appreciate more information', she added, and 'want some reassurance about the integrity and quality of what they're drinking'.[64]

Commitment to catering to an informed consumer explains why style bar staff undertook an educational role. 'We don't want to appeal to dickheads', decreed Christian Townsley, bar manager at Leeds's North Bar. 'The punters who show no interest in beer and don't want to be educated are the ones that we don't want.' Paul Gilchrist, manager of the Bierodrome, a chain of London style bars founded in 1999 in Islington devoted to popularizing Belgian beers, articulated similar sentiments, though more diplomatically. 'It's not [just] about pulling pints', he argued. Bierodrome disseminated knowledge about Belgian culture to customers cultivating a discerning palate. Taking its proselytizing mission seriously, the company gave its staff frequent beer seminars, even dispatching them on three-day visits to Belgium, where they both toured breweries and imbibed the country's culture (as well as some outstanding world beers). Each outlet offered a handful of draught beers and stocked another fifty bottled beers, all of them from Belgium.[65]

In involving customers in a personal relationship with bar staff, creating what Ellwood and Shekar recently called 'the community spirit of the experience',[66] style bar proprietors accomplished several objectives crucial to attracting the Generation Y woman: they diminished the emotional distance between themselves and the patron; with staff members placed in a friendly role, they encouraged her to see their bars as a third space, complementing home and office; and finally they fostered a feeling of belonging, much like the successful Starbucks' chain, where staff did not allegedly want so much to sell you coffee as be your friend. Such shrewd understanding of this new female generation underlined how outsiders to the industry appreciated more readily than traditional drink marketers that women were not a homogeneous group, that gender relations were changing and that the psychology of sales would provide both insight and impetus for new marketing strategies.

Staff informed about products also appealed to female customers generally. By providing information about beers, employees established a personal relationship with women customers, as two expert advertisers put it, 'through a sense of growth and learning'. Unlike men, women found this interaction both satisfying and emboldening because they had imbibed novel ideas and mastered facts about a new topic which had immediate applicability. This gender difference also emerged when buying wine: women were more willing than men to ask for guidance about different wines.[67]

The brand itself, however, must possess a distinctive image, certainly not one with widespread appeal. Christian Townsley knew well his clientele's attitudes at Leeds's North Bar. Imported beers reigned supreme at his establishment, and so he expressed strong dislike of the popular Kronenbourg 1664, brewed in the UK. He excluded the beer from his beverage list, but, as a compromise, reluctantly served it on tap. 'We hide it away at the end of the bar', he shamefacedly admitted. 'But', he vowed, 'we're going to get rid of it'.[68]

Intimate knowledge of the product and its image interacted with a third trait, a quest to explore new products. Booming sales in Belgian imports characterized the business at Inspire, a Coventry style bar where Duvel qualified hands down as the best seller. 'Imported beer drinkers', thought its licensee, 'tend to be open minded, adventurous, willing to try something new and are not scared to spend money'. To him, 'they are the new breed of independent drinkers'. Photographed for the story in the *Publican* were two young women, easily recognizable as Generation Y females. Unlike pubs, the bar catered to these speciality beers, all of them bottled and none of them household brands. One-third or even half of the twenty to thirty different selections changed each month. Sampling was encouraged, and exchanges made without charge. As at other style bars, the landlord ensured staff had knowledge about not just stocking and serving the beers, but most critically their appearance. Duvel, for example, was famed for its oversized head, a product of its bottle fermentation. With his continental beers, landlord John Leape was offering customers not merely different, exotic beverages, but an opportunity 'to reminisce about a holiday or trip where they first tasted the beers'. On return visits, he added, 'they bring along their friends and family so that they too can feel the ambience of that country'.[69]

Rising numbers of trips abroad fostered this popularity of foreign beers among the upmarket twenty-five to thirty-four year olds, who had high disposable income. Exposed to different tasting beers abroad, they returned home, eager to continue drinking these new beverages. By 2002, the doubling of imported beer sales since 1980 was part of a broader trend in which foreign food and beverages – notably Thai and Indonesian cuisine as well as speciality coffees – grew markedly in popularity. Another factor promoting imported beers was the trend of eating dishes with matching beers: diners, for example, consumed pizzas and pastas with Italy's Nastro Azzurro, the fourth most popular draught lager in pubs. As domestic beer consumption plateaued from 2005, imported beer sales soared over 20 per cent. From the perspective of drink retailers, foreign beer sales proved more lucrative because such beers carried higher profit margins.[70] This trend towards drinking such speciality beers in turn underscored a fourth trait, globalization.

In consuming the same beverages as men, women could be portrayed and, just as importantly, see themselves as having gained full gender equality. Speciality imported beers such as Belgian Hoegaarden and Leffe thus had enormous appeal to Generation Y women. New unisex drinking habits emerged in which men as well as women drank such beers and relished the taste. Some women had already demonstrated their fondness for speciality beers. Leeds's North Bar sponsored a competition in which contestants quickly quaffed two beers from each country. In 2001, a nineteen-year old woman bested all men.[71]

Style bars appeared in areas undergoing gentrification, most notably London's Brixton where loud music based around Coldharbour Lane hosted by DJs defined the nightlife for newly established young professionals from the mid-1990s. Brixton had become fashionable owing to its cheap housing and convenience for Oxford Circus. Again such venues sought to appeal to groups anxious to separate themselves from mainstream drinkers. 'People who come here are cool and open-minded', maintained John Sherdlow, owner of Helter Skelter, one of the pioneers of the night scene. 'Sure there are hookers and drug dealers outside, but in six years here none of my customers have been badly wounded or killed, and it filters out the wholesome, stale, and frankly boring people from Clapham and some other parts of South London', he asserted. These venues closely resembled the Bierodromes and Leeds's North Bar in looking abroad for inspiration and undertaking an educational role.[72]

Style bars experienced explosive growth. Indigenously brewed ale and lager sales declined, but imported beer sales soared, driven in part by their popularity among women. Because traditional domestic draught beers were consumed in pint or half-pint mugs, all linked in women's minds with males, females more easily turned to quaffing foreign beers, served in bottles. Women could drink directly out of the bottles or from tastefully designed branded glasses, free of male associations. As speciality imported beers, such as Hoegaarden and Leffe, gained popularity, consumption habits modified. New unisex drinking habits emerged in which men as well as women drank such beer and relished its taste.[73] At the White Horse Inn (Hendrerwydd, Denbighshire), the introduction of new crystal goblets in which to drink Pilsner Urquell sent sales skyrocketing, with a 33 per cent increase. 'A lot more women have started drinking the beer', noted the landlord.[74]

Marketing attractions helped foster this expansion. Niche beers had low volume but high profit margins, whereas standard beers sold in volume with small margins, enabling style bar proprietors to exploit the 'flight to quality' without sacrificing sales in house beers. These two categories thus complemented rather than competed against each other. 'Consumers', observed Freedom Brewery's Philip Parker, 'are trading up to higher quality and higher value products'. What they did not consume at style bars was traditional cask ale, which remained, as one reporter commented, 'a non-starter in the minds of the style bar beer buyer and many of their young customers'.[75]

Where large numbers of women congregated for leisure, beer in general simply had minimal appeal. In a 2008 survey of pubs and bars in which women constituted at least 50 per cent of the clientele, the top selling eleven female beverages included wines, vodka, champagne, gin, soft drinks, rum, and a mixed drink, but no beers whatsoever. At the top were white and then red wine, followed by Smirnoff Red Vodka, Moët and Chandon Champagne,

J20 Packaged Fruit Juice, Gordon's Gin and Coca Cola or Diet Coke Mixer. Magners Irish Cider ranked eighth. Seven beers made the final list, with just Carlsberg Draught Lager (ranked 39th) the only indigenously produced beer. Among women, Corona Extra, San Miguel Lager and Stella Artois outsold it.[76]

Ironically, women finally received greater credit as pivotal decision-makers because market research confirmed their influence over male companions. A Pizza Express survey in 2005 found that women in 95 per cent of the cases decided which pub or restaurant to visit. Fully two-thirds of the women, moreover, assumed control in ordering their partners' meals and in choosing the wine. Role reversal did not stop there when the wine bottle arrived: women would 'even taste it before serving'. What led to this transfer of decision-making authority? Women, now liberated, overwhelmingly displayed a willingness to pay for themselves: over nine of every ten went 'Dutch'. Differing gender traits re-enforced women's assumption of control. Men dithered over what to order when eating out, whereas women quickly decided: twice as many women as men could choose meals in five minutes. These findings prompted designation of an entirely new category, female ownership of people dining out, numbering some twelve million in the UK, with the heaviest concentration of such couples in the East Midlands (and the lowest, not surprisingly, in Scotland).[77] Nor were women in Britain displaying unique characteristics. Throughout the Western countries women acted as decision-makers in more than four of every five purchases.[78]

Women's influence over men when drinking alcohol, however, now went much further. Accompanying women into a bar, men abandoned their traditional beverage, a pint of British beer or lager, for wine or imported bottled beers. Unisex drinking habits thus arrived with couples sharing wine or beer, imported from the continent.[79] There was yet another irony about women as drinkers: beer wholesalers, instead of converting women to nationally branded beers, found that men themselves had discovered wine as a pub beverage. When surveyed in 2007, over half of the men confirmed that they switched to wine after drinking the first pint owing to beer's bloating effects. Two-thirds of the men, moreover, much preferred sharing a bottle of wine rather than ordering rounds of lager because they saw wine as a more sociable beverage. Women, too, confirmed new drinking habits. They began turning from Smirnoff Ice, easily the most popular Ready to Drink (RTD) beverage, to wine as they could share the beverage with partners or friends.[80]

Women were important not simply because they held sway over male companions, but because of anticipated demographic changes: non-married women, aged sixteen to sixty-four – nearly two of every five women in the UK (2005) – would soon comprise almost one in every two (2010). Both Generation X and Y women, argued Ellwood and Shekar, 'have taken control of their relationships and are no longer seen as passive but as active in choosing their lifestyle and the brands they associate with'.[81]

Recognition of new drinking habits and market trends led to the Orchid Group in 2006, one of the first pubcos in which women assumed vital managerial roles. The pubco embraced a novel philosophy, aimed specifically at females as customers as well as executives. This made sense, given that women contributed entirely different skills and attitudes to retailing. 'What we're trying to embed in our company is a female environment, so a female manager can relate to that environment and knows exactly what needs to be done', stressed Marie Wheatley, Orchid Personnel Director. No other pubco, management proudly asserted, employed more women as a percentage of the total workforce than Orchid. Women constituted two-fifths of management teams in its pubs, and fully one-half of the head office staff. Experience in working with Ha! Ha! Bar and Canteen as well as market research shaped the distinctive approach to retailing of its two chief executives. Men evaluated a pub on the basis of several factors, whereas women more exactingly had ten to twelve items on their checklist.[82]

This shrewd insight also explained the impressive success of Matchbar in generating a clientele overwhelmingly of women of diverse sexual orientation.[83] Its owner, Jonathan Downey, argued that, when it came to selecting a drinking venue, women stood three levels above men, whose sole interests in a pint of beer and male friends represented 'the lowest common denominator' in his bars. With much disposable income and a more discriminating eye, women became extremely valuable as patrons. Mindful of these gender differences, Downey ensured his bars provided the desirable amenities on females' checklist – a place to sit, attractive toilets, table service, good-quality house wine, a selection of wines and appealing cocktails.[84]

At Orchid, as at Matchbar, women encountered licensed premises appealing directly to Generation Y females as consumers. Highly trained staff, dressed in tailored uniforms, greeted customers, who entered rooms décorated with expensive John Lewis wallpaper. 'There is a strong emphasis on quality, ethical products (all coffee is Fairtrade) and healthier options', remarked one trainer. To attract mothers, Orchid provided children's meals following Food Standards Authority standards for fat, salt and sugar. Meat and vegetables came from Red Tractor Farms, ensuring the best quality. While landlords elsewhere complained about the smoking ban driving custom away, Orchid's managers now counted over half of all women bringing children. Hence, Orchid saw itself as creating not so much upmarket pubs as well-designed restaurants where non-alcoholic beverages featured prominently, especially at lunchtimes. Like style bars, Orchid pubs displayed a chameleon philosophy in which they catered to different types of customers during the day, with alcohol sales often incidental to the business. In the morning, speciality coffees and free wireless internet drew businesswomen and mothers. 'It's about trying to get that wider appeal and making people think that it's not just an alcohol-based environment', felt Sharon Hammond, Orchid's Concept Development manager.[85]

Orchid demonstrated how employing knowledgeable women throughout the company could generate vast custom from females. As had been discovered in pubcos years before, employing women on one side of the bar counter profoundly influenced those on the other. Within two years of its founding, Orchid had nearly doubled the percentage of its wine sales. Pubs with women as the dominant customers had one-third of total sales from wine. By then, too, Orchid was running a chain of nearly three hundred pubs with annual sales of £230 million, making it the six-largest pubco in the UK. Adam Bowers, Marketing Manager of Orchid, summarized the basis of the company's success: 'Everything is now done with female appeal in the back of people's minds when it comes to the local environment, right down to menu content and tonality of words'.[86]

In turning to women as challengers to the overwhelming masculinity dominating the industry, Orchid was scarcely unique. Peach, Punch, Greene King and Coors also embraced policies to promote more women as retailers. Greene King, a national brewery, boasted that single women comprised one out of every seven of its licensees. Committed to expanding this proportion, the brewery launched a new campaign, Public Housewives, with Debi Sicklemore (Grafton Arms, Euston), a 25-year veteran behind the bar, as one of its proponents.[87]

The likelihood of unescorted women being chatted up in traditional male pubs had long offended and alienated them, and here too lesbian bars provided new alternative venues. Lesbians and heterosexual women flocked to the Earl Ferrers (Streatham, South London), as its tenant acknowledged, 'because there's no macho element'. In patronizing the Via Fossa in Manchester's gay quarter, one straight woman candidly stated her rationale: 'You don't get hassled by dickheads'. According to the Ferrers's tenant, 'some of our female customers tell me ours is the only pub they go to by themselves to have a drink and a read'.

Staffing became vital in drawing women, whether lesbians or heterosexuals. At the King William IV (Hampstead Heath, London), owners as well as the bar staff were lesbians. In female-friendly surroundings, women might consume something other than wines. Manchester's Bar Fringe featured Belgian beers, while the Earl Ferrers stocked real ales. Twelve ciders and seven ales on tap enticed lesbians to the Cumberland Arms (Ouseburn), part of Newcastle-upon-Tyne's industrial valley. Lesbians could practise darts and compete on teams while sipping continental lagers at the Lord Clifdon (Hockley, Birmingham). Diverse entertainment was also offered: comedy, poetry, ping-pong and live music. The Odd Bar, in Manchester's Northern Quarter, innovatively donated its walls to the city's artists, and supplied a cinema screen in the basement for aspiring film makers. To the east in Yorkshire, Hebden Bridge's B@r Place catered specifically to the upwardly mobile, academics and 'creative media types' who could participate in speed dating and discos.[88]

The smoking ban as much as sexual orientation and female-friendly venues loomed large as a factor transforming the culture of brewing. Impetus for prohibiting smoking reflected the belief that 'women have become the prime target customer, indeed almost the main hope for the future of the trade', contended Andrew Pring, editor of the retailers' *Morning Advertiser* in 2007. That same year a poll established that the most likely group turning to pubs would be upmarket, married women in their forties, partly drawn by the imposition of the smoking prohibition. Though licensed premises would lose some youths as customers, parents confirmed that the elimination of smoking would make pubs more family-friendly. Orchid's rapid expansion also underlined how promoting women to upper levels of management enabled the pubco to embrace a philosophy welcoming to females as consumers. Pring noted the ever-widening impact of women on the industry. 'In the way pubs are designed, in what they sell, in how they reach out to new customers, in how they reinvent themselves, women executives are making their indelible mark on the face of the trade', he argued in 2008.[89]

Signifying accelerating changes, the *Morning Advertiser* compiled a list of women of substance in the industry in 2008. At the pinnacle were Ann Yerburg (Chair of Lancashire brewery Daniel Thwaites); Belinda Sutton (Managing Director of Cambridgeshire brewery Elgood & Sons); Lucy Knowles (Managing Director of Corney & Barrow wine bars); Deborah Kemp (Managing Director of Punch Taverns, then the country's largest pubco); Lynne D'Arcy (Joint Managing Director of Admiral Taverns, the third biggest pubco); and Carola Brown (Director of Ballard's Brewery, which she co-founded in 1980).

Beneath this exalted level, women held positions as directors in diverse fields – marketing, legal, human resources, public relations, retail operations, and recruitment and training. As this list testified, women were 'getting their hands on the reins of corporate power' to an unprecedented degree. More prosaically, women were increasingly establishing micro-breweries, typically forming partnerships with men. Nevertheless, women overall remained marginal as a factor in the corporate elite. Of the fifty most influential people in the pub industry in 2009, just two women appeared on the *Morning Advertiser*'s list.[90]

Entrenched opposition to women in the boardroom derived ironically not just from breweries, but from some pubcos. One of the largest pubcos, Spirit Group, owner of well over a thousand pubs, continued to point, not to more women as executives, but to cleanliness, safety, competitive prices and managerial efficiency, as the solution to drawing more customers. Another industry leader deprecating changes in both gender drinking and the overall structure of the drinks industry was Ian McKerracher, Chief Executive of the Restaurant Association. Throughout the industry, he confidently urged in 2002, 'there is no longer any sexual bias – it's more about aptitude and ability'.[91]

That gender played a decisive role in retailing was legitimized by subsequent market research. According to a *Morning Advertiser* survey in 2008, women were vastly superior to men across a wide spectrum. In defusing customer problems as well as organizational and front-of-house skills, women outperformed men by staggering percentages. Likewise, in catering, multi-tasking and finances, females held commanding leads. One participant succinctly summarized the cumulative findings. 'Many men are stuck in the old ways – women have better ideas and a new outlook on pub life in the 21st century.' There was, too, the feeling that women as homemakers naturally concentrated on customer service and standards, whereas men, as the female head of retailing for St Austell's Brewery knew, 'will look at the more macho options, edging towards technology, facilities and sports'. At a deeper level still, women assumed roles associated with nurturing. 'We are social workers, we are an ear to bend – a mother figure in a way', explained a female tenant of Fuller's Brewery. Some female retail executives drew an analogy between choosing the ideal female-friendly venue and evaluating a male as a potential mate. 'It must have a level of refinement, [and] be well-dressed, clean and smell good', pronounced Deborah Kemp, Managing Director of the Tenancy Division for pubco Punch. 'It would', she added, 'have personality with a great sense of humour – yet make her feel safe and secure'.[92]

Sexism, though declining, tenaciously persisted. Disconcerted that men vowed to abandon their local owing to fears that the new female manager was incapable of maintaining the cask ale in the best condition, Una Moir, Fuller's Operation Manager, faced the critics down. As a man's drink, beer had been historically cared for by the landlord, and so men viewed the entry of women into this sacred sanctum with deep suspicion.[93] Nicky Smiles likewise encountered the old sexist brewing culture soon after being named Operations Director of pubco Columbo at the age of twenty-four in 2008. 'When I meet people in the trade', she related, 'they tend to treat me as the person bringing in the coffee – especially suppliers.' Columbo's owners, two knowledgeable males, promoted her on the basis not of prior work experience, but of their strong conviction that 'she would end up running the company'. This was an enormous tribute, given the *Publican*'s characterization of Columbo as 'one of the most impressive operations in London'.[94]

Although market research and environmental psychology had afforded many insights into how to sell women alcohol, brewing industry executives had still steadfastly relied on males as the main consumers of their products. Only when forced to confront the long-term effect of wine bars and pubcos did some breweries realize the old order was disappearing, increasingly besieged by cultural and social developments which had elevated females' roles in other public spaces. The industry was, in fact, too much captive of its history in which men patronized pubs, bought beer and denigrated women. From these attitudes had come a culture of hostility to women, indeed of misogyny, dedicated to excluding them altogether from or at least marginalizing their access to pubs, the last bastion of the historic masculine republic.

From a women's perspective, the Beer Orders, far from the disaster as portrayed by detractors, introduced change into a static industry with new money, new people and new ideas. With them emerged a new culture of drinking in which women acquired greater social mobility and equal treatment with men in running or managing pubs; and as customers would be valued as vital in generating profits. By the early 2000s, women were regarded as critical in marketing, determining where and what their partners drank, and what was eaten. Ironically, in the end it was not the much-solicited men as the much overlooked women who proved so important in generating profits. Had brewers pitched their appeal to women much earlier, the problems of wooing them as customers would have been far easier. Instead, after decades of dismissing, denigrating and denying women's worth as drinkers, brewing executives confronted unpalatable alternatives: women who drank either wine or other beverages in pubs, or who consumed imported beers, chiefly from the continent, in style bars or clubs. Neither alternative was appealing. Following decades of insinuating both negative attitudes through advertising in women's minds and gendered drinking, so evocative of an overwhelming male culture, females could evaluate traditional pubs and beverages only from a jaundiced perspective. Consumption of foreign beers and wines – a conscious repudiation of endemic indigenous sexism – thus increasingly dominated the new culture of drinking, especially among Generation Y women and the men whom they so profoundly influenced.

There were several other ironies to this drawn-out tale of male prejudice against women's presence as drinkers, retailers and drink executives. Long stalwart supporters of the masculine republic in pubs and beerhouses, large breweries, owners of hundreds, sometimes thousands, of tied houses for almost two centuries and so dominant players in the market, vanished, save as manufacturers of beer itself. Most large breweries, except for Greene King and Fullers, had in turn been taken over by multinational concerns. Recent creations of the late twentieth century, pubcos lacked the long tradition of upholding the old masculine order, though enough sexism persisted to retard radical changes. The pub itself, however, had lost its centrality as a leisure venue. According to Peach Factory's *Eating Out and the Consumer Report, 2008*, twice as many people watched television (89 per cent) and almost the same proportion surfed the internet (83 per cent) as went to pubs (43 per cent). More people ate out at restaurants (57 per cent) and entertained friends at home or were entertained by them (52 per cent) than patronized pubs. As the report concluded, 'Britain has undergone an important cultural shift, where eating out rather than drinking out, has become the nation's number one out-of-home activity'. Pub going, in fact, proved no more popular than playing computer games![95]

Drinking habits, too, had fundamentally altered. Instead of visiting their local often during the week, regulars now confined drinking sessions to one

Table 6 Contraction of the local, 1970s-2018

Date	*On-Trade Beer Volumes (Barrels)*
Late 1970s	37 million
2008	17 million
Forecast 2018	10 million

Source: Paul Charity, 'Clarke: "Beer will Drop by 40%"', *Morning Advertiser*, 12 June 2008.

evening, usually Wednesdays, or more generally the weekend. Age became crucial as a predicator of going out. As age increased, so did drinking at home. Nearly two-and-a-half times as many drinkers under twenty-five years of age drank out in the previous month compared to those over fifty-five. Compared to Denmark, Britain looked commendably abstemious. Britons typically started their drinking day at 6:14 p.m., ninety minutes later than the Danes. Nearly two-and-a-half times as many Danes drank at lunchtime as Britons. Drinking out less had serious economic consequences. In 2008, Tim Clarke, Chief Executive of Mitchells & Butlers, prophesied that pubs would lose 40 per cent of their beer sales over the next decade, perhaps jeopardizing ten thousand locals (Table 6). This projected loss would hit pubs already staggering with the loss of one-third of their trade within two decades (1999–2018). These sobering trends and projections sat rather oddly with *The Enduring Appeal of the Local*, a Greene King survey published several months later.[96] Most likely survivors were those relying on food sales to drive alcohol consumption. Some managed chains, pre-eminently J. D. Wetherspoons, had already anticipated market changes, and of course made women as customers, staff and executives central to its business strategy. Already in the 1980s, JDW pubs were on average generating over one-fifth of their takings from food.[97]

Without a cross-section of the population, pubs, bars and clubs catered primarily to the young, thereby lacking the peer pressure capable of exerting social control over those displaying anti-social behaviour. The end result, youth binge drinking, would draw headlines, criticism and demands for instituting an entirely new drinking regime. But without older patrons as regulars, owners of drinking venues – whether pubs, bars or clubs – had strong motives for opposing restrictions, potentially cutting deeply into profits.

Notes

1 For the origins of the Beer Orders and the brewers' response, see David Hughes, 'Rolled Over by the Beerage', *Sunday Times*, 16 July 1989.

2 Derek Pain, 'Looking Back Across the Beers', *Morning Advertiser*, 2 Sept. 2004.

3 John Spicer, Chris Thurman, John Walters and Simon Ward, *Intervention in the Modern UK Brewing Industry* (New York: Palgrave Macmillan, 2012), p. 238.

4 The authors listed the 'winners' as the two biggest regional breweries, City professionals, redundant brewery executives, pubcos and foreign brewers (ibid., p. 242).

5 David Preece, Gordon Steven and Valerie Steven, *Work, Change and Competition: Managing for Bass* (London: Routledge, 1999), p. 26.

6 *Publican*, 13 Feb. 1986.

7 Ibid., 28 March 1995.

8 Ben McFarland, 'One for the Ladies', *Publican Newspaper*, 16 April 2001; Bob Williams, 'Return of Community Hub Pubs', *Publican*, 4 Oct. 1993.

9 John Shepherd, 'Last Chance Saloon', *Independent on Sunday*, 31 Oct. 1993; Edward Whitley, 'Time, Please, for the British Pub', *Spectator*, 268 (29 Feb. 1992), p. 16; Roderick Oram, 'Fresh Ferment for the Brewers', *Financial Times*, 19 Feb. 1995; Preece, Steven and Steven, *Work, Change and Competition*, pp. 13–14.

10 Shepherd, 'Last Chance Saloon'.

11 *Publican*, 25 July 1994.

12 Alan Cowell, 'Britain's Old-Fashioned Pubs Are Undergoing a Makeover', *New York Times International*, 8 Aug. 1999; Claudia Dowell, 'Grape Expectations', *Publican*, 19 May 1997; also see Spicer, Thurman, Walters and Ward (eds), *Intervention in the Modern UK Brewing Industry*, p. 233.

13 Michele Cheaney, 'Jobs for the Girls', *Publican Newspaper*, 28 April 1997; Robert Metcalfe, 'Wanted: Women Who Can Run Pubs', *Publican*, 11 Nov. 1989 and 26 Sept. 2005; also see Paul Jennings, *The Local: A History of the English Pub* (Stroud: Tempus, 2007), p. 222; Mike Bennett, 'Giving Tired Old Male Boozers the POW Factor', *Licensee and Morning Advertiser*, 6 Jan. 2000.

14 *Adventure*, 12 (Oct.–Dec. 1998), pp. 18–19; Adam Tinworth, 'Be Irresistible to Women', *Publican*, 3 July 1995; McFarland, 'One for the Ladies'.

15 Preece, Steven and Steven, *Work, Change and Competition*, p. 46.

16 Stanley Wright, *Running Your Own Pub* (London: Hutchinson & Co., 1984), p. 8; *Licensed Victuallers' Gazette*, Sept. 1961.

17 *Huntsman*, 27 (Autumn 1985), p. 12.

18 *Publican*, 16 Feb. 2004.

19 *Morning Advertiser*, 7 Sept. 2000; J. D. Pratten, 'Responding to Demand: New Types of Public Houses in the UK', *Journal of Food Products Marketing*, 9 (2003), p. 44.

20 Alistair Mutch, 'Trends and Tensions in UK Public House Management', *Hospitality Management*, 19 (2000), p. 368; Tinworth, 'Irresistible to Women'.

21 Cheaney, 'Jobs for the Girls'; Metcalfe, 'Women Who Can Run Pubs'; Tinworth, 'Irresistible to Women'; *Publican Newspaper*, 13 July 1998. See also Mutch, 'UK Public House Management', p. 368. Scottish & Newcastle likewise reported that women comprised about one-third of its applicants for pubs (*Publican*, 16 Feb. 2004).

22 Lorna Harrison, 'Those Were the Days', *Publican Newspaper*; 25 Sept. 2000; *Publican*, 16 Feb. 2004.

23 *Publican*, 7 March 1994.

24 Tinworth, 'Irresistible to Women'; Cheaney, 'Jobs for the Girls'.

25 MCM survey, quoted in the *Publican*, 13 June 1994; Catherine Turner, 'It's Your Round, Girls!', *Coventry Evening Telegraph*, 28 Sept. 2000; Andrew Burnyeat, 'Pubs Transformed by the Gentle Touch', *Publican Newspaper*, 8 May 2000.

26 John C. Everitt and Ian R. Bowler, 'Bitter-Sweet Conversions: Changing Times for the British Pub', *Journal of Popular Culture*, 32 (1996), p. 116; Mark Stretton, 'Bleak Streets', *Publican Newspaper*, 13 Jan. 2003.

27 David Flockhart, 'Beer', *Flavour*, 12 (June 2001), pp. 35–6; *Morning Advertiser*, 7 Oct. 2004.

28 Craig Thatcher, 'All Bar None', *Leisure & Management*, 16 (Dec. 1996), pp. 40–1; MORI, *Choice: Consumer's Views of Pub-Going* (London: Brewers' Society, 1992); Tim Knowles and David Egan, 'The Changing Structure of UK Brewing and Pub Retailing', *International Journal of Contemporary Hospitality Management*, 14:2 (2002), pp. 65–71; *Adventure*, 12 (Oct.–Dec. 1998), p. 19; Mintel *Leisure Report on Public Houses, Summer 1984*, quoted in *Publican*, 12 July 1984.

29 Key Note, *Public Houses* (London: Key Note Publications, 1991).

30 Turner, 'It's Your Round, Girls!' Critics of such beverages called it an alcopop.

31 Adam Withrington, 'Men: Drink More Wine', *Publican*, 14 Feb. 2005; *Publican*, 16 Aug. 2004.

32 *Glass: The Publican Newspaper Wine Magazine for 2003*; *Morning Advertiser*, 8 Aug. 2002.

33 Philip Ziegler and Desmond Seward (eds), *Brooks's: A Social History* (London: Constable, 1991): Christopher Wood, 'Brooks's Since the War', p. 105; and James Lees-Milne, 'The Second World War', p. 95.

34 Martin Peacock and Derren Selvarajah, '"Space I can call my Own": Private Social Clubs in London', *International Journal of Contemporary Hospitality Management*, 12 (2000), pp. 234–9.

35 Peacock and Selvarajah, 'Private Social Clubs in London', pp. 234–9; Kate Saunders, 'Running Circles Round Men: Gentlemen's Clubs for Female High-Flyers', *Sunday Times*, 25 Feb. 1990; Martin Peacock, 'London's New Private Social Clubs: Personal Space in the Age of "Hot Desking"', *Consumption and Participation: Leisure, Culture and Commerce, LSA*, No. 64 (2000), pp. 144–5, 150–1; Andy Knott, 'Women in the Industry', *Flavour*, 12 (June 2001), p. 57.

36 Knott, 'Women in the Industry', p. 57; Mark Ludmon, 'Players: Matt Saunders and Simon Patterson of Fat Cat Café Bars', *Flavour*, 10 (April 2001), pp. 36–9; *Publican*, 22 May 2006; *Publican*, 22 June 2009.

37 Flockhart, 'Beers', pp. 31–2.

38 Burnyeat, 'Bass to Cut Size of Its Flagship Chain'.

39 Gill Valentine, Sarah L. Holloway, Mark Jayne and Charlotte Knell, *Drinking Places: Where People Drink and Why* ([York]: Joseph Rowntree Foundation, 2007), p. 17; Graham Ridout, 'Border Crossings', *Morning Advertiser*, 12 Sept. 2002.

40 Mark Ludmon, 'Regional Breweries', *Flavour*, 13 (Aug. 2001), p. 61.

41 McFarland, 'One for the Ladies'; Knott, 'Women in the Industry', pp. 57–8.

42 Ellwood with Shekar, *Wonder Woman*, ch. 5.

43 Claire Hu, 'Madge's No Real-Ale Virgin', and 'Material Girl Boosts Landlord by 5 per cent', *Morning Advertiser*, 8 and 29 May 2003; Sarah Swainson (Marketing Managing of Bavaria UK) to Editor, *Publican*, 21 March 2005; Roger Protz, 'Women's Glasses Idea Is a Non Starter', *Morning Advertiser*, 17 March 2005.

44 Ellwood with Shekar, *Wonder Woman*, pp. 122, 126.

45 McFarland, 'One for the Ladies'; Flockhart, 'Beer', p. 36.

46 Turner, 'It's Your Round'; Tinworth, 'Irresistible to Women'.

47 See Chapter 9. Sarah L. Holloway, Gill Valentine and Mark Jayne, 'Masculinities, Femininities and the Geographies of Public and Private Drinking Landscapes', *Geoforum*, 40 (2009), pp. 824–5.

48 Surveys apparently did not give women the option of choosing whether they consumed alcohol as a method of establishing their identity (ibid., p. 826).
49 Ellwood with Shekar, *Wonder Woman*, ch. 4.
50 Judith Aldridge, Fiona Measham and Lisa Williams, *Illegal Leisure Revisited: Changing Patterns of Alcohol and Drug Use in Adolescents and Young Adults* (London: Routledge, 2011), p. 60.
51 Phil Mellows, 'Shopping for New Pubs Sites', *Publican Newspaper*, 2 Feb. 1998.
52 Marketpublic.com survey, quoted in Adam Withrington, 'What Do the People Think?', *Publican*, 4 Feb. 2007; Tinworth, 'Irresistible to Women'.
53 Holloway et al., 'Masculinities', pp. 825–6.
54 *Wetherspoon News*, June/July 2008, p. 11; Paul Charity, 'Profile: Wetherspoon' s Chairman Tim Martin', *Morning Advertiser*, 2 May 2002.
55 Sam Walton and John Huey, *Sam Walton, Made in America: My Story* (New York: Doubleday, 1992).
56 Steve Hemsley, 'Going by the Book', *Morning Advertiser*, 18 Oct. 2007; Claire Hu and Paul Charity, 'Laurel Calls for JDW to Make Pubs Smoke-Free', *Morning Advertiser*, 15 April 2004; Phil Mellows, 'Pubco Chief Slams Stone Age Staffing', *Publican Newspaper*, 27 Nov. 2000.
57 Paul Charity, 'Martin: Visionary or Gambler?' *Morning Advertiser*, 10 March 2005, and 'Profile: Wetherspoon's Chairman'.
58 *Wetherspoon News*, June/July 2008, pp. 42–3.
59 Paul Charity, 'Martin: Behind the Public Face', *Morning Advertiser*, 12 April 2007.
60 See Chapter 6, above, pp. 139–40.
61 *Wetherspoon News*, June/July, 2008, pp. 42–3.
62 Flockhart, 'Beers', pp. 33–4; also see Linada P. Morton, 'Targeting Generation X', *Public Relations Quarterly*, 48 (Winter 2003), pp. 43–5; Nelson Barber, Tim Dodd and Richard Ghiselli, 'Capturing the Younger Wine Consumer', *Journal of Wine Research*, 19 (2008), pp. 123, 130.
63 *Morning Advertiser*, 19 Oct. 2006.
64 Liz Moran, quoted in Tinworth, 'Irresistible to Women'.
65 Andy Knott, 'Bierodrome', *Flavour*, 13 (Aug. 2001), pp. 37–8, and 'Beer: North Bar, Leeds', 14 (Sept. 2001), pp. 35–6; also see Sally Bairstow, 'Increase Your Pulling Power', *Morning Advertiser*, 19 June 2003.
66 Ellwood with Shekar, *Wonder Woman*, p. 106.
67 Ibid., pp. 187–8, 203–4.
68 Knott, 'North Bar, Leeds', pp. 35–6.
69 *Publican*, 31 Jan. 2005.
70 *Morning Advertiser*: Tony Halstead, 'Rise of the Foreign Legion', 7 Aug. 2003; Kelly Smith, 'Be Famous … for World Beers', 24 Jan. 2008; 24 Aug. 2008; Ridout, 'Border Crossings'.
71 Flockhart, 'Beers', pp . 33–4; also see Tinworth, 'Irresistible to Women'.
72 Tom Innes, 'Location Report: Brixton', *Flavour*, 16 (Nov. 2001), pp. 22–4.
73 *Morning Advertiser*, 19 June 2003; Sarah Swainson (Marketing Managing of Bavaria UK) to Editor, *Publican*, 21 March 2005; Datamonitor Report quoted in David Tooley, 'Women Poised to Dominate Market', *Licensee & Morning Advertiser*, 27

April 2000; National Opinion Poll quoted in *Morning Advertiser*, 9 Nov. 2000.
74 Smith, 'Be Famous'.
75 Flockhart, 'Beers', pp. 31–4.
76 *Morning Advertiser*, 28 Aug. 2008.
77 Tony Halstead, 'Women Calling the Shots at Dining Out, Survey Shows', *Morning Advertiser*, 18 Aug. 2005.
78 Ellwood with Shekar, *Wonder Woman*, pp. 8–9; also see Lucy Britner, 'Sister Act', *Pubchef*, Sept. 2008.
79 Sally Bairstow, 'The Female Drinker', *Morning Advertiser*, 19 June 2003; Bairstow, 'Pulling Power'.
80 *Morning Advertiser*, 18 Oct. 2007; *Publican*, 19 Sept. 2005.
81 Ellwood with Shekar, *Wonder Woman*, p. 121.
82 Ewan Turney, 'Female Licensees "Better than Men"', *Morning Advertiser*, 28 Aug. 2008; Kelly Smith, 'Orchid Calls Women to the Bar', *Morning Advertiser*, 28 Aug. 2008.
83 See Chapter 6, p. 148.
84 Kate Oppenheim, 'Match Maker', *ICE*, Oct. 2000.
85 Smith, 'Women to the Bar'; Kelly Smith, 'Be Famous for ... Females', *Morning Advertiser*, 21 Feb. 2008.
86 Smith, 'Be Famous for ... Females'.
87 Andrew Pring, 'The Rise and Rise of Women', *Morning Advertiser*, 28 Aug. 2008; Kelly Smith, 'Anything Men Can Do: Do Women Make Better Hosts than Men?' *Morning Advertiser*, 28 Aug. 2008; *Publican*, 14 Sept. 2009.
88 Kelly Smith, 'A Gay Girl's Pub Guide', *Diva*, April 2010, pp. 57–9; 'Village Life', *Economist*, 9 March 1996.
89 Pring, 'Rise of Women'; Michelle Perrett, 'Changing Face of Pub-Goers', *Publican*, 19 March 2007.
90 'Women of Substance: Most Influential Women in the Pub Industry', *Morning Advertiser*, 28 Aug. 2008; Roger Protz, 'Ladies Who Brew', *Morning Advertiser*, 28 Aug. 2008; 'Top 50 Most Influential People in the Pub Industry', *Morning Advertiser*, 28 May 2009.
91 Tony Halstead, 'Rely on Girl Power to Drive Dining Market', *Morning Advertiser*, 23 May 2002.
92 Turney, 'Female Licensees'; Smith, 'Anything Men Can Do'; Smith, 'Be Famous for ... Females'.
93 Smith, 'Anything Men Can Do'.
94 Adam Withrington, 'The Youth Team', *Publican*, 27 April 2009.
95 Peter Martin, 'Out of the Wet and into the Dry', *Morning Advertiser*, 17 April 2008.
96 Ibid.; Tony Halstead, 'Listen Politicians – We Still Love Locals', *Morning Advertiser*, 3 July 2008; Paul Charity, 'Clarke: "Beer Will Drop by 40 per cent"', *Morning Advertiser*, 12 June 2008; Tony Halstead, 'Liquid Lunch Is a Thing of the Past', *Morning Advertiser*, 8 May 2008; Phil Mellows, 'In a Glass of Its Own', *Publican*, 19 Nov. 2001.
97 Charity, 'Profile: Wetherspoon's Chairman'.

9

A youth subculture of drinking

Pub and club going would become a mainstay of youth culture beginning in the 1980s, with four-fifths of all youths visiting them during the year. The fifteen- to twenty-four-year-olds were ten times more likely to go pubbing or clubbing than other age groups. Half of this age cohort frequented these venues at least monthly, with city centres of huge Northern cities – Liverpool, Manchester and Leeds, the club heartland – easily outdistancing London. From the mid-1990s, introduction of dance music revolutionized night clubs, which shed their images as venues for violent, drunken youths popping drugs, as commercialization and market segmentation fostered greater sophistication.[1]

Traditional drinkers ceased to be a major factor dominating drinking habits from the 1960s. With the decline of cinemas, courting couples made pubs their chief venue, and a new subculture of drinking emerged.[2] Those fifty-five and older, hitherto the backbone of the pub's clientele, accounted for falling amounts of alcohol consumption, a development especially striking owing to rising consumption in other age categories. Of the men fifty-five and over, 27 per cent patronized pubs in 1984, a percentage which halved in just four years. By the late 1990s, just 12 per cent of these men continued drinking in pubs.[3]

Young drinkers of wine and lager chiefly reshaped this new subculture of drinking. Of all age groups in the 1980s, the eighteen- to twenty-four-year-olds most increased their alcohol consumption.[4] Lager became the youth beverage of choice. Unlike the older generation, 'young people start off on lager, not bitter', remarked one marketing manager. 'The kind of thinking behind the promotion of these kegs and draught lagers is aimed at winning over younger people – ads concentrate on them almost exclusively, and … trying to get women to order it', contended David White.[5] The explosive growth of lager, which barely registered with 4 per cent of the market in the early 1960s, underlined this transformation. Within two decades, lager, the predominant youth drink, especially among males, claimed nearly half of the beer market. Lager was an alluring youth beverage: almost two-thirds of it was consumed by those under thirty-five, and it accounted for 40 per cent of the beer such men drank.[6]

Customarily, sex and class had set perimeters for pub drinkers, whereas age now became the chief delineator.[7] Youth wanted dancing as a part of their nighttime experience; traditional pubs simply did not embrace this value. Moreover, how women and men interacted in raves and dance clubs contrasted sharply with bars or pubs. Only here could women escape the social conventions making traditional masculine drink venues unwelcoming to females. 'The communal atmosphere of the rave', reflected historian Bill Osgerby, 'seemed to erode the predatory sexual relations of traditional night-club life and for many women the rave scene opened up access to the kind of thrills and pleasures that had previously been the preserve of masculine subcultures'.[8]

Rave clubs had no liquor licences, so youths resorted to drugs in pursuit of altering their conscious state. Because illicit drugs became more accessible and desirable, dance drugs – notably Ecstasy and cannabis and later heroin – consumed in dance clubs fueled the 'decade of dance' (1988–98), establishing this generation as the most prevalent drug users in the twentieth century. Illicit drug consumption among young adults (sixteen to twenty-four years) grew slowly but steadily from the 1960s, doubling every decade, until, in the early 1990s, the numbers doubled, reaching one-half of the entire group. The consequences of the dancing decade were horrific: heroin addicts had grown from 5000 (1975) to 280,000 (mid-2000s). Overall numbers proved as disturbing to critics as the inclusion in this new dance subculture of girls, women and individuals from well-heeled and professional backgrounds.[9]

By the early 1990s, the pub ceased to be a destination for vast numbers of youth. The Henley Report, issued in 1993, calculated that there were over fifty million attendances at raves, with spending of £1.8 billion annually. Instead of drinking Ind Coope's Double D, the youth opted for Double E, Evian and Ecstasy, quipped one reporter. To each rave, a typical participant was prepared to lay out £35, covering admission charges, soft drinks and, of course, 'dance drugs'. Reliable estimates put consumption of Ecstasy tablets at half a million weekly. In practical terms, this represented a staggering one million people weekly dancing and drinking, sometimes enhanced by Ecstasy, until 4 a.m. or even later.[10]

With vast sums being channelled into other pockets, pubs lost revenues, which slumped around 11 per cent in just five years (1987–92). To induce young drinkers to forsake drugs for alcohol, drink manufacturers engaged in what one reporter dubbed as a 'recreational drug war' from the early 1990s. 'The marketing of alcohol products as recreational drugs, complete with the motifs of youth clubbing culture, became a staple of brewing industry advertising campaigns', asserted Kevin Brain.[11]

In introducing or repackaging stronger alcoholic beverages, drink manufacturers deliberately sought to 'compete in the psychoactive market and appeal to the new generation of psychoactive consumers'. One of the most calculating efforts involved the marketing of Hooper's Hooch, the name itself evoking bootleggers' clandestine activities during the US prohibitionist era. Its manufacturer, Bass, 'originally used a yellow smiley fruit face logo which resembled the yellow smiley-face acid house logo'. Equally blatant if less popular was a potent fruity wine, Flavours for Ravers, offering purchasers free admission to a night club. Rave, Blastaway and the carefully named DNA – smacking of Ecstasy with its MDMA initials – likewise promoted the crossover from rave drugs to alcohol. So did skilfully crafted advertising for Grolsch lager, Holsten Pils and Vladivar Vodka, featuring psychedelic colours, techno music, and slogans redolent of drugs or even drug imagery, such as simpering smiles.[12]

New alcoholic 'designer drinks', reconfigured leisure venues and liberalised licensing policies all became part of a strategy dedicated to destroying the popularity of raves and acid house parties. This X generation, the product of the 'soft drinks revolution' of the 1960s and 1970s, drank refrigerated light-tasting, often sweet beverages, with a soft drinks base, served cold, typically with ice cubes.[13] From the early 1990s, drink manufacturers marketed new, more potent alcoholic beverages, aimed at wooing youth from dance clubs, acid house parties and raves, creating what one scholar has called a veritable 'revolution' in drinking beverages. Cider manufacturers, for example, facilitated this desire for stronger beverages, artificially enhancing the alcoholic content of cider. Assorted products advertised as lifestyle markers targeted segmented markets. One direct consequence would be excessive alcohol consumption. Rising sessional drinking, together with much stronger alcoholic beverages, illustrated how youth had altered what they consumed during a night out. Despite portrayals in the press, these products sought patronage from the eighteen- to thirty-five-year-olds, not from underage drinkers.[14]

Within 15 years, the range of beverages diversified as rapidly as their type and alcoholic strength. Remarkably little in the 1990s resembled the two previous decades. Designer bottled lagers, aperitifs and cocktails, higher in ABV and of greater potency, first became fashionable late in the 1980s.

Six distinct phases emerged over the next decade and a half.[15] First came premium (often imported) bottled beers (notably Budweiser), ice lagers, spirit mixers, white ciders (such as Diamond White), and fruit wines (named as in the case of Mad Dog 20/20 for their promised hallucinative effect). Fruit wines – Ravers and Thunderbird, for example – were quite potent, with their ABVs over 13 per cent. Alcopops, alcohol mixed with soft drinks or alcoholic lemonades, arrived in June 1995 from Australia, and targeted women under thirty-five. None became more controversial than Hooper's Hooch, quickly the best-selling of all alcopops. 'Sales in Bookers cash and carry stores', related *Bass Brewers News*, 'have ... been high with managers recounting stories of whole pallets of Hooch – 72 cases – disappearing in just ten minutes'. Bass aggressively promoted sales. Its brand manager instructed 'every Bass Brewers employee to keep asking for Hooch wherever they drink'. Within months, an informed expert estimated the alcopops market as worth £500 million annually.

By the decade's end, the second generation of alcopops, together with FABS (flavoured alcoholic beverages), had hit the market as a bridge beverage between club and pub. 'With its minimalist label and distinctive opaque red appearance', Bass's brand manager observed of a concoction of Guarani and Damiana (5 per cent ABV), 'Red's identity draws upon the subtleties of club culture with a distinctly underground feel'.

Early in the 2000s, in the third wave, shots, shooters and slammers gained popularity, especially with drink retailers who could anticipate profits of 75 per cent and more from each sale. Whether or not a conscious decision, the name 'shot' could evoke shooting up or injecting drugs. A shot consisted of a single drink, whereas a shooter contained several beverages. But within the drink industry the two terms were often used interchangeably. After Shock, a cinnamon-flavoured neutral liqueur with an ABV of 40 per cent, promised drinkers a hot rush replaced quickly by a cool one. Introduced first in 1997, After Shock easily outsold its distant rival, Sidekick, which with its 20 per cent ABV sought drinkers wanting a less alcoholic drink. Another popular beverage in the category was Goldschlager, cinnamon-flavoured schnapps from Switzerland with 40 per cent ABV. Slammers originated in Mexico, where tequila (less often white wine or champagne) mixed with a carbonated beverage was poured into a glass with the top part empty. As the drink fizzed, the drinker, hand over the top of the glass, slammed it down on the table, which mixed the bubbles with the liqueur leading to strong foaming and a down-in-one swift consumption, lest the beverage overflow the glass. The top slammer was Jose Cuervo Gold, its 40 per cent ABV making it a strong competitor to After

Shock, at least in strength. Shots, shooters and slammers – all served in small 1-ounce shot glasses – enticed drinkers with a single potent spirit or mixtures of liqueurs and spirits, heavily discounted if ordered for a group. For as little as £1 or £2, the drinker could mix different alcoholic spirits and liqueurs in one glass, sometimes forming the basis for a cocktail. Conscious of this category of beverages' link in the media and public mind with binge drinking, drink retailers avoided marketing them as 'between drinks' and instead stressed how each could be 'enjoyed as a drink in its own right'. Drinkers themselves knew better. Called 'party starters', 'routine breakers' or a 'social ritual', shots, shooters and slammers were consumed either with larger drinks, typically premium beers, wines or cocktails, or as a distinct break following consumption of other alcoholic beverages. Within the trade, all were rightly called down-in-one drinks, and targeted eighteen- to twenty-four-years-olds. Not surprisingly, high alcoholic strength sometimes formed part of the sales pitch. Producers of Metz 40, its name itself an advertisement of its alcoholic content, boasted of its superiority over other shots in being easily consumed, but still possessing "'the real kick you expect"'. Within months of their widespread appearance, shots, shooters and slammers 'are really going down a storm, especially among those in the eighteen- to twenty-four-year-old age bracket, and are becoming a permanent fixture on many a back bar', wrote the *Morning Advertiser*.

'Smart', 'buzz' or energy drinks, in which alcohol became mixed with caffeine or other stimulants such as guarana, one scholar contended, 'are a result of the attempt to capture the illegal drugs market'. This constituted the fourth phase. For youth, 'buzz' was synonymous with drunkenness. One such popular beverage, Virgin High Flyer, evoked the high that consumers associated with drug use. Over two-fifths of the market for alcopops and buzz drinks consisted of youths between eighteen and twenty-four. These young drinkers were displaying a new drinking pattern in which they consumed different types of drinks during the same evening. Such 'repertoire drinkers', as they soon became known, provided the commercial incentive for marketing new exotic alcoholic beverages in the early 2000s, RTDs (ready-to-drink potent bottled spirit mixers) and FABs (flavoured alcoholic beverages), notably Smirnoff Ice and Bacardi Breezer. Though originally distinct categories, these types of beverages eventually became merged under one rubric, alcopops, a term unpopular within the industry. But alcopops soon lost their fizz in part because of higher duty and adverse publicity, which led drink manufacturers to reduce advertising. 'These once-trendy beverages are clearly no longer seen as cool by the fickle target market of the eighteen–34–year olds, who have now ditched flavoured alcoholic beverages for more fashionable and sophisticated alternatives, such as cocktails', asserted Mintel analyst James McCoy. In response, drink manufacturers introduced spirit-based products, with vodka, gin, rum and bourbon among the leaders, and pre-mixed, branded cocktails in the mid-2000s. Wetherspoon's bar staff creatively invented and suitably named their own concoctions: Woo Woo, Blue Lagoon, Frisky Bison, Lust and Bulleit Breaker. These five best-sellers all contained juice or a soft drink mixed with vodka or bourbon; two of them added schnapps to the vodka.[16]

Many alcohol researchers became disturbed not so much that youth began experimenting with new beverages as that they were seemingly developing new unhealthy drinking patterns. Typical behaviour involved drinkers queuing at the bar and awaiting service, which often consumed time and so restrained consumption. Shots introduced a wholly new relationship between seller and consumer, table service, in which one of the bar staff circulated to 'drum up' sales. With a tray of different types of shots, much like restaurant staff displayed sweets, bar staff aggressively pushed sales, even venturing outdoors to hawk custom. Intervening in a group of male drinkers allowed a waitress to manipulate one of them into buying a round, lest he be embarrassed in front of his friends for misplaced frugality or lack of masculinity. One study discovered that approximately half of weekend drinkers consumed one shot or more during an evening. Three serious consequences ensued for drinkers: they were encouraged to mix different alcoholic beverages; shots, commonly downed in one gulp, promoted 'speed drinking' of spirits, far more potent than beers or wine which formed the mainstays of consumed beverages; and, as a supplement to beverages being consumed by the drinker, shots materially contributed to the rise of sessional alcohol consumption. Shot drinking has fostered what Fiona Measham called 'the new culture of intoxication'. Having to deal directly with this culture, Steven Green, Nottingham's Chief Constable, was blunter. For him, drink promotions, such as two for one or £1 a shot specials, ranked as 'a blatant inducement towards binge drinking'.[17]

Redesigned drink outlets, obscuring differences between traditional pubs and clubs, on one hand, and legal and illegal drugs, on the other, proliferated during the dance decade as well, constituting the second new facet of the night-time economy. Style and café bars, together with dance bars, soon represented about half of all drinking outlets in urban areas. To appeal to an entirely different clientele of young drinkers, breweries, pubcos and others replaced traditional 'spit and sawdust' plebean back-street boozers with high-tech 'chrome and cocktail' city-centre café and style bars, fronted with huge plate glass windows, the emblematic feature of the new drinking and leisure regime.[18] Terminology became a significant cultural cue to changes in women's drinking habits. Lager louts replaced hooligans in the press, and soon the female equivalent, the ladettes, emerged, encapsulating those women who drank excessively, initially beers but later including wines and cocktails. Drink sellers responded to this market with diverse tactics: respectable wine lists; better lighting; newspapers; comfortable sofas; menus with differing salad options and light meals; and upgraded toilets. Nottingham's two female managers of the Establishment recounted their wooing of women as customers. 'We are very female orientated', they admitted. 'Women like bright interiors, colour, stripped floorboards and flowers on the table. The Ladies loo is important. Professional women meet here and we have table service to cater for them.' 'Feminization' of the drink environment, as Jane McGregor has aptly observed, went further in some establishments, with pot pourri in women's loos and designated quiet chatting areas.[19]

Finally, liberalized licensing laws, representing the third change, promoted escalating drinking that breached safe consumption levels. 'The liberalization of alcohol-based licensing', contended Fiona Measham, 'enabled the revival of city centre cultural and night time economies and was in sharp contrast to the increased regulation and criminalization of unlicensed raves and dance events'. Dance clubs and dance drugs, linked with drug dealers and gang violence, thus provided the catalysts for more rigorous control aimed at curbing youth activities previously outside legal oversight. Nottingham acquired a well-deserved reputation as 'Binge Capital of Britain'. For its connotations with violence, others would dub it 'Sottingham'. For the first time in almost a century, the time-honoured concept of basing the number of licensing outlets on public 'need' was abolished. Key to this pivotal change was the licensing of one Nottingham nightclub, Liberty's, in 1996, as Jane McGregor cogently notes in her recent book.[20] The ensuing deregulation from the late 1990s facilitated the growth of new licensed venues, disproportionately concentrated in towns and cities. Special hours certificates, permitting venues to remain open until 2 or 3 a.m., remade the drinking landscape. Within three years, the 1121 special hours certificates issued in 1997–8 soared to 1929, an increase of some 70 per cent. Longer licensing hours enabled youth to transform city centres into a separate night-time economy.[21]

'Availability governed by market forces and competition led to price cuts, aggressive marketing and irresponsible retailing', asserted Roy Light. Cut-throat competition defied easy characterization: drinking games; reduced prices lasting less than three hours; two for one sales; specials on spirits (offering doubles at prices below those for two single shots); preset prices for unlimited drinking; and point of sale pressure. Critics of abusive drinking argued that these innovative, often aggressive, sales tactics belied the drink industry's much-vaunted claims of self-regulation as the most efficacious approach to binge drinking.[22] Subsequent government research confirmed that heavily discounted prices and sales promotions led to higher consumption of alcohol.[23] In the meantime, Wetherspoon had assumed the lead in renouncing most of these tactics.[24]

Later night hours, a wide array of new alcoholic beverages and late-night bars had transformed the market, and killed off both raves and night clubs as venues of choice for the young. So did the fact that 'there is a trend towards lounging rather than dancing', pointed out Peter Stringfellow, operator of Sheffield and London night clubs since 1960. Stringfellows, one of London's most popular night clubs during the 1980s, typified the market's metamorphosis. To draw business in the more competitive 1990s, he had introduced lap-dancing four nights a week, returning to his disco roots only on the weekends. Within two years (1997–8), 10 per cent of the country's night clubs and discos had closed.[25]

In appropriating rave culture, global breweries and other entrepreneurs had transformed it into a highly profitable commercial venture. 'Many UK cities began to reinvent themselves as places of consumption dependent on the development of a diverse and vibrant "after dark" economy, and this involved grappling with outdated laws and curtailments', concluded a recent sociological study of Leeds. Regeneration of decaying city centres for social interaction became central to the rhetoric justifying a radical departure. Emulation of European culture, concerns about deserted city centres, rejection of Thatcherite policies, New Labour's advocacy of a Third Way between free markets and state control, and integration of work, leisure, shopping and residence at one site – all these diverse forces inspired enthusiasm for reconceptualizing the city centre as a living, dynamic, expanding entity awaiting imaginative students of urbanization. According to one study, 'the idea of the "24 hour city" was designed to break away from the industrial city with its emphasis on manufacturing production and its strict temporal and spatial ordering'. Longer licensing hours naturally became a critical component of this redesigned nightlife of major urban cities.[26]

Popular youth areas in city centres of large cities appeared: Manchester's gay village; Liverpool's Concert Square; Newcastle's Bigg Market; Leeds's Exchange

Quarter and Boar Lane; Hull's George Street; Glasgow's Hope Street;[27] Nottingham's Lace Market; and Birmingham's Broad Street. Some bars drew 2500 customers nightly and made £3 million a year. Breweries focused on the eighteen- to twenty-five-year-old market, the most profitable age segment. Night-strips were populated by MVVDS – Mass Volume Vertical Drinkers – 'because they are encouraged to stand in large groups, swigging from bottles'. The essence of 'swig culture' was bar hopping, as drinkers moved quickly from one bar to another. Indeed, circuits or other areas with distinguishable dress codes, language or life styles, stimulated segmented markets, which socially demarcated public spaces in city centres.[28] Huge concentrations of bars facilitated circuit drinking. Six cities – Birmingham, Bradford, Cardiff, Glasgow, London and Manchester – had the greatest numbers of licensed venues on specific streets, nearly all of them the product of the post-1996 licensing expansion. Birmingham's Broad Street ranked first in the country in total numbers of drink outlets on one street, and provided the quintessential example of this explosion, more than doubling its drink venues. Some towns, such as Kingston-upon-Thames, claimed two distinct circuits, one for the traditional eighteen- to twenty-four-year-olds, and the other for twenty-four- to thirty-five-year-olds. Whether in Kingston or Birmingham, some forty companies competed for custom; the big players, such as Brannigans, Walkabout, Pitcher & Piano, J. D. Wetherspoons and O'Neill's, jostled with the more innovative venues, notably Po Na Na and Tiger Tiger. A 2002 survey established that such circuit bars accounted for nearly one-fifth of the pub market, second only to community locals.[29]

With the introduction of alcohol to 'dry' rave clubs, on one hand, and special hours certificates and late-night licences, on the other, a new bar scene emerged in which café and dance bars became the youth's new trendy venues of choice. Youths now often took drugs as part of the night out, with cannabis the most popular, followed very distantly by amphetamines, acid, Ecstasy and cocaine, though most were infrequent users.[30] 'Clubbers', commented Russell Pate, owner of Back to Basics, one of Leeds's first night clubs, 'are increasingly taking the bits they like about the clubbing experience, the music, the relaxed atmosphere and the up for it attitude and transplanting it to a more convivial location'. At late-night bars, club refugees could avoid lengthy queues, overpoweringly loud music and hefty cover charges, while embracing major elements of clubs – listening to DJs whose appearance print flyers had advertised. Unlike traditional pubs, late-night bars and café bars offered diverse alcoholic beverages, food combined with music, and sophisticated, expensive atmospheres styled by professional designers. Leeds' late night bars and night clubs, with capacity for 25,000 and 23,000 respectively, could accommodate nearly half of the city's sixteen- to twenty-four-year-old population.[31] In 1993, there were 142 million night club admission throughout the country, with the figure projected to reach 238 million in a decade. Between 1978 and 2001 the number of night clubs rose by 28 per cent, pubs and bars by 20 per cent and licensed restaurants and hotels by 68 per cent.[32]

The pattern of the night scene's revival in major city centres involved a two-stage process in the 1990s: initially a small group of independent entrepreneurs pioneered the redevelopment of decaying city centres such as Leeds and Nottingham, followed by corporations which bought some of these venues. City councils often preferred working with global breweries which invested heavily in new bars and clubs. Tetley's and Bass, for example, dominated the drinks scene in Leeds. Independent owners remained, usually on the periphery of the city centre where they thrived, owing to their ability to respond quickly to new trends.[33]

Some scholars portray the night-time economy as not so much an extension of day-time drinking hours as a distinct subculture, with its own rules, behaviour, drinking patterns, entertainment venues and clientele. Though initially intended as a cosmopolitan experiment in which revitalized city centres drew different types of customers, the night-time economy evolved in an altogether unexpected direction. Alcohol venues and the young, especially those with money to burn, defined a separate leisure zone catering to a narrow clientele. One consequence was that high alcohol intake, experimental sex and readily available drugs characterized drinkers in an ambience, where a carnivalesque tone prevailed and consumption became a key defining trait. Promoters of this night-time subculture deliberately encouraged a rejection of day-time traits, creating an inverted subculture in which restraint, moderation, disciplined behaviour and respect for prevailing social norms all disappeared. With cut-rate prices, specials on certain beverages and food as well as entertainment, drinkers had powerful incentives for embracing excess in all forms. Fostering this sense of uniqueness in the night-time economy, day-time drinking premises assumed different ambiences, called 'chameleon bars', with music louder, lights softer and dance space cleared. Little of the day-time environment would have been recognizable to participants in night-time drinking. Such bars drew drink revellers with better lighting and sound systems as well as numerous designer beers. Spectacle loomed large for night-time drinkers who invested their clothes, haircuts, beverages, drinking venues and personal display with the power to establish themselves securely in a social group. 'We don't just go out for a good time, nor even the best of times – we go out to put on a show', boasted one devotee of night-time drinking. 'Tonight, just like every Saturday night', he added, 'the curtain was set to go up on another superb performance'.[34]

A new drinking subculture, entirely different in age, gender, clothing and occupational traits, supplanted traditional Northern pub customers from the late 1970s. No longer confined predominantly to one sex and strikingly younger, eighteen- to twenty-five-year-old consumers became associated with image, created by the interaction of the environment and the participant's clothing, public comportment and beverage consumption. Style, fashion and age trumped gender, class and occupation. Northerners, wrote one reporter, 'like to display their money, spending it on clothes and going out, as opposed to southerners who are more restrained and tend to go for cars and mortgages'. Drinkers wore designer clothes and sports shoes and drank designer beers, such as the popular Red Stripe, an imported Jamaican lager. Women now joined men in drinking, but significantly in entirely new venues, wholly unassociated with neighbourhood locals. Conversation, the mainstay of traditional drinking culture, proved virtually impossible where loud, throbbing music filled the atmosphere. Young men drank canned, not draught, beer: it represented a rejection of tradionalists' habits, was less likely to spill and could be taken outside.[35]

Not only did younger people drink in distinctive ways, but their economic power revolutionized the layout, atmosphere, products and clientele of drinking venues. Huge crowds from Thursday through Saturday flooded city-centre drinking establishments. Young drinkers were mobile, equally spectators and spectacles, and part of shifting groups, so pub and club proprietors redesigned establishments to facilitate movement, eliminating tables and chairs, separate rooms and partitions which obstructed views. Since crowds were the norm in drinking premises, drinkers, who went from bar to bar, seldom stayed long, standing while consuming their beverages. Standing also facilitated eyeing the 'talent'. Music, lightshows, quizzes and cabarets became standard drawing features of trendy establishments.[36]

As the night time economy evolved, 'door pickers' or 'selectors', who replaced bouncers, facilitated the establishment of identity. Bouncers, untrained as doormen and physically intimidating, had earned respect for their muscular prowess, the ability to 'kill you with a biscuit'. Door pickers, in contrast, embodying a far more sophisticated approach, became valued for their social skills, sometimes based on counselling training. No longer was spotting potential troublemakers the overriding concern. Previously clothes had been fundamental to earning admission to clubs and bars, whereas now decisions came to depend on whether an individual conformed to the character profile of the specific venue. Having gained admission, entry became easier subsequently owing to being recognized at the door, and so the appreciative individual displayed loyalty which generated a sense of belonging and personal identity.[37]

Mobility pre-eminently defined youth drinking culture. To police the 50,000 weekenders in Nottingham city centre, drink establishments hired 400 bouncers. Manchester with its 100,000 weekend crowds required still more, estimated at 1000. By far the biggest, London's West End reputedly drew 500,000 weekend drinkers. In Sunderland, the city-centre population exploded from 5000 to 170,000 on weekends, overwhelming tradition agencies of social control. Pubs with modest takings of £250 nightly early in the week generated £3,000–£5,000 on weekends. Because crowds reached such unprecedented numbers, entry and ages of the drinkers had to be policed, often creating long queues which all became part of the new regime. Competition became keen on the drinking circuit, with food, happy hours and other enticements offered as inducements. Traditionalists had exerted control over drunkenness and behaviour in the old culture; police, overcome with numbers and reassured by New Labour's policy of corporate social responsibility, now ceded responsibility to bouncers, bar staff and proprietors, in many cases as much ill-trained and ill-suited as themselves to cope with extraordinary numbers of drinkers. As part of this mobility, drinkers spent as much, if not more, time on the street moving between venues as in the places themselves. This rootlessness, corroding any sense of personal loyalty, pervaded their entire behaviour: they displayed no awareness of how place, tradition, gender and work had formerly shaped relationships of their forebears and been projected into recognizable drinking rituals, which had helped their ancestors define themselves as part of the broader community. Drinking, now shorn of this wider symbolic significance, became dictated by fashion, trends, mating concerns and public appearance, nothing more distinctive here than in other parts of the UK, or indeed Western Europe or the United States.[38]

Divergent gender roles that had segregated men from women in traditional pubs did not so much vanish as become redefined. Young women now joined men in equal numbers in sex-segregated groups on Thursdays and Fridays and as dating couples on Saturdays, and so many pubs ceased to be masculine strongholds. In fact, women's adoption of hen parties as a parallel to men's stag nights could be seen less as emulation than as claims for their own independent public space. In stepping outside traditional gender boundaries, women were asserting 'a collective female public identity'.[39]

Virtually everything about the young's subculture of alcohol consumption conflicted with traditionalists' culture. Gone were the small groups of intimate friends and relatives who sat together in a ritualized tradition as an extension of the workplace that bound them physically and emotionally to place, the past and each other. Work, masculinity and community were all invoked in the comrade of drinking in pubs. 'In post-industrial societies drinking and drug taking become less of a male working class integrating mechanism and more of a consumerist search for time out', observed Kevin Brain.[40]

Young drinkers, segregated by age, not gender, went to pubs and clubs specifically to find women, 'talent' as men brazenly called them. To see and be seen became critical, as drinking merged into the broader pattern of dating rituals. Regardless of sex, on Fridays single-sex groups of young men and women ventured into a series of drinking places – called 'circuits' – rapidly consuming one beverage before moving on to the next one, perhaps totalling seven to ten over the course of an evening. Sunderland youths had wittingly dubbed Hylton Road, the main route into town, as the 'Ski Run', because 'you can drink your way down it before hitting the town'. Leeds students had their own equivalent pub crawl, the 'Otley Run', encompassing some 14 establishments. Drinking began at an agreed venue, quite separate from the circuit, where the group spent 45 minutes to an hour before visiting a 'stop-off' pub for a quick drink. Anonymity pervaded the experience: drinkers outside the group knew not each other or bar staff. What they consumed had nothing to do with a discerning palate, much less loyalty to brands or types of drinks, and everything with the eyes, which scanned the room for what others were consuming. Spectacle loomed large indeed in youth culture [41]

Young drinkers consumed beverages mindful most of their alcoholic potency. Formerly, drinkers developed an appreciation for a beer, which owing to its bitter taste took time to acquire. Taste now mattered nothing compared to the beverage's strength. Mixing drinks to produce powerfully intoxicating but appallingly tasting or appearing concoctions – Snakebite (lager mixed with cider) – became part of their normative behaviour. Thus, one undisguised purpose of drinking was to get drunk: on an extended weekend night men typically consumed five or six pints of beer, while women drank the equivalent of three-and-a-half to four pints of other beverages. Youth drank not just to enjoy psychoactive pleasure but to display the 'symbolic pleasure of consumption'. According to Kevin Brain, consumption in the post-Fordist era – the shift from production to services and consumption in the post-industrial years – constituted a conscious choice in which the consumer consumed with a deliberate eye to 'symbolically marking out lifestyle, status, and identity'. Masculinity, riches and social status – these, male drinkers of premium lagers all sought to project. For many Generation Y women, born after 1978, consumption, together with their occupation and leisure places, assumed a pivotal role in defining who they were in society.[42] Though both sexes now formed youth culture, women and men still drank different beverages. Men drank imported bottled lagers such as Becks, Coors, Pils, Red Stripe, Fosters and Budweiser, not so much because they viewed British tap beer as weak as because they wanted to advertise their choice of beverages. Hence, they held bottled beers with the labels showing outward. Two-fifths of drinkers who consumed Fosters, for instance, were in the eighteen- to twenty-four age group. Hooper's Hooch

> was sold at premium prices in glass bottles (like the premium lagers …) Sold in night-clubs, such packaging has the advantage of being seen by onlookers (advertised) and, unlike traditional alcoholic drinks which are served in glasses or tumblers, it is possible to walk around a club and even while consuming an alcopop without the certainty of spillage.

Malibu, Tequila Sunrise and Taboo, in contrast, were marketed as women's drinks, much like Babycham of an earlier generation. Baileys, Tia Maria and other sweet liqueurs were equally popular with women. Strange-sounding drinks resonated with names of venues bespeaking globalization: Sunderland now evoked New York. Pub names themselves lost their moorings in Britain's historic past and became part, too, of the image make-over.[43]

In the revitalized city centres, new style bars,[44]cafés, hybrid pubs, bars/restaurants and traditional pubs (committed to their masculinity, dislike of outsiders and long-standing beers) coexisted, reflecting the fragmented nature of drinking that began appearing from the early 1990s. But such development affected the social spectrum unevenly. 'The city centre is becoming a ghetto for cash-rich groups, whether they be townies, students or young professionals', contended one recent sociological study of Leeds.[45]

Given the relative affluence of these individuals, alcoholic abuse not only was possible but became a deliberate goal, as young drinkers sought excitement, activity and change. They craved escapism, sexual escapades and freedom to choose what fashion dictated, goals which traditionalists had emphatically rejected. Many outsiders attributed this youth subculture of heavy binge drinking, drunkenness, disorder and violence to anti-social behaviour. Extensive studies documented close relationships between soaring numbers of new licensed premises, on one hand, and rising amounts of deviance, on the other. It was not only that levels of intoxication rose but that the incidences of crime, violence and bloodshed likewise increased proportionately. From night-time drinking, a subculture arose with all the hallmarks of deviance that generated adverse publicity, social condemnation and lurid popular images encapsulated in the term 'binge drinking'.[46]

But youth culture, far from being monolithic, consisted of several subcultures, some of them more prone to violence and drunkenness than others. Age but not gender became a critical factor in predicting drunkenness and aggression for young adults whose behaviour really bespoke a highly ritualized mating encounter, with both men and women assessing each other as potential mates.[47] Two other key determinants of disorder and violence were location and time: city centres with heavy concentrations of licences; and Friday nights/Saturday mornings and Saturday nights/Sunday mornings between 9 p.m. and 3 a.m. Within these perimeters, disproportionate numbers of police incidents were logged.[48]

For those between eighteen and twenty-four living in Northern former industrial towns, 'getting pissed' or meeting the opposite sex ranked as major goals on 'the night out', generally Friday and Saturday nights, for both young men and young women. Same-sex groups went out in groups of three to five, neatly but not conspicuously dressed. Overcrowded premises of increasingly intoxicated, highly strung, young immature men, emboldened as part of a wider group of friends, contributed to the likelihood of conflict.[49]

Pubs and night clubs with most customers under twenty-one experienced more drunkenness and violence than those with older drinkers. When out drinking during an evening, young men moved about the drinking spaces, especially around the bar or pool table. 'There was a culture of "showing off"', observed one recent study. This took the form of drinking quickly and competitively, with round buying of identical beverages. Young women, in contrast, remained seated in groups, largely uninterested in showing off, and drank at varying speeds with a round sometimes skipped. This more disciplined form of drinking rendered drunkenness less likely. These gender differences were rooted in how each had approached drug taking in clubs and raves.[50]

Much like young bucks anxious to demonstrate courage or assert claims over available does, young men flaunted their masculinity as a way of winning respect from male friends while impressing nubile females. Men regarded excessive drinking in exactly the same way as they had earlier viewed dance drugs. Hilarity, swagger and pride contributed to defining their sense of masculinity. Perceived insults, attempts to hustle someone's girlfriend, spilling drinks or provocative, condescending behaviour frequently provoked confrontations, sometimes escalating into skirmishes (though seldom bloody violence). In night clubs catering to youths, 'fights were more frequent than in night clubs that had an older clientele', concluded a study of Wigan and Huddersfield. But the principal cause surely must have been that younger men (under twenty-one), immature, insecure and inexperienced, were overly sensitive, and so often misperceived unintended slights. Excessive alcohol consumption, moreover, eroded judgement. For some of these men with low status, the 'willingness to stand up for themselves' often involved desires either to protect their status or to assert claims for more. 'A lower status man', wrote two ethnographers 'would use aggression to acquire status as to be a "real man", and not be seen as of inferior value'. Inappropriate clothing or feeble responses to potential aggressors risked ridicule from mates as being a homosexual, the antithesis of the true masculine self to which they so aspired. Here, too, women of similar ages regarded such conduct as justifiable. Social class also played a role: many of these young females (under eighteen years of age) came from nearby 'rough' council estates, interpreted aggression as symptomatic of men who could suitably protect them, and sometimes when drinking engaged in violent behaviour against other women, though far less often than men. Drunkenness, frequent among these young women and those slightly older, likewise contributed to their propensity to brawl with other females, undoubtedly for the same reason as men: excessive intact of alcohol lowered inhibitions and restraint, promoting aggression, sometimes leading to violence.[51]

On the perimeter of city centre venues were pubs and clubs recognized as 'rough', representing another subculture of drinking altogether. Cheap, basic décor; unhygienic premises; a 'hard' clientele; few respectable women; drug dealing; and gangs – these commonly characterized such establishments.[52]

Drinking in the older birth cohorts exhibited dissimilar patterns. Nearly half of these drinkers consumed most of their alcohol at home, placing Britain in front of Germany, France and Spain. Regardless of whether urban or rural locations, drinkers displayed a distinct preference for domestic drinking, either at their own homes or those of friends or family. These drinkers, too, often drank before going out, called 'pre-loading', and sometimes on returning home. Class was clearly a factor, with those professionally or managerially employed the most predisposed to staying home, especially if living with someone else. In another distinct contrast with the young, older drinkers primarily consumed wine purchased through the off-trade, prompting one of them to quip that 'the supermarket is my local'. Accessibility provided one powerful incentive; cost proved another. As one study remarked,

> many middle-class respondents explained that drinking wine at home had changed from being a rare weekly treat to something which they could now afford on a regular basis as their own incomes [had] increased and perhaps more importantly as price of wine has [*sic*] fallen relative to average earnings.[53]

Not surprisingly, numerous scholarly studies have offered differing interpretations of rising youth drinking. Some geographers point to changing attitudes towards alcohol consumption over several generations as a compelling explanation for 'binge' drinking. An older generation, coming of drinking age in the 1950s and early 1960s, understood that parental expectations prohibited underage drinking. At the pub, sociability and a desire to fit in determined drinking: males consumed beer and women Cherry B. Drunkenness was condemned as unmanly, a violation of powerful social norms. Their children, the mid-generation, who began drinking in the two decades after 1974, were raised differently. Parents imposed strict prohibitions about underage drinking, but, with a greater diversity of drinks more readily available for experimentation and drinking accepted as a pervasive leisure activity, the mid-generation drank alcohol surreptitiously and defied parental norms. Young males consumed lager, beer or cider, while young females, who now drank more and in public, had spirits with sweet mixers, or Babycham. Their rationale for drinking remained the same as for the old generation. Types of beverages, motives, alcohol's importance as a factor in socializing with friends, parental attitudes and site of consumption – these now changed drastically for the third generation. With more liberal parental attitudes towards experimentation with alcohol, the young generation drinking in the so-called 'binge era' (2004–11) started consuming vodka and shots, with wine, alcopops and sprits with sweet mixers, beverages much stronger in alcoholic content than beer. What exacerbated the effect of this more potent mixture was that the young generation also drank more units of alcohol on average during a session than either the old or the mid-generation. Between 1990 and 2009, drink consumption for this cohort generation doubled. One reason for soaring consumption was that the young thought they had no choice but to drink as part of socializing with friends: they drank with 'determined drunkenness', in response to peer pressure, and hopeful of losing inhibitions. Round buying, home consumption and drinking games drove alcohol consumption still higher. In encouraging discussions with children and negotiating expected limitations with them, the cohort of mid-generation parents contributed to new consumption patterns.[54] As this study concluded,

> Within the majority population there has been a general extra-familiar shift in the emphasis of parenting between cohort generations – from disciplining young people to enabling their expressivity – which has produced a notable change in the ways that attitudes and practices about alcohol are communicated in intra-familiar contexts between family generations.[55]

As consumption for women matched increases for men, there was a gender convergence in drinking habits. Two factors – entry into the labour market and targeted advertising – fostered women's rising consumption, argued this same study. But other scholars point to additional factors as important. Women's greater emancipation – notably higher disposable incomes (linked with more education), social freedoms, and legal and political power – together with the erosion of the long-standing stigma against females' drinking and drunkenness in public, stimulated higher consumption levels. Delaying marriage, lighter domestic duties and valuing careers over children also contributed to what has been called 'genderquake' in redefining women's roles, including their drinking habits.[56]

Still other scholars view changes in the life cycle as more significant than child rearing habits over successive generations in explaining new drinking patterns. They point to the emergence of an extended adolescence in which those moving from adolescent to adulthood while pursuing an university degree had no choice but to rely increasingly on parents as government student financial support plummeted. Well over one in two of those in their mid-twenties lived with their parents, a 2005 survey documented. For these young people, career expectations had changed markedly: marriage, children and mortgage were deferred, while for some their personal debt rose. In prolonging stays with parents, these aspiring adults had two decided gains: increased disposable income, on one hand, and freedom to decide how to spend this money, on the other. Denied the opportunity to entertain friends at their own home, they turned to clubs, raves, acid house parties and then dance clubs and style bars as alternatives.[57]

But some scholars portray drink manufacturers as seeking excessive drinking with modern, stylish licensed premises, which had doubled in capacity in the late 1990s, and an ever-widening plethora of alcoholic beverages. These factors, together with unpleasant weather and limited leisure alternatives, all conspired to lure youth into drinking venues where they consumed twice as much alcohol in each session.[58]

In instituting greater security surveillance since '9/11', British authorities have paradoxically heightened insecurity in the young. As youth have surrendered control over their lives owing to the state's widening scrutiny of public behaviour, many have used drunkenness to reassert mastery over threatening external forces. Youth's avowed pursuit of drunkenness thus becomes not hedonistic but what one scholar calls 'self-actualization and self-expression'.[59] However imaginative as an explanation, this theory lacks evidence of the young perceiving their controlled intoxication from this perspective.

To some extent, youth's drinking in village pubs resembled their urban counterparts. In some villages, notably in the South-west, men drank deliberately to get drunk, the overriding purpose of such an outing. In drinking excessively, they could exhibit strength, belligerence, perseverance and group identity.[60]

Geography critically shaped drinking patterns. Village youth of both sexes in Cumbria and Leicestershire drank, not to get drunk but to relax and socialize. Deprived of alternative leisure activities, some of them did drink heavily, but the lack of anonymity, presence of older adults in pubs and knowledgeable landlords facilitated discipline, order and bloodless outings.[61]

Sharply diverging drinking cultures divided rural from urban areas in key ways. For young males, the village pub became the stage for establishing an identity, exclusive, hierarchical, sexist and racist in nature. Young men engaged in what one scholar called conversational cockfighting, embracing an overtly male discourse focusing on masculine genitalia with frequent mention of balls, bollocks and wanking. With this language, they defined their masculinity and established male solidarity, while excluding and reviling outsiders – women, gays and blacks – as inferiors. Sex segregation predominated, with young women drinking separately at the perimeters – the snugs, fireplaces or lounges – reminiscent of the pre-1918 drinking era.[62] To these young men, women represented objects to conquer, both sexually and physically. Young women's subordinate status inside the pub mirrored their inferiority in the village itself. Whether they waited on men as part of the bar staff or served as objects of male ridicule or derision, women had no entry into the pub's masculine world. Women's bodies, clothing and appearance attracted notice, not their personalities, thoughts or feelings. Avoiding the pub altogether earned no reprieve. Men's 'phallocentric discourse serves to emasculate and marginalize those who do not drink in the pub', contended Michael Leyshon.[63]

Ethnicity and religion equally formed drinking patterns. Among ethnic minorities in Britain, women generally eschewed alcohol, with the exception of black females, whose drinking patterns closely replicated those of the indigenous population.[64] Young Pakistani Muslim males conformed to the drinking patterns of other males in their age cohort, but, owing to Muslim beliefs, drank either privately or out of their locality. In some areas, such as Stoke-on-Trent, Muslim males had another reason to drink covertly, the fear of racism either causing confrontations or violent attacks from drunken drinkers. For Pakistani Muslim women, however, powerful religious norms – including being ultimately ostracized as an acceptable marriage partner – discouraged them from even contemplating consuming alcohol while participating in a social outing with drinkers.[65]

This new youth subculture of drinking displayed entirely novel traits, having little in common with other groups of drinkers. Licensing hours, leisure venues, access to alcohol, drug taking, beverages, gate keepers and composition of these drinkers – marked a sharp departure from the past, creating new social norms characteristic of just this one group. In some cases, government policies, notably in sanctioning longer licensing hours and allowing more licences, decisively moulded this subculture's emergence. So did drink sellers. With a broad range of increasingly potent beverages and aggressive sales promotions, they knowingly inspired heavier consumption of alcohol which contributed directly to rising insobriety. 'For the first time', writes James Nicholls, 'the alcohol industry began to market drunkenness as a primary aim of drinking as they sought to compete with other psychoactive youth markets'.[66] But the young themselves also powerfully influenced the nature of their drinking with a commitment to determined drunkenness.

Researchers have more convincingly described this new behaviour than offered compelling arguments which account for these distinctive drinking patterns. Changes in generational drinking certainly provide a persuasive viewpoint, but precisely why the mid-generation modified its childrearing attitudes and permitted greater freedom in their children's drinking habits remains unclear. More attention needs to be devoted to the cultural setting, contextualizing how drinking habits reflected wider social and economic changes since the Second World War. To what extent are changes in drinking patterns in contemporary England similar to those in other parts of the British Isles, Western Europe and North America? These and other questions need examination before the present-day debate on drinking can be placed in a proper perspective.

Notes

1 Robert Hollands, Paul Chatterton, Bernie C. Byrnes and Cait Read, *The London of the North? Youth Cultures, Urban Change and Nightlife in Leeds* (Newcastle-upon-Tyne, Centre for Urban and Regional Development Studies, Department of Sociology and Social Policy, University of Newcastle-upon-Tyne, 2001), pp. 52–3.

2 Elizabeth Roberts, *Women and Families: An Oral History, 1940–70* (Oxford: Blackwell, 1995), pp. 62–3.

3 MORI, *Public Attitudes to Pubs and Leisure* (June 1984 and April 1988).

4 Jane McCallion, 'Nearly 50 per cent of All Beer', *Publican*, 9 April 1987.

5 David White, 'The Pull of the Pub', *New Society*, 16 (1970), p. 318.

6 *Publican*, 27 March 1980; IPC Marketing, *The UK Beer Market* (Sept. 1977), p. 71; MORI, *Public Attitudes to Pubs and Leisure* (1984).

7 Alun Howkins, 'The Ploughman's Rest: Whose Round Is It Anyway? Brewers, Real Ale Campaigners, Lager Louts or the City?', *New Statesman*, 14 April 1989, p. 11; *Publican*, 27 March 1980; IPC Marketing, *The UK Beer Market* (Sept. 1977), p. 71.

8 Bill Osgerby, *Youth in Britain since 1945* (Oxford: Blackwells, 1998), p. 56.

9 Judith Aldridge, Fiona Measham and Lisa Williams, *Illegal Leisure Revisited: Changing Patterns of Alcohol and Drug Use in Adolescents and Young Adults* (London: Routledge, 2011), pp. 4–6.

10 Alex Spillius, 'The Bitter End?', *Observer*, 7 Nov. 1993; Aldridge, Measham and Williams, *Illegal Leisure Revisited*, p. 58; James Nicholls, *The Politics of Alcohol: A History of the Drink Question in England* (Manchester: Manchester University Press, 2009), pp. 223–4.

11 Kevin J. Brain, *Youth, Alcohol and the Emergence of the Post-Modern Alcohol Order* (St Ives, Cambridgeshire: Institute of Alcohol Studies, 2000), p. 4.

12 *Bass Brewers News*, June 1995, p. 9; Brain, *Youth*, pp. 4–5, 7, 10; Fiona Measham, 'The Decline of Ecstasy, the Rise of "Binge" Drinking and the Persistence of Pleasure', *Probation Journal*, 51 (2004), pp. 317–18; Alasdair J. M. Forsyth, 'A Design for Strife: Alcopops, Licit Drug – Familiar Scare Story', *International Journal of Drug Policy*, 12 (2001), p. 75; Fiona Measham, 'A History of Intoxication: Changing Attitudes to Drunkenness and Excess in the United Kingdom', in Marjana Martinic and Fiona Measham (eds), *Swimming with Crocodiles: The Culture of Extreme Drinking* (London: Routledge, 2008), pp. 26–7; Aldridge, Measham and Williams, *Illegal Leisure Revisited*, p. 14, n. 11.

13 See Chapter 3, above, p. 83.

14 Measham, 'Decline of Ecstasy', p. 317; Forsyth, 'Design for Strife', pp. 59–61, 76; Aldridge, Measham and Williams, *Illegal Leisure Revisited*, p. 59; *Publican*, 29 July 1996.

15 The following three paragraphs are based on the following: *Bass Brewers News*, Aug. 1995, pp. 1, 5, and Sept. 1996, p. 15; *Publican*, 29 July 1996; Measham, 'Decline of Ecstasy', p. 318; Graham Ridout, 'Shots Across the Bar', *Morning Advertiser*, 12 July 2001; J. E. McGregor, *Drink and the City: Alcohol and Alcohol Problems in Urban UK Since the 1950s* (Nottingham: Nottingham University Press, 2012), pp.141–57; Kevin Brain and Howard Parker, *Drinking with Design: Alcopops, Designer Drinks*

and Youth Culture (Manchester: Portman Group, 1997), pp. 11–12.

16 Brain, 'Youth', pp. 4–5, 7, 10; Measham, 'Decline of Ecstasy', pp. 317–18; Forsyth, 'Design for Strife', p. 75; Measham, 'History of Intoxication', pp. 26–7; Aldridge, Measham and Williams, *Illegal Leisure Revisited*, p. 14, n. 11; John Carvel, 'Sophisticated Young Drinkers Dump Alcopops for Cocktails', *Guardian*, 9 Nov. 2005.

17 Fiona Measham and Kevin Brain, '"Binge" Drinking, British Alcohol Policy and the New Culture of Intoxication', *Crime, Media, Culture*, 1 (2005), p. 271; Green quoted in McGregor, *Drink and the City*, p. 173.

18 Measham, 'Decline of Ecstasy', p. 318; Measham and Brain, '"Binge" Drinking', p. 267.

19 *Nottingahm Evening Post*, 14 Sept. 1998, quoted in Jane McGregor, 'From Dependence to Binge: Alcohol in Nottingham, 1970–2007' (Ph.D. dissertation, London School of Hygiene and Tropical Medicine, 2010), pp. 202–3.

20 Measham, 'Decline of Ecstasy', p. 318; McGregor, *Drink and the City*, pp. 152–5. James Nicholls examined the case in detail in 'Liberties and Licenses: Alcohol in Liberal Thought', *International Journal of Cultural Studies*, 9 (2006), pp. 131–51.

21 John Greenaway, 'Calling "Time" on Last Orders: The Rise and Fall of Public House Closing Hours in Britain', *Revue Française de Civilization Britannique*, 14 (2007), p. 193; Roy Light, 'The Licensing Act 2003: Liberal Constraint?' *Modern Law Review*, 68 (2005), p. 270; McGregor, *Drink and the City*, pp. 150–1, 174.

22 Rob Baggott, *Alcohol Strategy and the Drinks Industry: A Partnership for Prevention* (York: Joseph Rowntree Foundation, 2006), pp. 27, 29; Light, 'Licensing Act 2003', p. 27; M. Jackson, G. Hastings, C. Wheeler, D. Eadie and A. Mackintosh, 'Marketing Alcohol to Young People: Implications for Industry Regulation and Research Policy', *Addiction*, 95 (2000), supplement 4, pp. 5597–608.

23 See Rob Baggott, 'A Modern Approach to an Old Problem? Alcohol Policy and New Labour', *Policy & Politics*, 38 (2010), p. 145.

24 Baggott, *Alcohol Strategy*, p. 29.

25 Julia Finch, 'Death of the Disco: The Chameleon Pub Is Changing the Business behind a Big Night Out', *Guardian*, 23 Jan. 1999.

26 Hollands, Chatterton, Byrnes and Read, *London of the North?*, p. 32; John Spink and Peter Bramham, 'The Myth of the 24-hour City', in Peter Bramham and Wilf Murphy (eds), *Policy and Publics: Leisure, Culture and Commerce* ([Eastbourne]: Leisure Studies Association, 1999), pp. 140–1, 146, 150; Baggott, 'Alcohol Policy and New Labour', p. 136.

27 Glasgow was unusual in having several streets in the top ten. In addition to Hope Street, there were four others with large concentrations of drink outlets: Maryhill Road, Gallowgate, Sauchiehall Street and Argyle Street (*Morning Advertiser*, 15 Aug. 2002).

28 *Independent*, 17 July 2000; Hollands, Chatterton, Byrnes and Read, *London of the North?*, p. 54.

29 *Morning Advertiser*, 8 and 15 Aug. 2002.

30 Leslie Gofton and Douglas Stewart, 'Drink and the City', *New Society*, 74 (20/27 Dec. 1985), p. 504; Leslie Gofton, 'On the Town; Drink and the "New Lawlessness"', *Youth and Policy*, 29 (April 1990), p. 36; Robert G. Hollands, *Friday Night,*

Saturday Night: Youth Cultural Identification in the City (Newcastle-upon-Tyne: Department of Social Policy, University of Newcastle-upon-Tyne, 1995), pp. 37, 42–3; Hollands, Chatterton, Byrnes and Read, *London of the North?*, p. 78.

31 Hollands, Chatterton, Byrnes and Read, *London of the North?*, pp. 20–2, 24, 53.

32 Dick Hobbs, Phil Hadfield, Stuart Lister and SimonWinlow, *Bouncers: Violence and Governance in the Night-time Economy* (Oxford: Oxford University Press, 2003), p. 25.

33 Ibid., pp. 90–1; McGregor, *Drink and the City*, pp. 144–9.

34 Hobbs, Hadfield, Lister and Winlow, *Bouncers*, pp. 22–3, 26, 42, 46; Baggott, 'Alcohol Policy and New Labour', p. 140; McGregor, *Drink and the City*, pp. 146–7.

35 Gofton, '"New Lawlessness"', p. 36; Lois Miles, 'Drink Coping with Crowds on the Geordie Circuit', *Publican*, 11 Nov. 1989; Hollands, *Post-Industrial City*, p. 58.

36 Miles, 'Geordie Circuit'; Gofton, '"New Lawlessness"', p. 36; L. R. Gofton, 'Social Change, Market Change: Drinking Men in North East England', *Food and Foodways*, 1 (1986), p. 275.

37 Hobbs, Hadfield, Lister and Winlow, *Bouncers*, pp. 45–6.

38 Gofton and Douglas, 'Drink and the City', p. 504; Gofton, '"New Lawlessness"', pp. 36–7; Miles, 'Geordie Circuit'; Hobbs, Hadfield, Lister, and Winlow, *Bouncers*, pp. 43–4; Baggott, 'Alcohol Policy and New Labour', pp. 140, 143.

39 Hollands, *Post-Industrial City*, p. 67.

40 Brain, *Youth*, p. 12.

41 Hollands, *Post-Industrial City*, p. 37; Hollands, Chatterton, Byrnes and Read, *London of the North?*, p. 78.

42 See Chapter 8, above, p. 175.

43 Author's interview with Stuart Aitken, former Sales Director of the Whitbread Beer Co., 4 Aug. 2000; Forysth, 'Design for Strife', p. 75; Gofton and Douglas, 'Drink and the City', p. 504; Gofton, '"New Lawlessness"', pp. 36–7; Hollands, *Post-Industrial City*, pp. 39–40; *Courage News*, 55 (July 1991); Brain, 'Youth', p. 8.

44 These were recently established unbranded bars, with modern furnishings and stylish design. See Chapter 8, above, pp. 172–3, 178–81.

45 Hollands, Chatterton, Byrnes and Read, *London of the North?*, pp. 86–8, 94–5.

46 Hobbs, Hadfield, Lister and Winlow, *Bouncers*, pp. 37–8.

47 David Benson and John Archer, 'An Ethnographic Study of Sources of Conflict between Young Men in the Context of the Night Out', *Psychology, Evolution & Gender*, 4 (2002), pp. 7, 14, 21.

48 Hobbs, Hadfield, Lister and Winlow, *Bouncers*, pp. 39.

49 Benson and Archer, 'Ethnographic Study', pp. 9–10, 15.

50 Fiona Measham, '"Doing Gender" – "Doing Drugs": Conceptualizing the Gendering of Drugs Cultures', *Contemporary Drug Problems*, 29 (2002), p. 359; Gill Valentine, Sarah L. Holloway, Mark Jayne and Charlotte Knell, *Drinking Places: Where People Drink and Why* ([York]: Joseph Rowntree, 2007), pp. 45–6.

51 Measham, 'Conceptualizing the Gendering of Drugs Cultures', p. 359; Valentine, Holloway, Jayne and Knell, *Drinking Places*, pp. 45–6; Benson and Archer, 'Ethnographic Study', pp. 10, 12, 15, 18–19, 24.

52 Benson and Archer, 'Ethnographic Study', p. 17.
53 Valentine, Holloway, Jayne and Knell, *Drinking Places*, pp. 52–4, 57–8.
54 Gill Valentine, Sarah L. Holloway and Mark Jayne, 'Generational Patterns of Alcohol Consumption: Continuity and Change', *Health & Place*, 16 (2010), pp. 916–25.
55 Ibid., p. 924.
56 Ibid., p. 921; Paul Chatterton and Robert Hollands, *Urban Nightscapes: Youth Cultures, Pleasure Spaces and Corporate Power* (London: Routledge, 2003), pp. 148–51; Lesley Smith and David Foxcroft, *Drinking in the UK: An Exploration of Trends* ([York]: Joseph Rowntree Foundation, 2009), pp. 84–5.
57 Measham, 'History of Intoxication', p. 29.
58 Ibid.
59 Ibid., pp. 29–30.
60 Michael Leyshon, 'The Village Pub and Young People's Drinking Practices in the Countryside', *Annals of Leisure Research*, 11 (2008), p. 301; Michael Leyshon, '"No Place for a Girl": Rural Youth, Pubs and the Performance of Masculinity', in Jo Little and Carol Morris (eds), *Critical Studies in Rural Gender Issues* (Aldershot: Ashgate, 2005), p. 110.
61 Valentine, Holloway, Jayne and Knell, *Drinking Places*, pp. 34, 38, 40; Ian Bowler and John Everitt, 'Production and Consumption in Rural Service Provision: The Case of the English Village Pub', in Nigel Walford, John Everitt and Darrell Napton (eds), *Reshaping the Countryside: Perceptions and Processes of Rural Change* (New York: CABI Publishing, 1999), p. 153; Gill Valentine, Sarah Holloway, Charlotte Knell and Mark Jayne, 'Drinking Places: Young People and Cultures of Alcohol Consumption in Rural Environments', *Journal of Rural Studies*, 24 (2008), p. 37.
62 Evidence of the Royal Commission on Licensing, 22 May 1930, pp. 1129–30.
63 Michael Leyshon, '"We're Stuck in the Corner": Young Women, Embodiment and Drinking in the Countryside', *Drugs: Education, Prevention and Policy*, 15 (2008), pp. 267–89; Leyshon, 'Drinking Practices in the Countryside', p. 303; Leyshon, 'Masculinity', pp. 104–20.
64 Jim Orford, Mark Johnson and Bob Purser, 'Drinking in Second Generation Black and Asian Communities in the East Midlands', *Addiction Research and Theory*, 12 (2004), pp. 11–30.
65 Valentine, Holloway and Jayne, 'Generational Patterns', pp. 916–25; Valentine, Holloway, Jayne and Knell, *Drinking Places*, p. 48.
66 Nicholls, *Politics of Alcohol*, p. 226.

10

Yesterday's reforms, today's bingeing

Today, the debate on drinking, disorder and drunkenness has come full circle in less than a century. Parallel drinking concerns – accessible alcohol, redundant licences, cut-throat competition leading to slashed prices, pushing the sale of increasingly potent alcoholic beverages, a subculture of drunkenness publicly associated with one segment of society, drinking environments aimed at facilitating rapid consumption, deliberate weekend drunkenness and finally police, government and drink manufacturers highly tolerant of drunks – characterized the Edwardian era and the years from the 1990s onwards.[1] Nothing encapsulates the differing approaches to solving these circumstances better than the Licensing Acts of 1921 and 2003.

Radically different responses to the drink problem among one key group, the drink sellers, most distinguish the two periods. Nowadays, drink sellers see no serious drink problem for which they must assume responsibility. As Tim Martin (Chair of J. D. Wetherspoon) quipped, the trade, much like a disobedient student in class, pleaded innocence: 'It's not me, Sir, it's the supermarkets with their low prices'. Interwar Progressive brewers, in contrast, recognized drunkenness as a serious societal problem for which they took much responsibility, and devoted unstinted efforts to finding a solution. 'Passing the buck', the trade's current attitude, appealed as little to Progressive brewers as to Tim Martin.[2]

Declining beer consumption after 1899 leading to the collapse of London's licensed property created serious problems for the brewing industry.[3] Critics knew that cut-throat competition fostered aggressive price cutting, as numerous redundant pubs and beerhouses barely survived. In seeking to retain customers, some retailers radically reduced prices, offered credit, served drunks and sold alcohol outside licensing hours. Brewers responded with more potent beer. As W. Waters Butler lamented, 'competition makes him brew and sell a stronger liquor than in the interests of sobriety he would prefer'. Intent on quick turnover of business, breweries installed long bar counters for placing orders, stripped away tables and chairs, and converted all rooms into drinking space. 'Perpendicular drinking', as it commonly became known, facilitated both ordering and swift alcohol consumption.[4] Drinkers had virtually unlimited access to alcohol: licensed premises opened early and closed late; social clubs circumvented licensing-hour restrictions owing to authorities' inability legally to differentiate between bogus premises, catering to labourers, on one hand, and gentlemen's social clubs, with their propertied membership, on the other; and brewers had stimulated sales with hawkers, dispatched from the brewery, who canvassed working-class neighbourhoods for custom with promises of free delivery to the doorstep.[5]

Hide-bound brewers regarded these problems as rooted in unalterable circumstances: drunkenness was a product of character, not environment, and so an unavoidable feature of retailing alcohol; drinking premises functioned as a masculine republic, and so women belonged at home with children; the government was wholly untrustworthy, so brewers viewed it with pathological distrust; and retail outlets tied to breweries safeguarded distribution of the company beers. Finally, traditional brewers viewed drunkenness as lamentable but essential for profitability. Breweries sustained profits with heavy consumption of working-class males who all too frequently got drunk.[6]

Too many pubs and beerhouses selling beer to fewer drinkers consuming diminishing amounts of alcohol in Edwardian England had provoked intense cut-throat competition, drunkenness, demoralized retailers and a disorderly market place. The solution was painful but obvious: sharply reduce the number of licensed outlets; eliminate many small-scale, inefficient brewers and retailers; and redistribute licences outward from the city centre into new suburbs where few or no pubs and beerhouses existed.[7]

Experimentation in the nationalised areas during the First World War revolutionized received wisdom about sobriety, design of drink premises and the pub's clientele. The Central Control Board, appointed in 1915 with Lord D'Abernon as Chairman and soon an ardent Progressive reformer, had presided over new, shorter licensing hours which proved astonishingly successful. With licensing premises shut nearly three-fourths of the day, eliminating two-thirds of the old drinking hours, drinkers had drastically fewer hours in which to imbibe alcohol. Linked with restricted hours was the lengthy afternoon break, aimed at discouraging sozzling. Pubs opened for two-and-a-half hours from noon, closed for the late afternoon and then reopened for a three-hour session beginning at 6:00 or 6:30 p.m. Now, as John Greenaway noted, mealtimes corresponded with licensing hours. Consumption of food, one of the hallmarks of the Carlisle experiment, acted as a key factor in diluting the effects of alcohol.[8]

Advocate of a moderate, scientific approach replacing prewar extremism, D'Abernon saw four factors as vital to modifying the culture of drinking: the afternoon closure, sweeping licensing reduction, food and environmentalism. 'Regulate on sound physiological lines the modes and times and circumstances of drinking', he argued, 'and, within reasonable limits, the amount of consumption may with confidence be left to the operation of economic forces'.[9] Fewer licences in Carlisle likewise engendered sobriety. With half of them gone, alcohol consumption plummeted, so thought one informed source, Sir Edgar Sanders, General Manager of the Carlisle and District Management Scheme. Compared with 1913, he told a Government Commission in 1926, 'the consumption of beer and spirits had gone done by a third'.[10]

Food sales facilitated this transformation. Before 1914 heavy drinkers had consumed alcohol on empty stomachs and so succumbed to drunkenness. CCB wartime scientific experiments had demonstrated what the medical profession had long contended: food consumption slowed the ingestion of alcohol and retarded the likelihood of intoxication. 'The governing principle of psychological control should be dilution, including the specially important sort of dilution by food', D'Abernon maintained.[11] Embodied in *Alcohol: Its Action on the Human Organism* (1918), these conclusions would critically shape the mentality of Progressive brewers, and soon become accepted (as well as widely quoted) as the orthodox view on the subject. No other document presented the case more forcefully for environmental influence on drunkenness. Restricting access to alcohol (with fewer licences and the afternoon dry spell) and diluting its effect with food and weaker alcohol all reduced drunkenness.[12]

CCB researchers had demonstrated the role of a salutary environment as a potent weapon against insobriety. According to environmentalism, the individual was the product of the environment, which Progressives would change with social engineering as a method of altering behaviour. Drawing on his wartime experiences at the CCB, Sydney Nevile, Managing Director of Whitbread & Co., had come to see that 'cleanliness, space, and a humanising atmosphere tend to a higher tone amongst the consumers'.[13] Common to other such Progressive causes as the garden city movement, town planning, housing reform, model factory villages and settlement houses, environmentalism promised to address the socio-economic ills arising from industrialization, including drunkenness.[14]

Modifying the drinking environment became critical to inculcating new drinking norms. 'Men and women mainly fell into drunkenness in the absence of reasonable facilities for avoiding it', observed D'Abernon. Moral uplift took diverse forms: recreation (live orchestra music, newspapers, reading rooms, putting greens, billiard tables, bowling and a cinema); walls lined with artistic prints and lithographs; white table cloths; and flowers. Table service was also especially important. Sitting at tables engaged in sociability and placing orders with waitresses, customers exhibited discipline, redolent of restrained middle-class behaviour. Experience from Carlisle had shown that seated drinkers drank more slowly and typically consumed less alcohol than those who stood. Another counter-attraction, billiard tables, equally reduced alcohol consumption.[15]

Respectable working- and middle-class women, hitherto infrequent pub patrons, loomed large in CCB thinking about the environment. From the power of imitation, working-class male drinkers could develop order and discipline. Introducing women into drinking premises, D'Abernon felt, would have a 'civilizing influence', elevating the atmosphere which then became incompatible with drunkenness. Women's moral superiority, together with their skills in insinuating human virtues, would fundamentally transform the drinking ambience which had previously fostered intoxication. Encouragement of children in gardens or play areas too reflected the belief that their presence could act as an agency of respectability.[16]

Lord D'Abernon, a keen reformer, defied established conventions and prejudices in taking a bold stance on women drinking publicly. Imbuing women with enormous influence for heightened morals, he defended their presence on licensed premises against conservative authorities' strong opposition. In insisting on gender equality in drinking, D'Abernon set a precedent for their treatment in postwar Britain of enduring significance.[17]

Had it not been for the vital role of eight prominent brewers,[18] the Central Control Board's legacy would have been transitory Having failed to impose order, discipline and efficiency on the marketplace before the war, they despaired of reducing drunkenness, cut-throat competition and unethical behaviour, circumstances which besmirched their public reputation. Without governmental intervention, reducing excessive licences, permitting their removal to new suburban areas and sanctioning both the rebuilding and building of pubs, brewers had no prospect of rehabilitating their own reputations and the premises they owned, tens of thousands of pubs and beerhouses.[19]

Critics often assailed the brewer because, as owner of licensed premises, 'he cared for nothing but the sale of beer'. Why would they spend vast sums upgrading licensed property without reaping huge financial returns, Cecil Lubbock asked rhetorically before the Royal Commission in 1930? This question too has been raised by subsequent historians.[20] 'Anyone who has a job to do likes doing it well', he asserted. But, as Lubbock explained further, it also involved high ethical standards. 'It is a right thing to get houses into a good state.' These Progressive brewers committed millions of pounds to building, rebuilding and improving houses, not to make bigger profits or impress magistrates, but out of a sense of pride in being brewers. At the opening of the Welcome Inn (Eltham) in 1927, Nevile disclosed that the total cost of the new pub was £31,000. By any reckoning, it was a gigantic pub, spanning some 200,000 square feet. Nothing justified such a financial outlay. 'We can quite easily sell the amount of beer that we sell in this establishment in a space one-eighth the size, so … it requires a certain amount of vision and a certain amount sense of citizenship to run the risk of establishing places like this'. But he and other leading Progressive brewers undertook such risks, provided they could redeem themselves in their own eyes and in the public's as responsible, ethical businessmen.[21] Unlike traditional brewers, therefore, these Progressives possessed a strong social conscience, and took enormous pride in being reputable businessmen. It simply was not good enough to run profitable businesses; they also recognized their public commitment to the broader community. As Colonel W. H. 'Bill' Whitbread recalled in his appreciation, Nevile 'had a very strong sense of the social responsibility of the brewing trade to the country'. Nevile resolutely believed in the 'highest quality of product and the greatest integrity in business', recollected his obituarist. Immediately following the ending of the First World War, Nevile, in one of the most important speeches of his career, exhorted his fellow brewers at the Institute of Brewing to embrace a far-reaching perspective. When they all ultimately retired, he told them, 'it will be a satisfaction to feel that as commercial men, we have taken … perhaps an important part, in influencing for good the destinies of our own and future generations'.[22]

Drunkenness appalled these prideful brewers. 'Drunkenness is a curse we all desire to abolish', avowed Waters Butler (Mitchells & Butlers). Sydney Nevile, his colleague on the CCB, wholeheartedly agreed. 'Brewers', Nevile urged, 'should prefer England sober to England drunk'.[23] Progressive brewers articulated an ambitious agenda. Testifying before the Royal Commission on Licensing in 1930, Nevile offered his own personal goal: 'if I can cure drunkenness in the country in my time that will satisfy me'. Without government pressure and entirely of their own volition, Progressive brewers knew that they could go several steps further in facilitating sobriety. Nevile foresaw the likelihood of employing advertisements as a powerful method of stimulating public consumption of lighter, less intoxicating bottled beers. Drawing on his experience with the CCB, he remarked that 'it would be far better for the people to drink twice the amount of alcohol if they drank it diluted four times'. But, in a suggestion horrifying traditional brewers, Nevile advised the industry to assume a more direct role in combating drunkenness, hitherto regarded as an essential prerequisite for the industry's prosperity. 'We ought to take steps to encourage scientific study of the subject [of insobriety] in order to devise practical and effective steps to reduce excess to a minimum.'[24]

The war had demonstrated that prosperity and sobriety were compatible. For this reason, Progressive brewers came to see it as their duty to promote responsible use of their products. Their commitment, however, went well beyond passively extolling consumer self-restraint. 'It is in the financial interests of the trade not merely to accept, but if necessary to initiate, such regulation as will tend to discourage excessive consumption of alcoholic liquor falling short of actual insobriety without detrimentally affecting the service given to the public', Nevile pointedly noted before a packed meeting of brewers in 1919.[25] To traditional brewers, nothing could have been more short-sighted, misguided and outright dangerous. Not surprisingly, Nevile earned their opprobrium in many different ways.[26]

Whether in Britain, the US or many European countries, Progressives turned to government as a tactic to achieve one long-sought goal, a well-ordered marketplace. Order, discipline, fair competition, ethical behaviour and efficiency – these were what Progressive brewers pursued in a constructive relationship with the government.[27] This is not to portray huge breweries as altruistic. As the government imposed higher standards on all brewers, larger companies benefited most owing to elimination of their smaller rivals, which often engaged in questionable, if not illegal, sales practices. These leading Progressive firms – Whitbreads; Barclay Perkins; Watney, Combe & Reid; Charrington; and Mitchells & Butlers – all ranked in the forefront of shareholdings with £1 million or more, and so stood to benefit considerably.[28]

Central to understanding the transformation of Nevile, Butler and countless brewers into Progressives was what the CCB offered as an antidote to drunkenness, as great an evil to them as any other issue confronting the industry. Fewer and more evenly distributed licences meant fewer retailers with marginal incomes who survived solely by questionable business practices. Magisterial support encouraging the ethos of improved public houses, moreover, gave brewers a template for confronting drunkenness with higher standards, environmentalism and counter-attractions.

As part of this wider transformation, Progressive brewers understood their own part in fostering restraint, sobriety and healthy drinking habits among their customers. 'We hope to educate the public in the moderate indulgence in such consumption [of alcohol] as a cure for the abuse of excessive consumption', explained Edward W. Giffard, Chairman of Barclay Perkins. It was not coercive legislation but example setting – social pressure from surrounding respectable customers – that 'is the best policeman', stressed Nevile. This in turn depended directly on an elevated environment with adequate space, cleanliness and morally uplifting décor. At Whitbreads, Nevile advanced a more pithy description of what Progressives were offering the public: 'good service plus sobriety'.[29]

As part of this strategy to inculcate social norms against drunkenness, Progressive brewers sought a wider clientele, embracing the respectable classes, including women. Whatever business they lost in refusing to sell beer to drunkards could be recouped with more customers. Reiterated countless times, the improved pub movement's philosophy encapsulated succinctly Progressive brewers' goals: 'We do not want people to drink more beer – we want more people to drink beer'. And so they did. Through improved pubs, Nevile related in 1939, 'we cover a wider range of customers, as to age, sex and status'. By expanding the pub's clientele, brewers could offset lost sales as a result of more temperate habits if they sold both food and non-alcoholic beverages. Moreover, Progressive brewers expected that these new pub patrons would consume more expensive premium bottled beers. Given this profitable market, brewers cited commercial reasons as one key motivation for seeking more respectable customers. Frank Whitbread and William Sykes identified this concern in a letter to *The Times* in which they stated that 'insobriety drives away the best and most profitable customers'.[30]

Nothing more disheartened Progressive brewers than their seemingly insoluble commercial problems. They sought efficiency, product of a well-regulated marketplace, to ensure fair competition. Commercial circumstances in Edwardian England had denied them this. Whether in London, Birmingham or other large cities, over-capacity of breweries, together with falling beer consumption after 1899, created superfluous licences that intensified competition between publicans, who resorted to unethical behaviour such as the long pull.[31] A disordered market dominated liquor sales, angering magistrates, defaming brewers' public reputation and fostering drunkenness so detrimental to the public esteem which brewers so craved.

Progressive brewers learned more, too, from the salutary impact of government intervention during the war. Excessive licences obstructed efforts at reform both before and immediately after the war. Fewer licences – Butler estimated a reasonable estimate would cut fully one-half of the total in Birmingham – would permit remaining premises to be improved and new ones to be built, with each earning reasonable profits.[32] Such a solution would ensure efficiency, one key trait of Progressivism. For Nevile, as for Butler and other forward-thinking brewers, one tenable solution presented itself to the industry's interrelated problems of over-production, declining consumption and excessive licences – radically fewer licences more evenly distributed, especially in new suburban areas. The Central Control Board, with its sweeping powers of licensing reduction and innovative practices, established a standard which commercial brewers could keenly envy but never satisfactorily emulate. But the government could create a disciplined marketplace: directly through legislation requiring higher ethical standards, or indirectly through local magistrates imposing logical schemes, with licences fewer in number, redistributed to new growing suburban areas and permitted far more drinking space and amenities.

Lounge, Ham Hotel, Worthing, West Sussex, built by Kemp Town Brewery in 1925. 10

Draconian measures cutting licensing hours, increasing alcohol taxes, and diluting beer's strength, on one hand, and the CCB's introduction of food in Carlisle pubs, on the other, gave Nevile and Butler much to ponder. Pragmatism, interest in experimentation, devotion to scientific inquiry and advocacy of environmentalism, all characterized the Progressive outlook.[33] Each came together during the war under the guise of the CCB, where its Chairman, Lord D'Abernon, guided his board members with progressive policies.

Environmentalism took diverse forms of cultural uplift as a tactic for elevating the individual with bourgeois amenities, notably attractive murals, dancing, poetry recitals, theatrical plays, recreational games, live entertainment and newspapers (Plate 10). Where space permitted, generally in new suburban areas, Progressive brewers planned impressive gardens. This was particularly important for slum dwellers because only here could they enjoy what their homes denied them, the delights of flowers, plants and grass. Licensing laws forbade children from entering licensing premises under most circumstances, so gardens enabled sociability for the entire family. Adjoining gardens were frequently children's play areas, typically located in the back of the premises. Brewers, in fact, attached such weight to them that gardens, synonymous with middle-class lifestyles in Edwardian England, became the archetypal feature of improved pubs. Environmentalism and moral uplift marched hand in hand to inculcate order, discipline and restraint. 'A well-kept garden suggests the idea of care and good taste, which are the very things that a first-rate tenant or manager should wish to instil in his customers', maintained one brewer.

11 Smoke room, Merry Hill, Wolverhampton, rebuilt by William Butler & Co., in 1929.

Improved public houses, the indispensable weapon in the Progressive brewers' arsenal for attacking drunkenness, together with licensing reduction, would heighten the customer's own morals and décorum. 'The drunkard', thought Butler, would be 'ashamed to put his head in the place'.[34]

Food certainly did double duty in retarding drunkenness while attracting women. As Progressive reformers, Nevile and his colleagues appreciated the critical importance of modifying the drinking environment's pervasive masculinity as a deterrent to drunkenness. Men were more reluctant to drink excessively in the presence of women, whose introduction to the pub's clientele would transform the culture of drinking. Not only would women humanize the drinking context but they would serve as example setters and shape public opinion. Through the power of imitation, order and discipline could be imposed on working-class male drinkers. Women's moral superiority, together with their skills in insinuating human virtues, would fundamentally change the drinking ambience which had previously fostered intoxication. Progressive encouragement of children in gardens or play areas too reflected the belief that their presence could act as an agent of respectability.[35]

To draw women in drinking space previously reserved for men, brewers introduced the lounge (sometimes designated the smoke room), a term associated with upmarket hotels and luxury liners, immediately following the First World War (Plate 11). Here the 'masculine republic' was abolished: women drank with men in a refined, bourgeois environment, with tables, chairs, waiter service and carpeting. Spittoons and sawdust were banished as completely as pints of beer. Patrons drank wine, bottled beer and spirits, imitating a bourgeois social club, where drinkers sat, ordered from a waiter, exercised self-control and socialized with the opposite sex. This room acted as the progenitor of new drinking habits for all public-house customers in interwar England.[36]

In response to prewar drinking problems, authorities would impose an entirely new regime inaugurated on an experimental basis during the First World War. From this first-hand experience, Progressive brewers would articulate widely held goals: diminish markedly the overall numbers of redundant licences; redistribute them more evenly; permit the building, rebuilding and alteration of licensed premises; limit access to alcohol and so reduce drunkenness; and introduce food as an antidote to drunkenness. This became the genesis of the interwar improved public house, championed immediately at the war's end. To offer his blessing, none other than Lord D'Abernon, in many senses the philosophic head of this reform-minded group, advocated social engineering in which a new autonomous Licensing Commission would promote public-house improvement with funds from drink taxes.[37] Under the 1921 Licensing Act, access was limited through fewer drink outlets and truncated licensing hours. Cut-rate prices, given in the long pull, were outlawed. Heavier alcohol taxes, tied to alcoholic strength, accelerated the consumption of lighter alcoholic beverages. By the 1930s, the average gravity of beer was more than 10 per cent lower than in Edwardian England. In terms of strength, beer averaged 5 per cent before the war, and 4 per cent in the interwar era. But labourers drank what today would be called sessions beer, with an alcoholic content of 3–3.5 per cent. Arrests for drunkenness, reaching an apex of 205,000 on the eve of the war, fell by 85 per cent before the Armistice. New attitudes to drunkenness likewise emerged, with far less tolerance displayed to those drinking to excess.[38] Women continued to participate in public drinking, widening the cross-section of customers, especially from the respectable classes, who frequented improved pubs, the one striking change from Edwardian England. But in traditional working-class pubs and beerhouses, elder males demanded and received respect, assuming the role of disseminators of the proletarian culture among their sons.

But the success of the new interwar drinking regime derived not simply from legislation but from a productive partnership between enlightened brewers and government authorities, particularly licensing magistrates.[39] Both knew that drunkenness was rooted in the environment, and could be attacked with an entirely new form of drink outlet, the improved public house. An interwar partnership with the government committed to fostering a new drinking culture contrasted sharply with drink sellers today, who regard authorities with the same distrustful mentality as pre-1914 brewers. As Progressives, brewers would promote moral uplift, affording drinkers salutary alternatives to consuming alcohol. Prewar attitudes to customers were entirely rejected. Sydney Nevile, the quintessential spokesmen of the movement, expressed the Progressive philosophy:

> The improvement of the public-house did not merely consist of substituting tables and chairs for the bars. It was necessary to increase its utility by supplying a larger range of commodities and more amenities, and to raise the general standard by serving a larger section of the community.[40]

Armed with this strategy, he and other Progressive brewers would vigorously address drunkenness, which deeply affronted their social conscience. They also came to recognize a public responsibility for what they produced and distributed. Having witnessed the acceptance of weaker beers as a matter of government policy during the war, their perspective changed altogether. 'If they could produce a beer which met the requirements of the public without producing intoxicating effects until abnormal volumes had been consumed', Waters Butler argued, 'they ought to brew such a beer'. Less intoxicating beverages he and other Progressive brewers embraced, not to sell more beer or make higher profits but to achieve a socially desirable end – less drunkenness. Promoting beverages of high alcoholic content simply to reap higher financial returns – the strategy of twenty-first century drink manufacturers and retailers – would have struck Progressive brewers as socially irresponsible and morally contemptible, wholly incompatible with the precepts of good citizenship.[41]

Butler and Nevile had become Progressives owing to their wartime experience with D'Abernon and the Carlisle experiment. Today, their public-spirited attitude towards drink selling, this altruism, is altogether lacking, enabling the production of excessively powerful beverages. Instead of pondering what would be best for customers, today's drink sellers pander to the demands of immature consumers. Suffolk brewer Simon Loftus, former Chair of Adnams, is one striking exception. 'I don't want to rely on the "eight pints a night" brigade', he declared in 2002. 'Appealing to that crowd is socially irresponsible – all they're going for is the alcoholic hit rather than the quality of the beer'. Roger Protz, former editor of *What's Brewing* and a long-standing commentator on the brewing industry, shrewdly elaborated on this perspective. 'Brewers and pub owners, who do have a social responsibility, where sensible drinking is concerned, should question their craze for turning so many pubs into youth-only outlets where drinkers never mix with older and possibly wiser people', he urged.[42]

Progressive brewers cultivated a broader range of customers, particularly respectable working- and middle-class women. Their presence on licensed premises actively discouraged drunkenness, and had a humanizing effect on the environment. 'A higher level of conduct and manners is reached as the character of the licensed house in improved and a larger section of the community, including women, is catered for', maintained Nevile in an article addressing his approach to diminishing drunkenness.[43]

The absence today of a cross-section of the populace in city centres during weekend evenings, capable of asserting the Progressive brewers' concept of example setting and strong public disapproval of alcoholic excess, demonstrates the shortcomings of market segmentation. Instead of pubs and beerhouses attracting a cross-section of men and, to a lesser extent, of women as from the late 1960s to the early 1980s, new drink venues celebrated market segmentation, with bars aimed at attracting homosexuals, students, celebrators of Irish culture, and aficionados of sports and eroticism. No one, at least in the city centres, can impose informal social controls discouraging drunkenness. In villages, however, the Progressive philosophy did function. Recent scholarly studies of rural areas point to the role of older adult drinkers and well-informed landlords as critical in discouraging youths from engaging in anti-social behaviour and violence in village pubs.[44]

This explanation, in fact, also accounts for the rise of hooliganism at soccer matches since the 1960s. 'Juvenile hooliganism', contended Richard Holt, 'was mainly the consequence of the collapse of the controls which older family and time-served men had exerted'. More mature men had performed the same role as respectable older drinkers, especially of women, in exerting social pressure in pubs. What Holt called 'surveillance and supervision of the young' could be seen as exactly the same as strong social norms upheld by the respectable. Deindustrialization of the North had also undermined the informal apprenticeship, based on occupation, gender and place, which had bonded fathers and sons together through the rituals of going to soccer matches or to the pub.[45] Intoxication and drunkenness earned scorn and condemnation.

Today's drink reformers have turned the Carlisle experiment's approach to drunkenness on its head, with far less success and certainly less public approbation. From the early 1990s, the young had radically transformed drinking, but ironically their subculture of drinking stands in much the same place as the dominant drinking culture a century earlier. Parallels between the two eras – the pre-1914 era and 1990–2013 years – are striking:

- Access proved to be critical in facilitating drunkenness. One dimension of this was long licensing hours; even the lengthy pre-1914 hours did not extend into the early morning. Armed with a new philosophy, New Labour from the late 1990s liberalized drinking hours and encouraged more drink premises as a tactic to reduce drunkenness. Unlimited access to alcohol now became the undisputed norm. Vast numbers of redundant licences in city centres soon contributed to disorder, drunkenness and violence. Manchester city centre, for example, had more than double the number of licences in 2002 than a decade earlier. In the quarter of a century before passage of the 2003 Licensing Act, the number of on-licences throughout the country had risen by 30 per cent. Applications for new licences averaged five thousand annually, with pubs and bars the chief recipients.[46] Refuting traditional assumptions, which had attacked excessive intake of alcohol through restricted access with tight control over licensing and numbers of drink premises, the new reformers championed the proposition, as John Greenaway concisely put it, 'that the variable and more relaxed late night hours would result in more civilised and less frenetic drinking patterns'. Curiously, more, not fewer, licences seemed part of the cure for 'binge drinking'.[47]

- Excessive licences intensified competition, prompting retailers to slash prices. The concept in both eras was similar, though the strategies now became more sophisticated and innovative. One major difference was that the individual received price cuts for his or her purchase in Edwardian England, whereas groups benefited from them a century later. In essence, the individual drinker lost direct control over consumption, contributing to the greater likelihood of drunkenness.
- Drinking, often excessively, became the primary objective of a night out. Food slowed and could possibly reduce consumption, so alcohol became the centrepiece of the drinking occasion.
- Focusing on consumption, drink manufacturers featured potent alcoholic beverages. Average gravities of beer, a measure of strength, stood at unprecedented levels (average gravity of 1053–4°) in Edwardian England. To facilitate quicker turnover of custom, drink premises had to be stripped of tables, chairs and partitions, enabling drinkers to engage in 'perpendicular drinking'. Observations of drinking behaviour in the First World War, however, convinced Nevile, Butler and other Progressive brewers that drinkers drank more slowly when seated than when standing up, providing a powerful rationale for introducing tables and chairs in licensed premises as a strategy for reducing drunkenness. Home Office Research in 2008 likewise found that 'vertical drinking' promoted heavier alcohol consumption.[48]
- Drinkers were a selective group, unrepresentative of a cross-section of the population. Stress on gender and class in Edwardian England served the same role as age a century later.
- The serving of drunks, though illegal, remained integral to the revelries of a night out. In both eras, police, overwhelmed with drinking on weekends in concentrated areas, had no chance of imposing order, much less arresting most drunks. Besides, high levels of arrests would dampen drinkers' enjoyment of the 24–hour city.
- Drunkenness was recognized as a serious by-product of the drinking regime, but authorities proved surprisingly tolerant, provided it did not escalate into violence.[49]

There is also one final, though critical, difference with the interwar era. Progressive brewers concentrated on modifying the environment to instil discipline, order and control in drinkers, whereas modern policy researchers – in a return paradoxically to the pervasive Victorian ideology of self-inflicted poverty – see excess and drunkenness as the result of individual choice.[50] This was equally true of politicians. One interviewee told John Greenaway that they now saw alcohol consumption as 'an issue of individual behaviour rather than as a societal or structural one'.[51] Encapsulating this fundamental shift in perspectives was the transfer of licensing from the Home Office, the historic agency for dealing with regulation of drink sales, to the Department of Culture, Media and Sport, a newly created body concerned primarily with leisure and more broadly tourism.

This restricted perspective as much as the failure to contextualize the culture of drinking over a century prevents a better understanding of youth drinking today. In retrospect, one of the most revealing contrasts concerns how interwar brewers espoused a distinctive approach to the drink question, Progressivism, a mentality which involved their direct efforts to curb excess, promote moderation (especially with beers of lower alcoholic content as well as food), and secure a cross-section of the population as drinkers. Given these attitudes, Progressive brewers would surely have denigrated suggestions of introducing alcopops, more intoxicating alcoholic beverages and more licensed venues in areas already over-licensed. The mentality of today's drink sellers, as well as of the government and of heavy drinkers, was more than a century apart in so many ways.[52]

The Second World War and the subsequent building moratorium enduring into the 1950s ended the improved public house movement, but not Progressivism, at least not for the one surviving prominent brewer. Then, well into his eighties, Sydney Neville expressed disquiet within Whitbreads about the consequences of round buying, which he feared started with beer consumption and then shifted to spirit drinking. Again, as in the early 1920s, he raised the importance of the need for academic research. How, he asked rhetorically, could the industry spend £100,000 annually on improving beer quality, while virtually ignoring how to promote responsible drinking? Yet, when he proposed devoting £3000 to investigating this subject early in 1961, Whitbread's Research Committee rejected it.[53] For Nevile, the explanation for this opposition derived in part from the merger mania of the 1950s and 1960s. 'I deplore the present concentration of the brewing industry, and the consequent loss of personality and good will between the individual brewer, with his sense of citizenship, and the public', he lamented to Frank Beverley (Beverley Brothers).[54]

But another opportunity appeared several months later when Dr Howard Jones, Acting Directory of the School of Social Studies, University of Leicester, approached the Joseph Rowntree Social Service Trust, inquiring whether it might fund his research into drinking habits. On learning of Jones's plan, Nevile endorsed it enthusiastically. Jones required funding of some £4000 over a three-year period, a modest sum, Nevile knew, given what the industry spent on researching beer quality alone. To the old Progressive, here was a splendid chance, not to be missed, for obtaining rare scientific knowledge, without Whitbread itself becoming directly involved (and so possibly embarrassed by the findings). In studying this neglected subject, Nevile behaved very much like the quintessential transnational Progressives, pointing to similar research already completed in Canada and the US as compelling reasons for seeking more information. For Nevile, the rationale remained the same as in the interwar era.[55] Sir Frank Newsam, a close friend of Nevile, reiterated the old brewer's staunch beliefs which Newsam also shared: 'The Trade feels a sense of responsibility to the country and realizes that permanent security and prosperity can never be attained except by a high sense of citizenship'. Some months later, Whitbread's Board of Directors delivered its verdict: the brewery would not underwrite the cost of scientific research into drinking patterns.[56]

Ironically, the relentless disappearance of breweries, causing the withdrawal of public-spirited brewers whose long family connections with brewing had often given them a strong sense of social responsibility, befell Beverley Brothers seven years later, when Watney Mann took it over and closed it down. Two years later, Nevile himself, aged ninety-six, died, the sole survivor of an era long since vanished. For such men, their social conscience trumped profits, and as sellers of intoxicating liquor they exhibited strong commitment to discouraging drunkenness.

In the following decades, the relentless amalgamation of breweries accelerated as globalism created mammoth international companies, with diverse products sold throughout much of the world. Save for some smaller companies, notably Fullers, Charles Wells, Hydes and J. C. Lees, historic English brewing families have disappeared, with disastrous consequences. Roger Protz pointedly reminded the industry of its social responsibility to encourage drinking not merely by youths but by a broader spectrum of drinkers, older and more experienced, with social norms antithetical to excessive drinking.[57] Had he lived, Nevile would have sadly concurred.

Notes

1 Although police arrested over two hundred thousand in 1914 for drunkenness, this still grossly understated the actual figure. For discussion of the difficulty of policing drunks before 1914, see David W. Gutzke, *Protecting the Pub: Brewers and Publicans against Temperance* (Woodbridge: Royal Historical Society/Boydell Press, 1989), pp. 44–5.

2 David W. Gutzke, *Pubs and Progressives: Reinventing the Public House in England, 1896–1960* (DeKalb, Illinois: Northern Illinois University Press, 2006), pp. 102–3, 109–10; Tim Martin, 'Time for Some Lateral Drinking', *Morning Advertiser*, 20 March 2008.

3 Mark Girouard, *Victorian Pubs* (London: Studio Vista, 1975), pp. 181–4; T.R. Gourvish and R. G. Wilson, *The British Brewing Industry, 1830–1980* (Cambridge: Cambridge University Press, 1994), p. 602; Gutzke, *Protecting the Pub*, pp. 203–16.

4 *Brewers' Journal*, 15 Feb. 1903; Sir Frederick William Chance, 'Public House Reform at Carlisle', *Nineteenth Century*, 88 (1920), pp. 1073–4; Gutzke, *Protecting the Pub*, pp. 203–11; *Evidence of the Royal Commission on Liquor Licensing Laws*, 1896, 1 (C 8356), pp. 234–5, 241, 252.

5 National Repository, HO 185/353, Central Control Board (Liquor Traffic), Edgar Sander's Memorandum, 12 Oct. 1915.

6 Gutzke, *Pubs and Progressives*, pp. 96–9.

7 Ibid., pp. 100–1.

8 John Greenaway, 'Calling "Time" on Last Orders: The Rise and Fall of Public House Closing Hours in Britain', *Revue Française de Civilization Britannique*, 14 (2007), p. 187; Gutzke, *Pubs and Progressives*, ch. 3.

9 *Alcohol: Its Action on the Human Organism* (London: H.M. Stationery Office, 1918), p. 132; Lord D'Abernon, 'The Scientific Basis of Drink Control', *British Journal of Inebriety*, 17 (1920), pp. 83, 85; Gutzke, *Pubs and Progressives*, pp. 55, 64; Lord D'Abernon's speech, *The Times*, 28 Nov. 1918.

10 Modern Records Centre, University of Warwick, MSS 420/B5/4/43/6, Brewers' Society, Testimony of Sir Edgar Sanders, Transcript of Evidence, Southborough Committee, 8 July 1926, p. 522.

11 National Repository, HO 185/263, D'Abernon's speech at Longtown, 21 June 1917; *Alcohol: Its Action*, p. 132; D'Abernon, 'Scientific Basis of Drink Control', pp. 74–5; Noel Buxton, 'Public-Houses', *Contemporary Review*, 77 (1900), p. 560. D'Abernon was doubtless thinking of dilution resulting from the consumption of weaker beers. During the war, government restrictions had led to changes in the average strength of beer consumed falling from 5 per cent (pre-1914) to 2–3 per cent per cent (Sydney O. Nevile, 'Advances Made in the Sale and Distribution of Beer in Bulk and Bottle during the Last Fifty Years', *Journal of the Institute of Brewing*, 42 (1936), p. 521).

12 Michael E. Rose, 'The Success of Social Reform? The Central Control Board (Liquor Traffic), 1915–21', in M. R. D. Foot (ed.), *War and Society: Historical Essays in Honour and Memory of J. R. Western, 1928–71* (New York: Elek, 1973), p. 75; Gutzke, *Pubs and Progressives*, pp. 55–6.

13 *Brewing Trade Review*, 15 July 1926. Nevile's background is discussed in David W. Gutzke's 'Sydney Nevile: Squire in the Slums or Progressive Brewer?', *Business History*, 43 (2011), pp. 1–5 and *Pubs and Progressives*, pp. 17–18, 113–19.
14 David W. Gutzke, 'Progressivism in Britain and Abroad', in David W. Gutzke (ed.), *Britain and Transnational Progressivism* (London: Palgrave Macmillan, 2008), pp. 24, 33.
15 D'Abernon's speech, *The Times*, 28 Nov. 1918; Evidence of the Royal Commission on Licensing, 29 April 1930, pp. 1028, 1032, 1034, and 12 Nov. 1930, p. 2110.
16 Gutzke, *Pubs and Progressives*, p. 110; Stella Moss, '"A Grave Question": The Children Act and Public House Regulation, c. 1908–39', *Crimes and Misdemeanours*, 3 (2009), p. 111.
17 David W. Gutzke, 'Gender, Class and Public Drinking in Britain During the First World War', *Histoire Sociale/Social History*, 27 (1994), pp. 382–3; Gutzke, *Pubs and Progressives*, pp. 65–7.
18 These men are discussed in Gutzke, *Pubs and Progressives*, ch. 5.
19 Ibid., chs 4–5.
20 Stella Maria Moss, 'Cultures of Women's Drinking and the English Public House, 1914–39' (D.Phil., University of Oxford, 2009), p. 297.
21 *House of Whitbread*, 3 (Jan. 1928), p. 23; Evidence of the Royal Commission on Licensing, 18 March 1930, p. 809; Whitbread Archives, Notes by SON [Sydney O. Nevile] for Kenneth Hopkins, 9 Jan. 1957, p. 4; David W. Gutzke, 'Progressivism and the History of the Public House, 1850–1950', *Cultural and Social History*, 4 (2007), p. 91.
22 Obituary, 'Sir Sydney O. Nevile', *Whitbread News*, 82 (Sept. 1969); Colonel W. H. Whitbread, 'The Greatest Man in Our Trade', *Whitbread News*, 82 (Sept. 1969); Sydney O. Nevile, 'The Function of the Brewing Industry in National Reconstruction', *Journal of the Institute of Brewing*, 25 (1919), p. 131.
23 *Brewing Trade Review*, 1 Jan. 1903; Sydney O. Nevile, 'Beer Yesterday, Today and Tomorrow: Quality, Consistency, Variety', *Brewers' Journal*, 20 Dec. 1961.
24 Evidence of the Royal Commission on Licensing, 19 March and 12 Nov. 1930, pp. 820, 2134–5; Nevile, 'National Reconstruction', p. 124. In taking this pro-scientific stance, Nevile assumed a position in the forefront of supporters of the new modernionist paradigm which had consolidated control on the debate over the alcohol question during the war (Joanne Woiak, '"A Medical Cromwell to Depose King Alcohol": Medical Scientists, Temperance Reformers, and the Alcohol Problem in Britain', *Histoire Sociale/Social History*, 27 (1994), p. 365).
25 Nevile, 'National Reconstruction', pp. 123–4; also see Butler's comment in Nevile, 'National Reconstruction', p. 137.
26 Gutzke, *Pubs and Progressives*, pp. 118–19.
27 Gutzke, 'Progressivism in Britain', p. 23.
28 Gutzke, *Pubs and Progressives*, pp. 96, 106.
29 *Anchor Magazine*, 3 (Aug. 1923), p. 98; Sydney O. Nevile, *Seventy Rolling Years* (London: Faber & Faber, 1958), p. 174; *Brewing Trade Review*, 1 July 1926; also see Edwyn Barclay, 'The Future of the Public House', *Nineteenth Century*, 65 (1909), p. 1004.

30 Nevile, 'National Reconstruction', p. 140; Nevile, *Seventy Rolling Years*, p. 67; Sydney O. Nevile, 'How I Would Deal with Drunkenness', *A Monthly Bulletin*, 34 (1934), p. 58; F. J. Dawson, 'Mr Sydney O. Nevile Discusses Improved Licensed Houses', *Inns of Today, Supplement to Hotel Review*, April 1939; F. P. Whitbread and W. Sykes to Editor, *The Times*, 7 Nov. 1919; *One Hundred and Fifty Years of Brewing, 1788–1938: Souvenir Book of the Bristol Brewery Georges & Company* (Bristol: Bristol Brewery, Georges & Company, 1938), handwritten comments by its chairman, N. Hadley, inside back cover.

31 Gutzke, *Pubs and Progressives*, p. 106; Evidence of the Royal Commission on Licensing, 19 March 1930, p. 821; *Brewing Trade Review*, 1 Jan. 1919. The long pull, sometimes called over-measure, began in the late Victorian era in response to escalating competition, and involved an indirect form of price-cutting: retailers gave customers more beer than ordered without additional charge. The amount varied but could be considerable – the dispensing of a pint when just a half pint was requested was hardly unusual (David W. Gutzke, 'Public House Reform and Transnational Progressivism', unpublished paper).

32 Butler's comments on Nevile, 'National Reconstruction', p. 137.

33 Gutzke, *Pubs and Progressives*, pp. 100–1.

34 Moss, 'Children Act', p. 113; Thomas Skurray, 'My Ideals for an Improved Public House', *A Monthly Bulletin*, 2 (Oct. 1932), pp. 157–8; *Brewing Trade Review*, 1 Jan. 1903; Gutzke, *Pubs and Progressives*, pp. 169–70, 175–6; Gutzke, 'Progressivism and the History of the Public House', p. 87.

35 Moss, 'Children Act', p. 111; Gutzke, *Pubs and Progressives*, pp. 50–1, 110; Nevile, *Seventy Rolling Years*, p. 67; *Fellowship*, 6 (Feb. 1926), p. 38.

36 Gutzke, *Pubs and Progressives*, pp. 158–62, 183.

37 Greenaway, 'Calling Last Orders', p. 188.

38 Nevile, 'Advances Made in the Sale and Distribution of Beer', p. 521.

39 Nevile, 'National Reconstruction', p. 125.

40 *Brewing Trade Review*, 1 Oct. 1920.

41 Butler's comment on Nevile, 'National Reconstruction', p. 137; Gutzke, *Pubs and Progressives*, pp. 104–5.

42 Andrew Pring, 'Loftus' Road to Shangri La', *Morning Advertiser*, 20 June 2002; Roger Protz, 'Inn I Know Isn't Ruin of Britain!' *Licensee & Morning Advertiser*, 18 May 2000.

43 Nevile, 'Deal with Drunkenness', p. 58.

44 Gill Valentine, Sarah L. Holloway, Mark Jayne and Charlotte Knell, *Drinking Places: Where People Drink and Why* ([York]: Joseph Rowntree, 2007), p. 34; Gill Valentine, Sarah Holloway, Charlotte Knell and Mark Jayne, 'Drinking Places: Young People and Cultures of Alcohol Consumption in Rural Environments', *Journal of Rural Studies*, 24 (2008), p. 37.

45 Richard Holt, *Sport and the British: A Modern History* (Oxford: Clarendon Press, 1989), pp. 335–7.

46 Dick Hobbs, Phil Hadfield, Stuart Lister and SimonWinlow, *Bouncers: Violence and Governance in the Night-Time Economy* (Oxford: Oxford University Press, 2003), pp. 25, 86.

47 Greenaway, 'Calling Last Orders', p. 195.

48 Mike Hough, Gillian Hunter, Jessica Jacobson and Stefano Cassalter, *The Impact of the Licensing Act, 2003, on Levels of Crime and Disorder: An Evaluation* (London: Home Office, 2008), Research Report 4; Peter Wilby, 'Under the Influence', *New Statesman*, 10 March 2008.

49 John Greenaway, *Drink and British Politics Since 1830: A Study in Policy-Making* (New York: Palgrave Macmillan, 2003), p. 181.

50 J. B. Brown, 'The Pig or the Stye: Drink and Poverty in Late Victorian England', *International Review of Social History*, 18 (1973), pp. 380–95; Gutzke, 'Progressivism and the History of the Public House', pp. 86–7.

51 Greenaway, 'Last Orders', pp. 194–5.

52 For a superb overview of these changes, see Greenaway, *Drink and British Politics*, pp. 175–82.

53 London Metropolitan Archives, Sir Sydney O. Nevile Papers, LMA/4453/A/09/065: S[ydney] O. N[evile's] Note on Whitbread's Research Unit, 23 Jan. 1961; SON's Note, The Need for a Collective Study of the Present Position and Future Prospects of the Licensed Trade, 20 March 1961, p. 2; Nevile to Gilbert McAllister, 24 March 1961.

54 LMA/4453/A/09/069, Nevile Papers: Nevile to Frank Beverley (Beverley Brothers, Eagle Brewery), 20 April 1961; also see Nevile to F. Cornwall (Threlfall's Brewery Co.), 17 March 1960. For a useful overview of the merger craze, see Gourvish and Wilson, *British Brewing Industry*, ch. 11.

55 LMA/4453/A/09/064, Nevile Papers: Mrs M. M. Heath (Steering Group on Alcoholism) to R. N. Farrington (Whitbread Research Unit), 20 June 1961; Note by SON, 30 Aug. 1961. Immediately following the First World War, Nevile had proposed in his capacity as President of the Institute of Brewing that it launch a scientific study of the causes of drunkenness, but traditional brewers thwarted this idea (Evidence of the Royal Commission on Licensing, 12 Nov. 1930, p. 2106).

56 Nevile Papers: LMA/4453/A/09/067, Nevile Papers, Sir Frank Newsam to SON, 9 Aug. 1956; LMA/4453/A/09/064, Howard Jones to Nevile, 3 Oct. 1961.

57 Protz, 'Ruin of Britain!' *Licensee & Morning Advertiser*, 18 May 2000.

11

Folk devils and moral panics: women and youth across a century of censure

First enunciated in 1972 as an explanation for specific types of public responses to fears or alarms, sociologist Stanley Cohen's concept of a 'moral panic' has attracted considerable attention from scholars.[1] Curiously, despite this impressive literature, many historians have embraced the concept without explaining clearly what they thought constituted a moral panic, especially in analyses of the First World War.

Since publication of his book, Cohen's concept has been refined in subsequent scholarship, by both himself and other scholars. Seven traits characterized such a phenomenon: public concern; hostility (with offenders dubbed folk devils); public consensus; exaggerated response; volatility; introspective soul-searching; and finally perception of the deviant behaviour as symptomatic of a broader malaise. The last two factors especially suggest the origins of panics. Those involved as actors regarded the prevailing value system as threatened.[2] As David Garland remarked, 'this fear that a cherished way of life is in jeopardy is central to Cohen's account of moral panics, their nature and their genesis'.[3]

Edwardian England's numerous moral panics must be seen in the context of growing international competition. As a leading manufacturing country, Britain had undergone a relative rather than an absolute decline as a world power in the late nineteenth century. Intensified rivalry with European powers and the US created the framework for reappraisal of the country's future. From this soul-searching emerged the national efficiency movement in which previous assumptions and principles as well as existing institutions came to be scrutinized, and often deemed inferior to a German (less often US) model. Wherever Britons looked, Germany appeared ahead, with a model army, social insurance and superior educational system. Nothing exacerbated this deep insecurity about the country's place in the world more than turbulent problems in South Africa. Pride, sense of accomplishment and even racial superiority – these Britons had derived from their Empire, and so external threats to it proved more devastating to their psyche.[4]

The Boer War (1899–1902) inaugurated what some sociologists called a grassroots moral panic. According to this conceptualization, such 'panics originate with the general public; the concern about a particular threat is a widespread, genuinely felt – if perhaps mistaken concern'.[5]

Three facets especially fostered the panic. From the war's outset, military blunders, disasters and miscalculations embarrassed British leaders. Dubbed the 'Black Week', three military operations in December 1899 – the Battles of Stormberg and of Magorsfontein as well as the relief of Ladysmith – cost the lives of some three thousand soldiers as well as Britons' sense of world power. 'Some of the finest units of the British Army had been out-manoeuvred and out-fought by the irregular troops of two tiny pastoral republics', remarked historian G. R. Searle. Ultimately, Britain did defeat the Boers, but derived scant consolation. In vanquishing a small country hardly one-fifth the size of what Britain committed with its troop deployments, it had spent well over two years and some £200 million.[6]

However disturbing and humiliating were such events for a great military power, the war also raised broader questions. From huge industrial cities came thousands of patriotic slum dwellers as recruits for the Army, only to be deemed physically unfit for service. Nearly three-fourths of Manchester's volunteers failed the physical, with two-thirds of the rest admitted only into the militia. Of the original eleven thousand recruits, just one thousand met the Army's physical standards.[7] Manchester was by no means exceptional. In 1901, B. Seebohm Rowntree published statistics of over one-fourth of men from other northern industrial towns – York, Leeds and Sheffield – flunking physicals, and nearly another third having just marginally passed.[8]

Recruitment of soldiers itself quickly escalated into a moral panic in 1902 when Major General Sir John Frederick Maurice stressed that previous statistics had seriously undercounted the proportion of unfit men. In an anonymous article published in the high-brow *Contemporary Review*, he noted that adding the 20 per cent–30 per cent of men turned away by recruiting sergeants to the 40 per cent rejected outright by doctors produced a failure rate of almost 60 per cent. The following year in another upmarket periodical, *Nineteenth Century*, George F. Shee provided compelling evidence of physical deterioration. Within one decade (1890–1900), the height of recruits had fallen four inches and their weight nearly two pounds. These men, too, literally stood taller than the general population. Compared to a standard height of 66 inches in 1845, the average stood at 60 inches in 1901.[9] Appointed in 1903, the Inter-Departmental Committee on Physical Deterioration issued a report one year later that substantiated these claims.[10]

Exaggeration, prerequisite of a genuine moral panic, soon emerged. In stating that it had explored 'the degeneracy of our race', Sir John Gorst, Unionist MP and former cabinet member, distorted the report's findings. Deterioration, the product of environment, was remediable, whereas degeneracy, the result of inherited disorders, was not. This vital distinction was lost on many of his contemporaries, too.[11]

In assessing the deleterious impact of urban life on the physical, mental and general well-being of the labouring classes, the Report focused attention on children, the progenitors of the country's next generation of soldiers who would staff positions in Britain's empire.[12] When these facts were juxtaposed with the country's declining birth rate, the dimensions of the moral panic assumed new directions. Edwardian families of two or three children replaced late Victorian ones of five or six, but size was less significant than class: birth rates fell fastest in the better educated, wealthier and more successful middle and upper classes. Statistics, argued Karl Pearson in 1897, projected that just 20–25 per cent of the present generation – disproportionately drawn from the most impoverished, unskilled, uneducated and physically flawed – would produce one-half of the next one. The birth rate's decline intensified anxiety over infant mortality. It was worrisome that the death rate for children between one and five had fallen 33 per cent in the previous four decades, whereas infant mortality levels (deaths at under twelve months) remained unchanged. Thus, with far fewer babies being born, critics pointed out that infant mortality killed a higher proportion of them. The 'population question', Richard Soloway contended, 'raised the frightful possibility that the British were not only decaying, but actually committing "race suicide"'. Such tabloids as the *Daily Mail* left no doubt that the plummeting birth rate represented an 'ominous threat' to the country.[13]

Amid anxiety about infants' survival, mothers were blamed for infant mortality and demonized as folk devils. Sociologist David Garland noted that 'a specific group of deviants is singled out for "folk devil" status, in large part, because it possesses characteristics that make it a suitable screen upon which society can project sentiments of guilt and ambivalence'. According to two theories debated for decades in late Victorian England, women risked their babies' lives through either working outside the home, prohibiting adequate maternal care, or inept child-rearing skills. The Report of the Inter-Departmental Committee on Physical Deterioration (1904) cautiously suggested working mothers had a lower chance of seeing infants survive than their non-working counterparts. Under no circumstance, it urged, should employment of mothers be countenanced. Two years later the First National Conference on Infant Mortality went a step further, endorsing a resolution in which it sought legislation barring new mothers from factory work for three full months. At this same conference, John Burns, President of the Local Government Board, epitomized the disproportionate response characteristic of the moral panic. In seeking explanations for not just infant mortality but rickety and anaemic children, Britons should look no further, Burns maintained, than working mothers.[14]

The second theory, 'faulty maternal hygiene', gained widespread currency from the Physical Deterioration Report. Repeatedly, so medical and other health authorities proclaimed, feckless mothers themselves caused death of their babies.[15]

Four central issues – infant mortality, economic inefficiency, racial deterioration and the faltering of the Empire – soon became linked with women's drinking habits. Mothers loomed larger and more critically significant because they raised the next generation of Britons, who competed with the country's international rivals, sustained the Anglo-Saxon racial stock and staffed positions perpetuating the Empire. Economic, racial and imperial questions pivoted on motherhood: how much and how often mothers drank quite clearly had wider, more disturbing implications, with maternal skills, devotion to child rearing and acquired knowledge all seen as vital in a widening debate on Britain's place in the world.

Public concern over female drinking first emerged in 1899, even before the panic over recruitment, with the publication of the long-awaited Report of the Royal Commission on Liquor Licensing Laws. Covered extensively in the national press, the Commission had consumed three years of work in examining 259 witnesses, the most comprehensive inquiry into drinking for decades. Repeatedly, witnesses had testified to greater women's drinking and drunkenness.[16]

Women drinkers soon provoked public hostility, becoming what Cohen depicted as folk devils. Within months of the Peel Commission's publication, Joseph Rowntree and Arthur Sherwell co-authored *The Temperance Problem and Social Reform* in which they stressed that female alcoholic mortality rates, expressed as a ratio of living persons, had risen 104 per cent. This stood twice as high as the comparable male rate. Such was public interest in drinking that the book went through six editions in as many months, selling well over 90,000 copies. It was, in short, a best seller, a remarkable feat for a statistically laden book, with rather dry prose running to five hundred pages and more. Rising numbers of women arrested for drunkenness in the 1890s gave further credibility to these statistics.[17]

A public consensus, another characteristic of a moral panic, emerged in the next several years. Among the first publicly to portray women as folk devils was Viscount Peel, who had chaired the Liquor Licensing Commission. In an address in 1901, he recalled testimony before this body to corroborate his view that 'we have had some … appalling evidence of the extent to which intemperance is increasing among women'. Two reform-minded brewers the same year reiterated this conclusion.[18] Sir Thomas Barlow, a leading authority on scurvy and physician-extraordinary to both Queen Victoria and Edward VII, was just the most prominent of many physicians who deprecated women as folk devils.[19] Other health authorities provided compelling evidence. Frances Zanetti, one of Manchester's health inspectors, noted that the city's female death rate from drunkenness had nearly doubled in 1901–2. To give the story the prominence it deserved, the newly founded *Journal of Inebriety* printed her timely article. Upmarket periodicals, such as the *Nineteenth Century and After*, published articles subscribing to this thesis.[20]

Throughout the panic exaggerated comments shaped the discourse. Initially, several famous commentators offered cautious findings, subsequently overlooked by critics. Female alcoholic rates, the most compelling fact in fostering a panic, had been challenged in Arthur Shadwell's *Drink, Temperance and Legislation*, published in 1902. Reworking the statistics, he concluded that female drunkenness as well as alcoholic mortalities had fallen markedly for decades, not risen as Rowntree and Sherwell had contended. Fabrication of statistics, according to one recent study, satisfies the criterion of disproportionality, central to determining whether this issue qualified as a moral panic.[21] In that same year, another authority, Charles Booth, in his final volume to his exhaustive multi-volume study, *Life and Labour of the People in London*, drew on wide evidence to offer the restrained conclusion that women were apparently consuming more alcohol. Whether this contributed to more drunkenness was not a topic on which he felt confident to venture an opinion. Nevertheless, the folk devil image persisted. In a review of Charles Booth's final volume, the *Temperance Record* asserted that 'in common with all … who see and hear what is going on around them, Mr. Booth emphasizes the terrible truth that intemperance is on the increase among women'.[22]

From the very beginning of the moral panic over women's drinking, introspective soul-searching did occur primarily because it resonated with other topics. Rowntree and Sherwell, key originators of the panic, equated insobriety with economic inefficiency, one sensitive area of growing public anxiety. 'Either we must grapple with the forces that undermine our national strength and weaken our industrial efficiency, or be content to fall behind in the struggle for commercial supremacy', they maintained.[23] This theme likewise figured in a pamphlet by Thomas P. Whittaker, leading prohibitionist on the Peel Commission, in 1902 in which he argued that drink impaired an individual's mental as well as physical powers. Prophetically, he pointed to drink as responsible for racial deterioration. That same year another prohibitionist, James Whyte, associated alcohol with industrial inefficiency and racial degeneracy. Here was the beginning of a novel perspective of alcohol, with international competition and racial survival the centerpieces of the new critique. This new departure duly appeared in other prohibitionist literature. 'The Great Truth', claimed the *Temperance Record* the following year, 'is that the alcoholic habits of generations have culminated in … a state of mental degeneracy which … produces in-efficiency'.[24]

Women's drinking habits aroused such public alarm because of links with breast feeding and infant mortality, two key dimensions in the ongoing argument that damned employed mothers for jeopardizing their babies' lives. Pivotal to publicizing these interrelated issues was the Royal Commission on Alien Immigration in 1902. Several physicians testified to breast feeding and maternal sobriety as key factors explaining why babies of immigrants, especially Jews, had lower infant mortality than those of native Britons.[25] Such leading periodicals as the *British Medical Journal* and the *British Journal of Inebriety* published articles extolling breast feeding and sobriety as factors reducing infant mortality. Maternal intemperance, claimed several of these authors, explained why Britain grappled with national inefficiency and racial deterioration.[26]

These topics received heightened public attention when the Committee on Physical Deterioration gathered evidence in 1903–4. Expressing a consensus of opinion on working-class women's escalating consumption of alcohol, two leading physicians, William McAdam Eccles and Robert Jones, advanced a damning indictment of mothers who drank alcohol. Since foetuses could receive alcohol from their mothers' circulatory system, damaged foetal cells or even miscarriages could ensue. Eccles and Jones also cited alcohol's presence in breast milk and destruction of its nutritive value as causes of not only numerous infant deaths but physical deterioration. So persuasive were Eccles and Jones that they successfully wrote this conclusion into the final report. Developing a powerful anti-alcohol critique, they and other medical witnesses convinced the Committee to view drinking mothers as true folk devils: 'If the mother as well as the father is given to drink, the progeny will deteriorate in every way and the future of the race is imperilled'.[27]

Anti-drink physicians disseminated and enlarged this new critique of alcohol in the following two years.[28] At the National Conference on Infant Mortality, Professor G. Sims Woodhead viewed babies born of drunken mothers as more vulnerable to fatal diseases than other infants owing to alcohol's blocking of the transfer of immunities.[29] Woodhead and Kelynack broke entirely new ground in which they linked escalating female drinking, breast feeding and infant mortality. From this new diagnosis, the nature of the moral panic over mounting women's alcohol consumption assumed an entirely new direction, challenging the view of those medical practitioners who blamed maternal ignorance for declining numbers of mothers who breast-fed.[30]

Research into this topic had existed for some years, but only in 1904, amid the widening moral panic about mothers, children and alcohol, was it translated into English. Swiss Professor Gustav von Bunge, holder of the University of Basle's Chair of Physiological Chemistry, inaugurated debate with publication of *Alcoholism and Degeneration* in 1900. Translated into French, Italian, Portuguese, Russian, Japanese and finally English, it went through five editions.[31]

Bunge's thesis was disturbingly straightforward: alcohol consumption eradicated the ability to breast-feed. According to abundant data, where fathers drank two pints or more of beer daily, nearly four-fifths of their daughters could not suckle. From this research, Bunge drew several logical but quite questionable conclusions: the inability to breast-feed was rising; the function, once lost, was irretrievable to future generations; and, finally, 'the chronic poisoning by alcohol of the father is the main cause of the inability of nursing in the daughter'. He pointed to one long-term consequence. If growing numbers of mothers could not suckle as a result of steady paternal drink consumption, the future was ominous: 'Children are insufficiently nourished, and so from generation to generation, the work of deterioration goes on, leading at length, after endless suffering, to the ultimate decay of the race'.[32]

Bunge's research inflamed the ongoing moral panic. He defined consumption of two pints daily of beer as inflicting 'chronic poisoning' on offspring. Given his prohibitionist beliefs and view of drinking even modest quantities of alcohol as toxic, he predictably had no medically defensible definition of acceptable consumption levels. Hence, whatever fathers drank ranked as excessive, dangerous and ultimately the source of racial deterioration when they sired daughters. That the inability to breast-feed, based on just 1600 families, was increasing in Switzerland was a dubious judgement, and absolutely without any foundation whatsoever in Britain where he presented no substantiating evidence.[33]

Two anti-drink authorities in England nevertheless promptly endorsed Bunge's findings. Dr W. C. Sullivan indiscriminately characterized fathers, whether consumers of just two pints or more, as chronic alcoholics. Likewise, Kelynack wrote as if any drinking were synonymous with alcoholism. 'The widespread prevalence of alcoholism among women, especially during the reproductive period of life', he alleged, 'is one of the most important factors making for racial-decay'.[34] This unqualified hostility to alcohol was symptomatic of Kelynack's other colleagues – Sims Woodhead, William McAdam Eccles and Robert Jones – who like him had become prominent in the Society for the Study of Inebriety.[35] Kelynack and Sullivan publicized their views in 1906, providing scientific credibility for subsequent animated debate.

With public awareness of maternal drinking of alcohol, breast-feeding, the birth rate and infant mortality all significantly raised, the moral panic intensified further early in 1907. In a series of emotive and disturbing articles in the *Tribune*, provocatively entitled 'The Cry of the Children', journalist George R. Sims gave the panic what it needed most, first-hand graphic testimony from the pen of a journalist skilled in arousing indignation and outrage. His articles, far from being a cover for boosting the paper's circulation, had a specific political purpose: the banning of children under fourteen years of age from licensed premises.[36] One of the first muckrakers in Britain with exposés on slums in the 1880s, Sims had again ventured into London's impoverished neighbourhoods to obtain eye-witness accounts of how infants were being 'slowly murdered in the dram shop in their mother's arms'.[37]

Returning from his descent among the poor to report to his public, Sims recounted seeing 'babies in arms being fed with beer, and little girls of four sipping the gin from their mothers' glasses'.[38] In carelessly exposing babies to pneumonia, bronchitis, even tuberculosis from spit-sodden sawdust, careless mothers endangered survival of their offspring.[39]

Exaggeration, key to labelling the issue as a moral panic, was the hallmark of Sims's journalism.[40] Escalating the panic to new levels, Sims misrepresented Bunge's findings, making the case against women still more compelling. Bunge had avowed that fathers' steady alcohol consumption could inhibit their daughters' breast-feeding, whereas Sims now claimed that Bunge had blamed alcoholism of either the mother or the father for causing this outcome. He pointed directly to 'bad motherhood' as responsible for high infant mortality rates, a dereliction of duty which threatened to extinguish not just much of the supply of Britain's future soldiers but imperial greatness. 'What can be the future of our Empire, if on a falling birth rate 120,000 infants continue to die annually in the first year of their lives!', he demanded. For Sims, this fate could be avoided only if mothers followed his rallying slogans: 'Out of the Dram Shop' and 'Back to the Breast'.

Sims's muckraking raised public opinion to a fever pitch. Within four weeks of publication of his articles in pamphlet form, the initial fifty thousand copies had been exhausted and a second edition printed. Sentimental appeal with photographs matched Sims's evocative prose. On the pamphlet's cover appeared two angels gazing at a child's coffin, placed on an altar with 'ignorance and neglect' engraved on it; in the background stood working-class mothers pressing alcohol on their small children (Plate 12). Other photographs displayed the

12 'The cry of the children', 1907.

Tribune's skills in mobilizing public outrage. Small children standing outside pubs waiting for their mothers appeared in the 13 April issue; other photographs caught children seated at tables with beer glasses at their lips.[41]

Moral panics, argued Stanley Cohen, had a deeper intrinsic meaning than the events themselves. The mentality of those involved in moral panics saw folk devils as symptomatic of more disturbing underlying societal changes. As sociologist David Garland remarked, moral panics originated 'in the anxious concern on the part of certain actors that an established value system is being threatened'.[42]

Women's greater freedom outside the home, notably in sports, provoked consternation, criticism and controversy. Marriage property rights, suffrage claims and declining birth rates, maintained commentators, all imperilled the family.[43] The multi-volume *Life and Labour of the People in London*, widely publicized for a decade, naturally had the greatest credibility owing to its massive scope, inexhaustible research and statistical data. Booth's final volume in 1902 contended that women's economic and occupational independence had conferred respectability on female public drinking. This analysis and Booth's reputation carried great weight with Dr Robert Jones, who pointed to women's enfranchisement and enlarged legal rights as causes of the collapse of 'communal vigilance'. 'Women', he noted grimly, 'are now the companions of men in … industrial pursuits, and the freedom to work on equal terms with men has caused … the same depressing physical and mental influences … for which stimulants offer a temporary relief'.[44]

Critics imputed men's diminished control of females to women's rising drink consumption. 'More women', Robert Jones felt, 'are now without family ties and cares … and this solitude causes them to drink'. In articles serialized in the prestigious *British Medical Journal*, later collected as a book, Aimee Watt Smyth expanded the discussion in January 1904, placing women's increasing drinking in the centre of the debate over infant deaths. For Watt Smyth, as for many other Edwardians, this anxiety over alcohol was rooted firmly in women's new social roles. Nothing was more revealing than her portrayal of the contemporary woman as a 'worker', 'breadwinner', 'comrade' and 'person of independent means'.[45]

Women who drank publicly excited anxiety because they occupied important but now contested public space. Threats to male authority operated subconsciously to foster strictures of female conduct. That some women were venturing into sacred male territory, pubs and beerhouses, as part of their widening emancipation intensified alarms, producing surprising public disquiet.[46]

One approach to limiting women's public access to alcohol and reasserting the Victorian doctrine of separate spheres involved banning children under fourteen years of age from licensed premises. This legislative prohibition prevented mothers from frequenting pubs because they could not enter with their children, and would be presumably reluctant to leave them unattended on the street. Dr Rutherford put the point pithily: 'To save the children, the women must be saved first'. As Anna Martin explained, detractors of working-class culture sought 'to make of women a wall to stand between the nation and the natural results of its drink policy'. What this meant in practice was that 'the intemperance of the father mattered little provided the wife keeps sober, for by hook or crook she will contrive to save the children'.[47]

Subsequent moral panics based on fears of women's drinking and drunkenness suggest that the Children's Bill largely failed in keeping mothers out of pubs and beerhouses. Hypocrisy dominated the debate. Castigating women for ignorantly exposing babies to alcohol overlooked the common practice of many physicians recommending that mothers consume stout to promote breast-feeding.[48] Dangerous health practices in which drinkers spat on floors laden with sawdust had been well publicized in leading medical journals for several years, but ignored in the rush to blame feckless mothers for endangering babies.[49] Finally, some brewers themselves experimented with more salubrious premises before the war,[50] but the trade as a whole became preoccupied with protecting itself against prohibition or ruinous liquor taxes.[51] Besides, Edwardian brewers as a whole possessed a hidebound mentality, unreceptive to new ideas, opposed to legislative remedies and pathologically fearful that co-operating with the government would undoubtedly weaken the industry's position.

A second moral panic emerged with the First World War.[52] Excessive consumption of alcohol as well as drunkenness of soldiers, their wives and workmen, together with fears of Britain's war effort being jeopardized, actuated public hysteria.

Pressure for restricting licensing hours came immediately from naval and military authorities, anxious about drunkenness in the services.[53] Invoking authority under the emergency wartime legislation enacted on 31 August 1914, London's Chief Commissioner of Police, Sir Edward Henry, cut the capital's closing time from 12:30 a.m. to 11 p.m. Such was the sense of urgency that this order, imposed four days after the legislation, was itself further amended on 19 October, with 10 p.m. now set for closure of licensed premises. Still stricter limits, 9 p.m., were established for port and arsenal areas.[54]

Attention soon focused on soldiers' wives, who became demonized as folk devils, accused of squandering separation allowances and allotments by consuming more alcohol. As suffragette Sylvia Pankhurst recalled, 'war-time hysterics gave currency to fabulous rumours'. Writing to Lord Kitchener late in October, 1914, the Archbishop of Canterbury expressed the pervasive popular view of women. 'The women dependants of our soldiers are getting more money than they can wisely handle, accustomed as they are to dealing with shillings where they now have in some cases pounds at a time'. As a result, he noted, drink now constituted a 'terrible mischief'.[55] To *The Times* the following month, he reiterated his concern about 'the magnitude and gravity of the evil'. This same view received support from the Bishop of London, who pointed to women's drinking during mornings as the principal difficulty. He, too, had overwhelming evidence of this drinking habit's soaring popularity.[56]

Public outcry against women drinkers provided a consensus, a chief feature of moral panics, prompting authorities to impose restrictions. In September, the War Office threatened soldiers' wives with loss of their separation allowance if convicted of drunkenness. Indignant protests led to modified rules the next month in which soldiers' or sailors' wives apprehended for drunkenness would be released but warned that a second offence meant no further financial aid.[57] Licensed premises, deemed the source of the problem, meanwhile drew attention. Early in November 1914, Sir Edward Henry, appeasing fearful military authorities, vowed to close London licensed premises entirely unless the trade voluntarily dealt with early morning women's drinking. Given this ultimatum, the capital's brewers and retailers agreed to ban women from purchasing alcohol before 11:30 a.m. Birmingham and Sheffield justices reached similar agreements with local liquor traders.[58]

A disproportionate response, exemplifying a moral panic, soon ensued. From retailers Liverpool magistrates extracted an agreement to give women no more than two drinks per visit. In some Birmingham districts, women faced tighter constraints: they would only be supplied at home once a week with alcohol by the brewery's supplier.[59]

Prostitutes possibly infecting military personnel with venereal diseases equally inspired curbs on women drinking.[60] Lord Claude Hamilton unsuccessfully sought Home Office authority to detain prostitutes at hospitals and reformatories. On another front, the Plymouth Watch Committee failed to persuade the Town Council to resurrect the Contagious Diseases Acts. Undeterred military authorities, first in Plymouth and then in Cardiff, Grantham and Sheffield, acted without authorization and proscribed all women from licensed premises after 6 or 7 p.m.[61] When these restrictions drove women and soldiers into homes, exacerbated the problem and hence made supervision of drinking and other activities harder, Grantham's commanding officer, in an unprecedented step, authorized police and military authorities to enter homes. Their mission was clear: ascertain whether women were in bed with soldiers. This action proved to be too much for the justice system. Early the following year, bans on women frequenting licensed premises were declared illegal.[62]

Just as the panic subsided, government's direct intervention provoked renewed public anxiety. Two well publicized speeches from David Lloyd George, Chancellor of the Exchequer, denouncing drink as an evil and demonizing its consumers as folk devils, escalated the panic. These speeches, their hyperbole deliberate and obvious, elevated public concern into a genuine moral panic. In his Bangor speech immortalized in the press on 28 February 1915, he pointed to a minority of munitions workers, who begged off working a full week and returned enfeebled owing to boozing, as a huge threat to the war effort. 'Drink', he proclaimed, 'is doing us more damage in the War than all the German submarines put together'. Later the following month, he returned to this theme when responding to the Shipbuilding Employers' Federation's deputation, urging Britain's adoption of prohibition as vitally important to pursuing victory in the war. 'We are fighting Germany, Austria and Drink; and, as far as I can see, the greatest of these deadly foes is Drink', he maintained.[63] This animus against alcohol, one scholar has suggested, derived from Lloyd George's efforts to recapture his image as a prewar social reformer. Unable to champion disestablishment of the Welsh Church owing to the war's intervention, he now offered Welsh supporters prohibition as a suitable substitute. That he choose to deliver his speech at the shipbuilders' deputation extolling prohibition was surely no coincidence.[64]

Within hours of this declaration, the moral panic widened to the highest levels. George V disclosed his personal response: he would voluntarily eschew alcohol for the war's duration. In the event, he regretted his impetuousity, since only Lord Kitchener (Secretary of State for War) and prominent Anglican religious leaders boldly emulated him. Powerless to retreat from his exposed position, George V ultimately rationalized that his self-denial of alcohol included all forms of liquor save champagne, drunk thankfully as a face-saver during the war.[65]

Letters from diverse critics in the press incited renewed attacks on women's alleged excessive drinking. Disaffected reactionaries, social workers and administrators of the separation allowance received by soldiers' wives each indicted working-class women as improvident wives and mothers, unpatriotic and selfish for spurning calls for self-denial. Freed from all domestic chores or male guidance, hitherto indigent but hard-working wives, they contended, had degenerated into lazy, brazenly drunk squanderers of their husbands' money while gossiping in pubs. Taking inspiration from Lloyd George's overblown rhetoric, one secretary of a women's war club proclaimed: 'More ruin is being wrought in an hour of the public-house drinking at home than could happen after a day's work in the fighting line, for our men'. Another critic, Secretary of the Free Church Council, offered his experience in Lambeth as evidence of mothers' failures. 'I have never seen so many bare-footed children in London as lately', he claimed. A 'slum parson' pointed instead to soaring numbers of women charged with drunkenness in London police courts as testifying to debauched behaviour. These complaints in turn inspired an editorial in *The Times* reproving police officials for overindulgence toward drunken wives of military personnel.[66]

Criticism of women often also involved another trait of the moral panic, the deep soul-searching to find explanations for women's conduct. Anglican officials suggested rising intemperance derived from inexperience in dealing with larger sums of money than ever before. 'We have got to safeguard them from spending that [additional] money on drink', remarked the Bishop of London. In advising critics to abstain from reproving women for feckless behaviour, he urged that they instead offer such women friendship. 'Remember they are anxious about their husbands', he observed. 'The suspense is terrible to them; they are nervous, and they have very little to do.'[67]

Symptomatic of moral panics was their origins in other, underlying disturbances, which seemingly imperilled society's value system.[68] This became apparent at a meeting between the country's chief constables and the Central Control Board in September 1915. To many chief constables, women who publicly drank were guilty not only of squandering their husbands' separation allowances but of 'neglecting their homes and … their children'. Free from husbands' control, wives moved beyond traditional gender boundaries and encroached visibly on inviolable male territory. Women invaded masculine territory without male escorts, ordered drinks for themselves and returned home at their own discretion. Across a wide spectrum, women violated drinking norms, and assumed male space and roles in the most sacred of all leisure activities, consuming alcohol at masculine pubs. In seeking to restrict women's access to pubs, chief constables and other legal authorities were acting as surrogate husbands in which they reasserted male control over wayward wives. Women's numbers as much as their novelty disturbed men. When complaining about women's behaviour to the CCB in September, 1915, Southampton's Chief Constable admitted that, 'although there is not an increase in prosecutions for drunkenness against women, there is a considerable increase in their habits of drinking'.[69] That numerous poor working-class women had patronized pubs in Edwardian England without inciting adverse comment until the moral panic over children and motherhood indicated that this new wartime anxiety had far deeper origins than females drinking in pubs.[70]

Women now became conspicuous for drinking publicly, provoking yet another moral panic. Respectable women from the upper working and middle classes began frequenting pubs and beerhouses in unparalleled numbers throughout the country. One investigator, Mrs Stanley, explored Woolwich in April 1918, and encountered surprising numbers of 'smartly-dressed' girls and women doing a pub crawl without displaying drunkenness. During one hour on a Saturday evening, she counted over three hundred women and girls in three pubs.[71] This influx of numerous respectable women into licensed premises from mid-1916 constituted a remarkable change in female drinking, the first such time popular drinking habits had fundamentally altered since the 1850s. As an anonymous writer to the *Brewers' Journal* remarked in April 1917, 'women to-day are using the licensed house in numbers that would have appeared incredible three years ago'.[72] Rising numbers of women pubgoers would continue into the interwar era.

Impetus for this transformation reflected diverse factors: women recently employed now had money of their own to spend; war work gave them a stature comparable to men and justification in their own eyes to enjoy the economic prerogatives previously exercised by men only; soldiers posted abroad deprived women of companionship to fend off loneliness; and death of a loved one created need for grieving and solitude, on one hand, and communal support nightly displayed in pubs and beerhouses, on the other. Plummeting drunkenness equally played a role in undermining the long-standing stigma of public drinking. Respectable women, argued the *Brewers' Journal* in July 1917, no longer regarded the public house as synonymous with 'the drink evil'.[73]

With wives of military personnel acquitted of excessive drinking as well as drunkenness and their equality seemingly assured when using pubs and beerhouses, thwarted authorities attacked on another front from early 1917. Hence, a different group orchestrated the panic, but it still remained an elite-driven episode. Throughout the North-east, especially in Durham and Lancashire, chief constables and magistrates vigorously assailed women for consuming alcohol immoderately as a prelude in many instances to drunkenness. At Blackburn, two thousand women had been counted in two hundred pubs, with 200 females in the most popular one. Designed to alter drastically the drinking regime and encourage women's patronage, reforms at Carlisle – introduction of food, removal of snugs and state purchase – would all soon draw condemnation from the town's licensing committee.[74] For them, reformed pubs with their appeal to both sexes constituted a far greater danger to restoring the prewar status quo than unreformed ones. South Shields women earned the chief magistrate's strictures for daring to drink alcohol 'when the men were fighting and laying down their lives for the country'.[75] With such sentiments, the process of demonizing women drinkers as folk devils was well under way.

Authorities in two towns expressed the deepest hostility to women's drinking. More women but fewer men in some licensed premises fostered alarm in Middlesbrough. Such was the panic in 1916 when a survey of 26 pubs and beerhouses revealed that female outnumbered male customers that Chief Constable Henry Riches, a staunch critic of soldiers' wives 'drinking away separation allowances' in 1915, reiterated his charge that women drinkers 'neglect their homes and families'. Female drunkenness had increased somewhat, but even so five times as many men as women were arrested for drunkenness. What disturbed Riches was not so much the level of intoxication as women's wider patronage of licensed premises, the same anxiety articulated at the September 1915 meeting with the CCB. This became transparent the following year when, on his advice that women be segregated in a separate room, local female convictions for drunkenness plummeted to 157, the lowest number since the war began. His response was telling: 'Prosecutions against women for drunkenness', he complained, were still 'excessive'. To accomplish his unstated goal, women's complete exclusion from licensed premises, Riches craftily had magistrates stipulate that women could be sold alcohol only with an ample meal. He knew that, since few pubs and beerhouses served food, most women would be unable to drink on licensed premises at all. Queried years later about this outcome before the Royal Commission on Licensing in 1930, Riches unabashedly stated: 'That was the very object of it'. By 1918, police arrested just seven women for drunkenness.[76]

Hartlepool also carried the war of the sexes into pubs and beerhouses, the masculine republic home. Reacting to pressure from its Chief Constable in October, licensed victuallers banned women drinking alcohol on licensed premises for the war's duration. Unable to corroborate females' expanding alcohol consumption, he rather feebly pointed to shortages as his motive for denying women any beer.[77] When women sought alcohol in nearby West Hartlepool, the Superintendent of Police went so far as to argue that the 95 females counted in three pubs on one Saturday had almost in aggregate deprived working men of their beer. Authorities in Hartlepool, as in other Northern towns, had clearly exaggerated the problem, a key feature of moral panics. Publicans themselves disputed the need for such drastic action, stressing that women consumed alcohol moderately. The Chief Constable still reviled women, despite not one case of their being convicted of drunkenness in 1917! Inspired by this disclosure at brewster sessions, he applauded retailers for 'their patriotism'.[78]

Overreaction to women drinking on licensed premises impelled chief constables from the North-east to meet with the CCB late in October 1917. Here they assailed women drinkers as 'low class', immoral, feckless mothers to justify the demand that females be banned from drinking alcohol during evening hours, save when consumed with a meal. Banning women from licensed premises altogether on Monday mornings – typically when wives pawned items with 'uncle' to supplement family income – was a second demand. To buttress the case, Newcastle's Chief Constable maintained that 'before the war the women of the North … were not accustomed to go to public houses, but they were now doing so'. He, of course, exaggerated. Some lower-class Edwardian women ventured into the 'outdoor', the small area where patrons purchased alcohol for off consumption, and there 'stood crushed together'.[79]

Just days earlier an experienced CCB representative, having visiting some three hundred pubs and beerhouses in nine areas in the North-east, had reported his findings in which he repudiated what the chief constables had contended. As in the prewar years, the clientele of most pubs and beerhouses consisted solely of men, he found. In not one of the drinking establishments did women outnumber men. Women loomed largest numerically on Saturday night, but even then amounted to no more than twenty in licensed premises. On other occasions, they remained insignificant, sometimes numbering no more than two or three. Remarkably few women, moreover, were young, disorderly or drunken. Compared to national drinking trends, more women from Leeds and Birmingham were patronising pubs than in the North-east. The CCB case bolstered, D'Abernon reaffirmed support for its own policy of avoiding 'differentiation between the sexes'.[80]

Rebuffed in their efforts to reimpose control over women's behaviour, chief constables nevertheless continued vilifying females who publicly drank as folk devils in the following months. Complaints about women's greater consumption of alcohol causing beer shortages dominated brewster sessions in the North-east in mid-February 1918, indicating a regional consensus of opinion. Magistrates at Darlington, Castle Eden, South Shields and Newcastle urged publicans and beerhouse keepers either to restrict women's purchase of alcohol to lunch or dinner hours, or ban them from doing so altogether.[81] It was left to Bootle magistrates to take the most draconian action. In response, not to women drinking excessively but to their excessive numbers, the town's magistrates punished retailers and denied eight of them renewal of their licences.[82]

With the second panic of the war, as with the first, authorities grossly overstated the problem. North-eastern authorities were hidebound conservatives, vehemently opposed to admitting women into sacred male space. Newcastle's Chief Constable acknowledged that women incurred odium because they patronized licensed premises suitable in their austerity, he thought, just for men. Rising numbers of women consuming alcohol moderately still provoked the Southport bench to assail them for wasting time. Unescorted females prompted the observation that 'it was undesirable that women should congregate in large numbers in public-houses for drink and gossip'. Young women also drew the ire of Rochdale authorities. Because singing and music attracted young (unescorted) females to licensed premises, magistrates resolved that women's presence be limited 'only sufficiently long for taking of reasonable refreshments'. Unescorted women similarly disturbed the Castle Eden bench, which objected to their attending meetings of clubs on licensed premises. Disclosing the source of their anxiety, magistrates confessed to regarding this behaviour as 'a serious matter when so many men were away from home on active service'.[83]

Middlesbrough magistrates blamed women drinkers for fostering a beer shortage as justification for proposing a national rationing plan for men only.[84] 'The complaint', remarked the *Brewing Trade Review*, 'seems to have been entirely against men visiting seven or more houses in an evening, with the result that munitioners working overtime could get no beer when they finished work'.[85] Blackburn magistrates adopted a contradictory stance in which they criticized vast numbers of women for frequenting pubs and beerhouses, on one hand, and denounced reforms instituted at Carlisle to elevate the drinking environment with food, music and reconstructed premises, on the other.[86] Whatever the complaints, they originated in anxiety over women's uncontrolled behaviour.

Novel drinking habits aroused public disquiet as much as 'khaki fever'. By posing promiscuity as an alternative to purity, 'khaki fever', in which young women allegedly overthrew restraints around soldiers at the war's outset, imperilled gender relations. Whether socially or sexually, women began asserting rights in difference spheres. They likewise threatened prewar conventions, with public drinking offered as alternative to domestic abstinence.[87]

It was not increased drinking that produced these moral panics but something seen as far more disturbing, women claiming their right to move beyond well-understood public space into quintessential male territory. In essence, this was a fundamental but unspoken debate about where women physically might venture without male escorts. Women's presence in licensed premises thus became emblematic of the wartime fluid gender lines, with women's employment in hitherto male jobs, greater earning potential and encroachment on men's space such as in restaurants all threatening the prewar status quo. At the root of all moral panics, argued Stanley Cohen, stood this fear of societal values being subverted. Given the potential risks involved, authorities overreacted, projecting deeper but unstated anxieties into their perceptions of women's novel behaviour.[88]

In assuming a new persona, women challenged not only traditional demarcations in public space but how they behaved and interacted with men. Fashionably clothed women, their dresses 'well above their knees', wearing cosmetics (hitherto associated with prostitutes and chorus girls), smoking cigarettes and uninhibitedly drinking in pubs, inspired deep distrust.[89]

Such attired women in Middlesbrough disconcerted its Chief Constable, who damned them not as 'common prostitutes' but for possessing loose morals. From these diverse images emerged the term 'flapper', formerly linked with either child prostitutes or innocent young women. Now, during the war, these women, their unconventional, unfeminine and presumed immoral behaviour conspicuous, came to be called 'flappers'. After all, he thought, had they not repudiated the décorum of the respectable in entering all rooms on licensed premises, even sometimes disdaining male escorts?[90]

Government policy rather than self-assured females had partly stimulated this new conduct. The CCB's order banning treating had an unintended effect in encouraging 'the free resort of women to licensed premises, since it has broken down conventionality which restrained women from standing at a bar and ordering their own refreshment', observed the *Licensing World*.[91]

Such was the enduring hostility of Middlesbrough authorities to women drinking that the de facto prohibition of females from licensed premises, allegedly an emergency wartime measure, endured until 1926.[92] Here, the war against women's drinking privileges sustained itself for a lengthy period with male prejudices.

Brewers pre-empted this antipathy with decisive action immediately following the war. Women's new drinking habits served as the catalyst for brewers' improvement of public houses in interwar England. It was not slumping per capita beer consumption during the war, much less fears of American prohibition being introduced into Britain, but the protection of respectable female customers that motivated pub reform. Brewers already had a new clientele of young women from the upper working and middle classes as pub patrons arising from the war, whose presence had provoked virtual hysteria. Two brewers, Sydney Nevile and W. Waters Butler, both members of the CCB, imbibed Progressive policies implemented in Carlisle, and adopted them as the framework for transforming prewar boozers into bigger premises with more amenities aimed specifically at appealing to respectable women.[93] They and other Progressive brewers fully grasped how traditional unreformed premises deterred respectable women from publicly drinking. 'We are', admitted Newcastle's Chief Constable, 'depriving the women of going into these [licensed] places simply because the places are not suitable'. To reformed pubs with elevated environments he would offer fewer objections.[94]

Brewers protected women with more salubrious premises; the government promoted sobriety for both sexes by institutionalizing wartime restrictions on drinking hours in the Licensing Act of 1921. This legislation, on one hand, can be seen as the product of a wartime regulatory regime that had facilitated the decline of drunkenness. But the long-term impact of the moral panic, on the other, equally galvanized the Lloyd George government into legislating against a non-existent problem. Drunkenness convictions had begun falling before the war, and diverse factors accelerated the trend. Higher taxes on liquor related to its strength, lengthy afternoon 'dry periods' and earlier closing inculcated more disciplined drinking habits (save among alcoholics). Of utmost importance, Britons' palate had recalibrated towards less intoxicating beers. Brewers' attitudes had likewise undergone a sea change. When a Chairman of a Licensing Magistrates asked the pre-Progressive Waters Butler (Mitchells & Butler) what he thought about brewing a much weaker beer (3–3.5 per cent alcohol with average gravity of 1043°), Butler had retorted that 'it was not worthy of the name of beer'.[95] Wartime rationing had forced limits on beer production and a shift to weaker beers, with alcohol sold at 2–3 per cent. By the war's end, Butler, now a Progressive in outlook, trumpeted the lower alcoholic beers as a major contributory factor in promoting sobriety. Never in the interwar years did the powerful prewar beers become standard for drinkers: strength averaged 3–3.5 per cent.[96]

Social change in women's drinking habits came still faster in the Second World War. Nothing was more conspicuous, related a Mass-Observation report on Scotland late in 1940, than widening numbers of young females who 'frequent the more respectable or better-class bars, sometimes in company with members of the armed forces or other men friends, but also often alone or with one or two other women'. What drove such women into bars was not the alcohol itself but the lowering of social barriers permitting their presence. Meanwhile, other young Scottish women continued a prewar tradition of accompanying their young men for a night out.[97]

Women's escalating use of pubs coincided with the arrival of US soldiers late in 1942. Where arms and munitions production provided both more employment and higher wages, as at Cardiff, women had begun frequenting pubs earlier.[98]

Across the country chief constables, police officials and licensing magistrates expressed apprehension at the 'considerable increase in the number of women between 18 and 25 attending licensed premises'. This panic, as in the First World War, originated with the elite. One Methodist minister provided raw statistical data with visits to a different Sheffield pub in the evening between 8 p.m. and closing time over a 12-day period. His findings confirmed women's growing patronage of pubs: young women accounted for two of every five patrons. 'Only in this war', wrote the *Brewers' Journal*, 'are women using licensed houses to an extent hitherto unparalleled'. By no means was the rise of females in pubs confined to the North. In June 1943, Mass-Observation completed a report on drinking in Chichester in which it documented nearly an even split between the sexes in pubs owing primarily to an influx of young women. Working-class women easily outnumbered those from the upper working or middle classes. Solitary women drinking in pubs appeared now in Chichester, though older females braved residual disapproval more willingly than younger ones.[99]

Geography was as much a factor as age. In London, its cosmopolitan ambience and anonymity diluting objection, some young women displayed their own liberation. 'Before the war', reflected a young working-class wife of a British soldier, 'I wouldn't have gone into a pub by myself but everybody does it nowadays'. Joining her in London's West End pubs 'for a "good time"' were young female factory workers whose higher incomes enabled their purchase of clothing appropriate for these more exclusive outings.[100]

Greater numbers of young women on licensed premises in the Second World War quickly incited a moral panic as they became denigrated as folk devils. Prejudice against women pub goers raised the hackles of many conservative males, who exaggerated changes in drinking habits as much as in morality. As one commentator acknowledged, 'the sad sequel to drunkenness – immorality and V.D. – is one of the most pressing and perplexing problems'. Liverpool, so critics thought, epitomized problems in the entire country. Here, young prostitutes brazenly solicited seamen first to buy them a drink and then to 'accompany them for baser purposes'. City publicans posted notices banning unescorted women from being served as a strategy to combat a 'serious increase of drinking' constituting what one trade official deemed 'the magnitude of a social evil'.[101]

By inflating women's presence in pubs, and so displaying disproportionality, key to defining the outburst as a moral panic, officials could upheld bogus charges of mishaviour – drunkenness, underage drinking and promiscuity with soldiers – to justify the need for heightened control of a 'growing problem'. Women could thus again be put back in their proper subordinate prewar place. 'The public-house had been in the main a man's sanctum', commented Newport's Chief Constable Harris, who had first voiced concern early in 1941. 'Now', he grumbled two years later, 'it would appear that women were not only doing men's work, but acquiring their habits'. Similar sentiments had been voiced around the country, with the added charge that women contributed to overcrowded pubs.[102] More women were certainly frequenting licensed premises, but the moral panic's exaggeration of this trend strongly suggests that wartime estimates of their tripling in numbers had no reliable basis.[103]

Assertive female behaviour as much as male resentment at wartime changes provoked such strictures. As a result of the war, women were earning more money and spending some of it in pubs, a rarity in some localities. 'Women frequenting public houses exhibit a provocative spirit of independence in their methods of spending increased incomes', protested Cardiff's Chief Constable, James Wilson.[104] Testing their new-found freedom, Scottish women assumed the guise of male colleagues, even to the extent of ordering their pint of beer in a pewter tankard. The woman exhibiting greatest aplomb 'scores many points'.[105] Soon, females south of the border replicated this behaviour.[106]

In response to the moral panic, the government opportunely intervened, appointing a committee to examine servicewomen's wartime morality and drinking habits early in 1942. Six month later its Chair, Violet Markham, delivered a report that, while conceding that women were consuming more alcohol, disproved allegations of excessive drinking and immorality. The report identified new attitudes to alcoholic beverages in which both women and men came to see drinking as emblematic of sociability.[107]

These findings were corroborated in *A Monthly Bulletin* in a special issue in August 1942, with commissioned reports from investigators in large industrial cities and ports, localities most associated in the public mind with women's expanding drink consumption. Like the Markham Committee Report, investigators established women as a growing proportion of pub patrons, but found no evidence of rising drunkenness.[108]

Again the moral panic arose from fears of wider problems – women's drinking behaviour became symptomatic of broader threats to gender relations and social values amid a national crisis requiring unity to defeat Hitler. In displaying resolute independence and self-confidence in drinking out – 'there is no secrecy about it, no embarrassment' – women raised the spectre of social equality with men, thereby unwittingly provoking comment, criticism and censure. Male rituals and barroom drinking norms were entirely disregarded. Women entered bars sometimes on their own; purchased alcohol for themselves; and when accompanied by men took their turn buying a round. 'It is now a common sight to see women and girls of all classes in bars, standing each other drinks and occupying the stools formerly sacred to men', recorded one investigator. Shifting gender boundaries disturbed many men, who had difficulty mentally accepting the radically new drinking regime in working-class pubs, previously uncontested male sanctuaries. On entering his customary city centre pub and encountering numerous women seated at the bar counter, a Liverpool man bewilderingly sought reassurance from the barman: '"Excuse me, but is it all right for men to come in here?"'[109]

Challenging gender boundaries had created disquiet when more women began smoking in public during the interwar era, and only in the war itself did criticism wane. The *Brewers' Journal* shrewdly remarked that 'whenever women commence to do anything [new] they are taken to task'. Women smoking cigarettes had become what the *True Temperance Quarterly* called 'a symbol of emancipation', and it drew a parallel between this controversial social habit and another more conspicuous one, females drinking in pubs.[110]

In *Death at the Dog*, published in 1941, novelist Joanna Cannan vividly expresses this male consternation at women's drinking behaviour with one character, Chief Constable Carruthers of Loamshire, her fictitious rendering of rural Oxfordshire, where middle-class females regularly visit the lounge of the Dog. '"Disgustin, the way these women drink"', said Carruthers. '"In my young days mem-sahibs didn't go beyound a sip of white wine with the fish and a glass of port with the dessert, but now nothing comes amiss to them – beer, whiskey, gin"'.[111] Cannan wants to show the depth of Carruthers's horror at the collapse of all standards by indicating that he thought women are drinking Irish 'whiskey'.

A moral panic over adolescent drinking soon replaced public interest in women's increased use of pubs. Drawn into the labour market owing to a shortage of adult males now in uniform, flush with high wartime wages, and eager to display their new-found economic independence, adolescents of both sexes flocked to pubs. From the war's onset, youth had shown an increased propensity to patronize pubs and drink alcohol. Twenty-seven adolescents (seventeen to twenty-one) in Lancashire had been prosecuted for drunkenness in 1940, nearly three-and-a-half times more than in the previous year. 'There has been a tremendous influx to the drinking bars' in Bristol, with youths 'determined to have as good a time as possible'. Large industrial towns or ports – from Leeds, Liverpool, Rotherham and Sheffield to Birmingham, Newcastle-upon-Tyne, Bristol and Cardiff – all reported soaring amounts of juvenile drinking.[112] Juvenile drinkers alarmed many observers not so much by how much they drank as by their disconcerting novel behaviour. Numerous adolescents in pubs proved provocative. After gazing at his Leeds barroom crowded with adolescents, one Leeds publican remarked that 'it seemed as though only the young folks could afford to drink nowadays'. What fostered awareness of this change was that newer, brighter, bigger, and more modern premises, located on main streets, attracted such youths, whereas traditional boozers drew an older clientele. Emboldened by the war, youths entered pubs alone, and, 'well supplied with money', ridiculed high prices. 'They fan their sense of manliness by the consumption of the more potent and dearer drinks and not infrequently will spend as much as ten shillings a night on whisky, taking to beer only when other drinks are … unobtainable', commented one disgusted witness. On outings with females, male youths, their swagger as well-heeled workers conspicuous, bought dates dearer priced wine and whisky.[113]

Outside pubs, juvenile behaviour also caused public disquiet.

> Most nights and at week-ends groups of youths – little more than boys and girls – may be seen in the centre of Sheffield obviously 'under the influence' to some extent. They are so noisy that people may be forgiven for judging them to be thoroughly drunk.

Closer scrutiny, this onlooker thought, would reveal such public display as merely 'high spirits'. He had to concede, however, that adolescents in some places were drinking excessively, especially at dance halls and nearby pubs, typically overcrowded and so difficult to police.[114]

By mid-1942, a genuine moral panic had emerged, with numerous signs of overreaction. Liverpool publicans voluntarily posted notices prohibiting the serving of alcohol to those under eighteen. Within twelve months, the Home Office responding to public outcry requested that publicans throughout the entire country follow Liverpool's lead.[115] Anxious to quell public consternation and fully prepared to sacrifice profits from questionable sources, Liverpool publicans assumed the initiative and banned serving of alcohol to anyone under twenty, four years above the statutory limit! Religious officials took up the issue in earnest. For girls under eighteen, urged the Bishop of Chelmsford, an 8 p.m. curfew ought to be enforced. The Archdeacon of Dudley had another solution, the reimposition of the First World War's 'No Treating' regulation. Fears of rising juvenile drinking in Liverpool induced the Bishop of Liverpool to join the 'No Treating' movement. Further support came from Dr Temple, Archbishop of Canterbury, who explained that 'often those who were treated were unused to any kind of alcohol and did not know what its effects might be'. Despite growing public pressure for such a government edict, the Home Secretary, Herbert Morrison, baulked. Public anxiety, nevertheless, prompted numerous publicans to pre-empt feared intervention with hastily posted notices condemning underage drinking.[116]

Diverse sources sustained the moral panic well into 1943 and beyond. At Blackburn, another northern industrial city, three thousand protesters met to denounce 'Youth and Drink'. Nearby at Liverpool early the following year, its chief magistrate characterized youth's consumption of alcohol as a 'grave national concern'.[117] The national press played a pivotal role in publicizing the topic and inflaming public anxiety. A letter from prominent social workers appeared in the *The Times* expressing concern about youth drinking. Another national newspaper, the *Manchester Guardian*, published a lengthy story in which it argued that 'there has been a considerable, even if it is not yet a disastrous, increase in juvenile drinking....' More vigorous efforts, advised the paper, were needed to pre-empt the problem's escalation. To bolster its case, the *Guardian* quoted an anonymous cabinet minister who pointed to the spreading popularity of cocktails as the cause of more adolescent drinking. Legal authorities, notably chief constables and magistrates, similarly voiced their alarm at a widening social problem. Under mounting pressure, Morrison recommended that retailers post notices warning both publicans and public that underage drinking violated the law. Adolescents under eighteen could neither buy alcohol for themselves nor have someone else buy it for them, unless served with a meal. Giving such youths alcohol as a goodwill gesture also warranted prosecution.[118]

Exaggeration, central to a moral panic, dominated public interest. So powerful was the hysteria that persuasive evidence challenging widespread youth drinking remained outside the debate.[119] Statistics of youth drinking in Salford, a heavy-drinking industrial city of some 200,000 where prosecutions of seventeen- to twenty-one year-olds had tripled in one year, suggested a quick reassertion of prewar drinking norms. In 1941, just ten youths had been arrested, a sharp decline of nearly 40 per cent. Notwithstanding high wages in the booming port of Plymouth and intensive bombing in spring, 1941, 'adolescent drinkers are spasmodic nuisances rather than persistent offenders', attested one observer. High alcohol prices, one strong deterrent to youth's heavy drinking, were often overlooked as a restraint on drinking, even for relatively well-paid factory workers. Besides, youths typically spent more heavily on tobacco – perhaps three or even four times as much – as on alcohol. Likewise in Nottingham, critics overstated fears of youth drunkenness. 'The number of young people charged with serious crime and with intemperance is so small as to be almost negligible', knew one informed lawyer.[120]

Often it was less what youths consumed than how they behaved that served as a catalyst of the panic. One Cardiff drinker thought that 'young people who used to be seen only in the smaller licensed houses are now regular customers in the leading hotel bars'.[121]

Adolescents frequenting pubs aroused deeper concerns about declining morality, mounting juvenile delinquency and imperilled societal standards. That 'they have more money than common sense' in downing innumerable beers and gins Cardiff's Chief Constable attributed to a collapse of parental supervision. To him, this was especially reprehensible, given soldiers' patriotism and willingness to accept financial sacrifice. In arresting escalating numbers of youths who committed grievous bodily harm, he identified one outstanding culprit – alcohol consumption. He applauded the recruitment of youths in Cadet Training Corps, their programmes imposing the requisite discipline to deter '"wanton criminal acts"'.[122]

Youth alcohol consumption raised the more troubling topic of seduction, the plying of young inexperienced girls with alcohol for sexual purposes. Displaying classic symptoms of a moral panic, brewers themselves or informally through friends gathered information about adolescent female drinking, and came to see treating as a perilous step towards immorality. 'Little imagination is needed to foresee what may happen when a girl, taken unawares by some drink much stronger than she supposes it to be, temporally loses her self-control.' Their solution, the voluntary abstention from treating, was advocated in October 1943.[123]

Recently, Claire Langhamer minimized the influx of numerous adolescents (sixteen to eighteen years old) into pubs. Her emphasis on the age of drinkers loomed large as a factor in determining the changing age and gender composition of the pub's clientele, but this reflected two misconceptions: that the influx of new drinkers consisted primarily of young women mainly in their twenties; and that young customers were drinking alcoholic beverages.[124] Insight into both topics would come from Dr J. Macalister Brew, whose overlooked but detailed study of youth drinking appeared at the height of the moral panic in the *Times Educational Supplement.*

Macalister Brew conducted an exhaustive study in which she spent a night in a hundred different public houses in a sizeable but unidentified industrial town over a six-month period in late 1941 and early 1942.[125] Hers was a study unmatched in scope and in-depth knowledge since Mass-Observation's own investigation of another comparable northern town, Bolton, in the mid-1930s. To her pubs went youths aged sixteen to twenty-five in groups of three or more, evenly divided between the sexes. Despite press reports of soaring juvenile drunkenness, she found them instead drinking respectably. Of the thousands of people in pubs over the six-month period, she witnessed just only one case of a juvenile excessively drinking.[126] 'It is they who sit for hours talking over a very little liquid; who play darts and tinker with the automatic machines; who encourage the pianist or put pennies in the pianola', she concluded.[127]

Young men drank beer generally, sometimes as shandy, while young women preferred port and lemon, less often shandy or cider. These drinking habits, Brew noted, mirrored those of the preceding generation when about the same age.[128]

Those under the drinking age of eighteen constituted half of the total, while another third ranged between eighteen and twenty-one. Sixteen- and seventeen-year-olds could drink beer or wine but not spirits, provided they ordered alcohol with a meal. Most apparently chose not to do so. Elsewhere, publicans, so concerned about underage drinkers, had proposed banning everyone under twenty-one, but not in her survey town. Of soaring juvenile drunkenness publicized in press reports, Brew found no evidence.[129] Even underage drinking she deemed extremely rare, with juveniles far more interested in conversation, games, music and darts than booze. Besides, pubs were tightly policed, even in wartime, discouraging much thought of illegal drinking. Hull's pubs, for example, received 12,336 police visits in one year alone.[130]

Given these circumstances, many adolescents under eighteen frequented licensed premises where they consumed soft drinks or other non-intoxicants. This, in part, explains a key paradox: why total numbers of young customers of pubs slumped after 1946. Growing numbers of young people, including adolescents, had patronized licensed premises during the war, but withdrew thereafter. In wartime Britain adolescents (fourteen to eighteen) of both sexes inflated the population of young people in pubs. With jobs readily available, dance halls packed with uniformed men, and surplus income and time, youths turned to pubs as a form of social club, chiefly to socialize. They did consume beverages on licensed premises, but rarely (when under drinking age) alcohol. Hence, many informed authorities could record astonishingly more young people on licensed premises, while actual numbers of drinkers of alcohol expanded more slowly. When the war ended and soldiers returned to their civilian jobs, adolescents sacrificed their employment, spare money and visits to the pub.[131] As a result, Mass-Observation recorded declining pub-going among women overall in the immediate postwar years, but failed to note female adolescents played a role in this slump.[132] This in turn explains why later public opinion polls in 1949 and 1956 recorded far fewer women (and adolescents) drinking at pubs, with the proportions of 37 per cent just slightly higher by 4 per cent than a prewar survey.[133] During the war shortages of spirits and wine had compelled girls and women to consume beer, a pronounced shift in drinking that inflated total beer consumption. The withdrawal of youths and women following the war contributed to falling consumption.[134]

Moral panics did not disappear entirely with the war's end. A moral panic over prostitution in the 1950s, seen as threatening to the fragile nuclear family and culminating in the Street Offences Act (1959), drove women out of public places, notably pubs, making it increasingly difficult to participate in leisure activities outside the home, unless closely supervised by husbands or male escorts. Pubs, ever reflectors of society's mores, reclaimed their masculine subculture, thereby depriving women of their choice of whether to frequent pubs.[135]

Alarm over youth drinking appeared decades later in the 1980s when focus on behaviour in public spaces re-emerged. Lager louts, football hooligans and underage drinkers all attracted widening public attention and media comment, creating a context in the following decade for alarm over binge drinking.[136]

Heightened scrutiny of youth's consumption of alcohol received impetus when the drinks industry began marketing alcopops, fruit-laced alcohol beverages in 1995. All the traits of a moral panic – anxiety, demonizing of youth drinkers of alcopops as folk devils, exaggeration especially in tabloids, volatile coverage and soul searching (including speculation about the link between the club scene and these new beverages) – all duly appeared. Finally, alcopops became 'a potent symbol to carry the moral debate along', with street drinking, public disorder, inadequate parenting and drinking delinquents as wider societal concerns. This moral panic, moreover, contrasted with earlier ones involving alcohol because it reflected the power of diverse interest groups, intent on compelling authorities to enforce laws prohibiting underage drinking, drunkenness and violence.[137]

Binge drinking likewise came to be seen as a moral panic. In a recent scholarly study, *Drinking Places*, several scholars examined two areas, one urban (Stoke-on-Trent) and one rural (Eden, Cumbria), and discovered that rural youths were more than twice as likely to exceed safe levels of alcohol consumption as urban ones. Rural inhabitants displayed no sense of a moral panic primarily because public displays of drunkenness did not happen. In rural areas such as Eden, where pub culture flourished owing to few alternatives, inhabitants from diverse age groups drank together in an environment lacking anonymity of large urban areas. 'Sharing space in this way', the authors stated, 'appears to inhibit or control young people's behaviour because they are aware that drunken rowdiness may be witnessed by friends of the family or potential future employers'. Landlords, familiar with their clientele's names, imposed behavioural norms, which older drinkers reinforced. Since oldsters themselves had participated in a drinking culture in which heavy consumption of alcohol had been the norm, they showed much tolerance when youths displayed similar behaviour. Focus on binge drinking as an urban phenomenon, moreover, distracted attention from domestic drinking, the principal venue for alcohol consumption in both Eden and Stoke. Whatever problems arose from binge drinking, the authors concluded, most people – regardless of the context – drank responsibility.[138]

Scholars themselves contributed to causing moral panics about youth 'binge' drinking. Too often what appeared in academic journals was polemics masquerading as scholarly research. Unsubstantiated assertions were frequently made without concrete evidence.[139] The fact, too, that scholars specializing in this field could cite authors and publications without specific page references enabled generalizations to acquire a scholarly veneer that would not pass blind refereeing in historical periodicals. Extremely limited 'samples' also served as the basis for broad generalizations.[140]

Politicians equally manipulated fears for their own ends. Study of newspaper coverage in the *Express*, a leading newspaper, suggested that Tony Blair's government cleverly manipulated alarm over binge drinking as a tactic to further legitimize its own policy for combating climbing youth drunkenness – the lengthening of licensing hours. Rising concern over binge drinking crested in 2005, nicely timed to coincide with the 2003 Licensing Act being implemented.[141]

Writing about binge drinking as a moral panic also derived legitimacy from bogus historical parallels. Undoubtedly the classic 'analogy' was between the gin craze of the mid-eighteenth century, on one hand, and drug abuse and binge drinking of the late twentieth and early twenty-first centuries, on the other. Yet, as Peter Borsay recently emphasized, 'binge drinking is not the same as gin drinking'. Nor for that matter is there a legitimate parallel between gin consumption, a legal beverage, and crack cocaine, an illegal substance. Drawing similarities across not just centuries but cultures and countries contributes significantly to fears of abusive drinking.[142]

Fiona Measham has also appropriately challenged the usefulness of binge drinking as a concept. Youths, far from being a homogenous group, were divided into sub-categories, with gender, ethnicity, occupation, income and geography key variables shaping drinking habits. To suggest that all youths exhibited similar traits had no basis in reality.[143]

For most of the century amid wars and most recently with the emergence of youth culture, fears about the drinking of women and youths have fostered recurring moral panics. Each has been rooted in anxiety and apprehension about women and youths moving outside their allotted public space. Writing about the emergence of the modern women in the 1920s, two historians observed that 'following periods of actual or alleged advances for women, anxieties surface about the disintegration of the foundations of the gender order. Hostile reactions are not uncommon, as women's apparent gains are perceived to be at the expense of men'.[144] Wars in particular accentuated male antagonism towards women, creating powerful psychic stresses impelling authorities and others to challenge new female behaviour. Drinking was thus never the primary issue. Though commentators expressed dismay at new behaviour, the ultimate source of fears came from altogether different sources. The family, motherhood, empire, physical deterioration, gender roles, female subordination, emancipation and emergence of a distinct youth culture – all these as scholars remarked threatened an 'established value system'. Initially, these moral panics arose at the grassroots, but later elites exploited widespread fears in both world wars. Interest groups orchestrated panics still later, with alcopops and binge drinking the outstanding examples. Understandably, the contested public space, the male republic of the pub, exacerbated the power, depth and intensity of the reaction. Women and youths were not simply assuming new roles but invading sacrosanct male space, where oldsters had taught the next generation the essence of masculinity. After 1945, however, youth culture emerged to contest control not of drinking space but of the dominant norms of society. Youth disdain of prevailing habits expressed itself in diverse ways, one of them through new drinking patterns.

Notes

1 Stanley Cohen, *Folk Devils and Moral Panics: The Creation of the Mods and Rockers* (London: MacGibbon & Kee, 1972).

2 Erich Goode and Nachman Ben-Yehuda, *Moral Panics: The Social Construction of Deviance* (Oxford: Blackwell, 1994), pp. 33–41; David Garland, 'On the Concept of Moral Panic', *Crime Media Culture*, 4 (2008), pp. 9–30.

3 Garland, 'Moral Panic', p. 11.

4 G. R. Searle, *The Quest for National Efficiency: A Study in British Politics and British Political Thought, 1899–1914* (Oxford: Basil Blackwell, 1971), pp. 54–6.

5 Goode and Ben-Yehuda, *Moral Panics*, p. 127.

6 Searle, *The Quest for National Efficiency*, pp. 34–8.

7 Ibid., p. 60.

8 B. Seebohm Rowntree, *Poverty: A Study of Town Life* (London: Macmillan and Co., 1901), pp. 216–21. These figures are placed in a broad historical context in Roderick Floud, Kenneth Wachter and Annabel Gregory, *Height, Health and History: Nutritional Status in the United Kingdom, 1750–1980* (Cambridge: Cambridge University Press, 1990), chs 2–3.

9 George F. Shee, 'The Deterioration in National Physique', *Nineteenth Century*, 53 (1903), pp. 798–801; [Major General Sir John Frederick Maurice], 'Where to Get Men?', *Contemporary Review*, 81 (1902), pp. 78–86; Richard Soloway, 'Counting the Degenerates: The Statistics of Race Deterioration in Edwardian England', *Journal of Contemporary History*, 17 (1982), p. 148. From Manchester and Salford came the 'smallest soldiers in the British forces' during the First World War, with almost 90 per cent of the Bantam regiments, five feet being the specified minimum, recruited from these areas (Robert Roberts, *A Ragged Schooling: Growing up in the Classic Slum* (Manchester: Manchester University Press, 1976), p. 138).

10 *Report of the Inter-Departmental Committee on Physical Deterioration*, 1904, 32, Cd 2175.

11 Goode and Ben-Yehuda, *Moral Panics*, pp. 43–4; Soloway, 'Race Deterioration in England', pp. 144, 149–51. Some scholars have also confused deterioration with degeneracy (Henry Yeomans, 'Spirited Measures and Victorian Hangovers: Public Attitudes to Alcohol, the Law and Moral Regulation' (Ph.D., University of Plymouth, 2012), p. 179).

12 Soloway, 'Race Deterioration in England', p. 149. See Anna Davin's 'Imperialism

and Motherhood', *History Workshop*, 5 (Spring 1978), pp. 12–22, for a discussion of children as the pivotal issue in this debate.

13 Carol Dyhouse, 'Working-Class Mothers and Infant Mortality in England, 1895–1914', *Journal of Social History*, 12 (1978), p. 248; Soloway, 'Race Deterioration in England', pp. 153–4.

14 Garland, 'Moral Panic', p. 15; Dyhouse, 'Infant Mortality in England', pp. 253–4, 257, 259.

15 Dyhouse, 'Infant Mortality in England', pp. 257–8.

16 Joseph Rowntree and Arthur Sherwell, *The Temperance Problem and Social Reform* (London: Hodder & Stoughton, 1899), p. 90; David Wright and Cathy Chorniawry, 'Women and Drink in Edwardian England', *Historical Papers/Communications Historiques* [Canada] (1985), p. 119.

17 Rowntree and Sherwell, *Temperance Problem and Social Reform*, p. 90; Anne Vernon, *A Quaker Business Man: The Life of Joseph Rowntree, 1836–1925* (London: Allen & Unwin, 1958), p. 134; George B. Wilson, *Alcohol and the Nation: A Contribution to the Study of the Liquor Problem in the United Kingdom from 1800 to 1935* (London: Nicholson and Watson, 1940), table 34.

18 Viscount Peel [Arthur Wellesley Peel], *Female Intemperance, Is It Increasing? An Address on the Royal Commission Evidence* (London: Church of England Temperance Society, [1901]), p. 3; Noel Buxton and Walter Hoare, 'Temperance Reform', in C. F. G. Masterman (ed.), *The Heart of the Empire: Discussions of Problems of Modern City Life in England* (London: Unwin, 1901), p. 177.

19 Sir Thomas Barlow, *The Prevailing Intemperance among Women; Its Causes and Its Remedy; A Paper Read at a Conference of the Women's Union* (London: Church of England Temperance Society, [1902]).

20 Frances Zanetti, 'Inebriety in Women and Its Influence on Child-Life', *British Journal of Inebriety*, 1 (1903), pp. 50, 54; Sir Thomas Hunter, 'The Present Position of the Licensing Question', *Nineteenth Century and After*, 53 (1903), p. 697.

21 Arthur Shadwell, *Drink, Temperance and Legislation* (London: Longmans, Green & Co, 1902), pp. 78–84, 87, 220; Goode and Ben-Yehuda, *Moral Panics*, pp. 43–4.

22 Charles Booth (ed.), *Life and Labour of the People in London*, Final Volume: *Notes on Social Influences and Conclusion* (London: Macmillan & Co., 1902), pp. 59–65; *Temperance Record*, 1 (Aug. 1903), p. 333; also see the 1902 Report of the Preston Health Committee, quoted in H. L. Heath, *The Infant, the Parent and the State: A Social Survey and Review* (London: P. S. King, 1907), p. 5.

23 Rowntree and Sherwell, *Temperance Problem*, pp. 53–4.

24 Thomas P. Whittaker, *The Economic Aspect of the Drink Problem* (London: Church of England Temperance Society, [1902]), pp. 39–42; James Whyte, *The United Kingdom Alliance Vindicated* (Manchester: United Kingdom Alliance, [1902]), pp. 15–16; *Temperance Record*, 1 (July 1903), p. 278.

25 *Evidence of the Royal Commission on Alien Immigration*, 1902–3, 9, Cd 1742, pp. 152, 794.

26 Zanetti, 'Inebriety in Women', pp. 50, 54; [A. W. Smyth], 'Physical Degeneration', *British Medical Journal*, 23 Jan. 1904, p. 197.

27 *Evidence of the Interdepartmental Committee on Physical Deterioration*, 1904, 32,

Cd 2210, pp. 388–93, 400; *Report of the Interdepartmental Committee on Physical Deterioration*, 1904, 32, Cd 2175, pp. 31–2, and Appendix 16.

28 T. N. Kelynack, *The Alcohol Problem in Its Biological Aspect* (London: Richard J. James, 1906), pp. 44–5, 50; William McAdam Eccles, 'Alcohol as a Factor in the Causation of Deterioration in the Individual and the Race', *British Journal of Inebriety*, 2 (1905), p. 149; Robert Jones, 'Alcohol and National Deterioration', *British Journal of Inebriety*, 2 (1905), p. 158.

29 German Sims Woodhead, 'Alcoholism in Relation to Infantile Mortality', *National Conference on Infant Mortality: Report of the Proceedings of the National Conference on Infantile Mortality* (Westminster: P. S. King & Son, 1906), pp. 120–1.

30 George Newman, *Infant Mortality: A Social Problem* (London: Methuen & Co., 1906), p. 225.

31 *British Journal of Inebriety*, 5 (July 1907), pp. 29–30; Professor Gustav von Bunge, *Alcoholic Poisoning and Degeneration* (London: A. Owen & Co., [1904]).

32 Bunge, *Alcoholic Poisoning*, pp. 7–10, 17, 21–2.

33 Ibid., p. 21.

34 W. C. Sullivan, *Alcoholism: A Chapter in Social Pathology* (London: James Nisbet & Co., 1906), pp. 193–4; Kelynack, *Alcohol Problem*, p. 125.

35 David W. Gutzke, '"The Cry of the Children": The Edwardian Medical Campaign Against Maternal Drinking', *British Journal of Addiction*, 79 (1984), p. 74.

36 Unattributed quotations in the next two paragraphs come from George R. Sims, 'The Cry of the Children', *Tribune*, 4, 7, 11, 14, 18, 21 Feb. 1907.

37 David W. Gutzke, 'Britain's Social Housekeepers', in David W. Gutzke (ed.), *Britain and Transnational Progressivism* (London: Macmillan, 2008), p. 161; Gutzke, '"Cry of the Children"', p. 77; George R. Sims, *Horrible London* (London: *Daily News*, 1883), and *How the Poor Live* (London: Chatto, 1883).

38 George R. Sims, *My Life; Sixty Years' Recollections of Bohemian London* (London: Eveleigh Nash Co., 1917), pp. 335–6.

39 For discussion of babies' exposure to tuberculosis in pubs, see Gutzke, '"Cry of the Children"', p. 78.

40 Goode and Ben-Yehuda, *Moral Panics*, pp. 43–4.

41 Sims, 'Cry of the Children', *Tribune*, 3 and 13 April 1907.

42 Cohen, *Folk Devils*, pp. 191–8; Garland, 'Concept of the Moral Panic', p. 44.

43 David Rubinstein, *Before the Suffragettes: Women's Emancipation in the 1890s* (New York: St. Martin's Press, 1986), pp. 211–32. Women's role in local government is ably examined in Patricia Hollis, *Ladies Elect: Women in English Local Government, 1865–1914* (Oxford: Oxford University Press, 1987).

44 Booth, *Notes on Social Influences and Conclusion*, p. 59; Robert Jones, 'Alcohol and National Deterioration', in T. N. Kelynack (ed.), *The Drink Problem in its Medico-Sociological Aspect* (London: Methuen & Co., 1907), pp. 232–3. According to sociologists, women's growing demands for equality in late Victorian England provoked a backlash, leading to the establishment of rugby, a masculine sport played at public schools (K. G. Sheard and E. G. Dunning,'The Rugby Football Club as a Type of "Male Preserve": Some Sociological Notes', in John W. Loy, Jr, Gerald S. Kenyon and Barry D. McPherson (eds), *Sport, Culture and Society: A*

Reader on the Sociology of Sport (2nd rev. ed., Philadelphia: Lea & Febiger, 1981), pp. 163–4).

45 Jones, 'National Deterioration', pp. 232–3; [Smyth], 'Physical Deterioration', p. 198; also see Buxton and Hoare, 'Temperance Reform', p. 177.

46 See Chapter 1, above, pp. 21–2.

47 V. H. Rutherford, 'Alcohol and Legislation', in T. N. Kelynack (ed.), *The Drink Problem in Its Medico-Sociological Aspect* (London: Methuen & Co., 1907), p. 257; Anna Martin, 'Working Women and Drink', *Nineteenth Century and After*, 78 (1915), p. 1389.

48 M. Handfield-Jones, 'Some Points Regarding the Mother's Milk in the Early Weeks of Infant Life', *Practitioner*, 75 (1905), pp. 446–7.

49 Gutzke, '"Cry of the Children"', p. 78.

50 Some reform-minded brewers, eager to attract women as customers, did experiment with not quite a dozen pubs in Edwardian England, introducing food, tables and chairs, while eliminating partitions between bars (Mrs M. A. Cloudesley Brereton, 'Transforming the Public House', *Evening News*, 8 Dec. 1913; *Licensed Victuallers' Gazette*, 26 May 1911 and 14 June 1912; *Licensing World*, 27 May 1911; *Brewing Trade Review*, 1 Sept. 1918; *Hand in Hand*, 1 (Feb. 1920): 88–9; S. O. Nevile, *Seventy Rolling Years* (London: Faber and Faber, 1958), p. 70; Evidence of the Royal Commission on Licensing, 12 Nov. 1930, p. 2101).

51 David W. Gutzke, *Pubs and Progressives: Reinventing the Public House in England, 1896–1960* (DeKalb, Illinois: Northern Illinois University Press, 2006), pp. 96–8.

52 Another study with a different thesis also examines facets of the war as a moral panic. See Robert Duncan, *Pubs and Patriots: The Drink Crisis in Britain during the World War One* (Liverpool: Liverpool University Press, 2013).

53 Henry Carter, *The Control of the Drink Trade: A Contribution to National Efficiency, 1915–17* (London: Longmans, Green & Co., 1918), p. 28.

54 Ibid., pp. 28–30, 35–6.

55 E. Sylvia Pankhurst, *The Home Front: A Mirror to Life in England during the World War* (London: Hutchinson & Co., 1932), p. 98; Archbishop of Canterbury to Lord Kitchener, 23 Oct. 1914, quoted in G. K. A. Bell, *Randall Davidson: Archbishop of Canterbury* (New York: Oxford University Press, 1935), 2 vols, 2:747.

56 Archbishop of Canterbury to Editor, *The Times*, 14 Nov. 1914; Arthur F. Winnington-Ingram [Lord Bishop of London], *A Day of God: Being Five Addresses on the Subject of the Present War* (Milwaukee, Wisconsin: Young Churchman, 1914), pp. 62–3.

57 Susan Pedersen, 'Gender, Welfare and Citizenship in Britain during the Great War', *American Historical Review*, 95 (1990), pp. 996–7; *The Times*, 9 Dec. 1914.

58 Brewers' Company, Minute Book, 2 Nov. 1914, p. 35; Evidence of the Royal Commission on Liquor Licensing, 12 Nov. 1930, p. 2102; *Third Report of the Central Control Board (Liquor Traffic) Appointed under the Defence of the Realm (Amendment) (No. 3) Act, 1917–18*, 15, Cd 8558, p. 23; *Brewers' Journal*, 15 Nov. 1914.

59 Martin, 'Working Women', p. 1389; Birmingham Licensed Committee Report for 1914, quoted in *Brewing Trade Review*, 1 Feb. 1915; Lucy Bland, 'In the Name of Protection: The Policing of Women in the First World War', in Julia Brophy

and Carol Smart (eds), *Women-in-Law: Explorations in Law, Family and Sexuality* (London: Routledge & Kegan Paul, 1985), pp. 29–30.

60 Lynne Amy Amidon, '"Ladies in Blue": Feminism and Policing in Britain in the Late Nineteenth and Early Twentieth Centuries' (Ph.D. dissertation, State University of New York at Binghamton, 1986), ch. 4; Paul Ferris, *Sex and the British: A Twentieth-Century History* (London: Michael Joseph, 1993), ch. 4. For a discussion of breweries' delivery of beer to working-class neighbourhoods in Edwardian England, see David W. Gutzke, *Protecting the Pub: Brewers and Publicans against Temperance* (Woodbridge; Royal Historical Society/Boydell Press, 1989), pp. 205–14.

61 Carter, *Control of the Drink Trade*, pp. 25, 27; Pankhurst, *Home Front*, pp. 103–4; Bland, 'Policing of Women', p. 28.

62 Bland, 'Policing of Women', pp. 29–31, 33; Joan Lock, *The British Policewoman: Her Story* (London: Robert Hale, 1979), p. 28.

63 Goode and Ben-Yehuda, *Moral Panics*, pp. 43–4; *The Times*, 1 and 30 March 1915; Carter, *Control of the Drink Trade*, pp. 41, 50–1.

64 Stuart Mews, 'Urban Problems and Rural Solutions: Drink and Disestablishment in the First World War', in Derek Baker (ed.), *The Church in Town and Countryside: Papers Read at the Seventeenth Summer Meeting and the Eighteenth Winter Meeting of the Ecclesiastical History Society* (Oxford: Basil Blackwell, 1979), pp. 449–76.

65 Marvin Rintala, 'Taking the Pledge: H. H. Asquith and Drink', *Biography*, 16 (1993), pp. 107–8; Carter, *Control of the Drink Trade*, pp. 41–2.

66 Letters to Editor, *The Times*, 1915: Alice W. Harvey, 26 June; F. B. Meyer, 30 July; 'Slum Parson', 22 June; *The Times*, 21 Aug. 1915.

67 Winnington-Ingram, *Day of God*, pp. 62–3; Archbishop of Canterbury to Earl Kitchner, 23 Oct. 1914, quoted in Bell, *Davidson*, 2: 747.

68 Garland, 'Concept of Moral Panic', p. 99.

69 National Repository, HO 185/259, Conference of Chief Constables with CCB, 24 Sept. 1915, pp. 15–16, 34.

70 *Return of Women and Children in Public-Houses: Information Obtained from Certain Police Forces as to the Frequenting of Public-Houses by Women and Children*, 1908, Cd 3813.

71 National Repository, MEPO 2/1710, Report on Drinking Conditions among Women and Girls in Woolwich District, April 1918; Lock, *British Policewoman*, pp. 82–3.

72 Anonymous to Editor, *Brewers' Journal*, 15 April 1917; also see *Brewers' Journal*, 15 Oct. 1916; National Repository, HO 185/238: Woolwich Advisory Committee's Report on Drinking Conditions among Women and Girls in Woolwich and District, 1 May 1918, p. 2; F. C. Thornborough's Report on Allegations of Treating and Drinking among Young Girls, 9 May 1918. Employment of women in munitions production in Birmingham and probably elsewhere had fostered their growing presence on licensed premises from autumn 1915 ('Women and Drink: Excessive Consumption in Birmingham', *Birmingham Daily Post*, 5 Oct. 1915).

73 *Brewers' Journal*, 15 July 1917; David W. Gutzke, 'Gender, Class and Public Drinking in Britain during the First World War', in Jack S. Blocker and Cheryl Krasnick Warsh (eds), *The Changing Face of Drink: Substance, Imagery, and Behaviour*

(Ottawa: Social History/University of Ottawa, 1997), pp. 292–3.

74 *Brewers' Journal*, 15 Feb. 1917; *Brewing Trade Review*, 1 Feb. 1918. CCB reforms instituted at Carlisle are discussed in Gutzke, *Pubs and Progressives*, pp. 51–2, 56–63, and 'Gender, Class and Public Drinking', pp. 302–4.

75 *Brewers' Journal*, 15 Feb. 1917.

76 Evidence of the Royal Commission on Licensing, 22 Jan 1930, pp. 408–9, 420–1, 423, 425; *Brewers' Journal*, 15 March 1917.

77 *Licensed Victuallers' Gazette*, 5 Oct. 1917; *Brewing Trade Review*, 1 Nov. 1917. Stockton magistrates imposed a strict ban on women using licensed premises except for a half hour each at midday and evening meal times (*Licensing World*, 13 March 1920).

78 Goode and Ben-Yehuda, *Moral Panics*, pp. 43–4; *Brewers' Journal*, 15 Feb. 1918; *Licensed Victuallers' Gazette*, 12 Oct. 1917.

79 National Repository, HO 185/259, Restrictions of Sale of Liquor to Women in North East Coast Area, Deputation of County Constables from Newcastle, Middlesbrough, Hartlepool, Durham County and South Shields, 26 Oct. 1917; Robert Roberts, *The Classic Slum: Salford Life in the First Quarter of the Century* (Manchester: Manchester University Press, 1971), p. 121; Roberts, *Ragged Schooling*, pp. 67, 95; Kenneth Hudson, *Pawnbroking: An Aspect of British Social History* (London: Bodley Head, 1982), p. 76.

80 Nevile, *Seventy Years*, p. 108; *Brewers' Journal*, 15 Feb. 1918; National Repository, HO 185/259, F. C. Hultan (?), Report of Drinking amongst Women Report: North East Coast Area, 24 Oct. 1917, pp. 3–4; National Repository, HO 185/259, Restrictions of Sale of Liquor to Women in North East Coast Area, Deputation of County Constables from Newcastle, Middlesbrough, Hartlepool, Durham County and South Shields, 26 Oct. 1917.

81 *Brewers' Journal*, 15 April 1918; *Brewing Trade Review*, 1 March 1918.

82 *Brewers' Journal*, 15 April 1918.

83 Evidence of the Royal Commission on Licensing, 22 Jan. 1930, p. 434; *Brewers' Journal*, 15 Feb. 1917 and 15 Feb. 1918; *Brewing Trade Review*, 1 March 1918.

84 *Brewing Trade Review*, 1 March 1918. By March 1918, just 19 per cent of Middlesbrough licenses were still serving women alcohol for on-consumption (*Brewers' Journal*, 15 April 1918).

85 *Brewing Trade Review*, 1 March 1918.

86 *Brewers' Journal*, 15 Feb. 1917; *Brewing Trade Review*, 1 Feb. 1918.

87 Angela Woollacott, '"Khaki Fever" and Its Control: Gender, Class, Age and Sexual Morality on the British Homefront in the First World War', *Journal of Contemporary History*, 29 (1994), pp. 325–47.

88 Cohen, *Folk Devils*, pp. 192–3; Marwick, *Women at War*, p. 129.

89 Jerry White, *The Worst Street in North London: Campbell Bunk, Islington, Between the Wars* (London: Routledge & Kegan Paul, 1986), pp. 192–3; Roberts, *Classic Slum*, pp. 222, 224; Frances Donaldson, *Child of the Twenties* (1959; rept edn, London: Weidenfeld & Nicolson, 1986), pp. 80–2.

90 Sally Alexander, 'Becoming a Woman in London in the 1920s and 1930s', in David Feldman and Gareth Stedman Jones (eds), *Metropolis London, Histories and Representations Since 1800* (London: Routledge, 1989), p. 261; Evidence of the Royal

Commission on Licensing, 22 Jan. 1930, p. 408.

91 Woollacott, '"Khaki Fever" and Its Control', pp. 340–3; *Licensing World*, 28 April 1917; also see *Brewers' Journal*, 15 April 1917.

92 Evidence of the Royal Commission on Licensing, 22 Jan. 1930, pp. 408–9, 420–1, 423, 425.

93 Gutzke, *Pubs and Progressives*, pp. 49–68. See Chapter 10, above, pp. 223–9.

94 Evidence of the Royal Commission on Licensing, 22 Jan. 1930, p. 434.

95 Butler's comments on Nevile's speech, and Nevile's response, 'Function of the Brewing Industry', pp. 137, 141.

96 Gutzke, *Pubs and Progressives*, pp. 104–5.

97 University of Sussex, Mass-Observation Archives, Box 1, Intelligence Report: Public Opinion and the Drink Question in Scotland, Drinking Habits, 11 Oct. 1940, pp. 4–5.

98 'Adolescents in Public Houses', *A Monthly Bulletin*, Aug. 1942, pp. 3, 6–8, 11.

99 *Brewers' Journal*, 19 May and 16 June 1943; Mass-Observation Archives, FR 1837, Report on Juvenile Delinquency in Chichester, June 1943, p. 25. See also *True Temperance Quarterly*, 45–6 (Feb.–May 1944), p. 15, 47 (Aug. 1944), p. 5; 'Adolescents in Public Houses', p. 12.

100 Mass-Observation Archives, FR 1835, Report on Behaviour of Women in Certain London Houses, 11 June 1943, pp. 3–4.

101 'Adolescents in Public Houses', pp. 3, 6–8.

102 *Licensed Victuallers' Gazette*, 21 March 1941; *Brewer & Wine Merchant*, 1 March and 1 April 1943; Mass-Observation Archives, Report on Women in Public Houses, p. 7.

103 Claire Langhamer, '"A Public House Is for All Classes, Men and Women Alike": Women, Leisure and Drink in Second World War England', *Women's History Review*, 12 (2003), p. 430; Mass-Observation Archives, FR 1891, Report on Juvenile Drinking in Chichester, Aug. 1943,and FR 1837, Report on Juvenile Drinking, June 1943, p. 23. See also Chapter 2, above, pp. 60–1.

104 *True Temperance Quarterly*, 42 (May 1943), p. 5.

105 Drink Question in Scotland, 11 Oct. 1940, pp. 4–5; 'Adolescents in Public Houses', p. 9.

106 'Adolescents in Public Houses', pp. 9, 14.

107 *Brewers' Journal*, 18 Nov. 1942; 'Adolescents in Public Houses', pp. 6–7; *Report of the Committee on Amenities and Welfare Conditions in Three Women's Services*, 1942, Cmd 6384.

108 'Adolescents in Public Houses'; Gutzke, *Pubs and Progressives*, p. 126.

109 Drink Question in Scotland, 11 Oct. 1940, p. 5; 'Adolescents in Public Houses', pp. 2, 6, 8, 12, 14, 16–17.

110 *Brewers' Journal*, 16 June 1943; *True Temperance Quarterly*, 42 (May 1943), pp. 4, 8–9.

111 Joanna Cannan, *Death at the Dog* (1941, rept edn, Boulder, Colorado: Rue Morgue Press, 1999), p. 125; Tom and Enid Schantz, 'Meet Joanna Cannan', Joanna Cannan, *Death at the Dog*, p. 7.

112 'Adolescents in Public Houses', pp. 4–7, 9–11, 13–14, 16, 21–2.

113 Ibid., pp. 7, 14, 22; Mass-Observation Archives: Report on Behaviour of Women in Certain London Houses, 11 June 1943, FR 1835, p. 16; and Report on Juvenile Drinking in Chichester, FR 1891, Aug. 1943, pp. 5, 7.

114 'Adolescents in Public Houses', pp. 21–2.

115 'Drinking by the Young: Case for Campaign', *Manchester Guardian*, 17 Nov. 1943; 'Adolescents in Public Houses', pp. 6–7.

116 Brian Glover, *Brewing for Victory: Brewers, Beer and Pubs in the Second World War* (Cambridge: Lutterworth Press, 1995), pp. 28–9; 'Adolescents in Public Houses', p. 7.

117 *Birmingham Post*, 9 March 1943; *The Times*, 9 Feb. 1944; Langhamer, 'Women, Leisure and Drink', pp. 434–4; 'Drinking among Young People: The Problem as Liverpool Faces it', *Manchester Guardian*, 27 Nov. 1943.

118 'Drinking by the Young: Case for Campaign', *Manchester Guardian*, 17 Nov. 1943. Youths aged sixteen to eighteen could drink wine or beer with a meal.

119 This circumstance, vital here in qualifying the debate as a moral panic, has been ignored altogether in the scholarly literature. See Goode and Ben-Yehuda, *Moral Panics*, pp. 43–4.

120 'Adolescents in Public Houses', pp. 4, 17–19.

121 Ibid., pp. 12–13.

122 Ibid.

123 Brewers' Society, Memorandum, An Appeal for Voluntary Abstention from Treating, Modern Records Centre, University of Warwick, MSS 420, Box 297, 11 Oct. 1943.

124 Langhamer, 'Women, Leisure and Drink', pp. 430, 436–7.

125 She disclosed that the Northern factory town was well known for hard drinking and had a population under 150,000. Three towns – Middlesbrough (139,000), Stockport (135,000) and Oldham (120,600) – had populations closest to this figure.

126 J. Macalister Brew, 'Young People in Publichouses: Part 1: Why Do They Go There?' *Times Educational Supplement*, 21 Feb. 1942. A Mass-Observation report reached a similar conclusion the next year to the great disappointment of the British Temperance League which had commissioned it (Mass-Observation Archives, Report on Juvenile Drinking, FR 1837, June 1943, p. 93; Langhamer, 'Women, Leisure and Drink', p. 435).

127 Macalister Brew, 'Young People in Publichouses'.

128 Ibid.

129 'Drinking by the Young', and 'Among Young People', *Manchester Guardian*, 17 and 27 Nov. 1943; Brew, 'Young People'. Langhamer did not consult these sources.

130 *True Temperance Quarterly*, 49 (Feb. 1945); Brew, 'Young People'.

131 Few Birmingham adolescents surveyed late in the 1940s patronized pubs as a leisure activity (Bryan H. Reed (ed.), *Eighty Thousand Adolescents; A Study of Young People in the City of Birmingham by the Staff and Students of Westhill Training College, for the Edward Cadbury Charitable Trust* (London: Allen & Unwin, 1950), p. 39; Langhamer, 'Women, Leisure and Drink', pp. 436–7).

132 FR 3029, Mass-Observation Archives, A Report on Drinking Habits, Aug. 1948.

133 For sources, see Chapter 2, above, table 3, p. 62.

134 'Adolescents in Public Houses', p. 11.

135 Carol Smart, 'Law and the Control of Women's Sexuality: The Case of the 1950s', in Bridget Hutter and Gillian Williams (eds), *Controlling Women: The Normal and the Deviant* (London: Croom Helm, 1981), pp. 49–53. For a different interpretation, see Langhamer, 'Women, Leisure and Drink', pp. 436–7.

136 Virginia Berridge, Rachel Herring and Betsy Thom, 'Binge Drinking: A Confused Concept and Its Contemporary History', *Social History of Medicine*, 22 (2009), p. 600.

137 Ibid., p. 604; Goode and Ben-Yehuda, *Moral Panics*, pp. 138–9; Kevin Brain and Howard Parker, *Drinking with Design: Alcopops, Designer Drinks and Youth Culture* (Manchester: University of Manchester, 1997), pp. 17–23.

138 Gill Valentine, Sarah L. Holloway, Mark Jayne and Charlotte Knell (eds), *Drinking Places: Where People Drink and Why* (York: Joseph Rowntree Foundation, 2007), pp. 22, 32–6, 39–40, 52.

139 See, for example, Fiona Measham and Kevin Brain, '"Binge" Drinking, British Alcohol Policy and the New Culture of Intoxication', *Crime, Media, Culture*, 1 (2005), p. 267.

140 Ibid., pp. 269, 272.

141 C. Critcher, 'Moral Panics and Newspaper Coverage of Binge Drinking', in Bob Franklin (ed.), *Pulling Newspapers Apart* (London: Routledge, 2008), pp. 154–62.

142 Jessica Warner, *Craze: Gin and Debauchery in the Age of Reason* (2002; rept edn, New York: Random House, 2003), pp. 4, 193, 211, 217; Peter Borsay, 'Binge Drinking and Moral Panics: Historical Parallels?' *History & Policy* (Sept. 2007), wwww.historyandpolicy.org/papers/policy-paper-62.html.

143 Fiona Measham, 'The Decline of Ecstasy, the Rise of 'Binge' Drinking and the Persistence of Pleasure', *Probation Journal*, 51 (2004), p. 319.

144 Carolyn Jackson and Penny Tinkler, '"Ladettes" and "Modern Girls": "Troublesome" Young Femininities', *Sociological Review*, 55 (2007), p. 265.

Conclusion

In over a century of drinking out, women's consumption habits varied considerably. Respectable late Victorian and Edwardian women seldom frequented pubs, save on weekends when accompanying husbands. Introduction of saloon bars with more attractive décor did prompt some respectable women to use them, but the trend towards creating ladies' bars in more fashionable areas indicated that most respectable women preferred privacy if drinking out. About 40 per cent of women patronized pubs late in the 1930s and perhaps as many as 60 per cent during the Second World War, whereas after the war and through the early 1970s the level stabilized at less than 20 per cent (Figure 2).

Diverse catalysts transformed these drinking habits. Both world wars prompted numerous respectable women to enter public houses for the first time, creating moral panics in which critics demonized females and demanded their exclusion from licensed premises. Appointment of the Central Control Board to regulate drinking with Lord D'Abernon as Chairman proved crucial during the First World War in protecting women against authorities who sought to reimpose prewar drinking norms. Imbibing his Progressive outlook and policies, Sydney Nevile and W. Waters Butler, the two brewers on the CCB, spearheaded the interwar public house improvement movement as a conscious strategy to upgrade licensed premises to attract respectable women and men from the upper working and middle classes. Spending more money on improvements than economic returns justified, at least in the short run, Progressive brewers succeeded in enlarging the base of the pub's customers, with perhaps as many as 40 per cent of all women frequenting pubs on a monthly basis.

Women's drinking developed in much the same way during the Second World War, with one crucial difference. The new generation of brewers failed to embrace a reform philosophy to safeguard the larger numbers of women who had patronized wartime pubs and whose behaviour had provoked another

Figure 2 Women who visited pubs at least weekly, 1949-2013

Sources: Market Information Services, *What People Think about Public Houses*, 1949, table 6; S. H. Benson, *Combined Tabulations of the Behaviour and Attitudes of the Adult Population in Relation to Public Houses and Other Licensed Premises and Their Drinking Habits (Feb. 1956–May 1957)*, table 1; British Market Research Bureau Ltd, *Licensed Premises: Report of an Attitude Survey, August, 1960*, p. 66; Interscan, *Attitude Survey on Pub Going Habits and Brewery Control and Ownership of Public Houses, Aug. 1970*, table 4; Market and Opinion Research International, *Public Attitudes to Pubs and Leisure, June, 1984 and April, 1988; Observer*, 10 Sept. 1995; CAMRA Public Opinion Survey, *Publican*, 29 Jan. 2001; Mintel, *Pub Visiting, Leisure Intelligence, 2010–13.*

moral panic. By early 1948, two of five people surveyed opposed women drinking in bars.[1]

Progressivism disappeared from the industry for numerous reasons. The older generation of leading Progressive breweries, save for Sydney Nevile, had died. Wartime dislocation, together with government restrictions on building or rebuilding premises, stymied any possible revival of pub improvement into the 1950s, though several London and Birmingham breweries continued with the Progressive tradition of offering cultural uplift in pubs.[2] By the time breweries could resume fundamental changes in licensed premises, prevailing sentiment both inside and outside the industry had shifted decisively against large premises with cavernous interiors. Building costs had now more than tripled, forcing economies in size, materials and amenities. Eating out, perhaps owing to continued rationing, lost popularity, with newly built licensed premises, much smaller in size, often devoid of dining rooms.[3]

Without Progressives championing women's rights to drink publicly, the proportion of women using licensed premises soon plummeted, especially with a new moral panic over prostitution early in the 1950s deterring females from visiting pubs until well into the 1970s. Accordingly, women's abstention from alcohol altogether soared, reaching an unprecedented 70 per cent (Figure 3).

Steadily expanding domestic drinking from the 1970s ironically followed a similar if somewhat lower curve to women's growing use of pubs (Figure 4). It was thus not so much that men won women over to joining them in pubs as that reciprocity prevailed: more women began drinking in pubs regularly, while more men started joining women drinking at home. By the early 2000s, as many drinkers were consuming alcohol at home as at pubs, bars or clubs.[4] There was yet further irony. Drinking habits had come full circle, with women drinking at home exactly as their earlier counterparts before the First World War. The key difference, of course, was that females now drank with male companions.

Figure 3 Women who abstained from alcohol, 1939–84

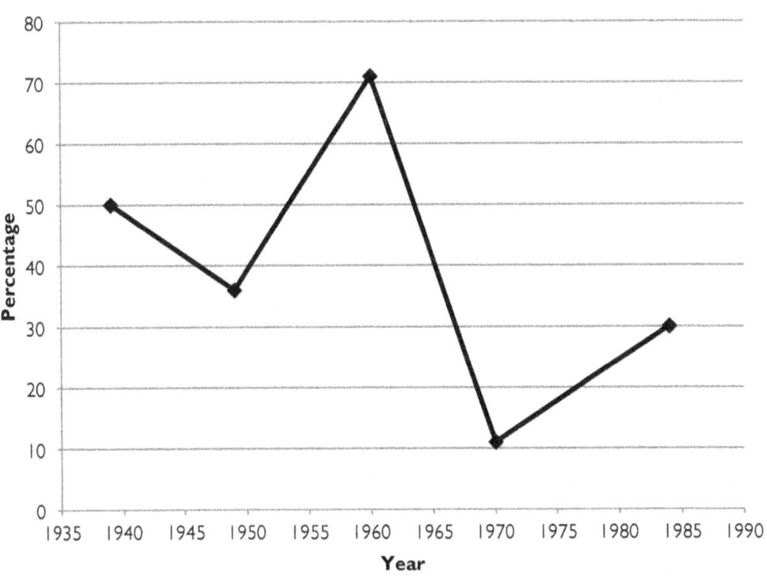

Sources: British Institute of Public Opinion Survey, quoted in *News Chronicle*, 26 June 1939; George H. Gallup, *The Gallup International Public Opinion Polls: Great Britain, 1937–75* (New York: Random House, 1976), vol. 1, p. 167; Market Information Services, What People Think about Public Houses (1950), table 6; Market and Opinion Research International, *Public Attitudes to Pubs and Leisure, June, 1984*, p. 81.

Women's drinking habits were revolutionized in the last quarter of the twentieth century, creating an entirely new subculture of drinking (Table 7).[5] As then *Publican* editor Caroline Nodder recalled about the mid-1970s, 'There were no alcopops. No gastropubs. No table service. No health and safety risk assessments. No lager louts. No karaoke. No themed pub chains. No such things as female-friendly.' Each category reflected effort to modify licensed premises as a calculated strategy for generating more female customers. Recalling youthful indiscretions, Chris Hutt, whose book (*The Death of the English Pub*), published in 1973, became standard reading for critics of the 'Big 6' breweries, ruefully acknowledged that, had he followed his own advice into the early 1990s, his pubco, Unicorn Inns, would not have survived. He pointed to the 'rising prominence of women and family customers in pubs' as one key factor shaping Britons' new drinking habits.[6]

As consumers primarily of wine, sherry and spirits, women had few options until supermarkets and wine bars stocked New World wines, especially from Australia, the US and South America, which became enormously popular. Such choices slowly appeared in the on-trade, and women enthusiastically consumed them, propelling wine ahead of spirits as the most female beverage by the late 1980s (Table 8).[7] Women could also choose from FABs (flavoured alcoholic beverages) – a sector led by Bacardi Breezer and Smirnoff Ice – and PPS (premium packaged spirits). RTD (ready to drink) beverages also appeared,

Figure 4 Rise of domestic drinking, 1960–2003

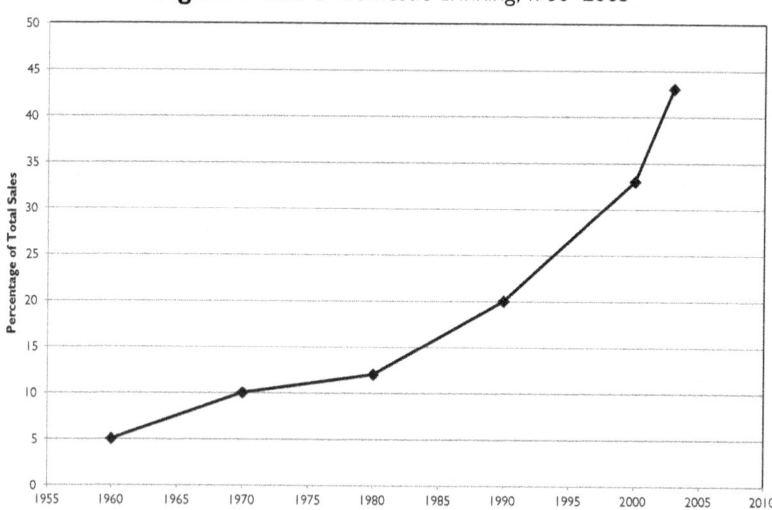

Source: *British Beer and Pub Association: Centenary, 1904-2004* (Crawley, West Sussex: William Reed, 2004), p. 28.

Table 7 Revolution in women's public drinking habits, 1975–2000

	1975	*2000*
Women in pubs/bars	Rare	Common
Competitors to pubs	Few	Numerous
Bar design	Traditional masculine	Female-friendly; style bars; wine bars; clubs
Masculine culture	Dominant but declining	Sharply contracting
Wholesaler/retailer relationship	Brewery tenancies	Multiple operators (pubcos)
Gay venues	Underground, grotty and shabby; bars in Canal Street (Manchester), Soho (London) and Brighton	Viable market for investors; designated areas in large cities; few lesbian-orientated bars or clubs
Families	Rare	Increasing numbers[1]
Consumption patterns of beverages	Strict gender divisions	Blurred
Soft drinks	Uncommon	Ubiquitous
Staples	Wine, Sherry, Babycham, and Spirits	Wine, alcopops (peaking 1996); FABs & PMS[2] (from 1996)
Brands	Not dominant	Standard[3]
Wine bars	Virtually invisible	Numerous
Wines	Limited selection: European; Hirondelle; Stowells; Mateus Rosé	Wider selection: New World wines, especially Australian, South African and Californian
Method of drinking	Glasses	Bottles
Food	Few venues with limited offerings	Ubiquitous and diverse

Notes

1 One-third of all pubs offered either a children's play area or a family room.

2 FABS (flavoured alcoholic beverages) with Bacardi Breezer, Smirnoff Ice and Metz the market leaders; and PMS (premixed spirit beverages).

3 According to Ben McFarland, 'increased brand awareness remains the biggest change across all categories in the industry over the last quarter of a century'. When customers ordered, brand names dominated most in lagers and ales (75%), followed by spirits (50%) (McFarland, 'Brands of Time', and 'A Glass of Their Own', *Publican Newspaper*, 23 Sept. 2002).

Sources: Ben McFarland, 'The Brands of Time', *Publican Newspaper*, 25 Sept. 2000, and 'One for the Ladies', *Publican Newspaper*, 16 Apr. 2001; *Morning Advertiser*, 9 Nov. 2000; David Tooley, 'Women Poised to Dominate Market', *Licensee & Morning Advertiser*, 27 Apr. 2000; Michele Cheaney 'Pub Grub – Food for Thought', *Publican Newspaper*, 24 March 1997; Davidson's *Directory: A Guide to Lesbian and Gay Organisations, Clubs, Pubs, Groups and Venues in the UK* (Downham Market: D & I Publications, 1989); Andy Knott, 'The Pink Pound', *Flavour*, 10 (Apr. 2001), pp. 50-2; *3Sixty*, 35 (Feb. 2005), p. 10, and 36 (March, 2005), p. 22.

Table 8 Leading beverages women most commonly consumed in pubs, 1973–88, where known (%)

	1973	*1975*	*1978*	*1981*	*1985*	*1988*
Beer	9	32		29	32	31
Lager	12	13	18	17	20	21
Spirits	46		26	33	34	33
Wine, sherry	14		25	24	36	37
Soft drinks	10		13	24	34	21
Vermouth, Martini					18	24
Cider					11	7

Notes: In 1975 wine and spirits were combined at 43 per cent. *Sources*: Market Opinion Research International (MORI), *Attitudes to the British Brewing Industry, 1973*, p. 32; MORI, *Attitudes to the British Brewing Industry, 1975*, p. 34; Paul Wilson, *Drinking in England and Wales: An Enquiry Carried Out on Behalf of the Department of Health and Social Security* (London: HMSO, 1980), p. 22; MORI, *Attitudes to the British Brewing Industry, 1981*, p. 6; MORI, *Public Attitudes to Pubs and Leisure, June, 1984*, p. 47; MORI, *Public Attitudes to Pubs and Leisure, 1988*, pp. 39, 41.

aimed specifically at the eighteen- to twenty-five-year-old female. Smirnoff Ice commanded the market. Women avoided beer as consistently as men shunned spirit-based beverages. RTD beverages had a customer base of 98 per cent women.[8] Interestingly, drink manufacturers, not breweries, courted women as pub patrons. Despite widespread belief in a beverage appealing across gender lines, men and women consumed very different alcoholic drinks up to the end of the period. Limited selections of alcohol and some soft drinks were supplanted when Wetherspoon pubs on the high streets pioneered breakfasts with non-alcoholic drinks (coffee, teas and fruit juices) and attractive foods such as cakes. Lunches and dinners likewise drew more women on to licensed premises, with the predicable fish and chips and pie and chips of the 1970s replaced with greater variety of dishes. Pubs serving nothing but booze became a shrinking minority, the last bastions of the masculine republic of drinking. At the end of the women's drinking revolution, nearly 90 per cent of pubs served food, generating 25 per cent of the industry's sales.[9]

Food sales became an integral part of women's culture of drinking with the rise of female-friendly pubs, first with J. D. Wetherspoon and Pitcher & Piano in the 1980s and then All Bar One, followed by Wizard, Orchard and many others. With gastro-pubs in the vanguard and those in the country with a chef (often formerly resident at a leading restaurant) providing inspiration as well as expertise, pub grub moved upwards in quality, so that eventually all but about 20 per cent of the on-licensed trade was featuring palatable dishes.[10] Underlining the ascent of food as an item at pubs, J. D. Wetherspoon ranked second only to McDonald's as the most popular place for eating out. People spent more money in restaurants than pubs. Tim Martin's Wetherspoon pubco best epitomized this transformation. 'Wetherspoon', maintained market consultant Peter Martin, 'is not just part of everyday British life – it is part of everyday eating-out life'. In remaking the British pub, Tim Martin rightly earned the epithet 'the founding father of the modern pub'.[11]

From the mid-1980s, women increasingly frequented licensed premises without male escorts, an unprecedented development since the lowering of gender barriers during the Second World War. Geography critically determined women's drinking habits. 'In the North', wrote one knowledgeable landlord, 'they are just about tolerated whereas in the South it is the women who specify which pub is allowable'.[12] Insight into women's anxieties about ordering at bar counters, interacting with bar staff and sitting alone became part of the female-friendly approach at Wetherspoon and Pitcher & Piano. Other chains emulated these pioneers in the 1990s, as did style bars and social clubs.

To attract women, JDW and Pitcher & Piano eliminated the overpowering masculine façades of traditional pubs, substituting friendlier staff, transparent windows to enable 'window shopping' prior to entering, and better ventilation. Changes in colours, décor, layout and furnishings constituted what one reporter called 'a revolution in pub design', deliberately aimed at making pubs 'considerably more welcoming to women'. Many of these ideas had originated in wine bars. Carpeting was extended throughout the premises, and partitions between different drinking rooms disappeared. As Chris Hutt argued in 1993, 'today's bar layouts were decided in the days of gin palaces and take no account of social change'.[13]

Martin intuitively sensed what later psychological and market research studies confirmed about the cues in the sales environment. Women loathed the smell of smoke and stale beer, both redolent of the masculine republic. When trying to order at the bar counter, women exposed themselves to unwanted male attention and comments, what one female area Manager of Allied Domecq Inns characterised as the 'intimidating scrum at the bar'. To address these female concerns, Wetherspoon pubs banned smoking at the bar counter as well as bar stools. Women, moreover, paid for drinks and meals at the bar counter where the cash register faced outwards, enabling staff to establish eye contact with them.[14]

In promoting a clientele more evenly balanced between the sexes, retailers recognized the vital importance of providing family-friendly facilities. Both the growing prevalence of soft drinks and healthier foods reflected the pub's new role as a weekend destination for families. With the heightened importance of the pub in family leisure, food itself no longer became an option for licensees. 'A high standard food menu', commented *Publican Newspaper* reporter Ben McFarland, 'is often the deciding factor between survival and closure'.[15] Wives joining husbands on an outing had to be accommodated with special facilities. By the late 1990s, over one-third of all pubs offered families either a children's play area or a family room. Women's growing importance as customers earlier had prompted Progressive brewers to make children's play areas a feature of new suburban improved pubs in interwar England.[16] In the 3 July 1995 issue of the *Publican*, an advertisement signalled the enormous shift transforming the cultures of drinking. Southern Sanitary Specialists advertised its baby changing facilities, noting that such a fold-down board 'is fast becoming an essential part of the customer service offered by pubs'.[17]

Women entering pubs sought a safe, reassuring atmosphere, and knew precisely what this meant. 'One of the main measuring sticks for a pub is its cleanliness – particularly the toilets', knew Louise Ashworth, CAMRA's marketing manager. Women had in mind something far different from what would satisfy men. Following an intensive 18-month survey, Allied Domecq Inns released a report in April 1999 in which it urged that toilets be 'easy to find, clean and plentiful, with good lighting, full-length mirrors, flowers and carpets'.[18] Toilet conditions improved overall, though still fell far short of what women wanted, save in new style bars, leading pubcos or chains in which women became the focus of the clientele.

What caused this remarkable transformation over a quarter of a century? No one factor was decisive; instead, economic, demographic and marketing developments all contributed to changing how women drank. In marrying later at twenty-eight rather than twenty-two and entering and remaining employed in the job market, women acquired a higher disposable income, which outstripped the growth of men's by one-third in the first half of the 1990s. Emboldened like interwar counterparts by their role as wage earners, women expressed their autonomy in adopting new drinking habits.[19]

Changes in the North's economic base transformed women's drinking habits. In the postwar era, married women seldom worked outside the home for wages, a fact which many husbands thought automatically disqualified spouses participating on the same basis in men's leisure. The North also represented the heartland of working-men's clubs, the late Victorian institutions in which men's prescriptive rights reigned as unchecked as in pubs.[20] To such august establishments, women came solely as guests, never as members. Pub and club prevailed as the dominant sites for men's leisure into the 1980s in the home of the Geordie, the areas spanning not just Newcastle-upon-Tyne, but North and South Tyneside and Gateshead. For their part, Tyneside women resorted to uncontested drinking areas, hotel bars and restaurants.[21]

Unescorted Geordie women interested in drinking never did so in pubs. 'Unaccompanied single women in pubs were associated with prostitution, alcoholism, or some other form of deviance', asserted sociologist Leslie Gofton who had conducted a thousand interviews in this area early in the 1980s. Certainly older women shared these prejudices. The White Swan in central Newcastle typified working-class pubs in posting a sign, 'no unaccompanied ladies'.[22] Other local landlords hung conspicuous signs barring women just during lunchtime hours.[23]

As capitalism shifted from producing commodities to financial services in the 1960s, deindustrialization simultaneously reduced the number of manufacturing jobs and the scale industrial production in areas formerly connected with both. In the fifteen years before 1988, employment in manufacturing contracted by 40 per cent in the North-east, with 250,000 jobs eliminated, while industrial production fell by well over 10 per cent.[24]

Since gender identity as well as a masculinity rooted in both the workplace and pub had stemmed from the region's historic manufacturing economy, the collapse of traditional industries had far-reaching consequences. Women gained employment from an expanding service sector and office work, and, as male work slumped, they soon accounted for almost half of the labour force. Gender relations were radically subverted, with the sexual integration of work and loss of their role as breadwinners (owing to part-time work or unemployment) dethroning men from their supremacy as much as new widening demands in parenting duties.[25]

The collapse of the North's economic base led to a new drinking sub-culture in which defining characteristics of age, sex, clothing and occupation displaced those of oldsters from the late 1970s. These eighteen- to twenty-five-year-old drinkers were primarily concerned not with gender, class or occupation but with style. Designer clothes, sports shoes and imported beers all projected their persona. To entirely new venues, quite separate from neighbourhood locals, went both sexes.[26]

Gender roles, dividing men from women, now became reconceptualised with masculine watering holes quickly disappearing. With hen parties, women claimed not only their autonomous public space but their 'collective female identity'.[27]

Facilitating the emergence of new women's drinking habits was legislation prohibiting sexual discrimination that led to the demise of one influential symbol of the masculine republic, men-only bars, in 1976. This was no mere pyrrhic victory. Bill Thomas, licensee of the Red Lion Hotel in Salisbury, exemplified the passing of the old order throughout the country. As his sister-in-law recalled in her memoirs,

> Bill held out as long as possible but when he could no longer resist there came the terrible day when the Men Only Bar was smartened up and made suitable for female drinkers. Old customs take a long time to die and it was at least a year before Jan and I and our women friends felt we were not brazen intruders.[28]

Government legislation had other immediate consequences for women. As pub architectural historian Geoff Brandwood concluded, women could 'expect toilet facilities: there can now scarcely be a pub anywhere without a ladies'. 'Men-only' drinking rooms in pubs disappeared faster than rules excluding women from working-men's social clubs. Eventually, decades later, working-men's clubs, confronted with slumping memberships, competition from style bars and government-imposed smoking bans, could no longer defy an image as 'ageing bastions for a by-gone era', and so joined the 'men-only' drinking bars as an antiquated institution.[29]

Another catalyst of change came from an entirely unexpected source, Thatcher's Beer Orders. 'The breakup of the brewers' monopoly has resulted in a much more competitive marketplace for wines', the leading beverage of choice for females, reflected Philip Goodband, wine consultant to Matthew Clark Wholesale. With the end of the brewers' monopoly of tied houses in the late 1980s, new entrepreneurs with big purses, often foreigners, entered the industry, unencumbered by the stultifying masculinity that had so obstructed meaningful changes for so long. But the industry was already being transformed with Tim Martin and his JDW pub chain as well as Crispin Tweddle and his Pitcher & Piano concept. Both men, who pioneered what came to be called pubcos, drew heavily from ideas outside the industry to introduce a revolutionary new concept, 'female-friendly' venues. Amid Ben Davis's advocacy of brooding browns in pub interiors and almost misogynistic attitudes towards women as part of the pub clientele, Martin and Tweddle as outsiders struck out independently in an entirely new direction. They innately perceived how a modified décor, feminized environment, food and impeccable toilets could woo vast numbers of women as customers. But their insights went well beyond the environment, grasping and modifying the subtle cues prevailing in the masculine culture of drinking that literally drove women out of the door, never to return. Women on the retail side of the bar counter – as part of the bar staff, managers and executives – were deliberately recruited to recast the culture of drinking so that women on the other side as customers could derive safety and security in what had been a notoriously masculine institution, unwelcoming to women and what they sought when drinking out. 'Finding a woman in charge behind the bar only has encouraged' more female customers, maintained the *Publican* in 2004.[30]

In advertising alcohol to women, marketers, who perceived salient differences between baby boomer, Generation X and Generation Y women, could exploit decisive generational factors to market beer. Turning established wisdom on its head, the trendiest bars for appealing to Generation Y women appeared first in the conservative North rather than in the more liberated South. Style bars in Leeds, Manchester and Liverpool promoted imported continental beers, notably Duvel, Leffe Blond and Paulaner with enormous success. Stocking ten to fifteen speciality beers, none of them leading brands, these bars understood the psychology of sales. 'The way they are retailed, the branded glassware, the theatre of serve, the point-of-sale – it all has a massive impact', remarked Geoff Brown, Punch Marketing Manager. Such beers were foreign and imported, wholly unassociated in women's minds with Britain's masculine culture of drinking. Brewed abroad, the Belgian beers in particular were ironically the unpasteurized 'real ales' that CAMRA had for so long championed as part of Britain's brewing heritage. Nothing better highlighted the psychological distaste that British women experienced towards British men, beer and the masculine republic of drinking than the repudiation of real ales. As Jane Street-Porter observed, 'the very idea of [British] beer conjures up unpleasant images of beer bellies and smelly, male-dominated boozers'. This aptly explains why British women accounted for just 13 per cent of beer sales in 2009, compared to 25 per cent in the US and 36 per cent in the Irish Republic. Over three-fourths of British women seldom or never consumed beer.[31]

Throughout the post-1945 era, breweries and landlords seemed fixated on selling men beer. Even when surveyed in the early 1990s, female-friendly bars then fashionable, landlords avoided a perception they were seeking more female custom lest they 'scare off the men!'[32] Of brewers more than a decade later, Louise Ashworth could still write that 'just because the majority of their drinkers are men, it seems they need to pander to this and indulge in the realms of male fantasy' when advertising their products. Eager to expand real ale sales, one CAMRA official expressed exasperation at brewers' ongoing dismissal of women in advertising.[33] Some years later, Caroline Nodder, editor of the *Publican*, criticized many breweries for sponsoring advertisements that concentrated 'almost entirely on males, male drinking occasions and imagery such as football games or stag nights'. Breweries continued to miss the point: she, like so many other women, found such an approach as much exasperating as affronting.[34]

Sexist advertisements, far from declining, became raunchier, with some banned for their blatant sexual content. Men could applaud Ninkasis, Goddess of Beer, while women expressed disgust. Brewers generally never solved the problem of how to appeal simultaneously to both sexes, largely because the dominant culture of drinking as overwhelmingly male persisted for most of the century.

As management began recruiting growing numbers of women, particularly in running pubs, from the 1980s, male customer perceptions of females as managers and licensees altered. For well over a century, women had interacted with men in traditional pubs or working-class clubs as inferiors – barmaids, prostitutes or subordinate wives – granted admission on special occasions, encouraging condescending, patronizing attitudes to females. Previously, *Publican* reporter Michele Cheaney reflected, 'women were often viewed as useful accessories whose main job was to sell beer to male customers, look attractive and be there to listen to their problems and jokes'.[35] Pervasive sexism inside pubs and clubs had mirrored society as a whole. The status of females in society overall rose perceptibly when their employment as well as educational and legal positions improved. Sexism, while not disappearing, was muted. Now, male patrons began encountering women in pubs and bars in roles which automatically commanded respect. According to one trainee manager, 'women are particularly drawn into this career path because it offers plenty of opportunities and challenges'.[36] Women's enhanced standing as managers and licensees in turn fostered vastly different subcultures of drinking in all but the most unregenerate traditional male pubs and style bars, where male prejudices and age-old sexist beliefs still often prevailed.

Sexism, the overwhelming masculinity of licensed premises and patronizing advertisements – all had limited women's visits to pubs. In response, women shunned alcohol in striking numbers until 1970, resisted publicity campaigns to promote drinking of beer and lager, and displayed more interest in drinking at home with other females or alone than accompanying menfolk for an evening out. Why, they reasonably thought, drink soft drinks in preference to unpalatable wine at pubs than simply stay at home consuming what they wanted? Britons' consumption of wine thus steadily expanded from the 1960s without numerous wine bars. Demographic changes – longer life expectancy and fewer children per family – propelled what would become the wine bar revolution, especially in London, from the late 1970s. Compared to masculine, sombre-coloured pub interiors, wine bars targeted women with feminine atmospheres and wider selections of wine with appealing meals. Here, too, women knew that men, who were keen to consume beer and chat up females, would avoid invading what became feminine space, though wine-drinking men with some cultural pretensions could patronize wine bars enjoying good wine and food to match.

Changes in this culture stemmed not just from more women frequenting licensed premises. The masculine republic of drinking was deeply entrenched, with men not merely on both sides of the bar counter but monopolizing the entire wholesale apparatus of production and distribution. This dominance contributed enormously to insulating the masculine republic from criticism, much less to the possibility of entertaining another perspective to marketing and retailing alcohol. In analysing how women's culture of drinking evolved over decades, it is vital to look closely at the nature of advertising, what beverages women drank publicly and the impact of imported beers. Because men chiefly tenanted and managed pubs, few had much insight into how gender differences – layout, colours, furnishings, food and critically toilets – all loomed large in women's assessment of drinking venues. Public opinion polls began querying women about such matters from the 1970s, though not about issues that aroused deep-seated feminine fears – ordering at the bar counter, arriving without an escort, sitting alone and repelling unwanted male attention. Women were consciously aware of encroaching on sacred male territory as outsiders, feelings which aggravated their sense of insecurity. Residual fears of being accosted as a prostitute likewise exacerbated anxiety well into the 1950s and 1960s. That pubs offered little beyond beer and often indifferent wine in austere, unattractive surroundings left women with few reasons for accompanying husbands, except on weekends. For their part, men much preferred drinking with their mates, a perspective reinforced repeatedly in brewers' advertising.

That men and women frequently saw female drinking quite differently should surprise less than that most males seemed insouciant about the impact of decades of blatant sexist advertisements, about drinking norms unwelcoming to women in licensed premises and about females' strong antipathy to pubs in general, and beer in particular. Men as husbands, executives of breweries or retailers of beer had instilled strong negative associations of British beer, men and pubs in the female psyche. To women, pubs and beerhouses were redolent of cramped, oppressively coloured, smoky rooms overflowing with beer-swilling men preoccupied with nothing more appealing than drinking, primarily with mates. Surely it was no accident that, when women finally turned to drinking in pubs in significant numbers, they preferred imported wine to indigenously brewed beer, or, if given a choice, imported beers, wholly free of associations with Britain's masculine republic of drinking. There was yet another irony: decades of pronounced sexism contributed not to converting most women into beer drinkers but to changing most men into wine drinkers, at least in female company, after the first pint in the pub.[37] Seldom had advertising and the masculine culture of drinking such an astonishing but unintended consequence.

In retrospect, looking back over a century and more, outsiders acted as the catalysts for transforming the cultures of drinking. Brewers Sydney Nevile and W. Waters Butler challenged the conservative, wealthy elite of brewers, upholders of the male status quo of drinking and dominators of policy as well as attitudes in the industry. The First World War afforded the opportunity for experimenting with radically different drinking habits, with women's influx on to licensed premises encouraging a vastly new conception of public houses. In participating as members of the Central Control Board, Nevile and Butler imbibed a new philosophy, Progressivism, which equipped them with ideas for building new and reforming old public houses. From Progressivism, reform-minded brewers acquired a mentality antithetical to the old prewar boozers. With environmentalism, moral uplift, discipline, order, pragmatism and experimentation, Progressive brewers vigorously attacked drunkenness, insalubrious licensed premises, and the image of drinking as déclassé. Motivated not by the desire to reap bigger profits but by commitment to elevating their reputation as brewers (with a public-spiritedness in which they sought to do 'the job well'), Nevile, Butler and other Progressive brewers greatly transformed the cultures of drinking throughout England between the wars.[38]

Similarly, Tim Martin, another outsider, became the intellectual heir of Sydney Nevile. Both men envisaged pubs with a wider clientele incorporating women as the rationale for changes: feminizing the drink environment with tables, chairs and flowers; promoting food as an antidote to drunkenness; de-emphasizing drink as the principal, if not sole, reason for a night out; and upgrading toilets. Other parallels also existed. Nevile and Martin drew ideas from abroad in formulating a business philosophy, with the latter impressed as much with California's successful smoking ban as with Sam Walton's practice of listening to employees. Both thought larger premises without partitions would have a salutary impact in modifying the cultures of drinking. Each became recognized in his own lifetime as the most influential individual in shaping drinking. As the heir of Nevile and Progressive thought, Martin would display a social conscience in recruiting more women not just as barmaids but throughout the company. Fetzer, produced in the US, became the chain's house wine owing to its commitment to CSR, corporate social responsibility. Like Nevile, he would consciously widen the pub's clientele, focusing especially on attracting women. His belief in the soundness of this marketing strategy was owed to recent studies of pubs in which those with a cross-section of the population – from young adults to old-age pensioners – rather than just young drinkers had displayed superior behaviour. For this reason too, he had come to see the importance of discouraging anti-social behaviour in his pubs with installation of CCTV throughout his pub chain. Experimentation, another interwar Progressive trait, had influenced him. At Bournemouth, licensing authorities had stipulated he must agree to install CCTV as a precondition of being granted a licence, and its success convinced Martin to implement this as a security measure in all his JDW pubs. His pubco also led in founding groups called Pubwatch, private, voluntary organizations dedicated to ensuring safe drinking environments that worked closely with police in discouraging anti-social behaviour, including drunkenness, drug taking, theft, verbal abuse, violence and vandalism. Perpetrators of such conduct could be banned altogether from licensed premises overseen by the local Pubwatch for a period.[39]

His 'socially responsible attitude to the problems of alcohol consumption' – the same commitment earlier of Nevile and other Progressive brewers – prompted a new, more aggressive policy about smoking adopted in 2004. Concerned about its health risks, Martin assumed leadership in phasing in a total smoking ban in all his JDW pubs. Dissatisfied with what he saw as Tony Blair's unworkable compromise, apparently designed to placate working-class drinkers who wanted no food, he discredited the government's prevarication. 'The dotty solution in Britain', he wrote in 2005, 'is to ban smoking from 2008, unless a pub sells no food. Great idea, Tony [Blair]; so we can stop selling food, allow smoking, and this will improve the health of the nation?' His stand forced the government's hand, leading to prohibition of smoking in pubs altogether. This broader social commitment to the wider community, doing 'the right thing' as Nevile's colleague had put it, likewise impelled him to engage directly in the binge drinking controversy and promote sensible consumption, abandoning JDW's retailing practices of offering two-for-one bottles and discounted doubles. Had Nevile been alive, surely he would have applauded this concerted effort to sell alcohol responsibly as he himself had tried from the 1920s.[40]

This is not to argue that Martin or Nevile were opposed to earning profits, but their outlook rested on a wider base, which in turn drove changes in retailing alcohol. Both had greater understanding of women's attitudes to drinking publicly than the rest of the industry. In introducing the lounge as part of the improved pub programme, Nevile grafted on to traditional male drinking space an entirely separate gender-neutral room where women could drink alone or with men without incurring social stigma. Martin exemplifies my thesis that changes in all facets of the cultures of drinking would be imperative for women to influence significantly public drinking. In implementing a new approach, Martin as an outsider displayed remarkably sensitive feelings – virtually absent among rival drink retailers – towards women. Whether placing cash registers on bars facing customers, eliminating staff name tags in bars or employing women in all positions of the company, Martin created a feminized environment where the masculine culture of drinking was confronted and subtly undermined. His would be a constantly innovative marketing strategy, with JDW pubs pioneering breakfast coffees and snacks. Here he unwittingly emulated Nevile's conviction that pubs ought to assume broader functions, especially in serving food and non-alcoholic beverages.

Women's own contributions to promoting these social changes altered over the century. Women seem to have responded approvingly to the improved pub rather assertively championing it, while they more actively intervened from the 1970s onwards in pressing for greater drinking equality. Partly no doubt it was that they now had jobs and money, whereas many women most likely to have been attracted by the improved pub would have thought that the right and proper way for their lives to develop was to get married and move into a world where a man acted as the breadwinner.

Change came to the brewing industry with increasing numbers of women drinking publicly, not just in pubs but in clubs as well as wine and style bars from the 1970s onwards. That women preferred drinking wine and other beverages to beer was partly the product of decades of sexist advertising, male prejudice, men serving as the mainstay of beer sales, buoyant beer consumption until the late 1970s and beer's fattening properties, diverse factors which entrenched the conservative mentality among breweries opposed to dismantling, even altering, the masculine culture of drinking. In many senses a mirror of social life in Britain, the pub would have change forced upon it by outsiders – pubcos and government legislation, together with demographic as well as economic factors. Unable to anticipate how these new circumstances would fundamentally transform the cultures of drinking, breweries and retailers procrastinated with disastrous long-term consequences. In the new culture of drinking that emerged in the twenty-first century, the pub, though still important, had a shrunken place as a venue for socializing, courtship and relaxation.[41] With heavy alcohol taxes, rigorously enforced drunk driving laws and limited selection of wines, often overpriced and of dubious quality, drinking to many Britons has become increasingly a social ritual best conducted in the confines of the home, where equality between the sexes and freedom from sexual harassment at last prevail for many women.

Notes

1 George H. Gallup, *The Gallup International Public Opinion Polls: Great Britain, 1937–75* (New York: Random House, 1976), vol. 1, p. 167.

2 Whitbreads' pubs performed theatrical plays and continued poetry reading in its pubs into the 1960s, while Barclays exhibited paintings and arranged for Shakespearean recitals ('Art and the Public-House', *House of Whitbread*, 8 (Summer 1946), pp. 28–30; *House of Whitbread*, 9 (Spring 1947), pp. 28–9, 11 (Spring 1951), pp. 40–1, and 12 (Summer 1952), pp. 33–5; Paul Jennings, 'The Barrow Poets', *Whitbread's Magazine*, 26 (Sept. 1966), pp. 14–15; *Anchor Magazine*, 20 (Jan. 1946), pp. 11, 13; April 1946, p. 9 and April 1947, p. 7); Anthony Sutcliffe and Roger Smith, *History of Birmingham*, vol. 3, *1939–70* (London: Oxford University Press, 1974), p. 255.

3 David W. Gutzke, *Pubs and Progressives: Reinventing the Public House in England, 1896–1960* (DeKalb, Illinois: Northern Illinois University Press, 2006), pp. 232–5.

4 *Publican Newspaper*, 12 Nov. 2001.

5 See Ben McFarland's useful overview, 'One for the Ladies', *Publican Newspaper*, 16 April 2001; Caroline Nodder, 'We're 30!' *Publican*, 26 Sept. 2005.

6 *Publican*, 1 March 1993; Nodder, 'We're 30!'

7 McFarland, 'One for the Ladies', 16 April 2001.

8 Adam Withrington, 'RTDS–What Would Licensees Like to See?', *Publican*, 19 Sept. 2005.

9 Chris Hutt, 'Inn to the Future', *Publican Newspaper*, 7 Oct. 2002; Mintel Report, 1996, quoted in *Publican Newspaper*, 24 March 1997.

10 Ben McFarland, 'The Brands of Time, 1975–2000', *Publican Newspaper*, 25 Sept. 2000.

11 Peter Martin, 'Out of the Wet and Into the Dry', *Morning Advertiser*, 17 April 2008; Nodder, 'We're 30!'

12 Tom Porter (Bakers Arms, Lytchett Minster) to Editor, *Publican*, 10 Oct. 1985.

13 McFarland, 'One for the Ladies'; *Publican*, 1 March 1993; Paul Allonby, 'Half a Million Spent to Make Women Happy!', *Licensee and Morning Advertiser*, 12 April 1999; Peter Martin, 'How "Revolutionary" Does Pub Design Need to Be?', *Publican*, 8 Nov. 1984.

14 Allonby, 'Make Women Happy!'

15 McFarland, 'Brands of Time'. Enactment of stricter drink driving laws in 1967 had created greater awareness of food: it provided an alternative to drinking, and slowed the body's absorption of alcohol.

16 McFarland, 'Brands of Time'; Gutzke, *Pubs and Progressives*, pp. 165–6.

17 Advertisement, 'Southern Sanitary Specialists', *Publican*, 3 July 1995.

18 Louise Ashworth, 'What Women Want', *Morning Advertiser*, 4 Nov. 2004; Allonby, 'Make Women Happy!'

19 McFarland, 'Brands of Time'.

20 *A Monthly Bulletin*, 27 (Dec. 1956), pp. 167–8; Leslie R. Gofton, 'Folk Devils and the Demon Drink: Drinking Rituals and Social Integration in North East England', *Drogalkohol*, 12 (1988), p. 188.

21 S. H. Benson, *Summary Report on Attitudes Towards Public Houses and Drinking Habits* (Feb. 1958), p. 8.

22 L. R. Gofton, 'Social Change, Market Change: Drinking Men in North East England', *Food and Foodways*, 1 (1986), p. 259; Leslie Gofton, 'On the Town; Drink and the "New Lawlessness"', *Youth and Policy*, 29 (April 1990), p. 36; Brian Bennison, *Heady Days: A History of Newcastle's Public Houses* (Newcastle: Newcastle Libraries & Information Service, 1996), 22.

23 Anne Garvey, 'Out of the Way: Women in Pubs', *New Society*, 27 (21 Feb. 1974), p. 460.

24 Fred Robinson, 'Industrial Structure', in Fred Robinson (ed.), *Post-Industrial Tyneside: An Economic and Social Survey of Tyneside in the 1980s* (Newcastle-upon-Tyne: Newcastle-upon-Tyne City Libraries and Arts, 1988), p. 18; David Byrne, 'What Sort of Future?', in Robert Colls and Bill Lancaster (eds), *Geordies: Roots of Regionalism* (Edinburgh: Edinburgh University Press, 1992), pp. 45–6, 48–9.

25 Anoop Nayak, 'Last of the "Real Geordies"? White Masculinities and the Subcultural Response to Deindustrialization', *Environment and Planning D: Society and Space*, 21 (2003), p. 9.

26 Gofton, '"New Lawlessness"', p. 36; Lois Miles, 'Coping with Crowds on the Geordie Circuit', *Publican*, 11 Nov. 1989; Robert G. Hollands, *Friday Night, Saturday Night: Youth Cultural Identification in the Post-Industrial City* (Newcastle-upon-Tyne: Department of Social Policy, University of Newcastle-upon-Tyne, 1995), p. 58.

27 Hollands, *Post-Industrial City*, p. 67.

28 Molly Maidment, *Child of the Red Lion: An Hotelier's Story* (Bradford on Avon: Ex Libris Press, 1989), p. 111.

29 Geoff Brandwood, 'The Vanishing Faces of the Traditional Pub', *Journal of the*

Brewery History Society, 123 (Summer 2006), p. 123; Dominic Roskrow, 'Whatever Happened to the Working Men's Club?', *Morning Advertiser*, 30 Oct. 2008.

30 *Publican*, 16 Feb. 2004.

31 Muireann Bolger, 'Reversing the Trend', *Publican*, 23 March 2009; *Publican*, 23 March 2009.

32 Caroline Nodder, 'Female Market Up Over "Friendly" Bars', *Publican Newspaper*, 10 Aug. 1998.

33 Ashworth, 'What Women Want'; Adam Withrington,'Beautiful Beer', *Publican*, 24 May 2005.

34 *Publican*, 23 March 2009; also see Bolger, 'Reversing the Trend'.

35 Michele Cheaney, 'Jobs for the Girls', *Publican Newspaper*, 28 April 1997.

36 *Publican Newspaper*, 8 Dec. 1997.

37 *Morning Advertiser*, 18 Oct. 2007. Over half (54 per cent) of the men in a 2007 survey reported switching to wine after a pint of beer in the pub. When imbibing at home, drinkers increasingly preferred wine, cider or spirits rather than beer (Mintel 2002 survey quoted in *Publican*, 28 Jan. 2002).

38 *Anchor Magazine*, 10 (June 1930), p. 121; David W. Gutzke, 'Sydney Nevile: Squire in the Slums or Progressive Brewer?', *Business History*, 43 (2011), pp. 6–8.

39 Tim Martin, 'Memo to All JDW Staff: "We Are Responsible Retailers"', *Morning Advertiser*, 30 Sept. 2004; Lorna Harrison, 'Dear John', *Publican*, 3 Jan. 2004.

40 Evidence of the Royal Commission on Licensing, 18 March 1930, p. 809; Paul Charity, 'Martin: Visionary or Gambler?', *Morning Adertiser*, 10 March 2005; also see Sydney O. Nevile, 'The Function of the Brewing Industry in National Reconstruction', *Journal of the Institute of Brewing*, 25 (1919), p. 131.

41 According to a 2005 survey, drinkers ranked home as the most popular place to socialize, with the disparity between the runner-ups, the pub (26 per cent) and restaurant (17 per cent), quite close (Harris Interactive survey, quoted in Rosie Davenport, 'A Real Home from Home', *Morning Advertiser*, 17 Nov. 2005).

Select bibliography of primary sources

Archival collections

British Beer & Pub Association
- Précis of Newspapers

Eldridge, Pope & Co.
- Advertisements

Glasgow University Archives Services
- Advertisements

Greenall, Whitley & Co.
- Magee, Marshall & Co.: Photographs

Heineken UK archives
- Advertisements
- Courage, Barclay & Simonds Records

London Metropolitan Archives
- Courage, Barclay & Simonds: Minutes of the Board of Directors
- National Federation of Licensed Victuallers: Executive Committee Minute Book

London School of Economics and Political Science
- New Survey of London Archives

Merseyside Record Office
- Peter Walker & Son

National Brewery Centre, Burton on Trent
- Advertisements

National Repository
- Liquor Traffic Central Control Board Archives

Northamptonshire Record Office
- Northamptonshire Brewers' Association
- Northamptonshire Brewing Company

Staffordshire Record Office
- Advertisements
- Shropshire Wholesale Brewers' Association

University of Sussex
- Mass-Observation Archives

University of Warwick Library, Modern Records Centre
- Brewers' Society Archives

Whitbread Archive
Press Advertisements
Sydney Nevile Papers

Newspapers

Architect & Building News
Architects' Journal
Bartender
Brewer & Wine Merchant
Brewers' Guardian
Brewers' Journal
Brewing Trade Review
Builder
Building
Caterer & Hotel Keeper Gazette
Christian World
Daily Express
Diva
Economist
Evening Standard (London)
Fellowship of Freedom and Reform
Financial Times
Flavour: The Magazine of Bar Professionals
Glass: The Publican Newspaper Wine Magazine
Guardian
Hotel
Hotel & Catering Management
Hotel & Catering Weekly Hotel Review
Indoors: The Trust House Review
Kentish Mercury
Labour Woman
Licensed Victuallers' Gazette
Licensee and Morning Advertiser
Licensing World
Luncheon & Tea Room
A Monthly Bulletin
Morning Advertiser
Morning Post
New Statesman
New York Times
Pubchef
Pub Leader
Publican
Publican Newspaper
Sussex Daily News

Temperance Record
3Sixty
The Times
Town & City Magazine
Tribune
True Temperance Quarterly
Which?
Wine and Spirit Trade Review
Yorkshire Evening News
Yorkshire Herald

House magazines of breweries and pubcos

Adventure (Allied Domecq)
Advertising Monthly (McEwan & Company)
Anchor Magazine (Barclay, Perkins & Co.)
Argosy (Allied Breweries)
Barclay's Magazine (Barclay, Perkins & Co.)
Bass Brewers (Bass Charrington)
Bass Brewers News (Bass Charrington)
Beer and Skittles (Watney, Combe & Reid)
Brewery Record (Henty & Constable)
Butler's (William Butler & Co.)
Courage News (Courage & Co.)
Deerstalker (Mitchells & Butlers)
Golden Cockerel (Courage & Co.)
Guinness Time (Arthur Guinness & Co.)
Hand in Hand (Watney, Combe & Reid)
House of Whitbread (Whitbread & Co.)
Huntsman (Allied Domecq)
Ind Coope News (Ind, Coope & Co.)
Malster (Drybrough's Brewery)
Malt & Hops (John Davenports Brewery)
Mash Tun (Ushers Brewery)
Mine Host (Ind Coope)
The News (Tennent Caledonian Breweries)
Red Hand (Watney, Combe, Reid & Co.)
Runcorn Newsletter (Bass's Runcorn Brewery)
Staff News (Courage, Barclay & Simonds, Ltd)
Tennent's Times (Tennent Caledonian Breweries)
Things That Affect Us (Vaux Breweries)
Toby Jug (Tennent Caledonian Breweries)
Truman Times (Truman, Hanbury & Buxton)
Truman Topics (Truman, Hanbury & Buxton)
Wetherspoon News (J. D. Wetherspoon & Co.)
Whitbread's Magazine (Whitbread & Co.)

Reference

'Bars – A Glossary', *The Times (Beer in Britain Supplement)*, 29 April 1958.
Gutzke, David W., *Alcohol in the British Isles from Roman Times to 1996: An Annotated Bibliography*, Westport, Connecticut: Greenwood Press, 1996.
Kelley's Directories
London's Yellow Pages
McWhirter, Kathryn, *The Good Wine Bar Guide, 1986*, London: Consumers' Association, 1985.
Post Office Directories of London
Ronay, Egon, *Pub and Tourist Sights in Britain, 1973*, London: British Tourist Authority, 1973.

Marketing and public opinion surveys

Acumen Marketing Group, *A Report on the British Market for Food in Pubs and Wine Bars, March 1978.*
Bradley, Michael, and Fenwick, David, *Public Attitudes to Liquor Licensing Laws in Great Britain: An Enquiry Carried Out in October–November, 1970 by OPCS Social Survey Division on Behalf of the Home Office and the Scottish Home and Health Department, 1974.*
Breeze, Elizabeth, *Women and Drinking: An Enquiry Carried Out on Behalf of the Department of Health and Social Security*, 1985.
British Institute of Public Opinion, Survey of Drinking Habits, 1939.
British Market Research Bureau, *Licensed Premises: Report of an Attitude Survey, August 1960.*
Daily Herald Readers and the Market for Beer and Stout, Aug. 1960.
Gallup, George H., *The Gallup International Public Opinion Polls: Great Britain, 1937–75*, 2 vols, New York: Random House, 1976.
Interscan, *Attitude Survey on Pub Going Habits and Brewery Control and Ownership of Public Houses, Aug. 1970.*
IPC Marketing, *The UK Beer Market, September, 1977.*
Lader, D., and Goddard, E., *Omnibus Survey Report No. 31. Drinking: Adults' Behaviour and Knowledge in 2006: A Report Using the ONS Omnibus Survey Produced by the Office for National Statistics on Behalf of the Information Centre for Health and Social Care*, London: Office of National Statistics, 2006.
The Lager Market in Scotland, Public Attitude Surveys, June 1967.
Market Information Services, *The Problem of Declining Beer Consumption: A Memorandum Prepared for Messrs. Gee & Partners on Behalf of the Brewers' Society, March 1950.*
Market Information Services, *What People Think about Public Houses: The Results of a Large-Scale Sample Survey Carried Out among the Adult Population of England and Wales during November, 1949.*
Market Opinion Research International, *Attitudes to the British Brewing Industry, 1973.*
Market Opinion Research International, *Attitudes to the British Brewing Industry, 1975.*

Market Opinion Research International, *Attitudes to the British Brewing Industry, 1981.*
Market and Opinion Research International, *Public Attitudes to Pubs and Leisure, June 1984.*
Market and Opinion Research International, *Public Attitudes to Pubs and Leisure, 1988.*
Mass-Observation, A Report on Drinking Habits, Aug. 1948
Mass-Observation, A Survey of Drinking Habits, 1949.
Mintel, *Pub Visiting, Leisure Intelligence, November, 2009.*
Odhams Press Survey, 1960.
S. H. Benson, *The Brewers' Society 1957 Advertising Campaign Market Research Charts, July, 1956.*
S. H. Benson, *A Summary Report on Attitudes towards Public Houses and Drinking Habits, February, 1958.*
S. H. Benson, *A Test on the Use of the Words 'Pub' and 'Social', London, Nov. 1959.*
Wilson, Paul, *Drinking in England and Wales: An Enquiry Carried Out on Behalf of the Department of Health and Social Security*, 1980.

Parliamentary papers and official publications

Alcohol: Its Action on the Human Organism, London: H.M. Stationery Office, 1918.
Evidence of the Interdepartmental Committee on Physical Deterioration, 1904, 32, Cd 2210.
Evidence of the Royal Commission on Alien Immigration, 1902–3, 9, Cd 1742.
Evidence of the Royal Commission on Licensing, 1929–31.
Evidence of the Royal Commission on Liquor Licensing Laws, 1897, 34, C 8355–6; 1898, 36, C 8694.
Evidence of the Select Committee of the House of Lords on Intemperance, 1877, 11 (171, 271, 418).
Evidence of the Select Committee on Sales of Liquors on Sunday Bill, 1868, 14 (402).
National Board for Prices and Incomes, Report No. 13: Costs, Prices and Profits in the Brewing Industry, 1966, Cmnd 2965, 1966–7.
Report of the Central Control Board (Liquor Traffic) Appointed under the Defence of the Realm (Amendment) (No. 3) Act: Second, 1916, 12, Cd 8243; *Third, 1917–18*, 15, Cd 8558.
Report of the Committee on Amenities and Welfare Conditions in Three Women's Services, 1942, Cmd 6384.
Report of the Inter-Departmental Committee on Physical Deterioration, 1904, 32, Cd 2175.
Report of the Monopolies and Mergers Commission on the Supply of Beer for Retail Sale in the UK, Cm 651, 1989.
Report of the Proceedings of the Monopolies and Mergers Commission on the Proposed Merger between Scottish & Newcastle Breweries PLC and Matthew Brown PLC, Cmnd 9645, 1985.
Return of Women and Children in Public-houses: Information Obtained from Certain Police Forces as to the Frequenting of Public-houses by Women and Children, 1908, Cd 3813.

Oral history interviews

Aitken, Stuart, former Sales Director with Whitbread Beer Company, 4 Aug. 2000.

Avis, Tony, former executive with Bass Charrington, 26–27 July 1997, Ilkley, West Yorkshire.

Hyde, Neal, former chairman of Hydes' Anvil Brewery, 15 Aug. 1998, Altrincham, Cheshire.

Index

Note: 'n.' following a page reference indicates the number of a note on that page.

Lightning Source UK Ltd.
Milton Keynes UK
UKOW05f0612050617
302667UK00017B/434/P

9 780719 052651